American Realism

American Realism

Selected, Edited,
and with Introductions by

Jane Benardete

G. P. PUTNAM'S SONS, New York

Contents

Introduction

"Realism," in the context of nineteenth-century American literature, describes a literary movement that flourished in the last three decades of the century and includes a great authorial triumvirate: William Dean Howells, Mark Twain, and Henry James. But "realism" is also a term that belongs to aesthetics and literary speculation, which, if not timeless, at least transcends the vogue of a moment, a decade or a small group of like-thinking writers. In this more general sense, the problem of realism is that of imitation itself. Simply put, it is the record of life, the real, the true. Such a definition, however, only opens new difficulties. We might suggest that the term excludes anything visionary or prophetic, though even that point could be argued, and we may assert that our interests are only literary, thus skirting (however awkwardly) a more technical, philosophic discussion of reality. Even so, many problems remain. To name a few: Is a story realistic because it accurately describes the appearance of a specific place at a certain time? Does realism necessarily include historically accurate, and therefore verifiable, houses and streetcars, clothes and furniture, place names, slang, economic and social facts? (Is the census realistic?) And even if all the facts are demonstrably accurate, what of the things that are left out, as some data must be if a book is to come to an end? Or is a work realistic, whatever its other properties, if it captures some essential element of life? If so, what essence? That of a heroic life or a mundane one, of an idea or the sense of a man thinking? And is there a necessary order in these things that makes one "more realistic" than another?

All of these problems were suggested, and none of them resolved, in the critical debate that accompanied the realistic movement in American fiction during the 1870's, 1880's, and 1890's. It is, however, important to realize that, at the time, the

9

proponents of realism were less concerned with transcendent problems of their art than with the social function of popular letters, especially novels and short stories. Like many earlier American writers and critics they insisted upon the didactic function of literature in a nation which seemed otherwise to lack a cohesive moral center. Without an established church, torn by the debates of contending political parties, yet constantly striving to absorb the immigrant strangers that Europe's economic and political strife drove to their shores, Americans seemed especially to need the calm moral and intellectual guidance of an articulate educated elite. In an earlier generation, Ralph Waldo Emerson writing of "The Poet" had proposed a literary figure who undertook some traditional functions of the ministry and recorded (whether in verse or prose made no difference) the divine message of universal truth. Emerson's essay marks a high point of hope for a semisacerdotal literary class. Yet in their different ways, both Walt Whitman and William Dean Howells, writing in the 1870's and 1880's, reflected Emerson's ideas. Both discuss the social effect of literature; its artistic value is subordinate, or it depends upon the work's popular effect. Both see literature shaping the "average" American character. Both fear the influence of the popular romance.

Critical opposition to the romance is, in fact, one aspect of responsible patriotism of the post-Civil War era. Emerging from four years of internecine war with dark memories of battles fought in their own backyards and cornfields, most Americans were ready to agree that their old attitudes and assumptions were no longer acceptable. Not all Americans traced the nation's moral character to its popular literature, but to those who did it seemed very clear that in the stories and novels which had so great an impact upon young boys and girls (and wives if not husbands), new standards should prevail. For half a century before the war, the romance, derived and adapted from the tales of Sir Walter Scott, had dominated American fiction. In the hands of writers like James Fenimore Cooper (1789-1851) and William Gilmore Simms (1806-1870), it had given the nation an epic past and the vision of a future founded on the universal influence of romantic nature. Others, like Nathaniel Hawthorne (1804-1864) and Herman Melville (1819-1891), had explored a darker side of the human spirit and the less reassuring aspects of American history. Yet they, too, worked within the idealistic conception of life and portrayed men moved to heroic gestures by their conviction of absolute moral positions emanating from an ultimate creative force. Just such inflated notions and exaggerated moral posturing, it seemed to some critics of the 1870's, had drawn Americans into an unnecessary war—had led them to fight when they might have negotiated, to seek empty glory though it cost them their lives.

No serious modern historian would try to demonstrate the "literary causes of the Civil War," yet time and again, commentators of the postwar era suggest wide-ranging, destructive effects of the romance. Many of them complain of the "feudal" element in popular literature. The word "feudal" is useful and interesting because it covers a number of qualities these critics anathematized. "Feudalism" is evident in the idealized medievalism of historical romances, like Scott's *Ivanhoe* which depicts the sources of a national aristocracy. But "feudalism" may also be found in such an admiring treatment of personal heroism as Lew Wallace's enormously successful story *Ben Hur* (1880). Walt Whitman attacked the "feudal" standard of character he found both in popular fiction and Shakespeare's plays (though these, at least, described the life of their times). Mark Twain, in *Life on the Mississippi* and the Grangerford episodes of *Huckleberry Finn*, blamed Sir Walter Scott for the bellicose "chivalry doings" of the American South. For those who attacked the "feudalism" of the romance, the opposite term, describing all they desired, was "democracy." By this they meant an anti-aristocratic literature, impatient of the unusual or improbable and unalterably opposed to the heroic gesture. These were the qualities realists tried to capture in their pictures of the healthy American average and the commonplace.

Among his many, generously conceived "literary passions," William Dean Howells counted Jane Austen, as the exemplary realist, and, in the 1890's, Leo Tolstoy. Both choices are significant, for Tolstoy best embodied that moral idealism in conjunction with the accurate description of social conditions which Howells also attempted. Austen, his earlier mentor, provided the basis for his description of middle-class American life. Her portrait of the English squirearchy—those sensible and literate families, neither rich nor poor, admirably well-informed of their "place" and their opportunities—is echoed in Howells' picture of a solidly commonsensical American middle class. His chronicles may, in fact, owe more to Austen's works than to the intensely competitive conditions and the rapidly changing structure of contemporary American society. Howells was, however, among the first to write of and for the new American bourgeoisie. They were, in the 1870's, newcomers among the well-to-do, families who had benefited by the expansion of industry at the end of the Civil War. Like the Laphams (described in *The Rise of Silas Lapham*, 1885) these Americans found the patterns of their lives reversed at the war's end. They had been village people, small-time entrepreneurs. They became little millionaires, profiting by the new possibilities of a national, rather than regional, economy. Rural or small town people, by birth and tradition, they were suddenly urbanized and exposed to the possibilities of a richer culture, of art, music, and literature. Yet, as Howells draws them, they were shaken by self-doubt. They enjoyed wealth, clothes, houses, and fine horses, but they had lost their moral identity, the village church, and old-time Protestantism. Like Penelope Lapham, they might read and criticize the silly assumptions of a romance like *Tears, Idle Tears*, but they had to suffer before they could adopt a more sophisticated attitude toward personal morality, even a notion so shallow as the "economy of pain."

Much the same class of old Americans, though somewhat more prosperous and intellectually accomplished, make up the cast of characters in Henry James' early fictions. Again the theme is the contrast of cultures. Howells compared rural or village and urban life; James placed genteel, somewhat pious provincial Americans amidst European aristocrats with an age-old standard of urbane manners and "worldly" ways. The Americans Howells and James drew were not, of course, economically "average." In what sense then do they represent the commonplace life of the nation? Howells might find in them "human nature known to us all"; James might point to their "sense of life." More precisely, for these authors and many of their readers, the prosperous bourgeoisie provided a standard of comfortable and cultivated existence to which even less fortunate Americans could well aspire. Glancing ahead to the poverty often depicted in naturalistic writing, it is well to establish the contrasting materials of realistic fiction. In Howells' hands, or James', realism was concerned with sensitive, intelligent, prosperous city dwellers. It was interested in their manners and issues arising in their private lives. It rarely descended to the marketplace. Above all, it tacitly assured American readers of our "well-to-do actualities."

Such bourgeois fiction is but one type of American realism. Another group of writers, generally known as "local colorists," early attracted the support of influential writers and editors like Thomas Wentworth Higginson (1823-1911), Thomas Bailey Aldrich (1836-1907), and William Dean Howells, all early converts to the realistic cause. Generally, "local color" fiction was concerned with the life of a small, well-defined region or province. Its characteristic setting was the isolated small town. The vogue for local color, coming at the end of the Civil War, seems to have reflected a lingering, sentimental sectionalism which saw political nationalism as a threat to the independent village life of an earlier America. Local colorists were consciously nostalgic, historians of a vanishing movement, recorders of a present that faded before their eyes. Yet for all their sentimentality, they were dedicated to minutely accurate descriptions of the life of their regions. They worked from personal experience; they recorded the facts of a unique environment and suggested that native life was shaped by the curious conditions of the locale. Their materials were necessarily limited: Sarah Orne Jewett (1849-1909) confined herself to life on the Maine seacoast, George Washington Cable (1844-1925) described the Creole culture of New Orleans. Yet, though their topics were necessarily disparate, local colorists had certain common artistic concerns. They shared a crypto-Jeffersonian fondness for the old democratic America; they laboriously described local peculiarities; above all, they recorded regional dialects. Reams of almost unreadable dialogue, littered with apostrophes and strange misspellings, testify to their interest in American vernacular. But for all these typographical horrors, local color writing marked a solid advance toward Americanism in the language of fiction. Earlier dialect writers, like Seba Smith (1792-1868) or "Petroleum V. Nasby" (really David Ross Locke, 1833-88), were journalistic, comic, admittedly transient writers. The local colorists were respectable, educated, and artistic. They were approved by powerful editors, published in the *Atlantic Monthly*. Their interest in dialect was not therefore a populistic attack upon academic diction, which they had fully mastered, but an appeal for the artistic integrity of native American speech. Ernest Hemmingway's tribute to Mark Twain's flexible, colloquial prose is well known. Behind Twain's achievement lay the work of many local colorists who established a place for American vernacular in serious literature.

Twain himself might be regarded as the apotheosis of local color. His literary voice is "Western" or "Southern," never academic. His most successful fictions—*Tom Sawyer* and *Huckleberry Finn*—are set in the past, gilded with nostalgia for his boyhood in Hannibal, Missouri (the significantly named "St. Petersburg" of these novels). Usually, however, the "local color" label is reserved for lesser writers, many of them women, whose stories reflect the delicate feelings Victorian ladies were understood to enjoy. They afford a link between realism and popular sentimentalism, for the accuracy and contemporaneity of their descriptive methods was constantly belied by fond yearnings for simpler, bygone days.

There is yet another school of realists which might be described as the embittered local colorists. This group—Western in origin, victims of the agricultural hard times of the 1870's and 1880's—includes Joseph Kirkland (1830-1894), author of *Zury: The Meanest Man in Spring County* (1887); Ed. Howe (1853-1937), best known for *The Story of a Country Town* (1883); and Hamlin Garland, whose early stories also recorded the drab laborious life of the "Middle Border." The place of this group of literary populists in the history of American realism may be debated. To some critics their work seems central. Alfred Kazin, for example, in *On Native Grounds* (1942) argues that "Realism in America . . . poured sullenly out of agrarian bitterness" and that the Western writers, especially, helped to shape later literary styles:

> It is to these lone protestants of their time, who did not always know that they were writing "realism," to Jeffersonian hearts plagued by a strangely cold and despotic America, to writers some of whom lacked every capacity for literature save a compelling passion to tell the truth, that the emancipated and metropolitan literature of contemporary America owes its very inception.*

Yet even in these embittered agrarians there was an optimistic strain. Hamlin Garland, in his manifesto *Crumbling Idols*, tried

*Alfred Kazin, *On Native Grounds* (New York: Reynal and Hitchcock, 1942), pp. 16-17.

to capture the new mood of the West, but his vision of "the majesty, the immensity, the infinite charm of the life" around him owed a great deal to Whitman's rolling lists of America's splendid regions. "Take," Garland suggests to the young writer in search of a subject,

> . . . the history of the lumbering district of the northern lakes,—a picturesque and peculiar life . . . The subtle changes of thought and old life that have come with the rise of a city like St. Paul or Minneapolis; the life of the great saw-mills and shingle-mills; and the river life of the upper Mississippi . . . Then there is the mixture of races; the coming in of the German, the Scandinavian; the subtle changes of character . . .*

These are familiar and patriotic formulas, with lingering overtones of the idealistic faith in American nature that characterized pre-Civil War rhetoric. In neither his manifesto nor his fiction was Garland really revolutionary. Yet the appearance of a significant group of Western writers, for which Garland tried to speak, marked a real change in the character of American fiction. The regions they described were less settled and civilized than the East. They had no eighteenth-century past, and no tradition of academic letters. Even their cities were relatively rough, a quality Carl Sandburg later captured in describing Chicago, capital of the Middle West, as "stormy, husky, brawling . . . half-naked, sweating, proud to be Hog Butcher, Tool Maker, Stacker of Wheat, Player with Railroads and Freight Handler to the Nation."† Garland was quite right, in 1894, to announce the passing of Boston as a literary center. New York, more metropolitan and less academic than the "Hub," had become the capital of American publishing. At the same time, Chicago was attracting young Middle Western artists and expanding the cultural interests it celebrated in the Columbian Exposition (1893). It is significant that, though their careers carried them East, the four most recent authors included in this volume—Hamlin Garland, Frank Norris, Theodore Dreiser, and John Steinbeck (like their older compatriot S. L. Clemens)— were all born in the Middle or Far West.

American realism in the last three decades of the nineteenth

---

* Hamlin Garland, *Crumbling Idols* (Stone & Kimball & Chicago, 1894), p. 15.
† Carl Sandburg, *Chicago* (1914), collected in *Chicago Poems* (1916).

century reflected various contemporary social and political
issues. There is evidence of the fear of renewed strife and of the
growing uniformity of national life; of urban prosperity and
agricultural depression; of the decay of New England and the
rise of the West. As important as any of these themes, yet far
more difficult to measure, was the impact of evolutionary
theory which helped to shape both realistic and naturalistic
writing, and, indeed, all aspects of American thought for half a
century.

Although it was published in 1859, the reception of Darwin's
Origin of Species in the United States was delayed for some
years by the overwhelming interests of the Civil War. When
thoughtful Americans began to read Darwin—and to understand
that his attack upon the theory of special creation would
further undermine the already infirm structure of traditional
Protestant theology—they also drank in the social philosophy of
Herbert Spencer. It was, indeed, Spencer, more than Darwin,
whose ideas dominated the American adaptations of evolutionary theory. His popularity in this country was, according to
Perry Miller, "staggering":

> Not only village agnostics, but scientists, many theologians,
> and most captains of industry paid him as great homage as
> the revolutionary generation paid to Locke. It would hardly
> be too much to say that the bulk of American "thought" in
> this period, measured solely by the weight of printed paper,
> was not thought at all, but only a recapitulation of Spencer.
> When Justice Holmes said, in his memorable dissent of 1906,
> in *Lockner v. New York*, that "the fourteenth Amendment
> does not enact Mr. Herbert Spencer's Social Statics," he was
> not only trying to get back to the original meaning of the
> amendment, but was blurting out his irritation with the
> decades in which Spencer had permeated the minds of
> businessmen and lawyers.*

And not only businessman and lawyers, of course, or agnostics
and scientists, but authors and artists as well, indeed virtually all
thinking Americans. What Spencer particularly offered to optimistic realists was a theory of social evolution which seemed to
justify the structure of nineteenth-century American society.

---

* Perry Miller, ed., *American Thought: Civil War to World War I* (New York:
Rinehart and Co., 1954), p. xxiii.

Even less optimistic writers, like Dreiser in *Sister Carrie*, found the social statics useful because Spencer's theory disposed of the need for moral laws or reforms. Nature, as Spencer described it, was organized around the "persistence of force": simple forms of life are propelled by "forces" until they become more and more complex, and so mature into an ultimate form which, apparently, becomes stable. The operation of these forces is inevitable and self-adjusting. Darwin's description of the "survival of the fittest" in nature, now transferred to society, seems to justify unbridled economic competition, not only because this is nature's way, but also because free competition ensures the improvement of the race. In Darwin's phrase, "the vigorous, the healthy and the happy survive and multiply."

One evidence of the wide-ranging effect of evolutionary theory was its application in rather inappropriate areas, like literary criticism. There is little resemblance between art and economic competition (though Spencer himself applied evolutionary theory to the arts). We may refuse to impose a tariff, but it is hard to remove the artist from conscious control of his work. Nonetheless, evolutionary suggestions are everywhere, as if these formulas had become a necessary part of the language. Howells, for example, offers a mildly optimistic theory of literary evolution to explain the inevitable progression from the romance to realism, and Garland appeals directly to Spencer for assurance that literary evolution is inevitable and not cruel: the old "idols," like the New England literary elite, simply *must* crumble. The full impact of popular evolutionary theory in literature came, however, at the turn of the century with the appearance of a group of younger writers who had read the European naturalists. For Norris it was apparently Zola that gave a new shape to fiction, for Dreiser a strange brew of Spencer, Balzac, and Thomas Hardy.

II

Naturalism, more than Realism, is a term which belongs to a literary epoch. Its major themes may be traced in nineteenth-century French literature. From the critic and historian, Hippolyte Taine (1828-1893), who is known for his theory of character shaped by *race*, *moment*, and *milieu*, writers learned the importance of demonstrating hereditary and environmental

influences in human development. To Gustave Flaubert
(1821-1880) and especially his novel *Madame Bovary* (1857)
interest in descriptive objectivity may be traced. But it was
Emile Zola (1840-1902) who, above all, formulated the naturalist's position and exemplified it in his mammoth fictional study
of two contemporary families marked by degenerate hereditary
traits, the *Rougon-MacQuart* novels. Zola's immediate literary
model was, of course, *La Comédie Humaine* by Honoré de
Balzac (1799-1850), over whose devotion to the "facts" Henry
James would wonder and lament. To this tradition of laborious
documentation, Zola brought a new element—clinical objectivity—founded, in part, on the work of Claude Bernard whose
Introduction à l'étude de la médecine expérimentale (1865)
helped to define an exact scientific method for medicine. Zola's
theory, as he stated it in *Le roman expérimental* (1880), made
of the novelist a kind of diagnostician in fiction. His attitude
was scientifically dispassionate. He assumed characters marked
by heredity and governed by natural laws beyond their control.
Both independent intelligence and free will were denied them.
Engaged in the struggle to survive amidst oppressive conditions,
they could not and did not pretend to ethical motives. They
were simply the hapless victims of impersonal forces, crushed
by their own weaknesses, society, and the inevitable greater
shape of things.

Because he was clinically objective, the naturalistic author felt
free to deal with materials which writers in a consciously ethical
literary tradition rejected. Zola, and other naturalists, chose
their subjects from the lower ranks of society. They portrayed
the miserable and despised, those who could not afford to
adopt the moral standard of the prosperous middle class. They
wrote of

> prostitutes, free love, social misery of many sorts, and
> burning questions of the day; they held the convenient
> belief that *"la morale n'avait plus rien à faire avec la
> littérature, pas plus qu'avec la science"* and that *"Le vice et
> la virtu sont les produits comme le vitriel et le sucre."*
> ["Morality has no more to do with literature than with
> science"; "Vice and virtue are products like vitriol and
> sugar."]*

---

* Lars Ahnebrink, *The Beginning of Naturalism in American Fiction* (New York:
Russell & Russell, 1961), p. 25.

There were, of course, good reasons for writing of misery and poverty. Such tales aroused the readers' sympathies. The poor and diseased were demonstrably victims of society and nature, while either the *bourgeoisie* or the very wealthy might seem to have at least a small measure of independence and ethical responsibility. It is, however, a critical truism that, in choosing to work with the life of the lower classes, naturalists loaded their literary dice, and that Zola, especially, for all his proclamations of objectivity, was a social reformer, a humanitarian, and so, in some sense, an optimist. It is only too easy to argue that, in claiming scientific objectivity, naturalists deceived—at any rate—themselves. Yet they worked meaningful changes in American literature. They introduced a new body of literary materials, drawn from society's lower depths, and espoused a somewhat self-conscious amorality. With these weapons in hand, they forcefully challenged the prevailing genteel standards of American publishing and criticism.

The impact of naturalism on American literature may be explained in various ways. We might, for example, assume a Spencerian attitude and explain the appearance of naturalism in the late 1890's as evidence of the law of change. Certainly, the old generation was passing away. Whitman died in 1892. Howells, now in his fifties, was deeply moved by a reforming social conscience which he dated from the Haymarket Affair of 1886, but he was unable to sympathize with the loose moral standards he found in French naturalism. Twain was also middle-aged and, in 1894, bankrupt. His economic difficulties and the death of his wife and daughter drove him ever deeper into cynicism, but when his despair took literary form it appeared as disillusioned idealism (like that of *The Mysterious Stranger*, published posthumously in 1916), which had little in common with the naturalistic acceptance of an amoral universe. Henry James, long resident abroad, had no meaningful connection with American literary movements. The younger writers, like Frank Norris, had grown up in an America where evolutionary theory was virtually the official philosophy, and so the step into naturalism was less difficult for them than for writers raised on the romance. To Westerners like Jack London (1876-1916) naturalism provided the basis for describing the rougher life of the frontier and the hard, adventurous existence which brought man close to the beasts.

The theme of human "bestiality," especially as an explanation of sexual desire, is one of the most familiar in American naturalism. In *McTeague* (1899), for example, Frank Norris described the relations of a crude dentist (who is compared to a draft-horse, a dog, a bear) with a superficially refined German-American girl who, awakened by his desires, is drawn into an animalistic affection for her "bear" husband. Theodore Dreiser's forgiving treatment of the career of his heroine in *Sister Carrie* (1900) also drew heavily upon the naturalistic understanding of sexuality. Carrie and her lovers are shown as victims of "forces." Their relations are illicit, but they are blameless for, at their imperfect stage of evolution, mind cannot guide behavior. The force of desire determines the liaisons they form. Such fictions obviously denied the semiofficial morality ("one life, one love") of the American middle class, but the strength of the naturalist's position was that it revised the basis of moral thought. To insist on rigid moral laws for men so weak and dominated by forces so strong seemed simply inhumane. Earlier evolutionists who accepted an inevitable, amoral social process without assuming an equally amoral attitude toward personal relations had been, undoubtedly, short-sighted. Before his death in 1920, Howells saw Dreiser and Mencken triumph over censorship, known to their generation as Comstockery, and proclaimed as leaders of a new truthfulness in American writing.

Indeed, a new kind of writer with a new kind of "truth" appeared with the naturalistic movement. Neither remote nor refined, either semi-educated or consciously rebelling against academic skills, he wrote (or claimed to write) directly from experience, with little plan and less theory. The legend of the production of *Sister Carrie* is a case in point. Dreiser simply put two words, the title, at the top of a page and the story began to unfold. It was completed in less than a year, with only about six months of actual work. Critics have long explained this achievement—as well as Dreiser's compassion for his characters—by pointing to autobiographical elements in the story. He had himself come, a wondering half-formed youth, to Chicago. Carrie's story resembles the careers of two of Dreiser's sisters. Elements of his own character may be found in both Drouet and Hurstwood. But critics also freely admit that the novel, though powerful, is unpolished. There are strange breaks in tone: Dreiser is sometimes objective, sometimes as sentimental as a Victorian "lady-writer." His prose is awkward—tedious, ungrammatical, repetitious, bombastic. And to the end of his life Dreiser remained an unpolished writer, a remarkable combination of gross artistic errors and undoubted dramatic power. Oddly, his contemporaries defended his errors as well as his genius. Sherwood Anderson, a deliberate writer whose own studied prose employs many complex literary devices, justified Dreiser's "crudity" because it seemed to capture the raw essence of American life. Randolph Bourne (1886-1918), a sophisticated academically trained critic, lamented Dreiser's naïveté but found grounds for praising his ineptitudes:

> There stirs in Dreiser's books a new American quality. It is not at all German. It is an authentic attempt to make something artistic out of the chaotic materials that lie around us in American life. Dreiser interests us because we can watch him grope and feel his clumsiness. He has the artist's vision without the sureness of the artist's technique. That is one of the tragedies of America. But his faults are those of his material and of uncouth bulk, and not of shoddiness. He expresses an America that is in process of forming. The interest he evokes is part of the eager interest we feel in that growth.*

Artistic crudity, that is to say, imitates national crudity. Even those too educated to become rough writers themselves would accept formlessness in art, if it provided the basis for a liberal critique of other formless elements in American society. Thus, artistic crudity was, in a measure, applauded by disaffected, well-educated Americans who wished to stand apart from a brawling, uncultivated materialistic society.

Into the 1930's, in writers like James T. Farrell (b. 1904), a tough journalistic style characterized the naturalists. Even so well-read an author as Frank Norris, with less firsthand experience of social injustice than of Zola, spoke as a proletarian. "Who cares for fine style!" the Harvard-trained Norris wrote. "Tell your yarn and let your style go to the devil. We don't want literature, we want life." Or again, in defiance of all establishments: "I never truckled. I never took off the hat to Fashion and held it out for pennies. I told the truth. They liked

---

* Randolph Bourne, "The Art of Theodore Dreiser" in *The Art of Theodore Dreiser* (Bloomington, Indiana: University of Indiana Press), p. 95.

it or they didn't like it. What had that to do with me? I told them the truth."*

As swaggering social critics and literary commoners, naturalists broadened the materials of literature and introduced a deliberately democratic style. The artistic value of these innovations might be questioned. Yet certainly one element in the naturalist's rejection of the realistic method has artistic merit. It is the theme of Frank Norris' essay on Zola: the rediscovery of, and the need for, "romance," both in the deeper probing of the human heart and in an overarching vision of life. Realists, trying to avoid exaggerated passions, minimized both the situations they treated and the passions life evokes. Urging a proper perspective on intense feelings and heightened emotions (the drama of love and ambition, for instance, which even prosperous middle-class society affords), they concentrated upon surfaces, manners, appearances. At its best such writing delicately implies the depths it does not treat. When it is less successful, it seems to omit, or to hide, too much.

Where moral problems are raised, the realist is deliberately pragmatic, seeking small solutions, avoiding grand moral gestures. The naturalistic novel, with its scientific overview of life, stretching far into the past and reaching forward into the most distant future, reintroduced eternal issues akin to those raised in the romance. The issues are not, of course, the same. For the idealistic world of the romance was based, either in acceptance or doubt, upon traditional Christian thinking. Its universe rested upon a creative spirit—whether benevolent or malevolent—and sought out the moral system his creation implied. Naturalistic objectivity denied morality, except in the distorted form of the need to "survive," as well as the personal, omnipresent creator. But it imagined great causes and reached out to an ultimate perfection. It did not judge the present moment alone, but set individual life in a pattern of change and becoming, and so opened out the very limited temporal structure of the contemporary novel. What opportunities this creates may be seen in John Steinbeck's best-known novel, *The Grapes of Wrath* (1939). The novel is set in the depression years and chronicles the almost unalleviated suffering of a migrant family, yet it presents their struggles as the action of a moment in the nation's history and constantly evokes, in contrast, the grandeur of American landscape, or eternal nature, itself.

* Quoted in Kazin, *On Native Grounds,* pp. 98, 102.

Yet in fairness, we should note that naturalism, too, founders on its theory. If realism too readily confines itself to a moment, naturalism finds easy answers in an eternal, self-regulating scheme. Despite their philosophic differences, American writers —realistic and naturalistic—were, in some measure, limited by the life they knew. It was Howells who urged American authors to do justice to their "well-to-do actualities," but the most striking proof of his point comes from Dreiser's apparently unconscious picture of Sister Carrie. For all her sufferings and degradation, her fate is immeasurably more fortunate than that of Zola's Nana. It is not, ultimately, their class or their vision of society that distinguishes realists from naturalists. The unavoidable difference between them lies in their vision of the "real," the "true." For realists, it is the immediately verifiable. Reality, truth, is found in the visible present and is ever available to an intelligent perceptor. It affects his moral judgment because this informed person will see the advantage of living wisely, sensibly in the current hour. For the naturalist, the real and true is always partially hidden from his eyes. It is the very shape of a system only partially revealed by facts now at hand. No man fully divines the ultimate end of that creation in which he is but a part. Caught in a process he cannot fully understand, much less control, the naturalist rests upon the inevitable and is bound by just one duty: to survive.

Jane Benardete

West Tisbury
Martha's Vineyard, Massachusetts
August, 1971

I. Walt Whitman: Prophet of the New

The emergence of realism in the 1870's is often presented as a wholly new departure in American literature. We are tempted to see the Civil War as a chasm which conveniently divided the intellectual life of the American nineteenth century into two contrasting periods: the first, romantic and idealistic, modifying yet preserving the traditional theology; the second, realistic and materialistic, deeply influenced by the new evolutionary science. As the second era appears, writers of the first fade away. Most of the authors who dominate our reading of the 1840's and 1850's did not, at least as creative writers, survive the Civil War. Emerson, Thoreau, Poe, Hawthorne, and Melville—all by 1870 had been silenced by age, death, or oblivion, and a new group of authors—Howells, Twain, James—had begun to appear. Such a "periodization" of history, however useful, is somewhat misleading. The process of intellectual change is continuous; even "revolutions" in popular philosophy, like that worked by Darwin and Spencer, have some basis in the ideas they seem to replace.

Walt Whitman (1819-1892) survived the "romantic" era and, somewhat consciously ancestral and prophetic, helped to usher in the new literary age. The critical ideas he expressed in *Democratic Vistas* (1871) are interesting in themselves. They also suggest some of the continuous concerns of American literature in the nineteenth century, ideas and interests that bridged the apparent gap between the pre- and the post-Civil War decades.

Whitman's great theme in *Democratic Vistas* is the relation of literature and society or, more emphatically, the unifying function of literature in a democratic society. From the literary debates of the early 1800's he inherited the vision of a national epic which would define the American character and become the basis of national culture. What Homer did for Greece, Virgil

24

for Rome, the author of the American epic would do for this new nation. His work would be both descriptive and ideal, realistic in its picture of American life and religious in its presentation of national aspirations. In the 1840's and 1850's Whitman had been a newspaperman (the editor, for a time, of the Brooklyn *Eagle*) deeply involved in politically oriented reforms like the temperance movement and, of course, abolition. Although the first edition of *Leaves of Grass* (1855) is mystical, this great autobiographical poem, like Wordsworth's *Prelude*, became, as it developed, a record of the poet's political, as well as his personal and religious, concerns. From his reading in Goethe, Hegel, Carlyle, and, above all, Ralph Waldo Emerson (who, Whitman claimed, brought him "to the boil" as a poet) he had learned that the spirit—"Soul"—moves equally in all forms of life, that literature and politics, like the manifold aspects of Nature itself, are but different forms of the same divine exfoliating Creation. Literature should not be reserved for the aesthete or those solely concerned with beauty. It must be inclusive, a mirror of all the forms life takes, for only so can it reflect the immanent spirit and become truly religious.

This idealistic assumption underlies Whitman's plea for a great native literature, but *Democratic Vistas* is also a tract addressed to a specific time, the early 1870's—the "Gilded Age"—a period characterized by rapid, conscienceless economic growth, political turpitude, and popular complacency. To Whitman, the contemporary spectacle was appalling and his description of it is venomous:

> The depravity of the business classes of our country is not less than has been supposed, but infinitely greater. The official services of America, national, state, and municipal, in all their branches and departments, except the judiciary, are saturated in corruption, bribery, falsehood, maladministration. In fashionable life, flippancy, tepid amours, weak infidelism, small aims, or no aims at all, only to kill time.

In contrast to this decadence, Whitman recalled the national mood of the war years (which he also celebrated in the "Drum Taps" section of *Leaves of Grass* and many passages of *Specimen Days*). Then the nation had actively sensed its political mission and private morality was high. The simple young Americans who suffered and died in the military hospitals

Whitman visited during the war were strong and uncomplaining. In the model of their unselfish devotion, Whitman found reason for faith in the American future. The "brotherhood" or "love of comrades" that bound Americans in battle might, he believed, reform the spirit of materialistic America. Whitman's tone is, of course, more prophetic than analytic. A great *literatus* (for all his nationalism, Whitman enjoyed the dignity of Latin!) or many *literati* must arise to hymn the American character and give moral unity to the still sectionalized nation.

The problem of "character" has a special place in Whitman's politics. Democracy, "the leveler," may enforce "the unyielding principle of the average" and create a tyrannical majority. Thus the merely equalizing principle of democracy must be complemented by respect for the special identity of each individual, "the pride and centripetal isolation of a human being in himself." To this preservative notion of individuality Whitman gives the name "personalism." It is a quality which may be realized in our literature by the praise of healthy, average Americans. "Personalism" is loosely equated with individualism, but Whitman does not indicate that technical interest in "individual" vision or "point of view" which is inherent in "impressionism" or Hamlin Garland's later coinage, "veritism." Nonetheless, there is a common quality in these terms, all of which emphasize the unique interest of each life and so suggest a kind of spiritual democracy.

In American society the opponent of literary "personalism" is for Whitman, "Culture." (Even naming it, in *Democratic Vistas*, he feels himself in close quarters with the enemy.) "Culture" is equivalent to conservative, established opinion in literature and the arts, the genteel, Anglicized taste which characterized writers of the "New England School." (We may find the style, for example, in the poetry of Henry Wadsworth Longfellow, "the American Tennyson," or the criticism of James Russell Lowell.) Whitman objects to this official culture because it perpetuates the literary and social standards of the "Old World," and especially a "feudal" ideal character. Again, his comment resembles the literary ideas of younger critics, though his statement of the danger of "feudalism" in literature is far less particular than, for example, William Dean Howells' attack on the romance.

The interest of Whitman's ideas to younger American writers, who thought themselves revolutionary, is suggested by Hamlin

Garland's reminiscence of the poet "old and poor." By the 1880's Whitman had become the "Good Gray Poet of Camden," to whom foreign literary radicals, like the English poet Swinburne, addressed their tributes. Sick and mild, the perfect figure of a martyr, Whitman had suffered for the cause of free speech in literature. He had endured censorship; Garland notes that Whitman's work was on the "double starred"—or "scholars only"—list in the Boston Public Library. He had confronted the tyrannical literary establishment. In his conversation with Whitman, Garland chides him gently for his harsh criticism of Richard Watson Gilder (1844-1909) and Edmund Clarence Stedman (1833-1908), two influential editors and minor genteel poets. Whitman's generous disclaimer is less characteristic than his rumored attack, for both Gilder and Stedman were imitative writers of empty "poesy." Also typical is Whitman's dislike of abnormality or exaggeration in the work of regional writers. Garland names the Middle Westerner Joseph Kirkland (1830-1894), two Southerners—George Washington Cable (1844-1925) and Joel Chandler Harris (1848-1908)—and a New Englander, Mary E. Wilkins [Freeman] (1852-1930). Sensationalism and "personalism" are, of course, incompatible so, once again, Whitman asks that the "really heroic character of the common Americans be depicted in novel and drama." Young local colorists who wished to publish in popular magazines would have found Whitman's standards hard to meet, yet they took inspiration from his vision of their careers in healthy democratic communities in "Ohio, Illinois, Missouri, or somewhere . . . outvying, in cheapest, vulgar life, all that has been hitherto shown in the vast ideal pictures."

Whitman's program for American literature is represented in *Democratic Vistas*. His example as an American author was, however, more important than any critical statement. In his poetry he was truly revolutionary and "modern," fulfilling as no other American writer has, the requirements he laid down for a great national *literatus*. For an example of "personalism" we should surely turn to *Leaves of Grass* and note in its catalogues the careful delineation of individual lives and Whitman's reverence for the heroic struggles of healthy average men. Much of Whitman's material forecasts the interest of writers of the early twentieth century, for he wrote of the body and sexuality in terms that antedate Freud, of urban poverty and the agricultural West, of the hard lives of whores and toughs.

His democratic attitudes, his subject matter, and the rolling cadences of his prophetic style influenced such poets as Edgar Lee Masters and Carl Sandburg and novelists such as Frank Norris and John Steinbeck. Yet for all his modernism, Whitman's essential philosophy belongs to the age of Emerson. His organic idealism was never seriously modified by Darwinism. His thought always echoes the curious blend of Transcendental naturalism and patriotism that is found in "The American Scholar" and "Self-Reliance." It is well to remember that "Emersonianism" was, in its popular form the semiofficial American philosophy of the later nineteenth century, and as Whitman's example suggests, it offered a path to many of the ideas and materials of twentieth-century literature which bypassed skepticism and evolutionary thought. Not that our major writers took this easy way. Yet their writing often reveals a genial optimistic strain that suggests the lingering idealism in their intellectual heritage.

Selection

1. *Democratic Vistas:*
ON THE NEED FOR A DEMOCRATIC LITERATURE*

. . . Today, ahead, though dimly yet, we see, in vistas, a copious, sane, gigantic offspring. For our New World I consider far less important for what it has done, or what it is, than for results to come. Sole among nationalities, these States have assumed the task to put in forms of lasting power and practicality, on areas of amplitude rivaling the operations of the physical kosmos, the moral political speculations of ages, long, long deferr'd, the democratic republican principle and the theory of development and perfection by voluntary standards, and self-reliance. Who else, indeed, except the United States, in history, so far, have accepted in unwitting faith, and, as we now see, stand, act upon, and go security for, these things?

But preluding no longer, let me strike the keynote of the following strain. First premising that, though the passages of it have been written at widely different times (it is, in fact, a collection of memoranda, perhaps for future designers, comprehenders), and though it may be open to the charge of one part contradicting another—for there are opposite sides to the great question of democracy, as to every great question—I feel the parts harmoniously blended in my own realization and convictions, and present them to be read only in such oneness, each page and each claim and assertion modified and temper'd by the others. Bear in mind, too, that they are not the result of studying up in political economy, but of the ordinary sense, observing, wandering among men, these States, these stirring years of war and peace. I will not gloss over the appaling dangers of universal suffrage in the United States. In fact, it is to admit and face these dangers I am writing. To him or her within whose thought rages the battle, advancing, retreating, between democracy's convictions, aspirations, and the people's

---

* This selection is taken from *Democratic Vistas* by Walt Whitman (1871).

crudeness, vice, caprices, I mainly write this essay. I shall use the words America and democracy as convertible terms. Not an ordinary one is the issue. The United States are destined either to surmount the gorgeous history of feudalism, or else prove the most tremendous failure of time. . . .

. . . Admitting all this, with the priceless value of our political institutions, general suffrage (and fully acknowledging the latest, widest opening of the doors), I say that, far deeper than these, what finally and only is to make of our Western world a nationality superior to any hitherto known, and outtopping the past, must be vigorous, yet unsuspected Literatures, perfect personalities and sociologies, original, transcendental, and expressing (what, in highest sense, are not yet express'd at all) democracy and the modern. With these, and out of these, I promulgate new races of Teachers, and of perfect Women, indispensable to endow the birth-stock of a New World. For feudalism, caste, the ecclesiastic traditions, though palpably retreating from political institutions, still hold essentially, by their spirit, even in this country, entire possession of the more important fields, indeed the very subsoil, of education, and of social standards and literature.

I say that democracy can never prove itself beyond cavil, until it founds and luxuriantly grows its own forms of art, poems, schools, theology, displacing all that exists, or that has been produced anywhere in the past, under opposite influences. It is curious to me that while so many voices, pens, minds, in the press, lecture rooms, in our Congress, etc., are discussing intellectual topics, pecuniary dangers, legislative problems, the suffrage, tariff and labor questions, and the various business and benevolent needs of America, with propositions, remedies, often worth deep attention, there is one need, a hiatus the profoundest, that no eye seems to perceive, no voice to state. Our fundamental want today in the United States, with closest, amplest reference to present conditions, and to the future, is of a class, and the clear idea of a class, of native authors, literatuses, far different, far higher in grade, than any yet known, sacerdotal, modern, fit to cope with our occasions, lands, permeating the whole mass of American mentality, taste, belief, breathing into it a new breath of life, giving it decision, affecting politics far more than the popular superficial suffrage, with results inside and underneath the elections of Presidents or

Congresses—radiating, begetting appropriate teachers, schools, manners, and, as its grandest result, accomplishing (what neither the schools nor the churches and their clergy have hitherto accomplish'd, and without which this nation will no more stand, permanently, soundly, than a house will stand without a sub-stratum), a religious and moral character beneath the political and productive and intellectual bases of the States. For know you not, dear, earnest reader, that the people of our land may all read and write, and may all possess the right to vote—and yet the main things may be entirely lacking?—(and this to suggest them).

View'd, today, from a point of view sufficiently over-arching, the problem of humanity all over the civilized world is social and religious, and is to be finally met and treated by literature. The priest departs, the divine literatus comes. Never was anything more wanted than, today, and here in the States, the poet of the modern is wanted, or the great literatus of the modern. At all times, perhaps, the central point in any nation, and that whence it is itself really sway'd the most, and whence it sways others, is its national literature, especially its archetypal poems. Above all previous lands, a great original literature is surely to become the justification and reliance (in some respects the sole reliance of American democracy).

Few are aware how the great literature penetrates all, gives hue to all, shapes aggregates and individuals, and, after subtle ways, with irresistible power, constructs, sustains, demolishes at will. Why tower, in reminiscence, above all the nations of the earth, two special lands, petty in themselves, yet inexpressibly gigantic, beautiful, columnar?. Immortal Judah lives, and Greece immortal lives, in a couple of poems.

Nearer than this. It is not generally realized, but it is true, as the genius of Greece, and all the sociology, personality, politics, and religion of those wonderful states, resided in their literature or aesthetics, that what was afterwards the main support of European chivalry, the feudal, ecclesiastical, dynastic world over there—forming its osseous structure, holding it together for hundreds, thousands of years, preserving its flesh and bloom, giving it form, decision, rounding it out, and so saturating it in the conscious and unconscious blood, breed, belief, and intuitions of men, that it still prevails powerful to this day, in defiance of the mighty changes of time—was its literature, permeat-

ing to the very marrow, especially that major part, its enhanc-
ing songs, ballads, and poems.*

To the ostent of the senses and eyes, I know, the influences
which stamp the world's history are wars, uprisings or downfalls
of dynasties, changeful movement of trade, important inventions, navigation, military or civil governments, advent of
powerful personalities, conquerors, etc. These of course play
their part; yet, it may be, a single new thought, imagination,
abstract principle, even literary style, fit for the time, put in
shape by some great literatus, and projected among mankind,
may duly cause changes, growths, removals, greater than the
longest and bloodiest war, or the most stupendous merely
political dynastic, or commercial overturn.

In short, as though it may not be realized, it is strictly true,
that a few first-class poets, philosophs, and authors have
substantially settled and given status to the entire religion,
education, law, sociology, etc., of the hitherto civilized world,
by tingeing and often creating the atmospheres out of which
they have arisen, such also must stamp, and more than ever
stamp, the interior and real democratic construction of this
American continent, today, and days to come. Remember also
this fact of difference, that, while through the antique and
through the mediaeval ages, highest thoughts and ideals realized
themselves, and their expression made its way by other arts, as
much as, or even more than by, technical literature (not open to
the mass of persons, or even to the majority of eminent
persons), such literature in our day and for current purposes is
not only more eligible than all the other arts put together, but
has become the only general means of morally influencing the
world. Painting, sculpture, and the dramatic theatre, it would
seem, no longer play an indispensable or even important part in

---

* See, for hereditaments, specimens, Walter Scott's Border Minstrelsy, Percy's
collection, Ellis's early English Metrical Romances, the European continental poems
of Walter of Aquitania, and the Nibelungen, of pagan stock, but monkish-feudal
redaction; the history of the Troubadours, by Fauriel; even the far-back cumbrous
old Hindu epics, as indicating the Asian eggs out of which European chivalry was
hatch'd; Ticknor's chapters on the Cid, and on the Spanish poems and poets of
Calderon's time. Then always, and, of course, as the superbest poetic culmination-ex-
pression of feudalism, the Shakespearean dramas, in the attitudes, dialogue, characters, etc., of the princes, lords, and gentlemen, the pervading atmosphere, the implied
and express'd standard of manners, the high port and proud stomach, the regal
embroidery of style, etc.

the workings and mediumship of intellect, utility, or even high aesthetics. Architecture remains, doubtless with capacities, and a real future. Then music, the combiner, nothing more spiritual, nothing more sensuous, a god, yet completely human, advances, prevails, holds highest place; supplying in certain wants and quarters what nothing else could supply. Yet in the civilization of today it is undeniable that, over all the arts, literature dominates, serves beyond all—shapes the character of church and school—or, in any rate, is capable of doing so. Including the literature of science, its scope is indeed unparallel'd.

Before proceeding further, it were perhaps well to discriminate on certain points. Literature tills its crops in many fields, and some may flourish, while others lag. What I say in these Vistas has its main bearing on imaginative literature, especially poetry, the stock of all. . . . I suggest, therefore, the possibility, should some two or three really original American poets (perhaps artists or lecturers) arise, mounting the horizon like planets, stars of the first magnitude, that, from their eminence, fusing contributions, races, far localities, etc., together, they would give more compaction and more moral identity (the quality to-day most needed) to these States, than all its Constitutions, legislative and judicial ties, and all its hitherto political, warlike, or materialistic experiences. As, for instance, there could hardly happen anything that would more serve the States, with all their variety of origins, their diverse climes, cities, standards, etc., than possessing an aggregate of heroes, characters, exploits, sufferings, prosperity or misfortune, glory or disgrace, common to all, typical of it all—no less, but even greater would it be to possess the aggregation of a cluster of mighty poets, artists, teachers, fit for us, national expressers, comprehending and effusing for the men and women of the States, what is universal, native, common to all, inland and seaboard, northern and southern. The historians say of ancient Greece, with her ever-jealous autonomies, cities and states, that the only positive unity she ever own'd or receiv'd, was the sad unity of a common subjection, at the last, to foreign conquerors. Subjection, aggregation of that sort, is impossible to America; but the fear of conflicting and irreconcilable interiors, and the lack of a common skeleton, knitting all close, continually haunts me. Or, if it does not, nothing is plainer than the need, a long period to come, of a fusion of the States into the only reliable identity, the moral and artistic one. For, I say, the true nationality of the States, the genuine union, when we come to a mortal crisis, is, and is to be, after all, neither the written law, nor (as is generally supposed) either self-interest, or common pecuniary or material objects—but the fervid and tremendous IDEA, melting everything else with resistless heat, and solving all lesser and definite distinctions in vast, indefinite, spiritual, emotional power.

It may be claim'd (and I admit the weight of the claim) that common and general worldly prosperity, and a populace well-to-do, and with all life's material comforts, is the main thing, and is enough. It may be argued that our republic is, in performance, really enacting today the grandest arts, poems, etc., by beating up the wilderness into fertile farms, and in her railroads, ships, machinery, etc. And it may be ask'd, Are these not better, indeed, for America, than any utterances even of greatest rhapsode, artist, or literatus?

I too hail those achievements with pride and joy: then answer that the soul of man will not with such only—nay, not with such at all—be finally satisfied; but needs what, (standing on these and on all things, as the feet stand on the ground), is addressed to the loftiest, to itself alone.

Out of such considerations, such truths, arises for treatment in these Vistas the important question of character, of an American stock-personality, with literatures and arts for outlets and return-expressions, and, of course, to correspond, within outlines common to all. To these, the main affair, the thinkers of the United States, in general so acute, have either given feeblest attention, or have remain'd, and remain, in a state of somnolence. . . .

Literature, strictly consider'd, has never recognized the People, and, whatever may be said, does not today. Speaking generally, the tendencies of literature, as hitherto pursued, have been to make mostly critical and querulous men. It seems as if, so far, there were some natural repugnance between a literary and professional life, and the rude rank spirit of the democracies. There is, in later literature, a treatment of benevolence, a charity business, rife enough it is true; but I know nothing more rare, even in this country, than a fit scientific estimate and reverent appreciation of the People—of their measureless wealth of latent power and capacity, their vast, artistic contrasts of lights and shades—with, in America, their entire reliability in emergencies, and a certain breadth of historic grandeur, of peace or war, far surpassing all the vaunted samples of book-heroes, or any *haut ton* coteries, in all the records of the world.

The movements of the late Secession War, and their results, to any sense that studies well and comprehends them, show that popular democracy, whatever its faults and dangers, practically justifies itself beyond the proudest claims and wildest hopes of its enthusiasts. Probably no future age can know, but I well know, how the gist of this fiercest and most resolute of the world's warlike contentions resided exclusively in the unnamed, unknown rank and file; and how the brunt of its labor of death was, to all essential purposes, volunteered. The People, of their own choice, fighting, dying for their own idea, insolently attack'd by the secession-slave-power, and its very existence imperil'd. Descending to detail, entering any of the armies, and mixing with the private soldiers, we see and have seen august spectacles. We have seen the alacrity with which the American-born populace, the peaceablest and most good-natured race in the world, and the most personally independent and intelligent, and the least fitted to submit to the irksomeness and exaspera-tion of regimental discipline, sprang, at the first tap of the drum, to arms—not for gain, nor even glory, nor to repel invasion—but for an emblem, a mere abstraction—for the life, *the safety of the flag.* We have seen the unequal'd docility and obedience of these soldiers. We have seen them tried long and long by hopelessness, mismanagement, and by defeat; have seen the incredible slaughter toward or through which the armies (as at first Fredericksburg, and afterward at the Wilderness), still unhesitatingly obey'd orders to advance. We have seen them in trench, or crouching behind breastwork, or tramping in deep mud, or amid pouring rain or thick-falling snow, or under forced marches in hottest summer (as on the road to get to Gettysburg—vast suffocating swarms, divisions, corps, with every single man so grimed and black with sweat and dust, his own mother would not have known him—his clothes all dirty, stain'd and torn, with sour, accumulated sweat for perfume—many a comrade, perhaps a brother, sun-struck, staggering out, dying, by the roadside, of exhaustion—yet the great bulk bearing steadily on, cheery enough, hollow-bellied from hunger, but sinewy with unconquerable resolution).

We have seen this race proved by wholesale, by drearier, yet more fearful tests—the wound, the amputation, the shatter'd

face or limb, the slow hot fever, long impatient anchorage in
bed, and all the forms of maiming, operation, and disease. Alas!
America have we seen, though only in her early youth, already
to hospital brought. There have we watch'd these soldiers, many
of them only boys in years—mark'd their decorum, their
religious nature and fortitude, and their sweet affection. Wholesale, truly. For at the front, and through the camps, in countless
tents, stood the regimental, brigade, and division hospitals;
while everywhere amid the land, in or near cities, rose clusters
of huge, whitewash'd, crowded, one-story wooden barracks; and
there ruled agony with bitter scourge, yet seldom brought a cry;
and there stalk'd death by day and night along the narrow aisles
between the rows of cots, or by the blankets on the ground, and
touch'd lightly many a poor sufferer, often with blessed,
welcome touch.

I know not whether I shall be understood, but I realize that it
is finally from what I learn'd personally mixing in such scenes
that I am now penning these pages. One night in the gloomiest
period of the war, in the Patent Office hospital in Washington
city, as I stood by the bedside of a Pennsylvania soldier, who
lay, conscious of quick approaching death, yet perfectly calm,
and with noble, spiritual manner, the veteran surgeon, turning
aside, said to me, that though he had witness'd many, many
deaths of soldiers, and had been a worker at Bull Run,
Antietam, Fredericksburg, etc., he had not seen yet the first
case of man or boy that met the approach of dissolution with
cowardly qualms or terror. My own observation fully bears out
the remark.

What have we here, if not, towering above all talk and
argument, the plentifully supplied, last-needed proof of democracy, in its personalities? Curiously enough, too, the proof on
this point comes, I should say, every bit as much from the
south, as from the north. Although I have spoken only of the
latter, yet I deliberately include all. Grand, common stock! to
me the accomplish'd and convincing growth, prophetic of the
future; proof undeniable to sharpest sense, of perfect beauty,
tenderness and pluck, that never feudal lord, nor Greek, nor
Roman breed, yet rival'd. Let no tongue ever speak in dispar-
agement of the American races, north or south, to one who has
been through the war in the great army hospitals. . . .

Did you, too, O friend, suppose democracy was only for
elections, for politics, and for a party name? I say democracy is

only of use there that it may pass on and come to its flower and fruits in manners, in the highest forms of interaction between men, and their beliefs—in religion, literature, colleges, and schools—democracy in all public and private life, and in the army and navy.* I have intimated that, as a paramount scheme, it has yet few or no full realizers and believers. I do not see, either, that it owes any serious thanks to noted propagandists or champions, or has been essentially help'd, though often harm'd, by them. It has been and is carried on by all the moral forces, and by trade, finance, machinery, intercommunications, and, in fact, by all the developments of history, and can no more be stopp'd than the tides, or the earth in its orbit. Doubtless, also, it resides, crude and latent, well down in the hearts of the fair average of the American-born people, mainly in the agricultural regions. But it is not yet, there or anywhere, the fully receiv'd, the fervid, the absolute faith.

I submit, therefore, that the fruition of democracy, on aught like a grand scale, resides altogether in the future. As, under any profound and comprehensive view of the gorgeous-composite feudal world, we see in it, through the long ages and cycles of ages, the results of a deep, integral, human and divine principle, or fountain, from which issued laws, ecclesia, manners, institutes, costumes, personalities, poems (hitherto unequal'd), faithfully partaking of their source, and indeed only arising either to betoken it, or to furnish parts of that varied-flowing display, whose center was one and absolute—so, long ages hence, shall the due historian or critic make at least an equal retrospect, an equal history for the democratic principle. It too must be adorn'd, credited with its results—then, when it, with imperial power, through amplest time, has dominated mankind—has been the source and test of all the moral, aesthetic, social, political, and religious expressions and institutes of the civilized world—has begotten them in spirit and in form, and has carried them to its own unprecedented heights—has had (it is possible) monastics and ascetics, more numerous, more devout than the monks and priests of all previous creeds—has sway'd the ages with a breadth and rectitude tallying Nature's own—has

* The whole present system of the officering and personnel of the army and navy of these States, and the spirit and letter of their trebly-aristocratic rules and regulations, is a monstrous exotic, a nuisance and revolt, and belong here just as much as orders of nobility, or the Pope's council of cardinals. I say if the present theory of our army and navy is sensible and true, then the rest of America is an unmitigated fraud.

fashion'd, systematized, and triumphantly finish'd and carried out, in its own interest, and with unparallel'd success, a new earth and a new man.

Thus we presume to write, as it were, upon things that exist not, and travel by maps yet unmade, and a blank. But the throes of birth are upon us; and we have something of this advantage in seasons of strong formations, doubts, suspense—for then the afflatus of such themes haply may fall upon us, more or less; and then, hot from surrounding war and revolution, our speech, though without polish'd coherence, and a failure by the standard called criticism, comes forth, real at least as the lightnings.

And maybe we, these days, have, too, our own reward—(for there are yet some, in all lands, worthy to be so encouraged). Though not for us the joy of entering at the last the conquered city—not ours the chance ever to see with our own eyes the peerless power and splendid *éclat* of the democratic principle, arriv'd at meridian, filling the world with effulgence and majesty far beyond those of past history's kings, or all dynastic sway—there is yet, to whoever is eligible among us, the prophetic vision, the joy of being toss'd in the brave turmoil of these times—the promulgation and the path, obedient, lowly reverent to the voice, the gesture of the god, or holy ghost, which others see not, hear not—with the proud consciousness that amid whatever clouds, seductions, or heart-wearying postponements, we have never deserted, never despair'd, never abandon'd the faith.

So much contributed, to be conn'd well, to help prepare and brace our edifice, our plann'd Idea—we still proceed to give it in another of its aspects—perhaps the main, the high façade of all. For to democracy, the leveler, the unyielding principle of the average, is surely join'd another principle, equally unyielding, closely tracking the first, indispensable to it, opposite (as the sexes are opposite), and whose existence, confronting and ever modifying the other, often clashing, paradoxical, yet neither of highest avail without the other, plainly supplies to these grand cosmic politics of ours, and to the launch'd forth mortal dangers of republicanism, today, or any day, the counterpart and offset whereby Nature restrains the deadly original relentlessness of all her first-class laws. This second principle is individuality, the pride and centripetal isolation of a human being in himself—identity—personalism. Whatever the name, its acceptance and thorough infusions through the organizations of political commonalty now shooting Aurora-like about the world, are of utmost importance, as the principle itself is needed for very life's sake. It forms, in a sort, or is to form, the compensating balance-wheel of the successful working machinery of aggregate America.

And, if we think of it, what does civilization itself rest upon—and what object has it, with its religions, arts, schools, etc., but rich, luxuriant, varied personalism? To that, all bends; and it is because toward such result democracy alone, on anything like Nature's scale, breaks up the limitless fallows of human-kind, and plants the seed, and gives fair play, that its claims now precede the rest. The literature, songs, aesthetics, etc., of a country are of importance principally because they furnish the materials and suggestions of personality for the women and men of that country, and enforce them in a thousand effective ways.* As the topmost claim of a strong consolidating of the nationality of these States, is, that only by such powerful compaction can the separate States secure that full and free swing within their spheres, which is becoming to

---

* After the rest is satiated, all interest culminates in the field of persons, and never flags there. Accordingly in this field have the great poets and literatuses signally toiled. They too, in all ages, all lands, have been creators, fashioning, making types of men and women, as Adam and Eve are made in the divine fable. Behold, shaped, bred by orientalism, feudalism, through their long growth and culmination, and breeding back in return—(when shall we have an equal series, typical of democracy?)—behold, commencing in primal Asia (apparently formulated, in what beginning we know, in the gods of the mythologies, and coming down thence), a few samples out of the countless product, bequeath'd to the moderns, bequeath'd to America as studies. For the men, Yudishtura, Rama, Arjuna, Solomon, most of the Old and New Testament characters; Achilles, Ulysses, Theseus, Prometheus, Hercules, Aeneas, Plutarch's heroes; the Merlin of Celtic bards; the Cid, Arthur and his knights, Siegried and Hagen in the Nibelungen; Roland and Oliver; Roustam in the Shah-Nemah; and so on to Milton's Satan, Cervantes' Don Quixote, Shakespeare's Hamlet, Richard II, Lear, Marc Antony, etc., and the modern Faust. These, I say, are models, combined, adjusted to other standards than America's, but of priceless value to her and hers.

Among women, the goddesses of the Egyptian, Indian, and Greek mythologies, certain Bible characters, especially the Holy Mother; Cleopatra, Penelope; the portraits of Brunhilde and Chriemhilde in the Nibelungen; Oriana, Una, etc.; the modern Consuelo, Walter Scott's Jeanie and Effie Deans, etc., etc. (Yet woman portrayed or outlin'd at her best, or as perfect human mother, does not hitherto, it seems to me, fully appear in literature.)

them, each after its kind, so will individuality, with unimpeded branchings, flourish best under imperial republican forms.

Assuming Democracy to be at present in its embryo condition, and that the only large and satisfactory justification of it resides in the future, mainly through the copious production of perfect characters among the people, and through the advent of a sane and pervading religiousness, it is with regard to the atmosphere and spaciousness fit for such characters, and of certain nutriment and cartoon-draftings proper for them, and indicating them for New World purposes, that I continue the present statement—an exploration, as of new ground, wherein, like other primitive surveyors, I must do the best I can, leaving it to those who come after me to do much better. (The service, in fact, if any, must be to break a sort of first path or track, no matter how rude and ungeometrical.)

We have frequently printed the word Democracy. Yet I cannot too often repeat that it is a word the real gist of which still sleeps, quite unawaken'd, notwithstanding the resonance and the many angry tempests out of which its syllables have come, from pen or tongue. It is a great word, whose history, I suppose, remains unwritten, because that history has yet to be enacted. It is, in some sort, younger brother of another great and often-used word, Nature, whose history also waits unwritten. As I perceive, the tendencies of our day, in the States (and I entirely respect them), are toward those vast and sweeping movements, influences, moral and physical, of humanity, now and always current over the planet, on the scale of the impulses of the elements. Then it is also good to reduce the whole matter to the consideration of a single self, a man, a woman, on permanent grounds. Even for the treatment of the universal, in politics, metaphysics, or anything, sooner or later we come down to one single, solitary soul.

There is, in sanest hours, a consciousness, a thought that rises, independent, lifted out from all else, calm, like the stars, shining eternal. This is the thought of identity—yours for you, whoever you are, as mine for me. Miracle of miracles, beyond statement, most spiritual and vaguest of earth's dreams, yet hardest basic fact, and only entrance to all facts. In such devout hours, in the midst of the significant wonders of heaven and earth (significant only because of the Me in the center), creeds, conventions, fall away and become of no account before this simple idea. Under the luminousness of real vision, it alone takes possession, takes value. Like the shadowy dwarf in the fable, once liberated and look'd upon, it expands over the whole earth, and spreads to the roof of heaven.

The quality of BEING, in the object's self, according to its own central idea and purpose, and of growing therefrom and thereto—not criticism by other standards, and adjustments thereto—is the lesson of Nature. True, the full man wisely gathers, culls, absorbs; but if, engaged disproportionately in that, he slights or overlays the precious idiocrasy and special nativity and intention that he is, the man's self, the main thing, is a failure, however wide his general cultivation. Thus, in our times, refinement and delicatesse are not only attended to sufficiently, but threaten to eat us up, like a cancer. Already, the democratic genius watches, ill-pleased, these tendencies. Provision for a little healthy rudeness, savage virtue, justification of what one has in one's self, whatever it is, is demanded. Negative qualities, even deficiencies, would be a relief. Singleness and normal simplicity and separation, amid this more and more complex, more and more artificialized state of society—how pensively we yearn for them! how we would welcome their return!

In some such direction, then—at any rate enough to preserve the balance—we feel called upon to throw what weight we can, not for absolute reasons, but current ones. To prune, gather, trim, conform, and ever cram and stuff, and be genteel and proper, is the pressure of our days. While aware that much can be said even in behalf of all this, we perceive that we have not now to consider the question of what is demanded to serve a half-starved and barbarous nation, or set of nations, but what is most applicable, most pertinent, for numerous congeries of conventional, over-corpulent societies, already becoming stifled and rotten with flatulent, infidelistic literature, and polite conformity and art. In addition to establish'd sciences, we suggest a science as it were of healthy average personalism, on original-universal grounds, the object of which should be to raise up and supply through the States a copious race of superb American men and women, cheerful, religious, ahead of any yet known.

America has yet morally and artistically originated nothing. She seems singularly unaware that the models of persons, books, manners, etc., appropriate for former conditions and for European lands, are but exiles and exotics here. No current of her life, as shown on the surfaces of what is authoritatively called her society, accepts or runs into social or aesthetic democracy; but all the currents set squarely against it. Never, in the Old World, was thoroughly upholster'd exterior appearance and show, mental and other, built entirely on the idea of caste, and on the sufficiency of mere outside acquisition—never were glibness, verbal intellect more the test, the emulation—more loftily elevated as head and sample—than they are on the surface of our republican States this day. The writers of a time hint the mottoes of its gods. The word of the modern, say these voices, is the word Culture.

We find ourselves abruptly in close quarters with the enemy. This word Culture, or what it has come to represent, involves, by contrast, our whole theme, and has been, indeed, the spur, urging us to engagement. Certain questions arise. As now taught, accepted and carried out, are not the processes of culture rapidly creating a class of supercilious infidels, who believe in nothing? Shall a man lose himself in countless masses of adjustments, and be so shaped with reference to this, that, and the other, that the simply good and healthy and brave parts of him are reduced and clipp'd away, like the bordering of box in a garden? You can cultivate corn and roses and orchards—but who shall cultivate the mountain peaks, the ocean, and the tumbling gorgeousness of the clouds? Lastly—is the readily given reply that culture only seeks to help, systematize, and put in attitude, the elements of fertility and power, a conclusive reply? . . .

Approaching thus the momentous spaces, and considering with reference to a new and greater personalism, the needs and possibilities of American imaginative literature, through the medium-light of what we have already broach'd, it will at once be appreciated that a vast gulf of difference separates the present accepted condition of these spaces, inclusive of what is floating in them, from any condition adjusted to, or fit for, the world, the America, there sought to be indicated, and the copious races of complete men and women, along these Vistas crudely outlined. It is, in some sort, no less a difference than lies between that long-continued nebular state and vagueness of the astronomical worlds, compared with the subsequent state, the definitely-form'd worlds themselves, duly compacted, clustering in systems, hung up there, chandeliers of the universe, beholding and mutually lit by each other's lights, serving for ground of all substantial foothold, all vulgar uses—yet serving still more as an undying chain and echelon of spiritual proofs and shows. A boundless field to fill! A new creation, with needed orbic works launch'd forth, to revolve in free and lawful circuits—to move, self-poised, through the ether, and shine like heaven's own suns! With such, and nothing less, we suggest that New World literature, fit to rise upon, cohere, and signalize in time, these States.

What, however, do we more definitely mean by New World literature? Are we not doing well enough here already? Are not the United States this day busily using, working, more printer's type, more presses, than any other country? uttering and absorbing more publications than any other? Do not our publishers fatten quicker and deeper? (helping themselves, under shelter of a delusive and sneaking law, or rather absence of law, to most of their forage, poetical, pictorial, historical, romantic, even comic, without money and without price—and fiercely resisting the timidest proposal to pay for it). Many will come under this delusion—but my purpose is to dispel it. I say that a nation may hold and circulate rivers and oceans of very readable print, journals, magazines, novels, library books, "poetry," etc.—such as the States today possess and circulate— of unquestionable aid and value—hundreds of new volumes annually composed and brought out here, respectable enough, indeed unsurpass'd in smartness and erudition—with further hundreds, or rather millions (as by free forage or theft aforementioned), also thrown into the market—and yet, all the while, the said nation, land, strictly speaking, may possess no literature at all.

Repeating our inquiry, what, then, do we mean by real literature? especially the democratic literature of the future? Hard questions to meet. The clues are inferential, and turn us to the past. At best, we can only offer suggestions, comparisons, circuits.

It must still be reiterated, as, for the purpose of these memoranda, the deep lesson of history and time, that all else in the contributions of a nation or age, through its politics, materials, heroic personalities, military *éclat*, etc., remains crude, and defers, in any close and thoroughgoing estimate, until vitalized by national, original achetypes in literature. They only put the nation in form, finally tell anything—prove, complete anything—perpetuate anything. Without doubt, some of the richest and most powerful and populous communities of the antique world, and some of the grandest personalities and events, have, to after and present times, left themselves entirely unbequeath'd. Doubtless, greater than any that have come down to us, were among those lands, heroisms, persons, that have not come down to us at all, even by name, date, or location. Others have arrived safely, as from voyages over wide, century-stretching seas. The little ships, the miracles that have buoy'd them, and by incredible chances safely convey'd them (or the best of them, their meaning and essence) over long wastes, darkness, lethargy, ignorance, etc., have been a few inscriptions—a few immortal compositions, small in size, yet compassing what measureless values of reminiscence, contemporary portraitures, manners, idioms, and beliefs, with deepest inference, hint, and thought, to tie and touch forever the old, new body, and the old, new soul! These! and still these! bearing the freight so dear—dearer than pride—dearer than love. All the best experience of humanity, folded, saved, freighted to us here. Some of these tiny ships we call Old and New Testament, Homer, Eschylus, Plato, Juvenal, etc. Precious minims! I think, if we were forced to choose, rather than have you, and the likes of you, and what belongs to, and has grown of you, blotted out and gone, we could better afford, appalling as that would be, to lose all actual ships, this day fasten'd by wharf, or floating on wave, and see them, with all their cargoes, scuttled and sent to the bottom.

Gathered by geniuses of city, race or age, and put by them in highest of art's forms, namely, the literary form, the peculiar combinations and the outshows of that city, age or race, its particular modes of the universal attributes and passions, its faiths, heroes, lovers and gods, wars, traditions, struggles, crimes, emotions, joys (or the subtle spirit of these), having been pass'd on to us to illumine our own selfhood, and its experiences—what they supply, indispensable and highest, if taken away, nothing else in all the world's boundless storehouses could make up to us, or ever again return.

For us, along the great highways of time, those monuments stand—those forms of majesty and beauty. For us those beacons burn through all the nights. Unknown Egyptians, graving hiero-glyphs; Hindus, with hymn and apothegm and endless epic; Hebrew prophet, with spirituality, as in flashes of lightning, conscience like red-hot iron, plaintive songs and screams of vengeance for tyrannies and enslavement; Christ, with bent head, brooding love and peace, like a dove; Greek, creating eternal shapes of physical and aesthetic proportion; Roman, lord of satire, the sword, and the codex;—of the figures, some far off and veil'd, others nearer and visible; Dante, stalking with lean form, nothing but fiber, not a grain of superfluous flesh; Angelo, and the great painters, architects, musicians; rich Shakspere, luxuriant as the sun, artist and singer of feudalism in its sunset, with all the gorgeous colors, owner thereof, and using them at will; and so to such as German Kant and Hegel, where they, though near us, leaping over the ages, sit again, impassive, imperturbable, like the Egyptian gods. Of these, and the like of these, it is too much, indeed, to return to our favorite figure, and view them as orbs and systems of orbs, moving in free paths in the spaces of that other heaven, the kosmic intellect, the soul?

Ye powerful and resplendent ones! ye were, in your atmospheres, grown not for America, but rather for her foes, the feudal and the old—while our genius is democratic and modern. Yet could ye, indeed, but breathe your breath of life into our New World's nostrils—not to enslave us, as now, but, for our needs, to breed a spirit like your own—perhaps (dare we to say it?) to dominate, even destroy, what you yourselves have left! On your plane, and no less, but even higher and wider, must we mete and measure for today and here. I demand races of orbic bards, with unconditional, uncompromising sway. Come forth, sweet democratic despots of the west!

By points like these we, in reflection, token what we mean by any land's or people's genuine literature. And thus compared and tested, judging amid the influence of loftiest products only, what do our current copious fields of print, covering in manifold forms, the United States, better, for an analogy, present, than, as in certain regions of the sea, those spreading, undulating masses of squid, through which the whale swimming, with head half out, feeds?

Not but that doubtless our current so-called literature (like an endless supply of small coin) performs a certain service, and maybe too, the service needed for the time, (the preparation-service, as children learn to spell). Everybody reads, and truly nearly everybody writes, either books, or for the magazines or journals. The matter has magnitude, too, after a sort. But is it really advancing? or, has it advanced for a long while? There is something impressive about the huge editions of the dailies and weeklies, the mountain-stacks of white paper piled in the press-vaults, and the proud, crashing, ten-cylinder presses, which I can stand and watch any time by the half hour. Then (though the States in the field of imagination present not a single first-class work, not a single great literatus), the main objects, to amuse, to titillate, to pass away time, to circulate the news, and rumors of news, to rhyme, and read rhyme, are yet attain'd, and on a scale of infinity. Today, in books, in the rivalry of writers, especially novelists, success (so-called) is for him or her who strikes the mean flat average, the sensational appetite for stimulus, incident, persiflage, etc., and depicts, to the common caliber, sensual, exterior life. To such, or the luckiest of them, as we see, the audiences are limitless and profitable; but they cease presently. While this day, or any day, to workmen portraying interior or spiritual life, the audiences were limited, and often laggard—but they last forever.

Compared with the past, our modern science soars, and our journals serve—but ideal and even ordinary romantic literature, does not, I think, substantially advance. Behold the prolific brood of the contemporary novel, magazine tale, theatre play, etc. The same endless thread of tangled and superlative love story, inherited, apparently from the Amadises and Palmerins of the 13th, 14th, and 15th centuries over there in Europe. The costumes and associations brought down to date, the seasoning hotter and more varied, the dragons and ogres left out—but the *thing*, I should say, has not advanced—is just as sensational, just as strain'd—remains about the same, nor more, nor less.

What is the reason our time, our lands, that we see no fresh local courage, sanity, of our own—the Mississippi, stalwart Western men, real mental and physical facts, Southerners, etc., in the body of our literature? especially the poetic part of it. But always, instead, a parcel of dandies and ennuyees, dapper little gentlemen from abroad, who flood us with their thin sentiment of parlors, parasols, piano songs, tinkling rhymes, the five-hundredth importation—or whimpering and crying about something, chasing one aborted conceit after another, and forever occupied in dyspeptic amours with dyspeptic women.

While, current and novel, the grandest events and revolutions, and stormiest passions of history, are crossing today with unparalleled rapidity and magnificence over the stages of our own and all the continents, offering new materials, opening new vistas, with largest needs, inviting the daring launching forth of conceptions in literature, inspired by them, soaring in highest regions, serving art in its highest (which is only the other name for serving God, and serving humanity), where is the man of letters, where is the book, with any nobler aim than to follow in the old track, repeat what has been said before—and, as its utmost triumph, sell well, and be erudite or elegant?

Mark the roads, the processes, through which these States have arrived, standing easy, henceforth ever-equal, ever-compact, in their range today. European adventures? the most antique? Asiatic or African? old history—miracles—romances? Rather, our own unquestion'd facts. They hasten, incredible, blazing bright as fire. From the deeds and days of Columbus down to the present, and including the present—and especially the late Secession War—when I con them, I feel, every leaf, like stopping to see if I have not made a mistake, and fall'n on the splendid figments of some dream. But it is no dream. We stand, live, move, in the huge flow of our age's materialism—in its spirituality. We have founded for us the most positive of lands. The founders have pass'd to other spheres—but what are these terrible duties they have left us?

Their policies the United States have, in my opinion, with all their faults, already substantially establish'd, for good, on their own native, sound, long-vista'd principles, never to be over-turn'd, offering a sure basis for all the rest. With that, their future religious forms, sociology, literature, teachers, schools, costumes, etc., are of course to make a compact whole, uniform, on tallying principles. For how can we remain, divided, contradicting ourselves this way?* I say we can only attain harmony and stability by consulting ensemble and the

---

* Note, today, an instructive, curious spectacle and conflict. Science (twin, in its fields, of Democracy in its)—Science, testing absolutely all thoughts, all works, has already burst well upon the world—a sun, mounting, most illuminating, most glorious—surely never again to set. But against it, deeply entrench'd, holding possession, yet remains (not only through the churches and schools, but by imaginative literature, and unregenerate poetry), the fossil theology of the mythic-materialistic, superstitious, untaught and credulous, fable-loving, primitive ages of humanity.

ethic purports, and faithfully building upon them. For the New
World, indeed, after two grand stages of preparation-strata, I
perceive that now a third stage, being ready for (and without
which the other two were useless), with unmistakable signs
appears. The First stage was the planning and putting on record
the political foundation rights of immense masses of people
—indeed all people—in the organization or republican National,
State, and municipal governments, all constructed with reference to each, and each to all. This is the American programme, not for classes, but for universal man, and is embodied
in the compacts of the Declaration of Independence, and, as it
began and has now grown, with its amendments, the Federal
Constitution—and in the State governments, with all their
interiors, and with general suffrage; those having the sense not
only of what is in themselves, but that their certain several
things started, planted, hundreds of others in the same direction
duly arise and follow. The Second stage relates to material
prosperity, wealth, produce, laborsaving machines, iron, cotton,
local, State, and continental railways, intercommunication and
trade with all lands, steamships, mining, general employment,
organization of great cities, cheap appliances for comfort,
numberless technical schools, books, newspapers, a currency for
money circulation, etc. The Third stage, rising out of the
previous ones, to make them and all illustrious, I, now, for one,
promulge, announcing a native expression-spirit, getting into
form, adult, and through mentality, for these States, self-
contain'd, different from others, more expansive, more rich
and free, to be evidenced by original authors and poets to come,
by American personalities, plenty of them, male and female,
traversing the States, none excepted—and by native superber
tableaux and growths of language, songs, operas, orations,
lectures, architecture—and by a sublime and serious Religious
Democracy sternly taking command, dissolving the old,
sloughing off surfaces, and from its own interior and vital
principles, reconstructing, democratizing society.

For America, type of progress, and of essential faith in man,
above all his errors and wickedness—few suspect how deep, how
deep it really strikes. The world evidently supposes, and we
have evidently supposed so too, that the States are merely to
achieve the equal franchise, an elective government—to inau-
gurate the respectability of labor, and become a nation of
practical operatives, law-abiding, orderly, and well-off. Yes,

those are indeed parts of the task of America; but they not only do not exhaust the progressive conception, but rather arise, teeming with it, as the mediums of deeper, higher progress. Daughter of a physical revolution—mother of the true revolutions, which are of the interior life, and of the arts. For so long as the spirit is not changed, any change of appearance is of no avail.

The old men, I remember as a boy, were always talking of American independence. What is independence? Freedom from all laws or bonds except those of one's own being, control'd by the universal ones. To lands, to man, to woman, what is there at last to each, but the inherent soul, nativity, idiosyncrasy, free, highest poised, soaring its own flight, following out itself?

At present, these States, in their theology and social standards (of greater importance than their political institutions) are entirely held possession of by foreign lands. We see the sons and daughters of the New World, ignorant of its genius, not yet inaugurating the native, the universal, and the near still importing the distant, the partial, and the dead. We see London, Paris, Italy—not original, superb, as where they belong—but second-hand here, where they do not belong. We see the shreds of Hebrews, Romans, Greeks; but where, on her own soil, do we see, in any faithful, highest, proud expression, America herself? I sometimes question whether she has a corner in her own house.

Not but that in one sense, and a very grand one, good theology, good art, or good literature, has certain features shared in common. The combination fraternizes, ties the races—is, in many particulars, under laws applicable indifferently to all, irrespective of climate or date, and, from whatever source, appeals to emotions, pride, love, spirituality, common to human-kind. Nevertheless, they touch a man closest (perhaps only actually touch him), even in these, in their expression through autochthonic lights and shades, flavors, fondnesses, aversions, specific incidents, illustrations, out of his own nationality, geography, surroundings, antecedents, etc. The spirit and the form are one, and depend far more on association, identity, and place, than is supposed. Subtly interwoven with the materiality and personality of a land, a race—Teuton, Turk, Californian, or what not—there is always something—I can hardly tell what it is—history but describes the results of it—it is the same as the untellable look of some human faces. Nature, too, in his stolid forms, is full of it—but to most it is there a secret. This something is rooted in the invisible roots, the profoundest meanings of that place, race, or nationality; and to absorb and again effuse it, uttering words and products as from its midst, and carrying it into highest regions, is the work, or a main part of the work, of any country's true author, poet, historian, lecturer, and perhaps even priest and philosoph. Here, and here only, are the foundations for our really valuable and permanent verse, drama, etc.

But at present (judged by any higher scale than that which finds the chief ends of existence to be to feverishly make money during one half of it, and by some "amusement," or perhaps foreign travel, flippantly kill time, the other half), and considered with reference to purposes of patriotism, health, a noble personality, religion, and the democratic adjustments, all these swarms of poems, literary magazines, dramatic plays, resultant so far from American intellect, and the formation of our best ideas, are useless and a mockery. They strengthen and nourish no one, express nothing characteristic, give decision and purpose to no one, and suffice only the lowest level of vacant minds.

Of what is called the drama, or dramatic presentation in the United States, as now put forth at the theatres, I should say it deserves to be treated with the same gravity, and on a par with the questions of ornamental confectionery at public dinners, or the arrangement of curtains and hangings in a ballroom—nor more, nor less. Of the other, I will not insult the reader's intelligence (once really entering into the atmosphere of these Vistas), by supposing it necessary to show, in detail, why the copious dribble, either of our little or well-known rhymesters, does not fulfill, in any respect, the needs and august occasions of this land. America demands a poetry that is bold, modern, and all-surrounding and kosmical, as she is herself. It must in no respect ignore science or the modern, but inspire itself with science and the modern. It must bend its vision toward the future, more than the past. Like America, it must extricate itself from even the greatest models of the past, and, while courteous to them, must have entire faith in itself, and the products of its own democratic spirit only. Like her, it must place in the van, and hold up at all hazards, the banner of the divine pride of man in himself (the radical foundation of the

new religion). Long enough have the People been listening to
poems in which common humanity, deferential, bends low,
humiliated, acknowledging superiors. But America listens to no
such poems. Erect, inflated, and fully self-esteeming be the
chant; and then America will listen with pleased ears.

Nor may the genuine gold, the gems, when brought to light at
last, be probably usher'd forth from any of the quarters
currently counted on. Today, doubtless, the infant genius of
American poetic expression (eluding those highly refined
imported and gilt-edged themes, and sentimental and butterfly
flights, pleasant to orthodox publishers—causing tender spasms
in the coteries, and warranted not to chafe the sensitive cuticle
of the most exquisitely artificial gossamer delicacy), lies
sleeping far away, happily unrecognized and uninjur'd by the
coteries, the art-writers, the talkers and critics of the saloons, or
the lecturers in the colleges—lies sleeping, aside, unrecking itself,
in some western idiom, or native Michigan or Tennessee
repartee, or stump speech—or in Kentucky or Georgia, or the
Carolinas—or in some slang or local song or allusion of the
Manhattan, Boston, Philadelphia, or Baltimore mechanic—or up
in the Maine woods—or off in the hut of the California miner,
or crossing the Rocky Mountains, or along the Pacific railroad—
or on the breasts of the young farmers of the northwest, or
Canada, or boatmen of the lakes. Rude and coarse nursing beds,
these; but only from such beginnings and stocks, indigenous
here, may haply arrive, be grafted, and sprout in time, flowers
of genuine American aroma, and fruits truly and fully our own.

I say it were a standing disgrace to these States—I say it were a
disgrace to any nation, distinguish'd above others by the variety
and vastness of its territories, its materials, its inventive activity,
and the splendid practicality of its people, not to rise and soar
above others, also in its original styles in literature and art, and
its own supply of intellectual and aesthetic masterpieces, archetypal, and consistent with itself. I know not a land except ours
that has not, to some extent, however small, made its title clear.
The Scotch have their born ballads, subtly expressing their past
and present, and expressing character. The Irish have theirs.
England, Italy, France, Spain, theirs. What has America? With
exhaustless mines of the richest ore of epic, lyric, tale, tune,
picture, etc., in the Four Years' War; with, indeed, I sometimes
think, the richest masses of material ever afforded a nation,

more variegated, and on a larger scale—the first sign of propor-
tionate, native, imaginative Soul, and first-class works to match,
is (I cannot too often repeat), so far wanting.

Long ere the second centennial arrives, there will be some
forty to fifty great States, among them Canada and Cuba. When
the present century closes, our population will be sixty or
seventy millions. The Pacific will be ours, and the Atlantic
mainly ours. There will be daily electric communication with
every part of the globe. What an age! What a land! Where,
elsewhere, one so great? The individuality of one nation must
then, as always, lead the world. Can there be any doubt who the
leader ought to be? Bear in mind, though, that nothing less than
the mightiest original non-subordinated SOUL has ever really,
gloriously led, or ever can lead. (This Soul—its other name, in
these Vistas, is LITERATURE.) . . .

The elevating and etherealizing ideas of the unknown and of
unreality must be brought forward with authority, as they are
the legitimate heirs of the known, and of reality, and at least as
great as their parents. Fearless of scoffing, and of the ostent, let
us take our stand, our ground, and never desert it, to confront
the growing excess and arrogance of realism. To the cry, now
victorious—the cry of sense, science, flesh, incomes, farms,
merchandise, logic, intellect, demonstrations, solid perpetuities,
buildings of brick and iron, or even the facts of the shows of
trees, earth, rocks, etc., fear not, my brethren, my sisters, to
sound out with equally determin'd voice, that conviction
brooding within the recesses of every envision'd soul—illusions!
apparitions! figments all! True, we must not condemn the show,
neither absolutely deny it, for the indispensability of its
meanings; but how clearly we see that, migrate in soul to what
we can already conceive of superior and spiritual points of view,
and palpable as it seems under present relations, it all and
several might, nay certainly would, fall apart and vanish.

I hail with joy the oceanic, variegated, intense practical
energy, the demand for facts, even the business materialism of
the current age, our States. But woe to the age and land in
which these things, movements, stopping at themselves, do not
tend to ideas. As fuel to flame, and flame to the heavens, so
much wealth, science, materialism—even this democracy of
which we make so much—unerringly feed the highest mind, the
soul. Infinitude the flight: fathomless the mystery. Man, so
diminutive, dilates beyond the sensible universe, competes with,

outcopes space and time, meditating even one great idea. Thus, and thus only, does a human being, his spirit, ascend above, and justify, objective Nature, which, probably nothing in itself, is incredibly and divinely serviceable, indispensable, real, here. And as the purport of objective Nature is doubtless folded, hidden, somewhere here—as somewhere here is what this globe and its manifold forms, and the light of day, and night's darkness, and life itself, with all its experiences, are for—it is here the great literature, especially verse, must get its inspiration and throbbing blood. Then may we attain to a poetry worthy the immortal soul of man, and which, while absorbing materials, and, in their own sense, the shows of Nature, will, above all, have, both directly and indirectly, a freeing, fluidizing, expanding, religious character, exulting with science, fructifying the moral elements, and stimulating aspirations, and meditations on the unknown.

The process, so far, is indirect and peculiar, and though it may be suggested, cannot be defined. Observing, rapport, and with intuition, the shows and forms presented by Nature, the sensuous luxuriance, the beautiful in living men and women, the actual play of passions, in history and life—and, above all, from those developments either in Nature or human personality in which power (dearest of all to the sense of the artist) transacts itself—out of these, and seizing what is in them, the poet, the aesthetic worker in any field, by the divine magic of his genius, projects them, their analogies, by curious removes, indirections, in literature and art. (No useless attempt to repeat the material creation, by daguerrotyping the exact likeness by mortal mental means.) This is the image-making faculty, coping with material creation, and rivaling, almost triumphing over it. This alone, when all the other parts of a specimen of literature or art are ready and waiting, can breathe into it the breath of life, and endow it with identity.

"The true question to ask," says the Librarian of Congress in a paper read before the Social Science Convention at New York, October 1869, "The true question to ask respecting a book, is *has it help'd any human soul?*" This is the hint, statement, not only of the great literatus, his book, but of every great artist. It may be that all works of art are to be first tried by their art qualities, their image-forming talent, and their dramatic, pictorial, plot-constructing, euphonious and other talents. Then, whenever claiming to be first-class works, they are to be strictly and sternly tried by their foundation in, and radiation, in the highest sense and always indirectly, of, the ethic principles and eligibility to free, arouse, dilate. . . .

There are still other standards, suggestions, for products of high literatuses. That which really balances and conserves the social and political world is not so much legislation, police, treaties, and dread of punishment, as the latent eternal intuitional sense, in humanity, of fairness, manliness, decorum, etc. Indeed, this perennial regulation, control, and oversight, by self-suppliance, is *sine qua non* to democracy; and a highest, widest aim of democratic literature may well be to bring forth, cultivate, brace, and strengthen this sense, in individuals and society. A strong mastership of the general inferior self by the superior self, is to be aided, secured, indirectly, but surely, by the literatus, in his works, shaping, for individual or aggregate democracy, a great passionate body, in and along with which goes a great masterful spirit.

And still, providing for contingencies, I fain confront the fact, the need of powerful native philosophs and orators and bards, these States, as rallying points to come, in times of danger, and to fend off ruin and defection. For history is long, long, long. Shift and turn the combinations of the statement as we may, the problem of the future of America is in certain respects as dark as it is vast. Pride, competition, segregation, vicious wilfulness, and license beyond example, brood already upon us. Unwieldly and immense, who shall hold in behemoth? who bridle leviathan? Flaunt it as we choose, athwart and over the roads of our progress loom huge uncertainty, and dreadful, threatening gloom. It is useless to deny it: Democracy grows rankly up the thickest, noxious, deadliest plants and fruits of all—brings worse and worse invaders—needs newer, larger, stronger, keener compensations and compellers.

Arrived now, definitely, at an apex for these Vistas, I confess that the promulgation and belief in such a class or institution—a new and greater literatus order—its possibility (nay certainty), underlies these entire speculations—and that the rest, the other parts, as superstructures, are all founded upon it. It really seems to me the condition, not only of our future national and democratic development, but of our perpetuation. In the highly artificial and materialistic bases of modern civilization, with the corresponding arrangements and methods of living, the force-infusion of intellect alone, the depraving influences of riches just as much as poverty, the absence of all high ideals in character—with the long series of tendencies, shapings, which few are strong enough to resist, and which now seem, with steam-engine speed, to be everywhere turning out the generations of humanity like uniform iron castings—all of which, as compared with the feudal ages, we can yet do nothing better than accept, make the best of, and even welcome, upon the whole, for their oceanic practical grandeur, and their restless wholesale kneading of the masses—I say of all this tremendous and dominant play of solely materialistic bearings upon current life in the United States, with the results as already seen, accumulating, and reaching far into the future, that they must either be confronted and met by at least an equally subtle and tremendous force-infusion for purposes of spiritualization, for the pure conscience, for genuine aesthetics, and for absolute and primal manliness and womanliness—or else our modern civilization, with all its improvements, is in vain, and we are on the road to a destiny, a status, equivalent, in its real world, to that of the fabled damned.

Prospecting thus the coming unsped days, and that new order in them—marking the endless train of exercise, development, unwind, in nation as in man, which life is for—we see, foreindicated, amid these prospects and hopes, new law-forces of spoken and written language—not merely the pedagogue-forms, correct, regular, familiar with precedents, made for matters of outside propriety, fine words, thoughts definitely told out—but a language fann'd by the breath of Nature, which leaps overhead, cares mostly for impetus and effects, and for what it plants and invigorates to grow—tallies life and character, and seldomer tells a things than suggests or necessitates it. In fact, a new theory of literary composition for imaginative works of the very first class, and especially for highest poems, is the sole course open to these States. Books are to be call'd for, and supplied, on the assumption that the process of reading is not a half-sleep, but, in highest sense, an exercise, a gymnast's struggle; that the reader is to do something for himself, must be on the alert, must himself or herself construct indeed the poem, argument, history, metaphysical essay—the text furnishing the hints, the clue, the start or framework. Not the book needs so much to be the complete thing, but the reader of the book does. That were to make a nation of supple and athletic minds, well-train'd, intuitive, used to depend on themselves, and not on a few coteries of writers.

Investigating here, we see, not that it is a little thing we have, in having the bequeath'd libraries, countless shelves of volumes, records, etc.; yet how serious the danger, depending entirely on them, of the bloodless vein, the nerveless arm, the false application, at second or third hand. We see that the real interest of this people of ours in the theology, history, poetry, politics, and personal models of the past (the British islands, for instance, and indeed all the past), is not necessarily to mold ourselves or our literature upon them, but to attain fuller, more definite comparisons, warnings, and the insight to ourselves, our own present, and our own far grander, different, future history), religion, social customs, etc. We see that almost everything that has been written, sung, or stated, of old, with reference to humanity under the feudal and oriental institutes, religions, and for other lands, needs to be rewritten, resung, restated, in terms consistent with the institution of these States, and to come in range and obedient uniformity with them.

We see, as in the universes of the material kosmos, after meteorological, vegetable, and animal cycles, man at last arises, born through them, to prove them, concentrate them, to turn upon them with wonder and love—to command them, adorn them, and carry them upward into superior realms—so, out of the series of the preceding social and political universes, now arise these States. We see that while many were supposing things established and completed, really the grandest things always remain; and discover that the work of the New World is not ended, but only fairly begun.

We see our land, America, her literature, aesthetics, etc., as, substantially, the getting in form, or effusement and statement, of deepest basic elements and loftiest final meanings, of history and man—and the portrayal (under the eternal laws and conditions of beauty) of our own physiognomy, the subjective tie and expression of the objective, as from our own combination, continuation, and points of view—and the deposit and record of the national mentality, character, appeals, heroism, wars, and even liberties—where these, and all, culminate in native literary and artistic formulation, she will flounder about, and her other, however imposing, eminent greatness, prove merely a passing gleam; but truly having which, she will understand herself, live nobly, nobly contribute, emanate, and, swinging, poised safely on herself, illumin'd and illuming, become a full-form'd world, and divine Mother not only of material but spiritual worlds, in ceaseless succession through time—the main thing being the average, the bodily, the concrete, the democratic, the popular, on which all the superstructures of the future are to permanently rest.

1

Contemporary Comment

2. HAMLIN GARLAND
Walt Whitman Old and Poor*

One of the very first books for which I had asked at the Boston Public Library was Walt Whitman's "Leaves of Grass." I had heard much of this book in the West but had never set eyes upon it, and even here in Boston it was "double starred" on the list and issued only to serious students of literature. Heaven knows I was serious enough, and so at the age of twenty-five I began my acquaintance with "the poet of Democracy."

Of the tremendous vitality of his message I was at once aware. Formless as the book appeared, its deeply patriotic spirit, its wide sympathy with working men and women, and especially its faith in the destiny of "these States" exalted me. I caught some part of the writer's faith in American manhood and the part America was to play in the world's future history.

From "Leaves of Grass" I passed to "Specimen Days" which made him still more admirable to me. That he profoundly influenced my thinking I freely acknowledge. I reread De Tocqueville in the light of "Democratic Vistas," perceiving that the local-color novel had sociologic value in that it aided the readers of one part of our widely separated States to understand the problems of another. I began at once to say these things to my students at Brown's school and elsewhere.

I went further. I wrote to Walt (as he called himself) telling him how inspiring I found his prose and that I considered it the very best avenue of approach to his poetry. This was on November 24, 1886.

"MR. WALT WHITMAN: . . .

"I am an enthusiastic reader of your books, both volumes of which I have within reach of hand. I am everywhere in my

* This selection is taken from Hamlin Garland, *Roadside Meetings*. It is reprinted here by permission of the author's daughters.

58

talking and writing making your claims felt and shall continue to do so. I have demonstrated (what of course you know) that there is no veil, no impediment between your mind and your audience, when your writings are *voiced*. The formlessness is only seeming, not real. I have never read a page of your poetry or quoted a line that has not commanded admiration. The music is there and the grandeur of thought is there if the reader reads, guided by the sense and not by the external lining or paragraphing. Even my young pupils feel the thrill of the deep rolling music though the thought may be too profound for them to grasp.

"In a course of lectures before the Boston School of Oratory last summer I made a test of the matter. I do not think a single pupil held out against my arguments supplemented by readings from your works. The trouble is they get at your work through the daily press or through the defenders of Longfellow or Tennyson (whom it is supposed you utterly antagonize). When it is brought to them by one who appreciates and measurably understands your methods and ideals, I do not think there is any doubt of the favorable result. I have found much opposition, but it was mostly ignorant or misled.

"I am a young man of very ordinary attainments, and do not presume to do more than give you a glimpse of the temper of that public which would not do you wrong, deliberately, but who, by reason of the causes hinted above, fail to get at the transcendent power of 'Leaves of Grass.' If I have given you the impression that I believe in you and strive to interpret you, you will not feel that I have overstepped the privilege of a pupil in the presence of a great teacher.

"The enclosed slip is a meager outline of a volume which I am writing and which I hope to get out this coming spring. As the motto page of this volume I have used a paragraph from your 'Collect.' While it is not strictly essential to the book, yet I should esteem it a favor if you would consent to its use. One sentence, 'In nothing is there more evolution than in the American mind,' I have also used in company with Spencer's great law of progress. It helped to decide the title, which is: 'The Evolution of American Thought;' an outline study of the leading phases of American literature, etc. In the latter part of the volume I have treated of the Age of Democracy and its thought, taking as foundation the splendid utterances of M. Taine upon the modern age. It is in this chapter that I place your work. I quote from you quite largely both in treating of your writings and in treating the general theme of present and future democratic ideals. I hope to be able to please you with my treatment of your great work. Besides this I am preparing special lectures upon the same subject. Have you any objections to the quotations which I find it necessary to use?

"In conclusion let me say that without any bias in your favor (rather the opposite from newspapers) your poems thrilled me, reversed many of my ideas, confirmed me in others, helped to make me what I am. I am a Border man, born in Wisconsin and raised on the prairie frontier. I am a disciple of Mr. Spencer and therefore strive at comparative methods of criticism. That your poems should thus convert me is to me a revelation of their power, especially when I can convince others in the same manner.

"And now, revered friend (for I feel you are a friend), think of me as one who radiates the principles of the modern age, and who will in his best manner (poor at best) strive to make his hearers and readers better aware of the 'Good Gray Poet' and his elemental lines.

"Your readers are increasing, and may you live to see the circle infinitely extended is my fervent hope. I do not expect a reply to this other than the signification whether I may quote you or not. I wish I might see and talk with you but that is not possible, except through your volumes."

This letter interested him and he replied, but it was not till long after that I learned how profoundly it had touched him. To him I was a "Boston professor" and a highly influential convert!

So far as I knew he had only one other public advocate of his books in all Boston. This was William Sloane Kennedy, a man of letters who acted as proof reader on the *Transcript*. Our common interest in Whitman drew us together and from him I learned that the poet was living in Camden, New Jersey, alone, broken in health and very poor. "He is confined to his room but enjoys meeting his friends. Go and see him if you are down that way."

II

This suggestion lay in my mind for two years before I found myself able to carry it out. Not till October, 1888, did I cross the river from Philadelphia in search of the poet whose presence had made Camden known throughout the world. The citizens from whom I inquired my way to Mickle Street directed me into a mean section of the town and when I came to the number designated, I could not believe that I had been rightly informed, so dim was the doorplate and so weather-worn the doorway. The street was ugly and narrow, and the house, a two-story frame structure, was such as a day laborer might have owned, and yet the poet's name was there.

In answer to my ring, a small gray man whom I guessed to be Whitman's attendant came clumping down the stairway and received my name impassively. "Wait here," he said, "I'll see if you can come up."

While he went back up the stairs, I studied the faded paper on the walls, and the worn carpet of the hall with growing astonishment. There was nothing to indicate that a poet of world-wide fame was living here. His sordid surroundings filled me with indignation. . . .

In spite of his surroundings, Whitman looked the hero of the poems, strong, self-poised, with a certain delicacy of action and speech. His face when turned toward me discovered a pleasant, searching glance. His mouth was hidden in his great beard, but his eyes were smiling and the lines on his brow were level. Nothing querulous showed in voice or word. His speech was nobly pure with nothing of the coarseness I had been led to expect. When he dropped into homely phrase or coined a word he did so with humorous intonation. It is because some of his interviewers failed to record his smile that so many misinterpretations of his conversation have been recorded. This use of the common phrase now and again lent additional charm to his speech.

He had no word of humor, however. He was grave without being low-spirited or grim, placidly serious in all that he said. He made no reference to his poverty or to his illness and nothing petulant or self-pitying came into his voice. . . .

. . . Naturally I led the talk toward things literary, and being "moved by the spirit," as he smilingly confessed, he talked freely of his contemporaries and gave me full permission to quote him.

I told him that many good people considered him unduly severe on American literature in general and "certain of our poets in particular, Stedman and Gilder for example."

He became grave. "You refer to a report by a German writer. I do not think Stedman was deceived, though many of his friends think I have the spirit to rasp him. It would have been ingratitude to have said such words even had I thought them, which I do not. I hold Stedman in high regard as a man of decided insight and culture. On personal grounds I owe him much. The traveler you mention either willfully or otherwise *twistified*," here he smiled, "what I said—if I said anything in his presence. I am beset with all kinds of visitors who go away thinking me fair game. It is one of the evils which men of any"—he hesitated again—"notoriety must bear patiently.

"As for American literature in general, I have insisted, as all my readers know, on the need of distinctive flavor in our poetry. There is an old Scotch word, Burns uses it occasionally, which expresses exactly what I mean—the word 'race.' A wild strawberry, a wild grape has the racy quality—this distinctive tang. Our poetry lacks *race*. Most of it might have been written in England or on the Continent. I myself like Cooper, Bryant, Emerson, and Whittier because they have this distinctive American quality."

This led me to bring up the work of George W. Cable, Joseph Kirkland, Joel Harris, Mary E. Wilkins, and others of my friends who were getting, it seemed to me, just that flavor he was demanding. "Their books are, in my judgment, forerunners of a powerful native literature."

After a pause he said, "It may be so, but I have not read many of them. Against some of them I *have* read I might bring a grave charge. They have a deplorable tendency toward the *outré*. I call their characters *delirium-tremen characters*. These writers seem not content with the normal man; they must take the exceptional, the diseased. They are not true, not American in the deeper sense at all. To illustrate, in a hunter's camp of twenty men there will always be some who are distorted, unusual, grotesque, but they are not typical of the camp. So in an 'army mess' there are always characters more or less abnormal, men who enjoy distorting their faces and cutting up antics. And yet in all my coming and going among the camps of the Civil War, I was everywhere struck with the decorum—a word I like to use—of the common soldier, his good manners, his quiet heroism, his generosity, even his good, real grammar. These are a few of the typical qualities of the American farmer and mechanic."

All this was said quietly but with deep earnestness, as if he were working the problem out while speaking. Then turning his glance on me he spoke with decision. "I say that the novel or drama claiming to depict American life is false if it deals mainly or largely with abnormal or grotesque characters. They should be used merely as foils."

This led me to say, "In the early stages of national literature it is natural to deal with the abnormal, the exceptional because it startles, claims the attention, so it may be that the novelists you speak of may be just in the preparatory stage and that they will pass on to something higher."

He fell into a profound muse, and at last said with deliberate precision as if making a concession which he had not hitherto directly stated, "I don't know but you are right. I can see that the novice would find the exceptional nearest his hand and most noticeable, and it may be that these books are preparatory to a new, indigenous fiction. The public itself, moreover, seems to demand and enjoy such work. It may be as you argue, that the writers and the public will grow toward a higher perception. At any rate I want to utter my protest against such work and to demand that the really heroic character of the common American be depicted in novel and drama." . . .

. . . Seeing that my interview was nearing an end, I said, "May I carry from you a friendly message to these young novelists?"

"You may, with this advice and plea: Tell them to go among the common men, as one of them, never looking down upon them. Tell them to study their lives and find out and celebrate their splendid primitive honesty, patience, and what I like to call their heroism. When our novelists shall do that in addition to being true to their time, their art will be worthy all praise from me or any other who is insisting on native anti-class poems, novels, and plays.

"And finally I would say to the young writer, don't depict evil for its own sake. Don't let evil overshadow your books. Make it a foil as Shakespeare did. His evil is always a foil for purity. Somewhere in your play or novel let the sunlight in." Here he raised his superb head and in a grandly suggestive gesture of his arm made his point clear. "As in some vast foundry whose walls are lost in blackness, a scuttle far.up in the roof lets the sun and the blue sky in."

As I rose to go I assured him that the circle of his admirers was swiftly widening, and that his influence on our literature was certain to deepen year by year. . . .

II. William Dean Howells: Spokesman for Realism

The realistic movement in American literature was to a great extent shaped by (and long identified with) William Dean Howells (1837-1920). As assistant editor and subsequently editor-in-chief of the *Atlantic Monthly* between 1866 and 1881, he wrote hundreds of critical reviews and helped other young realists, among them Mark Twain and Henry James, on the path to publication. When, after an interval of rest and travel, he joined *Harper's Monthly Magazine* in 1886 and took over its column of criticism, "The Editor's Study," it seemed to many that the center of American literary gravity was no longer Boston but New York. The effect of Howells' criticism was enlarged by his novels which provided a sympathetic chronicle of middle-class American life in the 1870's and 1880's. His subjects are contemporary and deliberately unromantic; his best work illustrates the changing economic and social conditions of the postwar years—the decline of the small town and the fading moral influence of traditional Protestantism, the rise of Big Business and the curiously impersonal injustices, as well as the rich local color and social contrasts, of the great new cities. Among his works most praised today are *A Modern Instance* (1881) which treats an unhappy marriage leading to divorce; *The Rise of Silas Lapham* (1885) which concerns the troubles of a middle-aged businessman who cannot accept the amoral corporate structure of the Gilded Age; and *A Hazard of New Fortunes* (1890) which shows Howells' concern with economic injustice and socialistic reform.

No other work represents so clearly the standards and values of American realism as *Criticism and Fiction* (1891). The volume was not written as a single statement, but was compiled by Howells from various pieces published in "The Editor's Study" between 1886 and 1891. This "cut and paste" method accounts for some awkward transitions in the volume. Even so, the continuity of Howells' thought in these years and the constancy of his devotion to realism is impressive.

Several important positions underlie Howells' defense of realism. One is his dissatisfaction with the "romance," a term which for him covers the work both of Sir Walter Scott and contemporary popular romancers. Howells' comments on the romance imply an optimistically revolutionary theory of literary style and taste. Scott's tales are crude as befits "the beginning of any art"; they also appeal to the cruder taste of an earlier readership and perhaps, quite properly, to children. But standards have advanced, readers have grown more critical, and so the day of the romance should be fading. At the same time, Howells fears the social effects of the romance. Like Walt Whitman in *Democratic Vistas*, he is concerned for the effect upon Americans of romantic (for Walt, "feudal") standards of character. The romance, Howells feels, may satisfy the Englishman who, presumably tainted by aristocracy and the past, "loves the passionate and heroic," but it does not properly reflect the calm, sensible average of American life. The romance offers false standards of conduct: it glorifies "Genius" —eccentric and immoral—and it exaggerates the value of devotion to a single virtue ("Love" or "Duty") although life, Howells insists, "is really concerned with a great many of other things." Most readers will gather that Howells shares Ulysses S. Grant's suspicion that those who read too much fiction waste their time and deform their emotions. As a military leader, Grant had proved himself wise, practical, and, above all, anti-romantic, avoiding those displays of military color other generals indulged. How effectively might this hero and former President protest false standards in fiction! In answer to Grant's fears, Howells, in section eighteen of *Criticism and Fiction*, gives "plain and simple" tests for fiction:

> If a novel flatters the passions, and exalts them above the principles, it is poisonous; it may not kill, but it will certainly injure . . . Then the whole spawn of so-called unmoral romances which imagine a world where the sins of sense are unvisited by the penalties following, swift or slow, but inexorably sure, in the real world, are deadly poison; these do kill.

If Howells' diagnosis seems to exaggerate the results of

addiction to the "novel habit," it is at least a measure of his belief in the tremendous moral impact of popular fiction.

Another aspect of Howells' comment in *Criticism and Fiction* resembles Whitman's theme in *Democratic Vistas*: the need for a new, nonderivative Americanism in literature. Howells briefly suggests a defense of realism on aesthetic grounds—"what is true is always beautiful and good, and nothing else is so"—but his definition of the "true" is tied to his understanding of American life and the need for a democratic literature. There is no justification for a literary elite or an establishment of taste for (Howells agrees with Burke) "the true standard of the arts is in every man's power." This is so only if truth is the standard, and if truth is, as Howells suggests, "human nature, known to us all." As a critical or philosophical principle, this statement raises more problems than it solves, but Howells' intent is social, more than aesthetic. He disowns an intellectual aristocracy in a democratic society and accordingly hopes that "the communistic era in taste . . . is approaching, and that it will occur within the lives of men now overawed by the foolish old superstition that literature and art are anything but the expression of life, and are to be judged by any other test than that of their fidelity to it."

Leveler though he was, or tried to be, Howells is popularly known as a conservative, partially because younger writers in the early years of this century found it useful to present him as the leader of a literary establishment against which they—as naturalists, moderns or simply a new generation—revolted. In fact, Howells was, if not elitist, undeniably "bookish" (his archrealist was Jane Austen, not an American contemporary). He was also, out of concern for the social effect of literature, always unwilling to open the novel to materials that seemed to him sordid or immoral. He has often been chastised for suggesting that the novel should treat no subject unfit for the eyes of a Young Girl (that "Iron Madonna who," in the words of the critic H. H. Boyesen, "strangles in her fond embrace the American novelist"). Howells' defense implies the genteel limits of his social experience, for if twentieth-century fiction may be taken as evidence, there is no reason to agree with him that "the manners of the novel have been improving with those of its readers." His benign optimism is again evident in the suggestion that our novelists should "concern themselves with the more smiling aspects of life, which are the more American . . . It is worth while, even at the risk of being called commonplace, to be true to our well-to-do actualities . . ." These views are, certainly, of a piece with his condemnation of exaggeration and false drama in the romance. Nonetheless, many Americans (Populists, "Muckrakers," and naturalists among them) found Howells' position politically and artistically shallow.

Howells' influence was, however, wide. Even those who disagreed found him stimulating. In *Roadside Meetings*, Hamlin Garland recalled that during "the summer of 1885 Howells became the subject of much literary gossip"; his novels

> were being read aloud in thousands of home circles, and clubs and social gatherings rang with argument as to whether or not his women characters could be found in New England society. It was agreed that his men existed, but their wives and daughters were woeful exaggerations—according to his critics. To use a good old phrase, his method and words created "regular katouse" in Boston and vicinity . . .*

The gentle satire entitled "Effie's Realistic Novel" suggests Howells' influence at a time when precocious children like Effie, as well as the readers of one of America's first serious children's magazines, lisped in realistic terms. Mark Twain's comment on Howells is the work of a friend and, like Howells' piece on Twain which appears later in this volume, casts light on the literary standards they shared. Twain, humorist and master of the American vernacular, praises Howells' humor and his sense of the "right word." For both of them, this humor is a distinctive national quality and attention to the "right word" evidence of their interest in native American speech.

* Hamlin Garland, *Roadside Meetings* (New York, Macmillan Co., 1930), p. 55.

Selections

3. *Criticism and Fiction:*
ON REALISM, CRITICISM AND THE
SOCIAL EFFECT OF LITERATURE*

The question of a final criterion for the appreciation of art is one that perpetually recurs to those interested in any sort of aesthetic endeavor. Mr. John Addington Symonds, in a chapter of The Renaissance in Italy treating of the Bolognese school of painting, which once had so great cry, and was vaunted the supreme exemplar of the grand style, but which he now believes fallen into lasting contempt for its emptiness and soullessness, seeks to determine whether there can be an enduring criterion or not; and his conclusion is applicable to literature as to the other arts. "Our hope," he says, "with regard to the unity of taste in the future then is, that all sentimental or academical seekings after the ideal having been abandoned, momentary theories founded upon idiosyncratic or temporary partialities exploded, and nothing accepted but what is solid and positive, the scientific spirit shall make men progressively more and more conscious of these bleibende Verhältnisse, more and more capable of living in the whole; also, that in proportion as we gain a firmer hold upon our own place in the world, we shall come to comprehend with more instinctive certitude what is simple, natural, and honest, welcoming with gladness all artistic products that exhibit these qualities. The perception of the enlightened man will then be the task of a healthy person who has made himself acquainted with the laws of evolution in art and in society, and is able to test the excellence of work in any stage from immaturity to decadence by discerning what there is of truth, sincerity, and natural vigor in it."

* The selection is taken from *Criticism and Fiction* by William Dean Howells (1891).

68

I

That is to say, as I understand, that moods and tastes and fashions change; people fancy now this and now that; but what is unpretentious and what is true is always beautiful and good, and nothing else is so. This is not saying that fantastic and monstrous and artificial things do not please; everybody knows that they do please immensely for a time, and then, after the lapse of a much longer time, they have the charm of the rococo. Nothing is more curious than the charm that fashion has. Fashion in women's dress, almost every fashion, is somehow delightful, else it would never have been the fashion; but if any one will look through a collection of old fashion plates, he must own that most fashions have been ugly. A few, which could be readily instanced, have been very pretty, and even beautiful, but it is doubtful if these have pleased the greatest number of people. The ugly delights as well as the beautiful, and not merely because the ugly in fashion is associated with the young loveliness of the women who wear the ugly fashions, and wins a grace from them, not because the vast majority of mankind are tasteless, but for some cause that is not perhaps ascertainable. It is quite as likely to return in the fashions of our clothes and houses and furniture, and poetry and fiction and painting, as the beautiful, and it may be from an instinctive or a reasoned sense of this that some of the extreme naturalists have refused to make the old discrimination against it, or to regard the ugly as any less worthy of celebration in art than the beautiful; some of them, in fact, seem to regard it as rather more worthy, if anything. Possibly there is no absolutely ugly, no absolutely beautiful; or possibly the ugly contains always an element of the beautiful better adapted to the general appreciation than the more perfectly beautiful. This is a somewhat discouraging conjecture, but I offer it for no more than it is worth; and I do not pin my faith to the saying of one whom I heard denying, the other day, that a thing of beauty was a joy forever. He contended that Keats's line should have read, "Some things of beauty are sometimes joys forever," and that any assertion beyond this was too hazardous.

II

I should, indeed, prefer another line of Keats's, if I were to profess any formulated creed, and should feel much safer with his "Beauty is Truth, Truth Beauty," than even with my friend's reformation of the more quoted verse. It brings us back to the solid ground taken by Mr. Symonds, which is not essentially different from that taken in the great Mr. Burke's Essay on the Sublime and the Beautiful—a singularly modern book, considering how long ago it was wrote (as the great Mr. Steele would have written the participle a little longer ago), and full of a certain well-mannered and agreeable instruction. In some things it is of that droll little eighteenth-century world, when philosophy had got the neat little universe into the hollow of its hand, and knew just what it was, and what it was for; but it is quite without arrogance. "As for those called critics," the author says, "they have generally sought the rule of the arts in the wrong place; they have sought among poems, pictures, engravings, statues, and buildings; but art can never give the rules that make an art. This is, I believe, the reason why artists in general, and poets principally, have been confined in so narrow a circle; they have been rather imitators of one another than of nature. Critics follow them, and therefore can do little as guides. I can judge but poorly of anything while I measure it by no other standard than itself. The true standard of the arts is in every man's power; and an easy observation of the most common, sometimes of the meanest things, in nature will give the truest lights, where the greatest sagacity and industry that slights such observation must leave us in the dark, or, what is worse, amuse and mislead us by false lights."

If this should happen to be true—and it certainly commends itself to acceptance—it might portend an immediate danger to the vested interests of criticism, only that it was written a hundred years ago; and we shall probably have the "sagacity and industry that slights the observation" of nature long enough yet to allow most critics the time to learn some more useful trade than criticism as they pursue it. Nevertheless, I am in hopes that the communistic era in taste foreshadowed by Burke is approaching, and that it will occur within the lives of men now overawed by the foolish old superstition that literature and art are anything but the expression of life, and are to be judged by any other test than that of their fidelity to it. The time is coming, I hope, when each new author, each new artist, will be considered, not in his proportion to any other author or artist, but in his relation to the human nature, known to us all, which it is his privilege, his high duty, to interpret. "The true standard of the artist is in every man's power" already, as Burke says; Michelangelo's "light of the piazza," the glance of the common eye, is and always was the best light on a statue; Goethe's "boys and blackbirds" have in all ages been the real connoisseurs of berries; but hitherto the mass of common men have been afraid to apply their own simplicity, naturalness, and honesty to the appreciation of the beautiful. They have always cast about for the instruction of some one who professed to know better, and who browbeat wholesome common-sense into the self-distrust that ends in sophistication. They have fallen generally to the worst of this bad species, and have been "amused and misled" (how pretty that quaint old use of amuse is!) "by the false lights" of critical vanity and self-righteousness. They have been taught to compare what they see and what they read, not with the things that they have observed and known, but with the things that some other artist or writer has done. Especially if they have themselves the artistic impulse in any direction they are taught to form themselves, not upon life, but upon the masters who became masters only by forming themselves upon life. The seeds of death are planted in them, and they can produce only the still-born, the academic. They are not told to take their work into the public square and see if it seems true to the chance passer, but to test it by the work of the very men who refused and decried any other test of their own work. The young writer who attempts to report the phrase and carriage of every-day life, who tries to tell just how he has heard men talk and seen them look, is made to feel guilty of something low and unworthy by the stupid people who would like to have him show how Shakespeare's men talked and looked, or Scott's, or Thackeray's, or Balzac's, or Hawthorne's, or Dickens's; he is instructed to idealize his personages, that is, to take the life-likeness out of them, and put the book-likeness into them. He is approached in the spirit of wretched pedantry into which learning, much or little, always decays when it withdraws itself and stands apart from experience in an attitude of imagined superiority, and which would say with the same confidence to the scientist: "I see that you are looking at a grasshopper there which you have found in the grass, and I suppose you intend to describe it. Now don't waste your time and sin against culture in that way. I've got a grasshopper here, which has been evolved at considerable pains and expense out of the grasshopper in general; in fact, it's a type. It's made up of wire and card-board, very prettily painted in a conventional tint, and it's perfectly indestructible. It isn't very much like a real grasshopper, but it's a great deal nicer, and it's served to represent the notion of a grasshopper ever since man emerged from barbarism. You may say that it's artificial. Well, it is artificial; but then it's ideal too; and what you want to do is to cultivate the ideal. You'll find the books full of my kind of grasshopper, and scarcely a trace of yours in any of them. The thing that you are proposing to do is commonplace; but if you say that it isn't commonplace, for the very reason that it hasn't been done before, you'll have to admit that it's photographic."

As I said, I hope the time is coming when not only the artist, but the common, average man, who always "has the standard of the arts in his power," will have also the courage to apply it, and will reject the ideal grasshopper wherever he finds it, in science, in literature, in art, because it is not "simple, natural, and honest," because it is not like a real grasshopper. But I will own that I think the time is yet far off, and that the people who have been brought up on the ideal grasshopper, the heroic grasshopper, the impassioned grasshopper, the self-devoted, adventureful, good old romantic card-board grasshopper, must die out before the simple, honest, and natural grasshopper can have a fair field. I am in no haste to compass the end of these good people, whom I find in the mean time very amusing. It is delightful to meet one of them, either in print or out of it—some sweet elderly lady or excellent gentleman whose youth was pastured on the literature of thirty or forty years ago—and to witness the confidence with which they preach their favorite authors as all the law and the prophets. They have commonly read little or nothing since, or, if they have, they have judged it by a standard taken from these authors, and never dreamed of judging it by nature; they are destitute of the documents in the case of the later writers; they suppose that Balzac was the beginning of realism, and that Zola is its wicked end; they are quite ignorant, but they are ready to talk you down, if you differ from them, with an assumption of knowledge sufficient for any occasion. The horror, the resentment, with which they receive any question of their literary saints is genuine; you descend at once very far in the moral and social scale, and anything short of offensive personality is too good for you; it is expressed to you that you are one to be avoided, and put down even a little lower than you have naturally fallen.

These worthy persons are not to blame; it is part of their intellectual mission to represent the petrifaction of taste, and to preserve an image of a smaller and cruder and emptier world than we now live in, a world which was feeling its way towards the simple, the natural, the honest, but was a good deal "amused and misled" by lights now no longer mistakable for heavenly luminaries. They belong to a time, just passing away, when certain authors were considered authorities in certain kinds, when they must be accepted entire and not questioned in any particular. Now we are beginning to see and to say that no author is an authority except in those moments when he held his ear close to Nature's lips and caught her very accent. These moments are not continuous with any authors in the past, and they are rare with all. Therefore I am not afraid to say now that the greatest classics are sometimes not at all great, and that we can profit by them only when we hold them, like our meanest contemporaries, to a strict accounting, and verify their work by the standard of the arts which we all have in our power, the simple, the natural, and the honest.

Those good people, those curious and interesting if somewhat musty back-numbers, must always have a hero, an idol of some sort, and it is droll to find Balzac, who suffered from their sort such bitter scorn and hate for his realism while he was alive, now become a fetich in his turn, to be shaken in the faces of those who will not blindly worship him. But it is no new thing in the history of literature: whatever is established is sacred with those who do not think. At the beginning of the century, when romance was making the same fight against effete classicism which realism is making to-day against effete romanticism, the Italian poet Monti declared that "the romantic was the cold grave of the Beautiful," just as the realistic is now supposed to be. The romantic of that day and the real of this are in certain degree the same. Romanticism then sought, as realism seeks now, to widen the bounds of sympathy, to level every barrier against aesthetic freedom, to escape from the paralysis of tradition. It exhausted itself in this impulse; and it remained for realism to assert that fidelity to experience and probability of motive are essential conditions of a great imaginative literature. It is not a new theory, but it has never before universally characterized literary endeavor. When realism becomes false to itself, when it heaps up facts merely, and maps life instead of picturing it, realism will perish too. Every true realist instinctively knows this, and it is perhaps the reason why he is careful of every fact, and feels himself bound to express or to indicate its meaning at the risk of over-moralizing. In life he finds nothing insignificant; all tells for destiny and character; nothing that God has made is contemptible. He cannot look upon human life and declare this thing or that thing unworthy of notice, any more than the scientist can declare a fact of the material world beneath the dignity of his inquiry. He feels in every nerve the equality of things and the unity of men; his soul is exalted, not by vain shows and shadows and ideals, but by realities, in which alone the truth lives. In criticism it is his business to break the images of false gods and misshapen heroes, to take away the poor silly toys that many grown people would still like to play with. He cannot keep terms with Jack the Giantkiller or Puss in Boots, under any name or in any place, even when they reappear as the convict Vautrec, or the Marquis de Montrivaut, or the Sworn Thirteen Noblemen. He must say to himself that Balzac, when he imagined these monsters, was not Balzac, he was Dumas; he was not realistic, he was romantic.

III

Such a critic will not respect Balzac's good work the less for contemning his bad work. He will easily account for the bad work historically, and when he has recognized it, will trouble himself no further with it. In his view no living man is a type, but a character; now noble, now ignoble; now grand, now little; complex, full of vicissitude. He will not expect Balzac to be always Balzac, and will be perhaps even more attracted to the study of him when he was trying to be Balzac than when he had become so. In César Birotteau, for instance, he will be interested to note how Balzac stood at the beginning of the great things that have followed since in fiction. There is an interesting likeness between his work in this and Nicolas Gogol's in Dead Souls, which serves to illustrate the simultaneity of the literary movement in men of such widely separated civilizations and conditions. Both represent their characters with the touch of exaggeration which typifies; but in bringing his story to a close, Balzac employs a beneficence unknown to the Russian, and almost as universal and as apt as that which smiles upon the fortunes of the good in the Vicar of Wakefield. It is not enough to have rehabilitated Birotteau pecuniarily and socially; he must make him die triumphantly, spectacularly, of an opportune hemorrhage, in the midst of the festivities which celebrate his restoration to his old home. Before this happens, human nature has been laid under contribution right and left for acts of generosity towards the righteous bankrupt; even the king sends him six thousand francs. It is very pretty; it is touching, and brings the lump into the reader's throat; but it is too much, and one perceives that Balzac lived too soon to profit by Balzac. The later men, especially the Russians, have known how to forbear the excesses of analysis, to withhold the weakly recurring descriptive and caressing epithets, to let the characters suffice for themselves. All this does not mean that César Birotteau is not a beautiful and pathetic story, full of shrewdly considered knowledge of men, and of a good art struggling to free itself from self-consciousness. But it does mean that Balzac, when he wrote it, was under the burden of the very traditions which he has helped fiction to throw off. He felt obliged to construct a mechanical plot, to surcharge his characters, to moralize openly and baldly; he permitted himself to "sympathize" with certain of his people, and to point out others for the abhorrence of his readers. This is not so bad in him as it would be in a novelist of our day. It is simply primitive and inevitable, and he is not to be judged by it.

IV

In the beginning of any art even the most gifted worker must be crude in his methods, and we ought to keep this fact always in mind when we turn, say, from the purblind worshippers of Scott to Scott himself, and recognize that he often wrote a style cumberous and diffuse; that he was tediously analytical where the modern novelist is dramatic, and evolved his characters by means of long-winded explanation and commentary; that, except in the case of his lower-class personages, he made them talk as seldom man and never woman talked; that he was

tiresomely descriptive; that on the simplest occasions he went
about half a mile to express a thought that could be uttered in
ten paces across lots; and that he trusted his readers' intuitions
so little that he was apt to rub in his appeals to them. He was
probably right: the generation which he wrote for was duller
than this; slower-witted, aesthetically untrained, and in maturity not so apprehensive of an artistic intention as the children
of today. All this is not saying Scott was not a great man; he
was a great man, and a very great novelist as compared with the
novelists who went before him. He can still amuse young
people, but they ought to be instructed how false and how
mistaken he often is, with his mediaeval ideals, his blind
Jacobitism, his intense devotion to aristocracy and royalty; his
acquiescence in the division of men into noble and ignoble,
patrician and plebeian, sovereign and subject, as if it were the
law of God; for all which, indeed, he is not to blame as he
would be if he were one of our contemporaries. Something of
this is true of another master, greater than Scott in being less
romantic, and inferior in being more German, namely, the great
Goethe himself. He taught us, in novels otherwise now an-
tiquated, and always full of German clumsiness, that it was false
to good art—which is never anything but the reflection of
life—to pursue and round the career of the persons introduced,
whom he often allowed to appear and disappear in our knowledge as people in the actual world do. This is a lesson which the
writers able to profit by it can never be too grateful for; and it
is equally a benefaction to readers; but there is very little else in
the conduct of the Goethean novels which is in advance of their
time; this remains almost their sole contribution to the science
of fiction. They are very primitive in certain characteristics, and
unite with their calm, deep insight, an amusing helplessness in
dramatization. "Wilhelm retired to his room, and indulged in
the following reflections," is a mode of analysis which would
not be practised nowadays; and all that fancifulness of no-
menclature in Wilhelm Meister is very drolly sentimental and
feeble. The adventures with robbers seem as if dreamed out of
books of chivalry, and the tendency to allegorization affects
one like an endeavor on the author's part to escape from the
unrealities which he must have felt harassingly, German as he
was. Mixed up with the shadows and illusions are honest,
wholesome, every-day people, who have the air of wandering
homelessly about among them, without definite direction; and

the mists are full of a luminosity which, in spite of them, we know for common-sense and poetry. What is useful in any review of Goethe's methods is the recognition of the fact, which it must bring, that the greatest master cannot produce a masterpiece in a new kind. The novel was too recently invented in Goethe's day not to be, even in his hands, full of the faults of apprentice work.

V

In fact, a great master may sin against the "modesty of nature" in many ways, and I have felt this painfully in reading Balzac's romance—it is not worthy the name of novel—Le Père Goriot, which is full of a malarial restlessness, wholly alien to healthful art. After that exquisitely careful and truthful setting of his story in the shabby boarding-house, he fills the scene with figures jerked about by the exaggerated passions and motives of the stage. We cannot have a cynic reasonably wicked, disagreeable, egoistic; we must have a lurid villain of melodrama, a disguised convict, with a vast criminal organization at his command, and

> "So dyèd double red"

in deed and purpose that he lights up the faces of the horrified spectators with his glare. A father fond of unworthy children, and leading a life of self-denial for their sake, as may probably and pathetically be, is not enough; there must be an imbecile, trembling dotard, willing to promote even the liaisons of his daughters to give them happiness and to teach the sublimity of the paternal instinct. The hero cannot sufficiently be a selfish young fellow, with alternating impulses of greed and generosity; he must superfluously intend a career of iniquitous splendor, and be swerved from it by nothing but the most cataclysmal interpositions. It can be said that without such personages the plot could not be transacted; but so much the worse for the plot. Such a plot had no business to be; and while actions so unnatural are imagined, no mastery can save fiction from contempt with those who really think about it. To Balzac it can be forgiven, not only because in his better mood he gave us such biographies as Eugénie Grandet, but because he wrote at a time when fiction was just beginning to verify the externals of life, to portray faithfully the outside of men and things. It was still held that in order to interest the reader the characters must be moved by the old romantic ideals; we were to be taught that "heroes" and "heroines" existed all around us, and that these abnormal beings needed only to be discovered in their several humble disguises, and then we should see every-day people actuated by the fine frenzy of the creatures of the poets. How false that notion was few but the critics, who are apt to be rather belated, need now be told. Some of these poor fellows, however, still contend that it ought to be done, and that human feelings and motives, as God made them and as men know them, are not good enough for novel-readers.

This is more explicable than would appear at first glance. The critics—and in speaking of them one always modestly leaves one's self out of the count for some reason—when they are not elders ossified in tradition, are apt to be young people, and young people are necessarily conservative in their tastes and theories. They have the tastes and theories of their instructors, who perhaps caught the truth of their day, but whose routine life has been alien to any other truth. There is probably no chair of literature in this country from which the principles now shaping the literary expression of every civilized people are not denounced and confounded with certain objectionable French novels, or which teaches young men anything of the universal impulse which has given us the work, not only of Zola, but of Tourguéneff and Tolstoï in Russia, of Björnson and Ibsen in Norway, of Valdés and Galdós in Spain, of Verga in Italy. Till these younger critics have learned to think as well as to write for themselves they will persist in heaving a sigh, more and more perfunctory, for the truth as it was in Sir Walter, and as it was in Dickens and in Hawthorne. Presently all will have been changed; they will have seen the new truth in larger and larger degree; and when it shall have become the old truth, they will perhaps see it all.

VI

In the mean time the average of criticism is not wholly bad with us. To be sure, the critic sometimes appears in the panoply of the savages whom we have supplanted on this continent; and it is hard to believe that his use of the tomahawk and the scalping-knife is a form of conservative surgery. It is still his conception of his office that he should assail with obloquy those who differ with him in matters of taste or opinion; that he must be rude with those he does not like, and that he ought to do them violence as a proof of his superiority. It is too largely his superstition that because he likes a thing it is good, and because he dislikes a thing it is bad; the reverse is quite possibly the case, but he is yet indefinitely far from knowing that in affairs of taste his personal preference enters very little. Commonly he has no principles, but only an assortment of prepossessions for and against; and this otherwise very perfect character is sometimes uncandid to the verge of dishonesty. He seems not to mind misstating the position of any one he supposes himself to disagree with, and then attacking him for what he never said, or even implied; the critic thinks this is droll, and appears not to suspect that it is immoral. He is not tolerant; he thinks it a virtue to be intolerant; it is hard for him to understand that the same thing may be admirable at one time and deplorable at another; and that it is really his business to classify and analyze the fruits of the human mind very much as the naturalist classifies the objects of his study, rather than to praise or blame them; that there is a measure of the same absurdity in his trampling on a poem, a novel, or an essay that does not please him as in the botanist's grinding a plant underfoot because he does not find it pretty. He does not conceive that it is his business rather to identify the species and then explain how and where the specimen is imperfect and irregular. If he could once acquire this simple idea of his duty he would be much more agreeable company than he now is, and a more useful member of society; though I hope I am not yet saying that he is not extremely delightful as he is, and wholly indispensable. He is certainly more ignorant than malevolent; and considering the hard conditions under which he works, his necessity of writing hurriedly from an imperfect examination of far more books, on a greater variety of subjects, than he can even hope to read, the average American critic—the ordinary critic of commerce, so to speak—is very well indeed. Collectively he is more than this; for the joint effect of our criticism is the pretty thorough appreciation of any book submitted to it.

VII

The misfortune rather than the fault of our individual critic is that he is the heir of the false theory and bad manners of the English school. The theory of that school has apparently been that almost any person of glib and lively expression is competent to write of almost any branch of polite literature; its manners are what we know. The American, whom it has largely formed, is by nature very glib and very lively, and commonly his criticism, viewed as imaginative work, is more agreeable than that of the Englishman; but it is, like the art of both countries, apt to be amateurish. In some degree our authors have freed themselves from English models; they have gained some notion of the more serious work of the Continent; but it is still the ambition of the American critic to write like the English critic, to show his wit if not his learning, to strive to eclipse the author under review rather than illustrate him. He has not yet caught on to the fact that it is really no part of his business to display himself, but that it is altogether his duty to place a book in such a light that the reader shall know its class, its function, its character. The vast good-nature of our people preserves us from the worst effects of this criticism without principles. Our critic, at his lowest, is rarely malignant; and when he is rude or untruthful, it is mostly without truculence; I suspect that he is often offensive without knowing that he is so. If he loves a shining mark because a fair shot with mud shows best on that kind of target, it is for the most part from a boyish mischievousness quite innocent of malice. Now and then he acts simply under instruction from higher authority, and denounces because it is the tradition of his publication to do so. In other cases the critic is obliged to support his journal's repute for severity, or for wit, or for morality, though he may himself be entirely amiable, dull, and wicked; this necessity more or less warps his verdicts.

The worst is that he is personal, perhaps because it is so easy and so natural to be personal, and so instantly attractive. In this respect our criticism has not improved from the accession of numbers of ladies to its ranks, though we still hope so much from women in our politics when they shall come to vote. They have come to write, and with the effect to increase the amount of little-digging, which rather superabounded in our literary criticism before. They "know what they like"—that pernicious maxim of those who do not know what they ought to like—and they pass readily from censuring an author's performance to censuring him. They bring a lively stock of misapprehensions and prejudices to their work; they would rather have heard about than known about a book; and they take kindly to the public wish to be amused rather than edified. But neither have they so much harm in them; they, too, are more ignorant than malevolent.

VIII

Our criticism is disabled by the unwillingness of the critic to learn from an author, and his readiness to mistrust him. A writer passes his whole life in fitting himself for a certain kind of performance; the critic does not ask why, or whether the performance is good or bad, but if he does not like the kind, he instructs the writer to go off and do some other sort of thing—usually the sort that has been done already, and done sufficiently. If he could once understand that a man who has written the book he dislikes, probably knows infinitely more about its kind and his own fitness for doing it than any one else, the critic might learn something, and might help the reader to learn; but by putting himself in a false position, a position of superiority, he is of no use. He ought, in the first place, to cast prayerfully about for humility, and especially to beseech the powers to preserve him from the sterility of arrogance and the deadness of contempt, for out of these nothing can proceed. He is not to suppose that an author has committed an offence against him by writing the kind of book he does not like; he will be far more profitably employed on behalf of the reader in finding out whether they had better not both like it. Let him conceive of an author as not in any wise on trial before him, but as a reflection of this or that aspect of life, and he will not be tempted to browbeat him or bully him.

The critic need not be impolite even to the youngest and weakest author. A little courtesy, or a good deal, a constant perception of the fact that a book is not a misdemeanor, a decent self-respect that must forbid the civilized man the savage pleasure of wounding, are what I would ask for our criticism, as something which will add sensibly to its present lustre. . . .

XIII

In fine, I would beseech the literary critics of our country to disabuse themselves of the mischievous notion that they are essential to the progress of literature in the way critics have vainly imagined. Canon Farrar confesses that with the best will in the world to profit by the many criticisms of his books, he has never profited in the least by any of them; and this is almost the universal experience of authors. It is not always the fault of the critics. They sometimes deal honestly and fairly by a book, and not so often they deal adequately. But in making a book, if it is at all a good book, the author has learned all that is knowable about it, and every strong point and every weak point in it, far more accurately than any one else can possibly learn them. He has learned to do better than well for the future; but if his book is bad, he cannot be taught anything about it from the outside. It will perish; and if he has not the root of literature in him, he will perish as an author with it.

But what is it that gives tendency in art, then? What is it makes people like this at one time, and that at another? Above all, what makes a better fashion change for a worse; how can the ugly come to be preferred to the beautiful; in other words, how can art decay?

This question came up in my mind lately with regard to English fiction and its form, or rather its formlessness. How, for instance, could people who had once known the simple verity, the refined perfection of Miss Austen, enjoy anything less refined and less perfect?

With her example before them, why should not English novelists have gone on writing simply, honestly, artistically, ever after? One would think it must have been impossible for them to do otherwise, if one did not remember, say, the lamentable behavior of the actors who support Mr. Jefferson, and their theatricality in the very presence of his beautiful naturalness. It is very difficult, that simplicity, and nothing is so hard as to be honest, as the reader, if he has ever happened to try it, must know. "The big bow-wow I can do myself, like any one going," said Scott, but he owned that the exquisite touch of Miss Austen was denied him; and it seems certainly to have been denied in greater or less measure to all her successors. But though reading and writing come by nature, as Dogberry justly said, a taste in them may be cultivated, or once cultivated, it may be preserved; and why was it not so among those poor islanders? One does not ask such things in order to be at the pains of answering them one's self, but with the hope that some one else will take the trouble to do so, and I propose to be rather a silent partner in the enterprise, which I shall leave mainly to Señor Armando Palacio Valdés. This delightful author will, however, only be able to answer my question indirectly from the essay on fiction with which he prefaces one of his novels, the charming story of The Sister of San Sulphizo, and I shall have some little labor in fitting his saws to my instances. It is an essay which I wish every one intending to read, or even to write, a novel, might acquaint himself with; for it contains some of the best and clearest things which have been said of the art of fiction in a time when nearly all who practise it have turned to talk about it.

Señor Valdés is a realist, but a realist according to his own conception of realism; and he has some words of just censure for the French naturalists, whom he finds unnecessarily, and suspects of being sometimes even mercenarily, nasty. He sees the wide difference that passes between this naturalism and the realism of the English and Spanish; and he goes somewhat further than I should go in condemning it. "The French naturalism represents only a moment, and an insignificant part of life. . . . It is characterized by sadness and narrowness. The prototype of this literature is the Madame Bovary of Flaubert. I am an admirer of this novelist, and especially of this novel; but often in thinking of it I have said, How dreary would literature be if it were no more than this! There is something antipathetic and gloomy and limited in it, as there is in modern French life"; but this seems to me exactly the best possible reason for its being. I believe with Señor Valdés that "no literature can live long without joy," not because of its mistaken aesthetics, however, but because no civilization can live long without joy. The expression of French life will change when French life changes; and French naturalism is better at its worst than French unnaturalism at its best. "No one," as Señor Valdés truly says, "can rise from the perusal of a naturalistic book . . . without a vivid desire to escape" from the wretched world depicted in it, "and a purpose, more or less vague, of helping to better the lot and morally elevate the abject beings who figure in it. Naturalistic art, then, is not immoral in itself, for then it would not merit the name of art; for though it is not the business of art to preach morality, still I think that, resting on a divine and spiritual principle, like the idea of the beautiful, it is perforce moral. I hold much more immoral other books which, under a glamour of something spiritual and beautiful and sublime, portray the vices in which we are allied to the beasts. Such, for example, are the works of Octave Feuillet, Arsène Houssaye, Georges Ohnet, and other contemporary novelists much in vogue among the higher classes of society."

But what is this idea of the beautiful which art rests upon, and so becomes moral? "The man of our time," says Señor Valdés, "wishes to know everything and enjoy everything: he turns the objective of a powerful equatorial towards the heavenly spaces where gravitate the infinitude of the stars, just as he applies the microscope to the infinitude of the smallest insects; for their laws are identical. His experience, united with intuition, has convinced him that in nature there is neither great nor small; all is equal. All is equally grand, all is equally just; all is equally beautiful, because all is equally divine." But beauty, Señor Valdés explains, exists in the human spirit, and is the beautiful effect which it receives from the true meaning of things; it does not matter what the things are, and it is the function of the artist who feels this effect to impart it to others. I may add that there is no joy in art except this perception of the meaning of things and its communication; when you have felt it, and portrayed it in a poem, a symphony, a novel, a statue, a picture, an edifice, you have fulfilled the purpose for which you were born an artist.

The reflection of exterior nature in the individual spirit, Señor Valdés believes to be the fundamental of art. "To say, then, that the artist must not copy but create is nonsense, because he can in no wise copy, and in no wise create. He who sets deliberately about modifying nature, shows that he has not felt her beauty, and therefore cannot make others feel it. The puerile desire which some artists without genius manifest to go about selecting in nature, not what seems to them beautiful, but what they think will seem beautiful to others, and rejecting what may displease them, ordinarily produces cold and insipid works. For, instead of exploring the illimitable fields of reality, they cling to the forms invented by other artists who have succeeded, and they make statues of statues, poems of poems, novels of novels. It is entirely false that the great romantic, symbolic, or classic poets modified nature; such as they have expressed her they felt her; and in this view they are as much realists as ourselves. In like manner if in the realistic tide that now bears us on there are some spirits who feel nature in another way, in the romantic way, or the classic way, they would not falsify her in expressing her so. Only those falsify her who, without feeling classic wise or romantic wise, set about being classic or romantic, wearisomely reproducing the models of former ages; and equally those who, without sharing the sentiment of realism, which now prevails, force themselves to be realists merely to follow the fashion."

The pseudo-realists, in fact, are the worse offenders, to my thinking, for they sin against the living; whereas those who continue to celebrate the heroic adventures of Puss in Boots and the hairbreadth escapes of Tom Thumb, under various aliases, only cast disrespect upon the immortals who have passed beyond these noises. . . .

XV

Which brings us again, after this long way about, to the divine Jane and her novels, and that troublesome question about them. She was great and they were beautiful, because she and they were honest, and dealt with nature nearly a hundred years ago as realism deals with it to-day. Realism is nothing more and nothing less than the truthful treatment of material, and Jane Austen was the first and the last of the English novelists to treat material with entire truthfulness. Because she did this, she remains the most artistic of the English novelists, and alone worthy to be matched with the great Scandinavian and Slavic and Latin artists. It is not a question of intellect, or not wholly that. The English have mind enough; but they have not taste enough; or, rather, their taste has been perverted by their false criticism, which is based upon personal perference, and not upon principle; which instructs a man to think that what he likes is good, instead of teaching him first to distinguish what is good before he likes it. The art of fiction, as Jane Austen knew it, declined from her through Scott, and Bulwer, and Dickens, and Charlotte Brontë, and Thackeray, and even George Eliot, because the mania of romanticism had seized upon all Europe, and these great writers could not escape the taint of their time; but it has shown few signs of recovery in England, because

English criticism, in the presence of the Continental master-
pieces, has continued provincial and special and personal, and
has expressed a love and hate which had to do with the quality
of the artist rather than the character of his work. It was
inevitable that in their time the English romanticists should
treat, as Señor Valdés says, "the barbarous customs of the
Middle Ages, softening and disfiguring them, as Walter Scott
and his kind did"; that they should "devote themselves to
falsifying nature, refining and subtilizing sentiment, and modifying psychology after their own fancy," like Bulwer and
Dickens, as well as like Rousseau and Madame de Staël, not to
mention Balzac, the worst of all that sort at his worst. This was
the natural course of the disease; but it really seems as if it were
their criticism that was to blame for the rest: not, indeed, for
the performance of this writer or that, for criticism can never
affect the actual doing of a thing; but for the esteem in which
this writer or that is held through the perpetuation of false
ideals. The only observer of English middle-class life since Jane
Austen worthy to be named with her was not George Eliot, who
was first ethical and then artistic, who transcended her in
everything but the form and method most essential to art, and
there fell hopelessly below her. It was Anthony Trollope who
was most like her in simple honesty and instinctive truth, as
unphilosophized as the light of common day; but he was so
warped from a wholesome ideal as to wish at times to be like
the caricaturist Thackeray, and to stand about in his scene,
talking it over with his hands in his pockets, interrupting the
action, and spoiling the illusion in which alone the truth of art
resides. Mainly, his instinct was too much for his ideal, and with
a low view of life in its civic relations and a thoroughly
bourgeois soul, he yet produced works whose beauty is surpassed only by the effect of a more poetic writer in the novels
of Thomas Hardy. Yet if a vote of English criticism even at this
late day, when all continental Europe has the light of aesthetic
truth, could be taken, the majority against these artists would
be overwhelmingly in favor of a writer who had so little artistic
sensibility, that he never hesitated on any occasion, great or
small, to make a foray among his characters, and catch them up
to show them to the reader and tell him how beautiful or ugly
they were; and cry out over their amazing properties.

Doubtless the ideal of those poor islanders will be finally
changed. If the truth could become a fad it would be accepted

by all their "smart people," but truth is something rather too large for that; and we must await the gradual advance of civilization among them. Then they will see that their criticism has misled them; and that it is to this false guide they owe, not precisely the decline of fiction among them, but its continued debasement as an art.

XVI

"How few materials," says Emerson, "are yet used by our arts! The mass of creatures and of qualities are still hid and expectant," and to break new ground is still one of the uncommonest and most heroic of the virtues. The artists are not alone to blame for the timidity that keeps them in the old furrows of the worn-out fields; most of those whom they live to please, or live by pleasing, prefer to have them remain there; it wants rare virtue to appreciate what is new, as well as to invent it; and the "easy things to understand" are the conventional things. This is why the ordinary English novel, with its hackneyed plot, scenes, and figures, is more comfortable to the ordinary American than an American novel, which deals, at its worst, with comparatively new interests and motives. To adjust one's self to the enjoyment of these costs an intellectual effort, and an intellectual effort is what no ordinary person likes to make. It is only the extraordinary person who can say, with Emerson: "I ask not for the great, the remote, the romantic. . . . I embrace the common; I sit at the feet of the familiar and the low. . . . Man is surprised to find that things near are not less beautiful and wondrous than things remote. . . . The perception of the worth of the vulgar is fruitful in discoveries. . . . The foolish man wonders at the unusual, but the wise man at the usual. . . . To-day always looks mean to the thoughtless; but to-day is a king in disguise. . . . Banks and tariffs, the newspaper and caucus, Methodism and Unitarianism, are flat and dull to dull people, but rest on the same foundations of wonder as the town of Troy and the temple of Delphos."

Perhaps we ought not to deny their town of Troy and their temple of Delphos to the dull people; but if we ought, and if we did, they would still insist upon having them. An English novel, full of titles and rank, is apparently essential to the happiness of such people; their weak and childish imagination is at home in its familiar environment; they know what they are reading; the fact that it is hash many times warmed over reassures them; whereas a story of our own life, honestly studied and faithfully represented, troubles them with varied misgiving. They are not sure that it is literature; they do not feel that it is good society; its characters, so like their own, strike them as commonplace; they say they do not wish to know such people.

Everything in England is appreciable to the literary sense, while the sense of the literary worth of things in America is still faint and weak with most people, with the vast majority who "ask for the great, the remote, the romantic," who cannot "embrace the common," cannot "sit at the feet of the familiar and the low," in the good company of Emerson. We are all, or nearly all, struggling to be distinguished from the mass, and to be set apart in select circles and upper classes like the fine people we have read about. We are really a mixture of the plebeian ingredients of the whole world; but that is not bad; our vulgarity consists in trying to ignore "the worth of the vulgar," in believing that the superfine is better.

XVII

Another Spanish novelist of our day, whose books have given me great pleasure, is so far from being of the same mind of Señor Valdés about fiction that he boldly declares himself, in the preface to his Pepita Ximenez, "an advocate of art for art's sake." I heartily agree with him that it is "in very bad taste, always impertinent and often pedantic, to attempt to prove these by writing stories," and yet I fancy that no reader whom Señor Valera would care to please could read his Pepita Ximenez without finding himself in possession of a great deal of serious thinking on a very serious subject, which is none the less serious because it is couched in terms of delicate irony. If it is true that "the object of a novel should be to charm through a faithful representation of human actions and human passions, and to create by this fidelity to nature a beautiful work," and if "the creation of the beautiful" is solely "the object of art," it never was and never can be solely its effect as long as men are men and women are women. If ever the race is resolved into abstract qualities, perhaps this may happen; but till then the finest effect of the "beautiful" will be ethical and not aesthetic merely. Morality penetrates all things, it is the soul of all things. Beauty may clothe it on, whether it is false morality and an evil soul, or whether it is true and a good soul. In the one case the beauty will corrupt, and in the other it will edify, and in either case it will infallibly and inevitably have an ethical effect, now light, now grave, according as the thing is light or grave. We cannot escape from this; we are shut up to it by the very conditions of our being. What is it that delights us in this very Pepita Ximenez, this exquisite masterpiece of Señor Valera's? Not merely that a certain Luis de Vargas, dedicated to the priesthood, finds a certain Pepita Ximenez lovelier than the priesthood, and abandons all his sacerdotal hopes and ambitions, all his poetic dreams of renunciation and devotion, to marry her. That is very pretty and very true, and it pleases; but what chiefly appeals to the heart is the assertion, however delicately and adroitly implied, that their right to each other through their love was far above his vocation. In spite of himself, without trying, and therefore without impertinence and without pedantry, Señor Valera has proved a thesis in his story. They of the Church will acquiesce with the reservation of Don Luis's uncle the Dean that his marriage was better than his vocation, because his vocation was a sentimental and fancied one; we of the Church-in-error will accept the result without any reservation whatever; and I think we shall have the greater enjoyment of the delicate irony, the fine humor, the amusing and unfailing subtlety, with which the argument is enforced. In recognizing these, however, in praising the story for the graphic skill with which Southern characters and passions are portrayed in the gay light of an Andalusian sky, for the charm with which a fresh and unhackneyed life is presented, and the fidelity with which novel conditions are sketched, I must not fail to add that the book is one of those who have come to the knowledge of good and evil, and to confess my regret that it fails of the remoter truth, "the eternal amenities" which only the avowed advocates of "art for art's sake" seem to forget. It leaves the reader to believe that Vargas can be happy with a woman who wins him in Pepita's way; and that is where it is false both to life and to art. For the moment, it is charming to have the story end happily, as it does, but after one has lived a certain number of years, and read a certain number of novels, it is not the prosperous or adverse fortune of the characters that affects one, but the good or bad faith of the novelist in dealing with them.

Will he play us false or will he be true in the operation of this or
that principle involved? I cannot hold him to less account than
this: he must be true to what life has taught me is the truth, and
after that he may let any fate betide his people; the novel ends
well that ends faithfully. The greater his power, the greater his
responsibility before the human conscience, which is God in us.
But men come and go, and what they do in their limited
physical lives is of comparatively little moment; it is what they
say that really survives to bless or to ban; and it is the evil which
Wordsworth felt in Goethe, that must long survive him. There is
a kind of thing—a kind of metaphysical lie against righteousness
and common-sense—which is called the Unmoral, and is supposed to be different from the Immoral; and it is this which is
supposed to cover many of the faults of Goethe. His Wilhelm
Meister, for example, is so far removed within the region of the
"ideal" that its unprincipled, its evil-principled, tenor in regard
to women is pronounced "unmorality," and is therefore infer-
ably harmless. But no study of Goethe is complete without
some recognition of the qualities which caused Wordsworth to
hurl the book across the room with an indignant perception of
its sensuality. For the sins of his life Goethe was perhaps
sufficiently punished in his life by his final marriage with
Christiane; for the sins of his literature many others must suffer.
I do not despair, however, of the day when the poor honest
herd of mankind shall give universal utterance to the universal
instinct, and shall hold selfish power in politics, in art, in
religion, for the devil that it is; when neither its crazy pride nor
its amusing vanity shall be flattered by the puissance of the
"geniuses" who have forgotten their duty to the common
weakness, and have abused it to their own glory. In that day we
shall shudder at many monsters of passion, of self-indulgence,
of heartlessness, whom we still more or less openly adore for
their "genius," and shall account no man worshipful whom we
do not feel and know to be good. The spectacle of strenuous
achievement will then not dazzle or mislead; it will not sanctify
or palliate iniquity; it will only render it the more hideous and
pitiable.

In fact, the whole belief in "genius" seems to me rather a
mischievous superstition, and if not mischievous always, still
always a superstition. From the account of those who talk
about it, "genius" appears to be the attribute of a sort of very
potent and admirable prodigy which God has created out of the

common for the astonishment and confusion of the rest of us poor human beings. But do they really believe it? Do they mean anything more or less than the Mastery which comes to any man according to his powers and diligence in any direction? If not, why not have an end of the superstition which has caused our race to go on so long writing and reading of the difference between talent and genius? It is within the memory of middle-aged men that the Maelstrom existed in the belief of the geographers, but we now get on perfectly well without it; and why should we still suffer under the notion of "genius" which keeps so many poor little authorlings trembling in question whether they have it, or have only "talent"?

One of the greatest captains who ever lived—a plain, taciturn, unaffected soul—has told the story of his wonderful life as unconsciously as if it were all an every-day affair, not different from other lives, except as a great exigency of the human race gave it importance. So far as he knew, he had no natural aptitude for arms, and certainly no love for the calling. But he went to West Point because, as he quaintly tells us, his father "rather thought he would go"; and he fought through one war with credit, but without glory. The other war, which was to claim his powers and his science, found him engaged in the most prosaic of peaceful occupations; he obeyed its call because he loved his country, and not because he loved war. All the world knows the rest, and all the world knows that greater military mastery has not been shown than his campaigns illustrated. He does not say this in his book, or hint it in any way; he gives you the facts, and leaves them with you. But the Personal Memoirs of U. S. Grant, written as simply and straightforwardly as his battles were fought, couched in the most unpretentious phrase, with never a touch of grandiosity or attitudinizing, familiar, homely in style, form a great piece of literature, because great literature is nothing more nor less than the clear expression of minds that have something great in them, whether religion, or beauty, or deep experience. Probably Grant would have said that he had no more vocation to literature than he had to war. He owns, with something like contrition, that he used to read a great many novels; but we think he would have denied the soft impeachment of literary power. Nevertheless, he shows it, as he showed military power, unexpectedly, almost miraculously. All the conditions here, then, are favorable to supposing a case of "genius." Yet who would trifle with that great heir of fame, that plain, grand, manly soul, by speaking of "genius" and him together? Who calls Washington a genius? or Franklin, or Bismarck, or Cavour, or Columbus, or Luther, or Darwin, or Lincoln? Were these men second-rate in their way? Or is "genius" that indefinable, preternatural quality, sacred to the musicians, the painters, the sculptors, the actors, the poets, and above all, the poets? Or is it that the poets, having most of the say in this world, abuse it to shameless self-flattery, and would persuade the inarticulate classes that they are on peculiar terms of confidence with the deity?

XVIII

In General Grant's confession of novel-reading there is a sort of inference that he had wasted his time, or else the guilty conscience of the novelist in me imagines such an inference. But however this may be, there is certainly no question concerning the intention of a correspondent who once wrote to me after reading some rather bragging claims I had made for fiction as a mental and moral means. "I have very grave doubts," he said, "as to the whole list of magnificent things that you seem to think novels have done for the race, and can witness in myself many evil things which they have done for me. Whatever in my mental make-up is wild and visionary, whatever is untrue, whatever is injurious, I can trace to the perusal of some work of fiction. Worse than that, they beget such high-strung and supersensitive ideas of life that plain industry and plodding perseverance are despised, and matter-of-fact poverty, or every-day, commonplace distress, meets with no sympathy, if indeed noticed at all, by one who has wept over the impossibly accumulated sufferings of some gaudy hero or heroine."

I am not sure that I had the controversy with this correspondent that he seemed to suppose; but novels are now so fully accepted by every one pretending to cultivated taste—and they really form the whole intellectual life of such immense numbers of people, without question of their influence, good or bad upon the mind—that it is refreshing to have them frankly denounced, and to be invited to revise one's ideas and feelings in regard to them. A little honesty, or a great deal of honesty, in this quest will do the novel, as we hope yet to have it, and as we have already begun to have it, no harm; and for my own part I will confess that I believe fiction in the past to have been largely injurious, as I believe the stage play to be still almost wholly injurious, through its falsehood, its folly, its wantonness, and its aimlessness. It may be safely assumed that most of the novel-reading which people fancy an intellectual pastime is the emptiest dissipation, hardly more related to thought or the wholesome exercise of the mental faculties than opium-eating; in either case the brain is drugged, and left weaker and crazier for the debauch. If this may be called the negative result of the fiction habit, the positive injury that most novels work is by no means so easily to be measured in the case of young men whose character they help so much to form or deform, and the women of all ages whom they keep so much in ignorance of the world they misrepresent. Grown men have little harm from them, but in the other cases, which are the vast majority, they hurt because they are not true—not because they are malevolent, but because they are idle lies about human nature and the social fabric, which it behooves us to know and to understand, that we may deal justly with ourselves and with one another. One need not go so far as our correspondent, and trace to the fiction habit "whatever is wild and visionary, whatever is untrue, whatever is injurious," in one's life; bad as the fiction habit is it is probably not responsible for the whole sum of evil in its victims, and I believe that if the reader will use care in choosing from this fungus-growth with which the fields of literature teem every day, he may nourish himself as with the true mushroom, at no risk from the poisonous species.

The tests are very plain and simple, and they are perfectly infallible. If a novel flatters the passions, and exalts them above the principles, it is poisonous; it may not kill, but it will certainly injure; and this test will alone exclude an entire class of fiction, of which eminent examples will occur to all. Then the whole spawn of so-called unmoral romances, which imagine a world where the sins of sense are unvisited by the penalties following, swift or slow, but inexorably sure, in the real world, are deadly poison: these do kill. The novels that merely tickle our prejudices and lull our judgment, or that coddle our sensibilities or pamper our gross appetite for the marvelous are not so fatal, but they are innutritious, and clog the soul with unwholesome vapors of all kinds. No doubt they too help to weaken the moral fibre, and make their readers indifferent to "plodding perseverance and plain industry," and to "matter-of-fact poverty and commonplace distress."

Without taking them too seriously, it still must be owned that the "gaudy hero and heroine" are to blame for a great deal of harm in the world. That heroine long taught by example, if not precept, that Love, or the passion or fancy she mistook for it, was the chief interest of a life, which is really concerned with a great many other things; that it was lasting in the way she knew it; that it was worthy of every sacrifice, and was altogether a finer thing than prudence, obedience, reason; that love alone was glorious and beautiful, and these were mean and ugly in comparison with it. More lately she has begun to idolize and illustrate Duty, and she is hardly less mischievous in this new role, opposing duty, as she did love, to prudence, obedience, and reason. The stock hero, whom, if we met him, we could not fail to see was a most deplorable person, has undoubtedly imposed himself upon the victims of the fiction habit as admirable. With him, too, love was and is the great affair, whether in its old romantic phase of chivalrous achievement or manifold suffering for love's sake, or its more recent development of the "virile," the bullying, and the brutal, or its still more recent agonies of self-sacrifice, as idle and useless as the moral experiences of the insane asylums. With his vain posturings and his ridiculous splendor he is really a painted barbarian, the prey of his passions and his delusions, full of obsolete ideals, and the motives and ethics of a savage, which the guilty author of his being does his best—or his worst—in spite of his own light and knowledge, to foist upon the reader as something generous and noble. I am not merely bringing this charge against that sort of fiction which is beneath literature and outside of it, "the shoreless lakes of ditch-water," whose miasms fill the air below the empyrean where the great ones sit; but I am accusing the work of some of the most famous, who have, in this instance or in that, sinned against the truth, which can alone exalt and purify men. I do not say that they have constantly done so, or even commonly done so; but that they have done so at all marks them as of the past, to be read with the due historical allowance of their epoch and their conditions. For I believe that, while inferior writers will and must continue to imitate them in their foibles and their errors, no one hereafter will be able to achieve greatness who is false to humanity, either in its facts or its duties. The light of civiliza-

tion has already broken even upon the novel, and no conscientious man can now set about painting an image of life without
perpetual question of the verity of his work, and without
feeling bound to distinguish so clearly that no reader of his may
be misled between what is right and what is wrong, what is
noble and what is base, what is health and what is perdition, in
the actions and the characters he portrays.

The fiction that aims merely to entertain—the fiction that is
to serious fiction as the opera-bouffe, the ballet, and the
pantomime are to the true drama—need not feel the burden of
this obligation so deeply; but even such fiction will not be gay
or trivial to any reader's hurt, and criticism will hold it to
account if it passes from painting to teaching folly.

More and more not only the criticism which prints its
opinions, but the infinitely vaster and powerfuler criticism
which thinks and feels them merely, will make this demand. I
confess that I do not care to judge any work of the imagination
without first of all applying this test to it. We must ask
ourselves before we ask anything else, Is it true?—true to the
motives, the impulses, the principles that shape the life of actual
men and women? This truth, which necessarily includes the
highest morality and the highest artistry—this truth given, the
book cannot be wicked and cannot be weak; and without it all
graces of style and feats of invention and cunning of construction are so many superfluities of naughtiness. It is well for the
truth to have all these, and shine in them, but for falsehood
they are merely meretricious, the bedizenment of the wanton;
they atone for nothing, they count for nothing. But in fact they
come naturally of truth, and grace it without solicitation; they
are added unto it. In the whole range of fiction we know of no
true picture of life—that is, of human nature—which is not also
a masterpiece of literature, full of divine and natural beauty. It
may have no touch or tint of this special civilization or of that;
it had better have this local color well ascertained; but the truth
is deeper and finer than aspects, and if the book is true to what
men and women know of one another's souls it will be true
enough, and it will be great and beautiful. It is the conception
of literature as something apart from life, superfinely aloof,
which makes it really unimportant to the great mass of
mankind, without a message or a meaning for them; and it is the
notion that a novel may be false in its portrayal of causes and
effects that makes literary art contemptible even to those whom

it amuses, that forbids them to regard the novelist as a serious or right-minded person. If they do not in some moment of indignation cry out against all novels, as my correspondent does, they remain besotted in the fume of the delusions purveyed to them, with no higher feeling for the author than such maudlin affection as the habitué of an opium-joint perhaps knows for the attendant who fills his pipe with the drug.

Or, as in the case of another correspondent who writes that in his youth he "read a great many novels, but always regarded it as an amusement, like horse-racing and card-playing," for which he had no time when he entered upon the serious business of life, it renders them merely contemptuous. His view of the matter may be commended to the brotherhood and sisterhood of novelists as full of wholesome if bitter suggestion; and we urge them not to dismiss it with high literary scorn as that of some Boeotian dull to the beauty of art. Refuse it as we may, it is still the feeling of the vast majority of people for whom life is earnest, and who find only a distorted and misleading likeness of it in our books. We may fold ourselves in our scholars' gowns, and close the doors of our studies, and affect to despise this rude voice; but we cannot shut it out. It comes to us from wherever men are at work, from wherever they are truly living, and accuses us of unfaithfulness, of triviality, of mere stage-play; and none of us can escape conviction except he prove himself worthy of his time—a time in which the great masters have brought literature back to life, and filled its ebbing veins with the red tides of reality. We cannot all equal them; we need not copy them; but we can all go to the sources of their inspiration and their power; and to draw from these no one need go far—no one need really go out of himself.

Fifty years ago, Carlyle in whom the truth was always alive, but in whom it was then unperverted by suffering, by celebrity, and by despair, wrote in his study of Diderot: "Were it not reasonable to prophesy that this exceeding great multitude of novel-writers and such like must, in a new generation, gradually do one of two things: either retire into the nurseries, and work for children, minors, and semi-fatuous persons of both sexes, or else, what were far better, sweep their novel-fabric into the dust-cart, and betake themselves with such faculty as they have to understand and record what is true, of which surely there is, and will forever be, a whole infinitude unknown to us of infinite importance to us? Poetry, it will more and more come to be understood, is nothing but higher knowledge; and the only genuine Romance (for grown persons), Reality."

If, after half a century, fiction still mainly works for "children, minors, and semi-fatuous persons of both sexes," it is nevertheless one of the hopefulest signs of the world's progress that it has begun to work for "grown persons," and if not exactly in the way that Carlyle might have solely intended in urging its writers to compile memoirs instead of building the "novel-fabric," still it has, in the highest and widest sense, already made Reality its Romance. I cannot judge it, I do not even care for it, except as it has done this; and I can hardly conceive of a literary self-respect in these days compatible with the old trade of make-believe, with the production of the kind of fiction which is too much honored by classification with card-playing and horse-racing. But let fiction cease to lie about life; let it portray men and women as they are, actuated by the motives and the passions in the measure we all know; let it leave off painting dolls and working them by springs and wires; let it show the different interests in their true proportions; let it forbear to preach pride and revenge, folly and insanity, egotism and prejudice, but frankly own these for what they are, in whatever figures and occasions they appear; let it not put on fine literary airs; let it speak the dialect, the language, that most Americans know—the language of unaffected people everywhere—and there can be no doubt of an unlimited future, not only of delightfulness but of usefulness, for it.

XX

Of the finer kinds of romance, as distinguished from the novel, I would even encourage the writing, though it is one of the hard conditions of romance that its personages starting with a parti pris can rarely be characters with a living growth, but are apt to be types, limited to the expression of one principle, simple, elemental, lacking the God-given complexity of motive which we find in all the human beings we know.

Hawthorne, the great master of the romance, had the insight and the power to create it anew as a kind in fiction; though I am not sure that The Scarlet Letter and the Blithedale Romance are not, strictly speaking, novels rather than romances. They do not play with some old superstition long outgrown, and they do not invent a new superstition to play with, but deal with things vital in every one's pulse. I am not saying that what may be called the fantastic romance—the romance that descends from Frankenstein rather than The Scarlet Letter—ought not to be. On the contrary, I should grieve to lose it, as I should grieve to lose the pantomime or the comic opera, or many other graceful things that amuse the passing hour, and help us to live agreeably in a world where men actually sin, suffer, and die. But it belongs to the decorative arts, and though it has a high place among them, it cannot be ranked with the works of the imagination—the works that represent and body forth human experience. Its ingenuity can always afford a refined pleasure, and it can often, at some risk to itself, convey a valuable truth.

Perhaps the whole region of historical romance might be reopened with advantage to readers and writers who cannot bear to be brought face to face with human nature, but require the haze of distance or a far perspective, in which all the disagreeable details shall be lost. There is no good reason why these harmless people should not be amused, or their little preferences indulged.

But here, again, I have my modest doubts, some recent instances are so fatuous, as far as the portrayal of character goes, though I find them admirably contrived in some respects. When I have owned the excellence of the staging in every respect, and the conscience with which the carpenter (as the theatrical folks say) has done his work, I am at the end of my praises. The people affect me like persons of our generation made up for the parts; well trained, well costumed, but actors, and almost amateurs. They have the quality that makes the histrionics of amateurs endurable; they are ladies and gentlemen; the worst, the wickedest of them, is a lady or gentleman behind the scene.

Yet, no doubt it is well that there should be a reversion to the earlier types of thinking and feeling, to earlier ways of looking at human nature, and I will not altogether refuse the pleasure offered me by the poetic romancer or the historical romancer because I find my pleasure chiefly in Tolstoï and James and Galdós and Valdés and Thomas Hardy and Tourguéneff, and Balzac at his best.

The reversions or counter-currents in the general tendency of a time are very curious, and are worthy tolerant study. They are always to be found; perhaps they form the exception that establishes the rule; at least they distinguish it. They give us performances having an archaic charm by which, by-and-by, things captivate for reasons unconnected with their inherent beauty. They become quaint, and this is reason enough for liking them, for returning to them, and in art for trying to do them again. But I confess that I like better to go forward than to go backward, and it is saying very little to say that I value more such a novel as Mr. James's Tragic Muse than all the romantic attempts since Hawthorne. I call Mr. James a novelist because there is yet no name for the literary kind he has invented, and so none for the inventor. The fatuity of the story merely as a story is something that must early impress the storyteller who does not live in the stone age of fiction and criticism. To spin a yarn for the yarn's sake, that is an ideal worthy of a nineteenth-century Englishman, doting in forgetfulness of the English masters and grovelling in ignorance of the Continental masters; but wholly impossible to an American of Mr. Henry James's modernity. To him it must seem like the lies swapped between men after the ladies have left the table and they are sinking deeper and deeper into their cups and growing dimmer and dimmer behind their cigars. To such a mind as his the story could never have value except as a means; it could not exist for him as an end; it could be used only illustratively; it could be the frame, not possibly the picture. But in the mean time the kind of thing he wished to do, and began to do, and has always done, amid a stupid clamor, which still lasts, that it was not a story, had to be called a novel; and the wretched victim of the novel habit (only a little less intellectually degraded than the still more miserable slave of the theatre habit), who wished neither to perceive nor to reflect, but only to be acted upon by plot and incident, was lost in an endless trouble about it. Here was a thing called a novel, written with extraordinary charm; interesting by the vigor and vivacity with which phases and situations and persons were handled in it; inviting him to the intimacy of characters divined with creative insight; making him witness of motives and emotions and experiences of the finest import; and then suddenly requiring him to be man enough to cope with the question itself; not solving it for him by a marriage or a murder, and not spoon-victualling him with a moral minced small and then thinned with milk and water, and familiarly flavored with sentimentality or religiosity. I can imagine the sort of shame with which such a writer as Mr.

James, so original and so clear-sighted, may sometimes have been tempted by the outcry of the nurslings of fable, to give them of the diet on which they had been pampered to imbecility; or to call together his characters for a sort of round-up in the last chapter.

XXI

It is no doubt such work as Mr. James's that an English essayist (Mr. E. Hughes) has chiefly in mind, in a study of the differences of the English and American novel. He defines the English novel as working from within outwardly, and the American novel as working from without inwardly. The definition is very surprisingly accurate; and the critic's discovery of this fundamental difference is carried into particulars with a distinctness which is as unfailing as the courtesy he has in recognizing the present superiority of American work. He seems to think, however, that the English principle is the better, though why he should think so he does not make so clear. It appears a belated and rather voluntary effect of patriotism, disappointing in a philosopher of his degree; but it does not keep him from very explicit justice to the best characteristics of our fiction. "The American novelist is distinguished for the intellectual grip which he has of his characters. . . . He penetrates below the crust, and he recognizes no necessity of the crust to anticipate what is beneath. . . . He utterly discards heroics; he often even discards anything like a plot. . . . His story proper is often no more than a natural predicament. . . . It is no stage view we have of his characters, but one behind the scenes. . . . We are brought into contact with no strained virtues, illumined by strained lights upon strained heights of situation. . . . Whenever he appeals to the emotions it would seem to be with an appeal to the intellect too . . . because he weaves his story of the finer, less self-evident though common threads of human nature, seldom calling into play the grosser and more powerful strain. . . . Everywhere in his pages we come across acquaintances undisguised. . . . The characters in an American novel are never unapproachable to the reader. . . . The naturalness, with the every-day atmosphere which surrounds it, is one great charm of the American novel. . . . It is throughout examinative, discursory, even more—quizzical. Its characters are

undergoing, at the hands of the author, calm, interested observation. . . . He is never caught identifying himself with them; he
must preserve impartiality at all costs . . . but . . . the touch of
nature is always felt, the feeling of kinship always follows. . . .
The strength of the American novel is its optimistic faith. . . . If
out of this persistent hopefulness it can evolve for men a new
order of trustfulness, a tenet that between man and man there
should be less suspicion, more confidence, since human nature
sanctions it, its mission will have been more than as aesthetic, it
will have been a moral one."

Not all of this will be found true of Mr. James, but all that
relates to artistic methods and characteristics will, and the rest
is true of American novels generally. For the most part in their
range and tendency they are admirable. I will not say they are
all good, or that any of them is wholly good; but I find in
nearly every one of them a disposition to regard our life
without the literary glasses so long thought desirable, and to see
character, not as it is in other fiction, but as it abounds outside
of all fiction. This disposition sometimes goes with poor enough
performance, but in some of our novels it goes with performance that is excellent; and at any rate it is for the present more
valuable than evenness of performance. It is what relates
American fiction to the only living movement in imaginative
literature, and distinguishes by a superior freshness and authen-
ticity any group of American novels from a similarly accidental
group of English novels, giving them the same good right to be
as the like number of recent Russian novels, French novels,
Spanish novels, Italian novels, Norwegian novels.

It is the difference of the American novelist's ideals from
those of the English novelist that gives him his advantage, and
seems to promise him the future. The love of the passionate and
the heroic, as the Englishman has it, is such a crude and
unwholesome thing, so deaf and blind to all the most delicate
and important facts of art and life, so insensible to the subtle
values in either that its presence or absence makes the whole
difference, and enables one who is not obsessed by it to thank
Heaven that he is not as that other man is.

There can be little question that many refinements of thought
and spirit which every American is sensible of in the fiction of
this continent, are necessarily lost upon our good kin beyond
seas, whose thumb-fingered apprehension requires something
gross and palpable for its assurance of reality. This is not their

fault, and I am not sure that it is wholly their misfortune: they are made so as not to miss what they do not find, and they are simply content without those subtleties of life and character which it gives us so keen a pleasure to have noted in literature. If they perceive them at all it is as something vague and diaphanous, something that filmily wavers before their sense and teases them, much as the beings of an invisible world might mock one of our material frame by intimations of their presence. It is with reason, therefore, on the part of an Englishman, that Mr. Henley complains of our fiction as a shadow-land, though we find more and more in it the faithful report of our life, its motives and emotions, and all the comparatively etherealized passions and ideals that influence it.

In fact, the American who chooses to enjoy his birthright to the full, lives in a world wholly different from the Englishman's, and speaks (too often through his nose) another language: he breathes a rarefied and nimble air full of shining possibilities and radiant promises which the fog-and-soot-clogged lungs of those less-favored islanders struggle in vain to fill themselves with. But he ought to be modest in his advantage, and patient with the coughing and sputtering of his cousin who complains of finding himself in an exhausted receiver on plunging into one of our novels. To be quite just to the poor fellow, I have had some such experience as that myself in the atmosphere of some of our more attenuated romances.

Yet every now and then I read a book with perfect comfort and much exhilaration, whose scenes the average Englishman would gasp in. Nothing happens; that is, nobody murders or debauches anybody else; there is no arson or pillage of any sort; there is not a ghost, or a ravening beast, or a hair-breadth escape, or a shipwreck, or a monster of self-sacrifice, or a lady five thousand years old in the whole course of the story; "no promenade, no band of music, nossing!" as Mr. Du Maurier's Frenchman said of the meet for a fox-hunt. Yet it is all alive with the keenest interest for those who enjoy the study of individual traits and general conditions as they make themselves known to American experience.

These conditions have been so favorable hitherto (though they are becoming always less so) that they easily account for the optimistic faith of our novel which Mr. Hughes notices. It used to be one of the disadvantages of the practice of romance in America, which Hawthorne more or less whimsically lamented, that there were so few shadows and inequalities in our broad level of prosperity; and it is one of the reflections suggested by Dostoïevsky's novel, The Crime and the Punishment, that whoever struck a note so profoundly tragic in American fiction would do a false and mistaken thing—as false and as mistaken in its way as dealing in American fiction with certain nudities which the Latin peoples seem to find edifying. Whatever their deserts, very few American novelists have been led out to be shot, or finally exiled to the rigors of a winter at Duluth; and in a land where journeymen carpenters and plumbers strike for four dollars a day the sum of hunger and cold is comparatively small, and the wrong from class to class has been almost inappreciable, though all this is changing for the worse. Our novelists, therefore, concern themselves with the more smiling aspects of life, which are the more American, and seek the universal in the individual rather than the social interests. It is worth while, even at the risk of being called commonplace, to be true to our well-to-do actualities; the very passions themselves seem to be softened and modified by conditions which formerly at least could not be said to wrong any one, to cramp endeavor, or to cross lawful desire. Sin and suffering and shame there must always be in the world, I suppose, but I believe that in this new world of ours it is still mainly from one to another one, and oftener still from one to one's self. We have death too in America, and a great deal of disagreeable and painful disease, which the multiplicity of our patent medicines does not seem to cure; but this is tragedy that comes in the very nature of things, and is not peculiarly American, as the large, cheerful average of health and success and happy life is. It will not do to boast, but it is well to be true to the facts, and to see that, apart from these purely mortal troubles, the race here has enjoyed conditions in which most of the ills that have darkened its annals might be averted by honest work and unselfish behavior.

Fine artists we have among us, and right-minded as far as they go; and we must not forget this at evil moments when it seems as if all the women had taken to writing hysterical improprieties, and some of the men were trying to be at least as hysterical in despair of being as improper. If we kept to the complexion of a certain school—which sadly needs a school-master—we might very well be despondent; but, after all, that school is not representative of our conditions or our intentions. Other traits are much more characteristic of our life and our fiction. In most American novels, vivid and graphic as the best of them are, the people are segregated if not sequestered, and the scene is sparsely populated. The effect may be in instinctive response to the vacancy of our social life, and I shall not make haste to blame it. There are few places, few occasions among us, in which a novelist can get a large number of polite people together, or at least keep them together. Unless he carries a snap-camera his picture of them has no probability; they affect one like the figures perfunctorily associated in such deadly old engravings as that of "Washington Irving and his Friends." Perhaps it is for this reason that we excel in small pieces with three or four figures, or in studies of rustic communities, where there is propinquity if not society. Our grasp of more urbane life is feeble; most attempts to assemble it in our pictures are failures, possibly because it is too transitory, too intangible in its nature with us, to be truthfully represented as really existent.

I am not sure that the Americans have not brought the short story nearer perfection in the all-round sense than almost any other people, and for reasons very simple and near at hand. It might be argued from the national hurry and impatience that it was a literary form peculiarly adapted to the American temperament, but I suspect that its extraordinary development among us is owing much more to more tangible facts. The success of American magazines, which is nothing less than prodigious, is only commensurate with their excellence. Their sort of success is not only from the courage to decide what ought to please, but from the knowledge of what does please; and it is probable that, aside from the pictures, it is the short stories which please the readers of our best magazines. The serial novels they must have, of course; but rather more of course they must have short stories, and by operation of the law of supply and demand, the short stories, abundant in quantity and excellent in quality, are forthcoming because they are wanted. By another operation of the same law, which political economists have more recently taken account of, the demand follows the supply, and short stories are sought for because there is a proven ability to furnish them, and people read them willingly because they are usually very good. The art of writing them is now so disciplined and diffused with us that there is no lack either for the magazines or for the newspaper "syndicates" which deal in them almost to the exclusion of the serials. In other countries the feuilleton of the journals is a novel continued from day to day, but with us the papers, whether daily or weekly, now more rarely print novels, whether they get them at first hand from the writers, as a great many do, or through the syndicates, which purvey a vast variety of literary wares, chiefly for the Sunday editions of the city journals. In the country papers the short story takes the place of the chapters of a serial which used to be given.

XXII

An interesting fact in regard to the different varieties of the short story among us is that the sketches and studies by the women seem faithfuler and more realistic than those of the men, in proportion to their number. Their tendency is more distinctly in that direction, and there is a solidity, an honest observation, in the work of such women as Mrs. Cooke, Miss Murfree, Miss Wilkins and Miss Jewett, which often leaves little to be desired. I should, upon the whole, be disposed to rank American short stories only below those of such Russian writers as I have read, and I should praise rather than blame their free use of our different local parlances, or "dialects," as people call them. I like this because I hope that our inherited English may be constantly freshened and revived from the native sources which our literary decentralization will help to keep open, and I will own that as I turn over novels coming from Philadelphia, from New Mexico, from Boston, from Tennessee, from rural New England, from New York, every local flavor of diction gives me courage and pleasure. M. Alphonse Daudet, in a conversation which Mr. H. H. Boyesen has set down in a recently recorded interview with him, said, in speaking of Tourguéneff: "What a luxury it must be to have a great big untrodden barbaric language to wade into! We poor fellows who work in the language of an old civilization, we may sit and chisel our little verbal felicities, only to find in the end that it is a borrowed jewel we are polishing. The crown of jewels of our French tongue have passed through the hands of so many generations of monarchs that it seems like presumption on the part of any late-born pretender to attempt to wear them."

This grief is, of course, a little whimsical, yet it has a certain measure of reason in it, and the same regret has been more seriously expressed by the Italian poet Aleardi:

"Muse of an aged people, in the eve
Of fading civilization, I was born.
. . . . . . Oh, fortunate,
My sisters, who in the heroic dawn
Of races sung! To them did destiny give
The virgin fire and chaste ingenuousness
Of their land's speech; and, reverenced, their hands
Ran over potent strings."

It will never do to allow that we are at such a desperate pass in English, but something of this divine despair we may feel too in thinking of "the spacious times of great Elizabeth," when the poets were trying the stops of the young language, and thrilling with the surprises of their own music. We may comfort ourselves, however, unless we prefer a luxury of grief, by remembering that no language is ever old on the lips of those who speak it, no matter how decrepit it drops from the pen. We have only to leave our studies, editorial and other, and go into the shops and fields to find the "spacious times" again; and from the beginning Realism, before she had put on her capital letter, had divined this near-at-hand truth along with the rest. Mr. Lowell, almost the greatest and finest realist who ever wrought in verse, showed us that Elizabeth was still Queen where he heard Yankee farmers talk. One need not invite slang into the company of its betters, though perhaps slang has been dropping its "s" and becoming language ever since the world began, and is certainly sometimes delightful and forcible beyond the reach of the dictionary. I would not have any one go about for new words, but if one of them came aptly, not to reject its help. For our novelists to try to write Americanly, from any motive, would be a dismal error, but being born Americans, I would have them use "Americanisms" whenever these serve their turn; and when their characters speak, I should like to hear them speak true American, with all the varying Tennesseean, Philadelphian, Bostonian, and New York accents. If we bother ourselves to write what the critics imagine to be "English," we shall be priggish and artificial, and still more so if we make our Americans talk "English." There is also this serious disadvantage about "English," that if we wrote the best "English" in the world, probably the English themselves would not know it, or, if they did, certainly would not own it. It has always been supposed by grammarians and purists that a language can be kept as they find it; but languages, while they live, are perpetually changing. God apparently meant them for the common people—whom Lincoln believed God liked because he had made so many of them; and the common people will use them freely as they use other gifts of God. On their lips our continental English will differ more and more from the insular English, and I believe that this is not deplorable, but desirable.

In fine, I would have our American novelists be as American as they unconsciously can. Matthew Arnold complained that he found no "distinction" in our life, and I would gladly persuade all artists intending greatness in any kind among us that the recognition of the fact pointed out by Mr. Arnold ought to be a source of inspiration to them, and not discouragement. We have been now some hundred years building up a state on the affirmation of the essential equality of men in their rights and duties, and whether we have been right or wrong the gods have taken us at our word, and have responded to us with a civilization in which there is no "distinction" perceptible to the eye that loves and values it. Such beauty and such grandeur as we have is common beauty, common grandeur, or the beauty and grandeur in which the quality of solidarity so prevails that neither distinguishes itself to the disadvantage of anything else. It seems to me that these conditions invite the artist to the study and the appreciation of the common, and to the portrayal in every art of those finer and higher aspects which unite rather than sever humanity, if he would thrive in our new order of things. The talent that is robust enough to front the every-day world and catch the charm of its work-worn, care-worn, brave, kindly face, need not fear the encounter, though it seems terrible to the sort nurtured in the superstition of the romantic, the bizarre, the heroic, the distinguished, as the things alone worthy of painting or carving or writing. The arts must become democratic, and then we shall have the expression of America in art; and the reproach which Mr. Arnold was half right in making us shall have no justice in it any longer; we shall be "distinguished.". . .

The art which in the mean time disdains the office of teacher is one of the last refuges of the aristocratic spirit which is disappearing from politics and society, and is now seeking to shelter itself in aesthetics. The pride of caste is becoming the pride of taste; but as before, it is averse to the mass of men; it consents to know them only in some conventionalized and artificial guise. It seeks to withdraw itself, to stand aloof; to be distinguished, and not to be identified. Democracy in literature is the reverse of all this. It wishes to know and to tell the truth, confident that consolation and delight are there; it does not care to paint the marvellous and impossible for the vulgar many, or to sentimentalize and falsify the actual for the vulgar few. Men are more like than unlike one another: let us make them know one another better, that they may all be humbled and strengthened with a sense of their fraternity. Neither arts, nor letters, nor sciences, except as they somehow, clearly or obscurely, tend to make the race better and kinder, are to be regarded as serious interests; they are all lower than the rudest crafts that feed and house and clothe, for except they do this office they are idle; and they cannot do this except from and through the truth.

4. ON GEORGE ELIOT AND NATHANIEL HAWTHORNE*

. . . I only wish to own that so far as I understand it, the chief part of my ethical experience has been from novels. The life and character I have found portrayed there have appealed always to the consciousness of right and wrong implanted in me; and from no one has this appeal been stronger than from George Eliot. Her influence continued through many years, and I can question it now only in the undue burden she seems to throw upon the individual, and her failure to account largely enough for motive from the social environment. There her work seems to me unphilosophical.

It shares whatever error there is in its perspective with that of Hawthorne, whose *Marble Faun* was a new book at the same time that *Adam Bede* was new, and whose books now came into my life and gave it their tinge. He was always dealing with the problem of evil, too, and I found a more potent charm in his more artistic handling of it than I found in George Eliot. Of course, I then preferred the region of pure romance where he liked to place his action; but I did not find his instances the less veritable because they shone out in

"The light that never was on sea or land."

I read the *Marble Faun* first, and then the *Scarlet Letter*, and then the *House of Seven Gables*, and then the *Blithedale Romance*; but I always liked best the last, which is more nearly a novel, and more realistic than the others. They all moved me with a sort of effect such as I had not felt before. They were so far from time and place that, although most of them related to our country and epoch, I could not imagine anything approximate from them; and Hawthorne himself seemed a remote and

* The selection is taken from *My Literary Passions* by William Dean Howells (1895).

impalpable agency, rather than a person whom one might actually meet, as not long afterward happened with me. I did not hold the sort of fancied converse with him that I held with other authors, and I cannot pretend that I had the affection for him that attracted me to them. But he held me by his potent spell, and for a time he dominated me as completely as any author I have read. More truly than any other American author he has been a passion with me, and lately I heard with a kind of pang a young man saying that he did not believe I should find the *Scarlet Letter* bear reading now. I did not assent to the possibility, but the notion gave me a shiver of dismay. I thought how much that book had been to me, how much all of Hawthorne's books had been, and to have parted with my faith in their perfection would have been something I would not willingly have risked doing.

Of course there is always something fatally weak in the scheme of the pure romance, which, after the color of the contemporary mood dies out of it, leaves it in danger of tumbling into the dust of allegory; and perhaps this inherent weakness was what that bold critic felt in the *Scarlet Letter*. But none of Hawthorne's fables are without a profound and distant reach into the recesses of nature and of being. He came back from his researches with no solution of the question, with no message, indeed, but the awful warning, "Be true, be true," which is the burden of the *Scarlet Letter*; yet in all his books there is the hue of thoughts that we think only in the presence of the mysteries of life and death. It is not his fault that this is not intelligence, that it knots the brow in sorer doubt rather than shapes the lips to utterance of the things that can never be said. Some of his shorter stories I have found thin and cold to my later reading, and I have never cared much for the *House of Seven Gables*, but the other day I was reading the *Blithedale Romance* again, and I found it as potent, as significant, as sadly and strangely true as when it first enthralled my soul.

5. ON ZOLA*

But what shall I say of Zola himself, and my admiration of his epic greatness? About his material there is no disputing among people of our Puritanic tradition. It is simply abhorrent, but when you have once granted him his material for his own use, it is idle and foolish to deny his power. Every literary theory of mine was contrary to him when I took up *L'Assommoir*, though unconsciously I had always been as much of a realist as I could, but the book possessed me with the same fascination that I felt the other day in reading his *L'Argent*. The critics know now that Zola is not the realist he used to fancy himself, and he is full of the best qualities of the romanticism he has hated so much; but for what he is, there is but one novelist of our time, or of any, that outmasters him, and that is Tolstoy. For my own part, I think that the books of Zola are not immoral, but they are indecent through the facts that they nakedly represent; they are infinitely more moral than the books of any other French novelist. This may not be saying a great deal, but it is saying the truth, and I do not mind owning that he has been one of my great literary passions, almost as great as Flaubert, and greater than Daudet or Maupassant, though I have profoundly appreciated the exquisite artistry of both these. No French writer, however, has moved me so much as the Spanish, for the French are wanting in the humor which endears these, and is the quintessence of their charm.

* The selection is taken from *My Literary Passions* by William Dean Howells (1895).

6. ALICE WELLINGTON ROLLINS
Effie's Realistic Novel*

"Mamma, I don't see why I couldn't write a novel, now that it is the fashion to put into novels just the plain things that everybody sees every day. You know we have been studying recent literature in Miss Owen's class at school, and it seems as if it would be ever so easy to write a story like those Mr. Howells writes."

"But why do you try to make a novel out of it, Effie? Perhaps you would not find it quite so easy after all. Why not take just a simple story?"

"Why, Mamma, a realistic novel *is* just a simple story. That's why I like it, and why I think I can do it. It's just an account of what real people do every day of their lives, and you don't have to invent anything at all. It's very absurd, Mr. Howells says, to put troubadours and knights and all sorts of unnatural adventures into a story nowadays. People are tired of such things."

"Well, but what will it be, Effie? A love story?"

"No; I think not a love story."

"How are you going to write a novel without a love story in it?"

"Why, Mamma, that's just it again! A realistic novel doesn't have to have lovers. Indeed, it mustn't have lovers. All that sort of thing is very old-fashioned in a novel."

"But, Effie," objected Lilian, Effie's older sister, "I'm quite sure Mr. Howells has lovers in his. Why, don't you remember, one of his stories was called 'Their Wedding Journey,' and I think somebody is always married in all of them."

"Well," said Effie, thoughtfully, "I'll tell you how I think it is: You can have people engaged and married, if you can't think of anything better for them to do, only you mustn't make a

---

* The selection constitutes the entire essay, first published in 1887. I am indebted to my student, Leocadia Borowski, who brought this story to my attention.

great fuss about it. There mustn't be all sorts of objections from the parents, and they mustn't turn pale with passion, and rave at each other in sonnets, and all that sort of thing. They must just get engaged sensibly and then go and get married, the way people really do."

"But what will you have your heroine do, if she doesn't fall in love or get married?"

"I don't know yet; I haven't made up my mind; but I think I shall have her go into a convent."

"Oh, Effie! Mr. Howells wouldn't do that. He wouldn't use a convent at all!"

"Why not? There *are* convents. It is perfectly realistic to take things that really do exist."

"But then there are so few convents; and comparatively few girls go into them nowadays. I think, if you are going to be realistic, you will have to tell just what the average girl, and not the exceptional girl, does."

"Oh, well; of course there are lots of other things she can do," said Effie. "I only happened to think of a convent just then."

A few days afterward, Effie brought her first chapter to her mother.

"The name of the novel is 'Margaret P. Wharton,' " she explained. "Don't you think it was very realistic, Mamma, to put in that 'P'? They don't generally, you know. They just call their heroine 'Margaret Wharton,' or 'Helen Rainsford,' or 'Priscilla Remington'; but real girls almost always have an initial, so I put one in."

"And what made you decide on a 'P'?" asked Papa, who was supposed to be reading the paper, but who was evidently listening.

"Why, because her middle name was Patterson!" answered Effie, promptly. "You wouldn't have me put in an 'A' or a 'G' or an 'R', would you, to stand for Patterson?"

"Not for worlds," answered Papa, gravely. "But, you see, I didn't know it was Patterson, and in a realistic novel you ought not to leave anything to the imagination. I might have supposed, you know, that her middle name was Porter or Prentice. But go on, my dear."

" 'Margaret Wharton was not what you would call a beauty,' " read Effie from her manuscript.

"Wait a minute, Effie; you forgot the 'P.' "

"Oh, well, Papa," exclaimed Effie, impatiently, "of course

you don't have to put in the 'P' every time. 'Margaret Wharton
was not what you would call a beauty.' You see, Papa," she
explained, "in a realistic novel you must never go to extremes
about anything. In the old-fashioned stories the heroine was
always perfectly beautiful; but real girls are not perfectly
beautiful, and so I couldn't let Margaret Wharton—"

"With a 'P,' Effie,—"

"—be as handsome as I should have liked to make her.
'Margaret Wharton,'" she began again, "'was not what you
would call a beauty. Yet there was something singularly attractive about her.'"

"Her clothes?" inquired Papa. But Effie continued, without
deigning to notice the interruption—"'Her hair, which was of
the most beautiful golden color, waved over her forehead in
little, short, lovely curls; while at the back it was coiled into a
shining knot that seemed to have caught the sunbeams and
imprisoned them in its toils. Her eyes, which were gloriously
black in color, were full of infinite expression and dreamy
loveliness, enhanced in effect by the beautifully arched eye-
brows, and by the long lashes that swept a cheek almost marble
in its pallor, yet tinged at times with rosy blushes, like an
exquisitely tinted shell.'"

"And her nose?" inquired Papa.

"I haven't come to her nose yet," answered Effie with dignity.
"'Her dainty little ears peeped out from her luxuriant tresses as
if they wanted to hear the pretty things people were sure to say
about so lovely a face—'"

"Brava, Effie!" interrupted Papa, clapping his hands. "That's
capital!—even if it isn't realistic," he added, under his breath.

"'—while the pure, sweet mouth, arched in the most exquisite
curves, hid from view teeth that were like a row of shining
pearls.'"

"How do you know they were like pearls, Effie, if they were
hid from view?" Papa suggested.

"'Her complexion,'" continued Effie, undismayed, "'was of
the purest rose and white, while her graceful head was poised on
a throat like that of a swan. Her—' Oh, dear!" interrupted the
young author, looking helplessly at her manuscript, "I do
believe I forgot her nose after all; I'm so glad you reminded me
of it. I can slip it in right here. Give me a pencil, please. 'Her
nose—'"

"Is that her nose?" inquired Papa, pointing to the ∧ with which Effie was inserting her new sentence about the nose.

" 'Her nose,' " repeated Effie, with a glance of terrible scorn at her father, " 'was of the purest Grecian type; while over all her exquisite features floated an expression of dreamy thought, of tender charm, which added tenfold to their inexpressible loveliness.' "

"Quite a pretty girl," murmured Papa, "for one who was not a beauty."

"Yes," said Effie, complacently. "She *was* pretty. There's no harm in her being pretty, you know, for lots of real girls are ever so pretty. And you couldn't expect me to make a heroine out of an ugly old poke."

"Certainly not," said Papa with emphasis. "And now I understand the full significance of the 'P' in the middle of her name; it is to remind us that she was only Pretty, and not Beautiful, if we are in danger of forgetting it after your description."

"But, Effie," said her mother, "I don't think realistic people talk much about tresses when they mean hair."

"And *I* don't think," said Lilian, emphatically, "that they ever describe people at all. I'm sure Mr. Howells doesn't. He never tells you how people look, or what they wear; he just begins and goes right ahead with letting them do something."

"Oh, no no, indeed, Lilian!" answered Effie, with full confidence that here, at least, she had unanswerable arguments for her methods. "That is just exactly what he doesn't do. All the critics say so. Mr. Howells's people *never* do anything. Why, Miss Owen told us that was the great objection that many people made to his work; that there is so little action in it, and his characters never seem to be doing anything in particular."

"What do they do, if they don't do anything?" inquired Papa.

"I said they didn't do anything *in particular*. They don't stab villains, nor jump overboard, nor get into railway accidents, nor have to marry a rich man they hate, to save their father's fortune, nor do all sorts of things that nobody ever really did do—except in the old-fashioned novels."

"Well, isn't it time, by the way, that we found out what Miss Margaret P. was doing? That will give us the right clew, perhaps. What was your realistic heroine doing, Effie, with her beaut—, I mean her pretty complexion and her bright eyes?"

"She was walking down Beacon street."

"Ah! that sounds more like it. On the right side, or the left side?"

"On the right side, of course, Papa; *nobody* ever walks on the left side of Beacon street, going down."

"I see. In the old-fashioned novel, Margaret would have walked on the left side of the street, and so, by her eccentricity, at once have excited a suspicion that she was about something unusual, which must not be in the modern work of art. Go on, my dear; this is very interesting. *Why* was this pretty girl walking down Beacon street on the right side, that lovely day? By the way, Effie, I am assuming that it *was* a lovely day because Miss Margaret was out; but is it well to leave even so much as that to our imagination? Ought you not to *say*, briefly but unmistakably, that it was a lovely day?"

"I'm coming to that," said Effie, apologetically. "But there is one more paragraph first. 'Her dress was of the costliest velvet, made simply but elegantly, and looped most gracefully at the back.' Don't you remember, Lilian, how nicely Mr. Howells always describes the way girls loop up their overskirts?" asked Effie, interrupting herself for sake of the sympathy she felt sure of at last.

"Ye-s," said Lilian, doubtfully. "But your description doesn't seem just like his. I think it's because you describe the wrong thing; you describe the velvet, and he described the looping."

"But, of course, I couldn't say just the same thing he did, could I?"

"N-o; but, you see, Mr. Howells is always so funny."

"Well, don't you think what I said about her little ears listening to hear what people said about her face was funny?"

"Yes, of course, it was funny; but then, you see, it wasn't *very* funny."

"And it ought not to be!" said Effie, triumphantly. "Nothing in a realistic novel ought to be *very* anything. You must never go to extremes. If it's a little funny, that's enough. Now I shall go on. 'Around her neck she wore the costliest fur; her little hands were cased in the daintiest gloves to be had at Hovey's—.' I think Hovey's makes it very realistic, don't you, Papa?—'while a long and dainty feather curled lovingly around her little hat, as if it liked to be there.' "

"I'm very glad she wore only a feather in her hat," replied Effie's father, adding, "though a severe critic might object that a realistic girl usually wears the whole bird. I am more than ever persuaded that it was an exceedingly fine day; still, Effie, don't you think it is time you told us something about the weather? I infer, from there being no mention of an umbrella in Miss Wharton's very complete outfit, that it was not raining; still, in a realistic novel, nothing ought to require an effort of the imagination."

"I am just coming to that, Papa. 'It was a lovely afternoon, towards the close of July,—' "

"July! Why, I thought she had on furs?"

"Oh dear, so she had! I must have the furs, so I'll just change July to January—they both begin with a J—'It was a lovely afternoon near the close of January. A splendid sunset glowed in the west—' "

"Did you ever know a sunset to glow in the east?"

"Oh, Papa! what a terrible critic you are! I don't believe you like Mr. Howells's style."

"Oh, yes, I like Mr. Howells's style very much; but this doesn't seem exactly in his style. For instance, Mr. Howells never speaks of sunsets."

"But, Papa, a sunset is just as real as a person. There *are* sunsets; it isn't anything I invented out of my own head."

"I know there are sunsets, and I have no doubt Mr. Howells likes a real genuine sunset to look at, very much; but he doesn't think sunsets belong to fiction. They are to look at, not to read about. Now I shouldn't wonder if you had a page or two there about the sunset."

"Yes, there are three pages of it, and it is just lovely! And I thought it must be realistic because it is a description of the very sunset you and I saw last summer at Mount Desert."

"But do you think a sunset at Mount Desert in August would be likely to be very similar to the sunsets on Beacon street in January?"

"Oh, dear! Then I might as well give it up. But, Papa, what do you suppose Mr. Howells would have said if he had been writing this story?"

"Well, I haven't a very clear idea as yet of your plot and general scope; but I should say, with what material you have exhibited as yet, Mr. Howells would have said just about this: 'Near five o'clock on a pleasant afternoon in January, Miss Margaret Wharton was walking on Beacon street.' "

"But, Papa, how does he ever fill up a whole novel with such short sentences as that?"

"Ah, there is his art! It is very easy to say what Mr. Howells doesn't put in; but it isn't so easy to say in advance what he does."

"Well," said Effie, with a sigh, "I don't see but it's just as hard to be realistic as it is to be artistic. I shall give up my novel, and try a story of adventure."

"But don't leave Margaret P. Wharton in the lurch quite yet, Effie. All I know about her so far is that she wasn't a beauty, though she wore elegant clothes; but, as you say, there is something singularly attractive about her, and I want to find out what it is. What were you going to have her do? Was it a case for 'aspirations'?"

"I wasn't going to have her do anything. In realistic novels, people don't have aspirations. Or, if they do have them," with a sudden recollection, "they don't amount to anything. I was just going to let her go to some teas and theatricals, and perhaps try to do a little artistic work, or something, and find she couldn't—"

"But isn't that very discouraging to your readers, Effie?"

"Yes, of course it's discouraging; but, then, it ought to be discouraging. In real life, people don't find they can do everything they desire; and it is very silly to do as the old-fashioned novelists did, and represent heroes and heroines as accomplishing everything they undertake without any trouble at all, and undertaking, too, the most unheard-of and difficult things. I was just going to let my heroine go to Mount Desert in the summer, and to Washington in the winter, and put in a few clever little sketches of society life, and then stop. A realistic novel doesn't have to come to a climax, you know."

"But what do you know yet about society, Effie? And how can you write about Washington when you have never been there? Wouldn't that require too much imagination for an author who means to be purely realistic?"

"No; because, you see, the things I should imagine would be real. I shouldn't invent dragons and duels and knights and talismans, and all sorts of things that never existed—"

"Oh, but, Effie!" interrupted Lilian, "knights and duels did exist once."

"Yes, *once*; but they were never very common, and they were never worth writing about anyhow. It's perfectly proper to invent things, because, of course, our imagination is a real thing, too, and it must be meant for something; only we must invent things just like those we see every day."

"Then I don't see where the invention comes in," remarked Lilian, promptly. "I don't think it takes much imagination to write about a girl's going to a tea; and, as you say, it seems to me we were meant to use our imagination for something."

"I'll come to your help, Effie, this time," said her father. "It's all right about using our imagination for common things; only you make a mistake in thinking that imagination is inventing things. Imagination is not *inventing* things; it is *seeing* things; but it is seeing things that are out of sight—it is seeing intellectual and spiritual things, just as the eye sees really visible things."

"Then, Papa," said Effie, triumphantly, "you ought not to have found fault with my imagination when I said Margaret Wharton's teeth were like pearls. They were 'hid from view,' but I could see with my imagination perfectly well what they were like."

"Quite true; and I didn't find fault with you for telling us they were like pearls. I only said that, from your own point of view, you ought not to tell us, because you said when you started out that you were only going to describe what you saw. I think you will find out, as you go on, that it requires a great deal more imagination to write a realistic novel than to write a fairy-tale; because the object of a realistic story is not to repeat common things, but to interest people in common things; not to create uncommon things, but to show people that common things are not by any means so uninteresting as they seem at first sight. The realistic writer must see, not new things, but new qualities in things; and to do that, he must have plenty of imagination. He must understand not only what his heroine's teeth are like, though they are 'hid from view,' but what her thoughts are like, though they also are hid from view. This is the difference, Effie: those whom you call the 'old-fashioned writers' imagined that they must describe the thoughts and looks and clothes and actions of a princess, or some creature out of the range of every-day life; but the realistic writers have discovered that the thoughts and clothes and looks and actions of a little beggar-girl can be made just as interesting to people, if only you can *see what is unseen* about them with your mind's eye. Now, which would you say had really the nobler imagination—a man who went into his library and wrote a remarkable poem about the golden apples of the Hesperides, that were pure creations of his fancy, or Sir Isaac Newton when he went and sat down under a common appletree, and set his imagination to work to find out what made the apple fall to the ground? The realistic writer is satisfied with the every-day appletree—that is quite certain; but here is your mistake about him, Effie: He *isn't* satisfied with telling you that the apples fell; he shows you how they fell, and what a great, beautiful, wonderful law of the universe caused them to fall; and he makes you feel that the law was all the more beautiful and wonderful for not applying merely to one particular apple, or even to the whole class of apple-trees, but to everything.''

''Only that sounds, Papa, as if the realists went into long and elaborate paragraphs about things, and I'm sure they don't. They never stop long enough to talk about a thing, or describe a law; they just make you see things, and they always seem to be the same old things you have always seen before.''

''But with a difference, Effie; with a difference. A little while ago you spoke of one of Mr. Howells's heroines who tried to do something and couldn't. I suppose you mean the poor rich girl who lost all her money, and found that all her fine education did not help her a bit when it came to earning her living. Now if Mr. Howells had merely meant by that to show girls how absurd it was for them to try to do anything, it would have been a very cruel story; but I think he merely meant to show the parents what scrappy sort of education they were giving their daughters, with all the money they were spending for it.''

''But don't you think you are very cruel to me now, Papa, when I am trying to do something, and you are doing all you can to discourage me?''

''You said a little while ago, Effie, that it was a good thing to discourage people; that that was what the realistic novel was for.''

Effie smiled through her tears.

''But only to discourage people from expecting too fine results, Papa; not to discourage them from *trying*.''

"And I don't wish to discourage you from trying. Only I wish you to try the right thing. When I said a common apple-tree was better than the Hesperides, I didn't mean to deny that the Hesperides are good in their way. I like realistic novels, *really* realistic novels, very much; but I like wholly imaginative stories too; and I think those pretty and delicate touches of yours about Margaret Wharton's little ears listening to what people said about her face, and the little feather that curled around her hat as if it liked to be there, show that you have a genuine gift at fancy; and if I were you, I wouldn't despise fancy, for it is really a very good trait in an author."

So it happened that next day at recess, Effie informed her friends:

"I've given up my novel, and I'm just going to try fairy-tales." And she added, with a little sigh, "Papa says that I may write very good fairy-tales, but that I haven't imagination enough to be a realistic writer."

7. MARK TWAIN
William Dean Howells*

Is it true that the sun of a man's mentality touches noon at forty and then begins to wane toward setting? Doctor Osler is charged with saying so. Maybe he said it, maybe he didn't; I don't know which it is. But if he said it, I can point him to a case which proves his rule. Proves it by being an exception to it. To this place I nominate Mr. Howells.

I read his *Venetian Days* about forty years ago. I compare it with his paper on Machiavelli in a late number of *Harper*, and I cannot find that his English has suffered any impairment. For forty years his English has been to me a continual delight and astonishment. In the sustained exhibition of certain great qualities—clearness, compression, verbal exactness, and unforced and seemingly unconscious felicity of phrasing—he is, in my belief, without his peer in the English-writing world. *Sustained.* I intrench myself behind that protecting word. There are others who exhibit those great qualities as greatly as does he, but only by intervaled distributions of rich moonlight, with stretches of veiled and dimmer landscape between; whereas Howells's moon sails cloudless skies all night and all the nights.

In the matter of verbal exactness Mr. Howells has no superior, I suppose. He seems to be almost always able to find that elusive and shifty grain of gold, the *right word*. Others have to put up with approximations, more or less frequently; he has better luck. To me, the others are miners working with the gold-pan—of necessity some of the gold washes over and escapes; whereas, in my fancy, he is quicksilver raiding down a riffle—no grain of the metal stands much chance of eluding him. A powerful agent is the right word: it lights the reader's way and makes it plain; a close approximation to it will answer, and

* The selection constitutes the entire essay "William Dean Howells" by Mark Twain (1906).

much traveling is done in a well-enough fashion by its help, but we do not welcome it and applaud it and rejoice in it as we do when *the* right one blazes out on us. Whenever we come upon one of those intensely right words in a book or a newspaper the resulting effect is physical as well as spiritual, and electrically prompt: it tingles exquisitely around through the walls of the mouth and tastes as tart and crisp and good as the autumn-butter that creams the sumac-berry. One has no time to examine the word and vote upon its rank and standing, the automatic recognition of its supremacy is so immediate. There is plenty of acceptable literature which deals largely in approximations, but it may be likened to a fine landscape seen through the rain; the right word would dismiss the rain, then you would see it better. It doesn't rain when Howells is at work.

And where does he get the easy and effortless flow of his speech? and its cadenced and undulating rhythm? and its architectural felicities of construction, its graces of expression, its pemmican quality of compression, and all that? Born to him, no doubt. All in shining good order in the beginning, all extraordinary; and all just as shining, just as extraordinary to-day, after forty years of diligent wear and tear and use. He passed his fortieth year long and long ago; but I think his English of to-day—his perfect English, I wish to say—can throw down the glove before his English of that antique time and not be afraid.

I will go back to the paper on Machiavelli now, and ask the reader to examine this passage from it which I append. I do not mean examine it in a bird's-eye way; I mean search it, study it. And, of course, read it aloud. I may be wrong, still it is my conviction that one cannot get out of finely wrought literature all that is in it by reading it mutely:

> Mr. Dyer is rather of the opinion, first luminously suggested by Macaulay, that Machiavelli was in earnest, but must not be judged as a political moralist of our time and race would be judged. He thinks that Machiavelli was in earnest, as none but an idealist can be, and he is the first to imagine him an idealist immersed in realities, who involuntarily transmutes the events under his eye into something like the visionary issues of reverie. The Machiavelli whom he depicts does not cease to be politically a republican and socially a just man because he holds up an atrocious despot

like Caesar Borgia as a mirror for rulers. What Machiavelli
beheld round him in Italy was a civic disorder in which there
was oppression without statecraft, and revolt without patriotism. When a miscreant like Borgia appeared upon the
scene and reduced both tyrants and rebels to an apparent
quiescence, he might very well seem to such a dreamer the
savior of society whom a certain sort of dreamers are always
looking for. Machiavelli was no less honest when he honored
the diabolical force of Caesar Borgia than Carlyle was when
at different times he extolled the strong man who destroys
liberty in creating order. But Carlyle has only just ceased to
be mistaken for a reformer, while it is still Machiavelli's hard
fate to be so trammeled in his material that his name stands
for whatever is most malevolent and perfidious in human
nature.

You see how easy and flowing it is; how unvexed by
ruggednesses, clumsinesses, broken meters; how simple and—so
far as you or I can make out—unstudied; how clear, how limpid,
how understandable, how unconfused by cross-currents, eddies,
undertows; how seemingly unadorned, yet is all adornnent, like
the lily-of-the-valley; and how compressed, how compact, without a complacency-signal hung out anywhere to call attention
to it.

There are twenty-three lines in the quoted passage. After
reading it several times aloud, one perceives that a good deal of
matter is crowded into that small space. I think it is a model of
compactness. When I take its materials apart and work them
over and put them together in my way, I find I cannot crowd
the result back into the same hole, there not being room
enough. I find it a case of a woman packing a man's trunk: he
can get the things out, but he can't ever get them back again.

The proffered paragraph is a just and fair sample; the rest of
the article is as compact as it is; there are no waste words. The
sample is just in other ways: limpid, fluent, graceful, and
rhythmical as it is, it holds no superiority in these respects over
the rest of the essay. Also, the choice phrasing noticeable in the
sample is not lonely; there is a plenty of its kin distributed
through the other paragraphs. This is claiming much when that
kin must face the challenge of a phrase like the one in the
middle sentence: "an idealist immersed in realities who invol-
untarily transmutes the events under his eye into something like

the visionary issues of reverie." With a hundred words to do it with, the literary artisan could catch that airy thought and tie it down and reduce it to a concrete condition, visible, substantial, understandable and all right, like a cabbage; but the artist does it with twenty, and the result is a flower.

The quoted phrase, like a thousand others that have come from the same source, has the quality of certain scraps of verse which take hold of us and stay in our memories, we do not understand why, at first: all the words being the right words, none of them is conspicuous, and so they all seem inconspicuous, therefore we wonder what it is about them that makes their message take hold.

> The mossy marbles rest
> On the lips that he has prest
> In their bloom,
> And the names he loved to hear
> Have been carved for many a year
> On the tomb.

It is like a dreamy strain of moving music, with no sharp notes in it. The words are all "right" words, and all the same size. We do not notice it at first. We get the effect, it goes straight home to us, but we do not know why. It is when the right words are conspicuous that they thunder:

The glory that was Greece and the grandeur that was Rome!

When I go back from Howells old to Howells young I find him arranging and clustering English words well, but not any better than now. He is not more felicitous in concreting abstractions now than he was in translating, then, the visions of the eyes of flesh into words that reproduced their forms and colors:

In Venetian streets they give the fallen snow no rest. It is at once shoveled into the canals by hundreds of half-naked *facchini*; and now in St. Mark's Place the music of unnumerable shovels smote upon my ear; and I saw the shivering legion of poverty as it engaged the elements in a struggle for the possession of the Piazza. But the snow continued to fall, and through the twilight of the descending flakes all this toil and encounter looked like that weary kind of effort in dreams, when the most determined industry seems only to renew the task. The lofty crest of the bell-tower was hidden in the folds of falling snow, and I could no longer see the golden angel upon its summit. But looked at across the Piazza, the beautiful outline of St. Mark's Church was perfectly penciled in the air, and the shifting threads of the snowfall were woven into a spell of novel enchantment around the structure that always seemed to me too exquisite in its fantastic loveliness to be anything but the creation of magic. The tender snow had compassionated the beautiful edifice for all the wrongs of time, and so hid the stains and ugliness of decay that it looked as if just from the hand of the builder—or, better said, just from the brain of the architect. There was marvelous freshness in the colors of the mosaics in the great arches of the façade, and all that gracious harmony into which the temple rises, of marble scrolls and leafy exuberance airily supporting the statues of the saints, was a hundred times etherealized by the purity and whiteness of the drifting flakes. The snow lay lightly on the golden globes that tremble like peacock-crests above the vast domes, and plumed them with softest white; it robed the saints in ermine; and it danced over all its work, as if exulting in its beauty—beauty which filled me with subtle, selfish yearning to keep such evanescent loveliness for the little-while-longer of my whole life, and with despair to think that even the poor lifeless shadow of it could never be fairly reflected in picture or poem.

Through the wavering snowfall, the Saint Theodore upon one of the granite pillars of the Piazzetta did not show so grim as his wont is, and the winged lion on the other might have been a winged lamb, so gentle and mild he looked by the tender light of the storm. The towers of the island churches loomed faint and far away in the dimness; the sailors in the rigging of the ships that lay in the Basin wrought like phantoms among the shrouds; the gondolas stole in and out of the opaque distance more noiselessly and dreamily than ever; and a silence, almost palpable, lay upon the mutest city in the world.

The spirit of Venice is there: of a city where Age and Decay, fagged with distributing damage and repulsiveness among the other cities of the planet in accordance with the policy and business of their profession, come for rest and play between seasons, and treat themselves to the luxury and relaxation of sinking the shop and inventing and squandering charms all about, instead of abolishing such as they find, as is their habit when not on vacation.

In the working season they do business in Boston sometimes, and a character in *The Undiscovered Country* takes accurate note of pathetic effects wrought by them upon the aspects of a street of once dignified and elegant homes whose occupants have moved away and left them a prey to neglect and gradual ruin and progressive degradation; a descent which reaches bottom at last, when the street becomes a roost for humble professionals of the faith-cure and fortune-telling sort.

What a queer, melancholy house, what a queer, melancholy street! I don't think I was ever in a street before where quite so many professional ladies, with English surnames, preferred Madam to Mrs. on their door-plates. And the poor old place has such a desperately conscious air of going to the deuce. Every house seems to wince as you go by, and button itself up to the chin for fear you should find out it had no shirt on—so to speak. I don't know what's the reason, but these material tokens of a social decay afflict me terribly: a tipsy woman isn't dreadfuler than a haggard old house, that's once been a home, in a street like this.

Mr. Howells's pictures are not mere stiff, hard, accurate photographs; they are photographs with feeling in them, and sentiment, photographs taken in a dream, one might say.

As concerns his humor, I will not try to say anything, yet I would try, if I had the words that might approximately reach up to its high place. I do not think any one else can play with humorous fancies so gracefully and delicately and deliciously as he does, nor has so many to play with, nor can come so near making them look as if they were doing the playing themselves and he was not aware that they were at it. For they are unobtrusive, and quiet in their ways, and well conducted. His is a humor which flows softly all around about and over and through the mesh of the page, pervasive, refreshing, health-giving, and makes no more show and no more noise than does the circulation of the blood.

There is another thing which is contentingly noticeable in Mr.

Howells's books. That is his "stage directions"—those artifices which authors employ to throw a kind of human naturalness around a scene and a conversation, and help the reader to see the one and get at meanings in the other which might not be perceived if intrusted unexplained to the bare words of the talk. Some authors overdo the stage directions, they elaborate them quite beyond necessity; they spend so much time and take up so much room in telling us how a person said a thing and how he looked and acted when he said it that we get tired and vexed and wish he hadn't said it at all. Other authors' directions are brief enough, but it is seldom that the brevity contains either wit or information. Writers of this school go in rags, in the matter of stage directions; the majority of them have nothing in stock but a cigar, a laugh, a blush, and a bursting into tears. In their poverty they work these sorry things to the bone. They say:

". . . replied Alfred, flipping the ash from his cigar." (This explains nothing; it only wastes space.)

". . . responded Richard, with a laugh." (There was nothing to laugh about; there never is. The writer puts it in from habit—automatically; he is paying no attention to his work, or he would see that there is nothing to laugh at; often, when a remark is unusually and poignantly flat and silly, he tries to deceive the reader by enlarging the stage direction and making Richard break into "frenzies of uncontrollable laughter." This makes the reader sad.)

". . . murmured Gladys, blushing." (This poor old shop-worn blush is a tiresome thing. We get so we would rather Gladys would fall out of the book and break her neck than do it again. She is always doing it, and usually irrelevantly. Whenever it is her turn to murmur she hangs out her blush; it is the only thing she's got. In a little while we hate her, just as we do Richard.)

". . . repeated Evelyn, bursting into tears." (This kind keep a book damp all the time. They can't say a thing without crying. They cry so much about nothing that by and by when they have something to cry *about* they have gone dry; they sob, and fetch nothing; we are not moved. We are only glad.)

They gravel me, these stale and overworked stage directions, these carbon films that got burnt out long ago and cannot now carry any faintest thread of light. It would be well if they could be relieved from duty and flung out in the literary back yard to rot and disappear along with the discarded and forgotten "steeds" and "halidomes" and similar stage-properties once so dear to our grandfathers. But I am friendly to Mr. Howells's stage directions; more friendly to them than to any one else's, I think. They are done with a competent and discriminating art, and are faithful to the requirements of a stage direction's proper and lawful office, which is to inform. Sometimes they convey a scene and its conditions so well that I believe I could see the scene and get the spirit and meaning of the accompanying dialogue if some one would read merely the stage directions to me and leave out the talk. For instance, a scene like this, from *The Undiscovered Country:*

". . . and she laid her arms with a beseeching gesture on her father's shoulder."

". . . she answered, following his gesture with a glance."

". . . she said, laughing nervously."

". . . she asked, turning swiftly upon him that strange, searching glance."

". . . she answered, vaguely."

". . . she reluctantly admitted."

". . . but her voice died wearily away, and she stood looking into his face with puzzled entreaty."

Mr. Howells does not repeat his forms, and does not need to; he can invent fresh ones without limit. It is mainly the repetition over and over again, by the third-rates, of worn and commonplace and juiceless forms that makes their novels such a weariness and vexation to us, I think. We do not mind one or two deliveries of their wares, but as we turn the pages over and keep on meeting them we presently get tired of them and wish they would do other things for a change:

". . . replied Alfred, flipping the ash from his cigar."

". . . responded Richard, with a laugh."

". . . murmured Gladys, blushing."

". . . repeated Evelyn, bursting into tears."

". . . replied the Earl, flipping the ash from his cigar."

". . . responded the undertaker, with a laugh."

". . . murmured the chambermaid, blushing."

". . . repeated the burglar, bursting into tears."

". . . replied the conductor, flipping the ash from his cigar."

". . . responded Arkwright, with a laugh."

". . . murmured the chief of police, blushing."

". . . repeated the house-cat, bursting into tears."

And so on and so on; till at last it ceases to excite. I always notice stage directions, because they fret me and keep me trying to get out of their way, just as the automobiles do. At first; then by and by they become monotonous and I get run over.

Mr. Howells has done much work, and the spirit of it is as beautiful as the make of it. I have held him in admiration and affection so many years that I know by the number of those years that he is old now; but his heart isn't, nor his pen; and years do not count. Let him have plenty of them: there is profit in them for us.

III. Mark Twain:
Realistic Humorist

As a writer, Samuel Langhorne Clemens (1835-1910) is almost unknown. He lives pseudonymously as Mark Twain. This confusion of names is an emblem of the "doubleness" which many critics have discovered in Twain's writings and, in their various ways, explained. Mark Twain was probably the most popular writer of his age. Though serious and cynical, he was known as a humorist and an entertainer. A short story, "The Celebrated Jumping Frog of Calaveras County" (1865) won him national recognition as a Western writer, working within the frontier tradition of the tall tale. A novel written with Charles Dudley Warner (1829-1900), entitled *The Gilded Age* (1873), gave its name to the post-Civil War era of speculation and political corruption. Twain capitalized upon the growing market for children's literature with a classic "boy's book," *The Adventures of Tom Sawyer* (1876) eight years before the publication of his masterpiece, *The Adventures of Huckleberry Finn* (1884), which he properly described as a boy's book written for adults. It is hard to regard an author who often rode the crest of popular literary waves as an independent or natural writer, yet at the height of his career Twain disowned conscious literary method. In an essay on "The Art of Authorship" he argued that the "training most in use" by successful authors was not "deliberate or consciously methodical" but "guided and governed and made by-and-by unconsciously systematic, by an automatically working taste—a taste which selects and rejects without asking you for any help, and patiently and steadily improves itself without troubling you to approve or applaud."*
A selection from his *Autobiography*, included here, describes his travails as a writer guided by sure but unformulated

---

* From *The Art of Authorship*, ed. George Bainton in Walter Blair, ed., *The Selected Shorter Writings of Mark Twain* (Boston: Houghton Mifflin Company, n.d.)

narrative principles. One such struggle culminates in the production of a little story that took twelve years to organize and four hours to write. In this account as in his other comments on authorship, Twain's key word is "taste" which seems to be a catch-all term for many different literary elements, such as diction, narrative organization, even the length of the necessarily unwritten "troublesome and aggravating and uncertain" little pause he celebrates in "How to Tell a Story." Taste also covers the writer's choice of material. It is the central issue in his advice to young Elinor Glyn, in a passage which indicates the genteel limits Twain imposed upon himself even in his skeptical and embittered old age.

Yet there is a strain of conscious artistry in Twain's denial of literary method or fully conscious control of his materials. In "How to Tell a Story" he comments tellingly on the apparent formlessness which seems to him "the basis of American art." Why is this quality American? Twain does not explain, but it seems possible that formlessness is important because it indicates the artist's rejection of academic and recognizable styles. That artist is also most American who imitates the commonplace and seems himself to belong to the average. Certainly, this was Twain's own achievement. Though he acquired great wealth, traveled abroad, and lived for many years in an exclusive area of Hartford, Connecticut, he remained in his public and literary guise a common American of the comparatively uncultured West. Even his most formal prose echoes the language of small towns in the American heartlands.

The rare statements that suggest Twain's literary judgments show him as a serious craftsman, scrupulously sensitive to language, as befits the author who prefaced *Huckleberry Finn* with a semiserious note on the dialects used therein: "the Missouri negro dialect; the extremest form of the backwoods South-Western dialect; the ordinary 'Pike County' dialect; and four modified varieties of this last." Such attention to the vernacular is, of course, realistic. American writing of the post-Civil War years often attempts to imitate indigenous American speech and there are many reasons for the vogue of literary dialect: such language is "true"; it is uniquely American; it is commonplace and distinctly unacademic. In contrast, the language of the romance was inflated, often deliberately artificial and grandiose. When Twain condemns James Fenimore Cooper's "word-sense" and concludes that his "English is a crime against the language" his judgment indicates the new standard for literary language as well as Cooper's shortcomings. In his own defense, the romancer could appeal to a literary convention which allows the writer to move from dialect to more formal speech when he wishes to show the universal spirit working in the individual soul. Cooper himself spoke, for example, of "the privilege of all writers of fiction, more particularly when their works aspire to the elevation of romances, to present the *beau-ideal* of their characters to the reader." Twain answers with a scathing ruling: "when a personage talks like an illustrated, gilt-edged, tree-calf, hand-tooled, seven-dollar Friendship's Offering in the beginning of a paragraph, he shall not talk like a negro minstrel in the end of it."

Indeed, the narrative standards of the realist are implicit in all of Twain's exaggeratedly academic "nineteen principles governing literary art in the domain of romantic fiction." He wants reportorial accuracy not only in "human talk," but also in "woodcraft or sailorcraft." Fictional cannonballs should act as everyday cannonballs do, and make-believe barges should be just as long and no longer than barges we have seen. These are the standards of "truth" as Howells defined it, which give the advantage to an author who avoids the far or strange and writes of places he knows, the life he has lived.

The lifelong friendship between William Dean Howells, the "bookish" critic, and Mark Twain, the "unconscious" artist, casts light on both authors. In 1869 when he met Twain for the first time, Howells was already established in New England as the assistant editor of the *Atlantic Monthly*. Almost at once he became Twain's trusted literary adviser and sometime editor. He reviewed his works as they appeared and, from one so influential, favorable notices were especially valuable. Howells' unflagging admiration for Twain's work may surprise us, for though *Huckleberry Finn* is unique in its mastery of vernacular realism, other fictions, like *The Prince and the Pauper* (1882) or *The Personal Recollections of Joan of Arc* (1896) might well be called romantic. Yet Howells found in Twain traces of the Southern and Western past and, in his humor, a sense of the incongruous which frontiersmen felt in a region where civilization and uncultivated nature came face to face. "Mark Twain: An Inquiry" was published in 1901, upon the appearance of a "uniform edition" of Twain's works. In his review Howells notes that apparent formlessness which Twain called American:

it is the "instinct of something chaotic, ironic, empiric in the order of experience," a quality which characterizes, without actually defining, the skeptical post-Darwinian attitudes Howells and Twain shared. Though anything but sacerdotal in tone, Twain came close to realizing Whitman's prophecy of a "divine literatus" who would unite the divided nation. He had been Southerner, Westerner, and Northerner; he was a successful writer who still seemed to remain one of the "divine average." His career passed beyond the simply literary and achieved some greater moral significance. At the end of his life, he was, in Howells' words, a "recognized authority in matters of public import." In his later elegiac memoir of their friendship, Howells described Twain's unique position: he was "sole, incomparable, the Lincoln of our literature."

Selections

8. FENIMORE COOPER'S LITERARY OFFENSES*

The Pathfinder and *The Deerslayer* stand at the head of Cooper's novels as artistic creations. There are others of his works which contain parts as perfect as are to be found in these, and scenes even more thrilling. Not one can be compared with either of them as a finished whole.

The defects in both of these tales are comparatively slight. They were pure works of art.—*Prof. Lounsbury*.

The five tales reveal an extraordinary fulness of invention.

. . . One of the very greatest characters in fiction, Natty Bumppo. . . .

The craft of the woodsman, the tricks of the trapper, all the delicate art of the forest, were familiar to Cooper from his youth up.—*Prof. Brander Matthews*.

Cooper is the greatest artist in the domain of romantic fiction yet produced by America.—*Wilkie Collins*.

It seems to me that it was far from right for the Professor of English Literature in Yale, the Professor of English Literature in Columbia, and Wilkie Collins to deliver opinions on Cooper's literature without having read some of it. It would have been much more decorous to keep silent and let persons talk who have read Cooper.

Cooper's art has some defects. In one place in *Deerslayer*, and in the restricted space of two-thirds of a page, Cooper has scored 114 offenses against literary art out of a possible 115. It breaks the record.

There are nineteen rules governing literary art in the domain of romantic fiction—some say twenty-two. In *Deerslayer* Cooper violated eighteen of them. These eighteen require:

* The selection is taken from the essay "Fenimore Cooper's Literary Offenses" by Mark Twain. First printed in *North American Review*, July 1895.

1. That a tale shall accomplish something and arrive somewhere. But the *Deerslayer* tale accomplishes nothing and arrives in the air.

2. They require that the episodes of a tale shall be necessary parts of the tale, and shall help to develop it. But as the *Deerslayer* tale is not a tale, and accomplishes nothing and arrives nowhere, the episodes have no rightful place in the work, since there was nothing for them to develop.

3. They require that the personages in a tale shall be alive, except in the case of corpses, and that always the reader shall be able to tell the corpses from the others. But this detail has often been overlooked in the *Deerslayer* tale.

4. They require that the personages in a tale, both dead and alive, shall exhibit a sufficient excuse for being there. But this detail also has been overlooked in the *Deerslayer* tale.

5. They require that when the personages of a tale deal in conversation, the talk shall sound like human talk, and be talk such as human beings would be likely to talk in the given circumstances, and have a discoverable meaning, also a discoverable purpose, and a show of relevancy, and remain in the neighborhood of the subject in hand, and be interesting to the reader, and help out the tale, and stop when the people cannot think of anything more to say. But this requirement has been ignored from the beginning of the *Deerslayer* tale to the end of it.

6. They require that when the author describes the character of a personage in his tale, the conduct and conversation of that personage shall justify said description. But this law gets little or no attention in the *Deerslayer* tale, as Natty Bumppo's case will amply prove.

7. They require that when a personage talks like an illustrated, gilt-edged, tree-calf, hand-tooled, seven-dollar Friendship's Offering in the beginning of a paragraph, he shall not talk like a negro minstrel in the end of it. But this rule is flung down and danced upon in the *Deerslayer* tale.

8. They require that crass stupidities shall not be played upon the reader as "the craft of the woodsman, the delicate art of the forest," by either the author or the people in the tale. But this rule is persistently violated in the *Deerslayer* tale.

9. They require that the personages of a tale shall confine themselves to possibilities and let miracles alone; or, if they venture a miracle, the author must so plausibly set it forth as to

make it look possible and reasonable. But these rules are not respected in the *Deerslayer* tale.

10. They require that the author shall make the reader feel a deep interest in the personages of his tale and in their fate; and that he shall make the reader love the good people in the tale and hate the bad ones. But the reader of the *Deerslayer* tale dislikes the good people in it, is indifferent to the others, and wishes they would all get drowned together.

11. They require that the characters in a tale shall be so clearly defined that the reader can tell beforehand what each will do in a given emergency. But in the *Deerslayer* tale this rule is vacated.

In addition to these large rules there are some little ones. These require that the author shall

12. *Say* what he is proposing to say, not merely come near it.

13. Use the right word, not its second cousin.

14. Eschew surplusage.

15. Not omit necessary details.

16. Avoid slovenliness of form.

17. Use good grammar.

18. Employ a simple and straightforward style.

Even these seven are coldly and persistently violated in the *Deerslayer* tale.

Cooper's gift in the way of invention was not a rich endowment; but such as it was he liked to work it, he was pleased with the effects, and indeed he did some quite sweet things with it. In his little box of stage-properties he kept six or eight cunning devices, tricks, artifices for his savages and woodsmen to deceive and circumvent each other with, and he was never so happy as when he was working these innocent things and seeing them go. A favorite one was to make a moccasined person tread in the tracks of the moccasined enemy, and thus hide his own trail. Cooper wore out barrels and barrels of moccasins in working that trick. Another stage-property that he pulled out of his box pretty frequently was his broken twig. He prized his broken twig above all the rest of his effects, and worked it the hardest. It is a restful chapter in any book of his when somebody doesn't step on a dry twig and alarm all the reds and whites for two hundred yards around. Every time a Cooper person is in peril, and absolute silence is worth four dollars a minute, he is sure to step on a dry twig. There may be a hundred handier things to step on, but that wouldn't satisfy Cooper. Cooper requires him to turn out and find a dry twig; and if he can't do it, go and borrow one. In fact, the Leather Stocking Series ought to have been called the Broken Twig Series.

I am sorry there is not room to put in a few dozen instances of the delicate art of the forest, as practiced by Natty Bumppo and some of the other Cooperian experts. Perhaps we may venture two or three samples. Cooper was a sailor—a naval officer; yet he gravely tells us how a vessel, driving toward a lee shore in a gale, is steered for a particular spot by her skipper because he knows of an *undertow* there which will hold her back against the gale and save her. For just pure woodcraft, or sailorcraft, or whatever it is, isn't that neat? For several years Cooper was daily in the society of artillery, and he ought to have noticed that when a cannon-ball strikes the ground it either buries itself or skips a hundred feet or so; skips again a hundred feet or so—and so on, till finally it gets tired and rolls. Now in one place he loses some "females"—as he always calls women—in the edge of a wood near a plain at night in a fog, on purpose to give Bumppo a chance to show off the delicate art of the forest before the reader. These mislaid people are hunting for a fort. They hear a cannon-blast, and a cannon-ball presently comes rolling into the wood and stops at their feet. To the females this suggests nothing. The case is very different with the admirable Bumppo. I wish I may never know peace again if he doesn't strike out promptly and *follow the track* of that cannon-ball across the plain through the dense fog and find the fort. Isn't it a daisy? If Cooper had any real knowledge of Nature's ways of doing things, he had a most delicate art in concealing the fact. For instance: one of his acute Indian experts, Chingachgook (pronounced Chicago, I think), has lost the trail of a person he is tracking through the forest. Apparently that trail is hopelessly lost. Neither you nor I could ever have guessed out the way to find it. It was very different with Chicago. Chicago was not stumped for long. He turned a running stream out of its course, and there, in the slush in its old bed, were that person's moccasin-tracks. The current did not wash them away, as it would have done in all other cases—no, even the eternal laws of Nature have to vacate when Cooper wants to put up a delicate job of woodcraft on the reader.

We must be a little wary when Brander Matthews tells us that Cooper's books "reveal an extraordinary fulness of invention."

As a rule, I am quite willing to accept Brander Matthews's
literary judgments and applaud his lucid and graceful phrasing
of them; but that particular statement needs to be taken with a
few tons of salt. Bless your heart, Cooper hadn't any more
invention than a horse; and I don't mean a high-class horse,
either; I mean a clothes-horse. It would be very difficult to find
a really clever "situation" in Cooper's books, and still more
difficult to find one of any kind which he has failed to render
absurd by his handling of it. Look at the episodes of "the
caves"; and at the celebrated scuffle between Maqua and those
others on the table-land a few days later; and at Hurry Harry's
queer water-transit from the castle to the ark; and at Deerslayer's half-hour with his first corpse; and at the quarrel
between Hurry Harry and Deerslayer later; and at—but choose
for yourself; you can't go amiss.

If Cooper had been an observer his inventive faculty would
have worked better; not more interestingly, but more rationally,
more plausibly. Cooper's proudest creations in the way of
"situations" suffer noticeably from the absence of the observer's protecting gift. Cooper's eye was splendidly inaccurate.
Cooper seldom saw anything correctly. He saw nearly all things
as through a glass eye, darkly. Of course a man who cannot see
the commonest little every-day matters accurately is working at
a disadvantage when he is constructing a "situation." In the
Deerslayer tale Cooper has a stream which is fifty feet wide
where it flows out of a lake; it presently narrows to twenty as it
meanders along for no given reason, and yet when a stream acts
like that it ought to be required to explain itself. Fourteen
pages later the width of the brook's outlet from the lake has
suddenly shrunk thirty feet, and become "the narrowest part of
the stream." This shrinkage is not accounted for. The stream
has bends in it, a sure indication that it has alluvial banks and
cuts them; yet these bends are only thirty and fifty feet long. If
Cooper had been a nice and punctilious observer he would have
noticed that the bends were oftener nine hundred feet long than
short of it.

Cooper made the exit of that stream fifty feet wide, in the
first place, for no particular reason; in the second place, he
narrowed it to less than twenty to accommodate some Indians.
He bends a "sapling" to the form of an arch over this narrow
passage, and conceals six Indians in its foliage. They are
"laying" for a settler's scow or ark which is coming up the

stream on its way to the lake; it is being hauled against the stiff
current by a rope whose stationary end is anchored in the lake;
its rate of progress cannot be more than a mile an hour. Cooper
describes the ark, but pretty obscurely. In the matter of
dimensions "it was little more than a modern canal-boat." Let
us guess, then, that it was about one hundred and forty feet
long. It was of "greater breadth than common." Let us guess,
then, that it was about sixteen feet wide. This leviathan had
been prowling down bends which were but a third as long as
itself, and scraping between banks where it had only two feet of
space to spare on each side. We cannot too much admire this
miracle. A low-roofed log dwelling occupies "two-thirds of the
ark's length"—a dwelling ninety feet long and sixteen feet wide,
let us say—a kind of vestibule train. The dwelling has two
rooms—each forty-five feet long and sixteen feet wide, let us
guess. One of them is the bedroom of the Hutter girls, Judith
and Hetty; the other is the parlor in the daytime, at night it is
papa's bedchamber. The ark is arriving at the stream's exit now,
whose width has been reduced to less than twenty feet to
accommodate the Indians—say to eighteen. There is a foot to
spare on each side of the boat. Did the Indians notice that there
was going to be a tight squeeze there? Did they notice that they
could make money by climbing down out of that arched sapling
and just stepping aboard when the ark scraped by? No, other
Indians would have noticed these things, but Cooper's Indians
never notice anything. Cooper thinks they are marvelous creatures for noticing, but he was almost always in error about his
Indians. There was seldom a sane one among them.

The ark is one hundred and forty feet long; the dwelling is
ninety feet long. The idea of the Indians is to drop softly and
secretly from the arched sapling to the dwelling as the ark
creeps along under it at the rate of a mile an hour, and butcher
the family. It will take the ark a minute and a half to pass
under. It will take the ninety-foot dwelling a minute to pass
under. Now, then, what did the six Indians do? It would take
you thirty years to guess, and even then you would have to give
it up, I believe. Therefore, I will tell you what the Indians did.
Their chief, a person of quite extraordinary intellect for a
Cooper Indian, warily watched the canal-boat as it squeezed
along under him, and when he had got his calculations fined
down to exactly the right shade, as he judged, he let go and
dropped. And *missed the house!* That is actually what he did.

He missed the house, and landed in the stern of the scow. It was not much of a fall, yet it knocked him silly. He lay there unconscious. If the house had been ninety-seven feet long he would have made the trip. The fault was Cooper's, not his. The error lay in the construction of the house. Cooper was no architect.

There still remained in the roost five Indians. The boat has passed under and is now out of their reach. Let me explain what the five did—you would not be able to reason it out for yourself. No. 1 jumped for the boat, but fell in the water astern of it. Then No. 2 jumped for the boat, but fell in the water still farther astern of it. Then No. 3 jumped for the boat, and fell a good way astern of it. Then No. 4 jumped for the boat, and fell in the water *away* astern. Then even No. 5 made a jump for the boat—for he was a Cooper Indian. In the matter of intellect, the difference between a Cooper Indian and the Indian that stands in front of the cigar-shop is not spacious. The scow episode is really a sublime burst of invention; but it does not thrill, because the inaccuracy of the details throws a sort of air of fictitiousness and general improbability over it. This comes of Cooper's inadequacy as an observer.

The reader will find some examples of Cooper's high talent for inaccurate observation in the account of the shooting-match in *The Pathfinder*.

"A common wrought nail was driven lightly into the target, its head having been first touched with paint."

The color of the paint is not stated—an important omission, but Cooper deals freely in important omissions. No, after all, it was not an important omission; for this nailhead is *a hundred yards from* the marksmen, and could not be seen by them at that distance, no matter what its color might be. How far can the best eyes see a common house-fly? A hundred yards? It is quite impossible. Very well; eyes that cannot see a house-fly that is a hundred yards away cannot see an ordinary nail head at that distance, for the size of the two objects is the same. It takes a keen eye to see a fly or a nail-head at fifty yards—one hundred and fifty feet. Can the reader do it?

The nail was lightly driven, its head painted, and game called. Then the Cooper miracles began. The bullet of the first marksman chipped an edge of the nail-head; the next man's bullet drove the nail a little way into the target—and removed all the paint. Haven't the miracles gone far enough now? Not to suit Cooper; for the purpose of this whole scheme is to show off his prodigy, Deerslayer-Hawkeye-Long-Rifle-Leather-Stocking-Pathfinder-Bumppo before the ladies.

" 'Be all ready to clench it, boys!' cried out Pathfinder, stepping into his friend's tracks the instant they were vacant. 'Never mind a new nail; I can see that, though the paint is gone, and what I can see I can hit at a hundred yards, though it were only a mosquito's eye. Be ready to clench!'

"The rifle cracked, the bullet sped its way, and the head of the nail was buried in the wood, covered by the piece of flattened lead."

There, you see, is a man who could hunt flies with a rifle, and command a ducal salary in a Wild West show today if we had him back with us.

The recorded feat is certainly surprising just as it stands; but it is not surprising enough for Cooper. Cooper adds a touch. He has made Pathfinder do this miracle with another man's rifle; and not only that, but Pathfinder did not have even the advantage of loading it himself. He had everything against him, and yet he made that impossible shot; and not only made it, but did it with absolute confidence, saying, "Be ready to clench." Now a person like that would have undertaken that same feat with a brick-bat, and with Cooper to help he would have achieved it, too.

Pathfinder showed off handsomely that day before the ladies. His very first feat was a thing which no Wild West show can touch. He was standing with the group of marksmen, observing—a hundred yards from the target, mind; one Jasper raised his rifle and drove the center of the bull's-eye. Then the Quarter-master fired. The target exhibited no result this time. There was a laugh. "It's a dead miss," said Major Lundie. Pathfinder waited an impressive moment or two; then said, in that calm, indifferent, know-it-all way of his, "No, Major, he has covered Jasper's bullet, as will be seen if anyone will take the trouble to examine the target."

Wasn't it remarkable! How *could* he see that little pellet fly through the air and enter that distant bullet-hole? Yet that is what he did; for nothing is impossible to a Cooper person. Did any of those people have any deep-seated doubts about this thing? No; for that would imply sanity, and these were all Cooper people.

> "The respect for Pathfinder's skill and for his *quickness and accuracy of sight*" (the italics are mine) "was so profound and general, that the instant he made this declaration the spectators began to distrust their own opinions, and a dozen rushed to the target in order to ascertain the fact. There, sure enough, it was found that the Quartermaster's bullet had gone through the hole made by Jasper's, and that, too, so accurately as to require a minute examination to be certain of the circumstance, which, however, was soon clearly established by discovering one bullet over the other in the stump against which the target was placed."

They made a "minute" examination; but never mind, how could they know that there were two bullets in that hole without digging the latest one out? for neither probe nor eyesight could prove the presence of any more than one bullet. Did they dig? No; as we shall see. It is the Pathfinder's turn now; he steps out before the ladies, takes aim, and fires.

But, alas! here is a disappointment; an incredible, an unimaginable disappointment—for the target's aspect is unchanged; there is nothing there but that same old bullet-hole!

> " 'If one dared to hint at such a thing,' cried Major Duncan, "I should say that the Pathfinder has also missed the target!' "

As nobody had missed it yet, the "also" was not necessary; but never mind about that, for the Pathfinder is going to speak.

> " 'No, no,' said he, confidently, 'that *would* be a risky declaration. I didn't load the piece, and can't say what was in it; but if it was lead, you will find the bullet driving down those of the Quartermaster and Jasper, else is not my name Pathfinder.'
>
> "A shout from the target announced the truth of this assertion."

Is the miracle sufficient as it stands? Not for Cooper. The Pathfinder speaks again, as he "now slowly advances towards the stage occupied by the females":

> " 'That's not all, boys, that's not all; if you find the target touched at all, I'll own to a miss. The Quartermaster cut the wood, but you'll find no wood cut by that last messenger.' "

The miracle is at last complete. He knew—doubtless *saw*—at the distance of a hundred yards—that his bullet had passed into the hole *without fraying the edges*. There were now three bullets in that one hole—three bullets embedded processionally in the body of the stump back of the target. Everybody knew this—somehow or other—and yet nobody had dug any of them out to make sure. Cooper is not a close observer, but he is interesting. He is certainly always that, no matter what happens. And he is more interesting when he is not noticing what he is about than when he is. This is a considerable merit.

The conversations in the Cooper books have a curious sound in our modern ears. To believe that such talk really ever came out of people's mouths would be to believe that there was a time when time was of no value to a person who thought he had something to say; when it was the custom to spread a two-minute remark out to ten; when a man's mouth was a rolling-mill, and busied itself all day long in turning four-foot pigs of thought into thirty-foot bars of conversational railroad iron by attenuation; when subjects were seldom faithfully stuck to, but the talk wandered all around and arrived nowhere; when conversations consisted mainly of irrelevancies, with here and there a relevancy, a relevancy with an embarrassed look, as not being able to explain how it got there.

Cooper was certainly not a master in the construction of dialogue. Inaccurate observation defeated him here as it defeated him in so many other enterprises of his. He even failed to notice that the man who talks corrupt English six days in the week must and will talk it on the seventh, and can't help himself. In the *Deerslayer* story he lets Deerslayer talk the showiest kind of book-talk sometimes, and at other times the basest of base dialects. For instance, when someone asks him if he has a sweetheart, and if so, where she abides, this is his majestic answer:

" 'She's in the forest—hanging from the boughs of the trees, in a soft rain—in the dew on the open grass—the clouds that float about in the blue heavens—the birds that sing in the woods—the sweet springs where I slake my thirst—and in all the other glorious gifts that come from God's Providence!' "

And he preceded that, a little before, with this:

" 'It consarns me as all things that touches a fri'nd consarns a fri'nd.' "

And this is another of his remarks:

" 'If I was Injin born, now, I might tell of this, or carry in the scalp and boast of the expl'ite afore the whole tribe; or if my inimy had only been a bear' "—and so on.

We cannot imagine such a thing as a veteran Scotch Commander-in-Chief comporting himself in the field like a windy melodramatic actor, but Cooper could. On one occasion Alice and Cora were being chased by the French through a fog in the neighborhood of their father's fort:

" '*Point de quartier aux coquins!*' cried an eager pursuer, who seemed to direct the operations of the enemy.
" 'Stand firm and be ready, my gallant 60ths!' suddenly exclaimed a voice above them; 'wait to see the enemy; fire low, and sweep the glacis.'
" 'Father! father!' exclaimed a piercing cry from out the mist; 'it is I! Alice! thy own Elsie! spare, O! save your daughters!'
" 'Hold!' shouted the former speaker, in the awful tones of parental agony, the sound reaching even to the woods, and rolling back in solemn echo. ' 'Tis she! God has restored me my children! Throw open the sally-port; to the field, 60ths, to the field! pull not a trigger, lest ye kill my lambs! Drive off these dogs of France with your steel!' "

Cooper's word-sense was singularly dull. When a person has a poor ear for music he will flat and sharp right along without knowing it. He keeps near the tune, but it is *not* the tune. When a person has a poor ear for words, the result is a literary flatting and sharping; you perceive what he is intending to say, but you also perceive that he doesn't *say* it. This is Cooper. He was not a word-musician. His ear was satisfied with the *approximate* word. I will furnish some circumstantial evidence in support of this charge. My instances are gathered from half a dozen pages of the tale called *Deerslayer*. He uses "verbal," for "oral"; "precision," for "facility"; "phenomena," for "marvels"; "necessary," for "predetermined"; "unsophisticated," for "primitive"; "preparation," for "expectancy,"; "rebuked," for "subdued"; "dependent on," for "resulting from"; "fact," for "condition"; "fact," for "conjecture"; "precaution," for "caution"; "explain," for "determine"; "mortified," for "disappointed"; "meretricious," for "factitious"; "materially," for "considerably"; "decreasing," for "deepening"; "increasing," for "disappearing"; "embedded," for "enclosed"; "treacherous," for "hostile"; "stood," for "stooped"; "softened," for "replaced"; "rejoined," for "remarked"; "situation," for "condition"; "different," for "differing"; "insensible," for "unsentient"; "brevity," for "celerity"; "distrusted," for "suspicious"; "mental imbecility," for "imbecility"; "eyes," for "sight"; "counteracting," for "opposing"; "funeral obsequies," for "obsequies."

There have been daring people in the world who claimed that Cooper could write English, but they are all dead now—all dead but Lounsbury. I don't remember that Lounsbury makes the claim in so many words, still he makes it, for he says that *Deerslayer* is a "pure work of art." Pure, in that connection, means faultless—faultless in all details—and language is a detail. If Mr. Lounsbury had only compared Cooper's English with the English which he writes himself—but it is plain that he didn't; and so it is likely that he imagines until this day that Cooper's is as clean and compact as his own. Now I feel sure, deep down in my heart, that Cooper wrote about the poorest English that exists in our language, and that the English of *Deerslayer* is the very worst that even Cooper ever wrote.

I may be mistaken, but it does seem to me that *Deerslayer* is not a work of art in any sense; it does seem to me that it is destitute of every detail that goes to the making of a work of art; in truth, it seems to me that *Deerslayer* is just simply a literary *delirium tremens*.

A work of art? It has no invention; it has no order, system, sequence, or result; it has no lifelikeness, no thrill, no stir, no seeming of reality; its characters are confusedly drawn, and by their acts and words they prove that they are not the sort of people the author claims that they are; its humor is pathetic; its pathos is funny; its conversations are—oh! indescribable; its love-scenes odious; its English a crime against the language.

Counting these out, what is left is Art. I think we must all admit that.

9. HOW TO TELL A STORY*
The Humorous Story an American Development.—Its Difference from Comic and Witty Stories

I do not claim that I can tell a story as it ought to be told. I only claim to know how a story ought to be told, for I have been almost daily in the company of the most expert story-tellers for many years.

There are several kinds of stories, but only one difficult kind—the humorous. I will talk mainly about that one. The humorous story is American, the comic story is English, the witty story is French. The humorous story depends for its effect upon the *manner* of the telling; the comic story and the witty story upon the *matter*.

The humorous story may be spun out to great length, and may wander around as much as it pleases, and arrive nowhere in particular; but the comic and witty stories must be brief and end with a point. The humorous story bubbles gently along, the others burst.

The humorous story is strictly a work of art—high and delicate art—and only an artist can tell it; but no art is necessary in telling the comic and the witty story; anybody can do it. The art of telling a humorous story—understand, I mean by word of mouth, not print—was created in America, and has remained at home.

The humorous story is told gravely; the teller does his best to conceal the fact that he even dimly suspects that there is anything funny about it; but the teller of the comic story tells you beforehand that it is one of the funniest things he has ever heard, then tells it with eager delight, and is the first person to laugh when he gets through. And sometimes, if he has had good success, he is so glad and happy that he will repeat the "nub" of it and glance around from face to face, collecting applause, and then repeat it again. It is a pathetic thing to see.

---

* The selection is taken from the essay "How to Tell a Story" by Mark Twain, first printed in *Youth's Companion*, October 3, 1895, 1897.

Very often, of course, the rambling and disjointed humorous story finishes with a nub, point, snapper, or whatever you like to call it. Then the listener must be alert, for in many cases the teller will divert attention from that nub by dropping it in a carefully casual and indifferent way, with the pretence that he does not know it is a nub.

Artemus Ward used that trick a good deal; then when the belated audience presently caught the joke he would look up with innocent surprise, as if wondering what they had found to laugh at. Dan Setchell used it before him, Nye and Riley and others use it to-day.

But the teller of the comic story does not slur the nub; he shouts it at you—every time. And when he prints it, in England, France, Germany, and Italy, he italicizes it, puts some whooping exclamation-points after it, and sometimes explains it in a parenthesis. All of which is very depressing, and makes one want to renounce joking and lead a better life.

Let me set down an instance of the comic method, using an anecdote which has been popular all over the world for twelve or fifteen hundred years. The teller tells it in this way:

THE WOUNDED SOLDIER

In the course of a certain battle a soldier whose leg had been shot off appealed to another soldier who was hurrying by to carry him to the rear, informing him at the same time of the loss which he had sustained; whereupon the generous son of Mars, shouldering the unfortunate, proceeded to carry out his desire. The bullets and cannon-balls were flying in all directions, and presently one of the latter took the wounded man's head off—without, however, his deliverer being aware of it. In no long time he was hailed by an officer, who said:

"Where are you going with that carcass?"

"To the rear, sir—he's lost his leg!"

"His leg, forsooth?" responded the astonished officer; "you mean his head, you booby."

Whereupon the soldier dispossessed himself of his burden, and stood looking down upon it in great perplexity. At length he said:

"It is true, sir, just as you have said." Then after a pause he added, *"But he* TOLD *me* IT WAS HIS LEG!!!!!"

—

Here the narrator bursts into explosion after explosion of thunderous horse-laughter, repeating the nub from time to time through his gaspings and shriekings and suffocatings.

It takes only a minute and a half to tell that in its comic-story form; and isn't worth the telling, after all. Put into the humorous-story form it takes ten minues, and is about the funniest thing I have ever listened to—as James Whitcomb Riley tells it.

He tells it in the character of a dull-witted old farmer who has just heard it for the first time, thinks it is unspeakably funny, and is trying to repeat it to a neighbor. But he can't remember it; so he gets all mixed up and wanders helplessly round and round, putting in tedious details that don't belong in the tale and only retard it; taking them out conscientiously and putting in others that are just as useless; making minor mistakes now and then and stopping to correct them and explain how he came to make them; remembering things which he forgot to put in in their proper place and going back to put them in there; stopping his narrative a good while in order to try to recall the name of the soldier that was hurt, and finally remembering that the soldier's name was not mentioned, and remarking placidly that the name is of no real importance, anyway—better, of course, if one knew it, but not essential, after all—and so on, and so on, and so on.

The teller is innocent and happy and pleased with himself, and has to stop every little while to hold himself in and keep from laughing outright; and does hold in, but his body quakes in a jelly-like way with interior chuckles; and at the end of the ten minutes the audience have laughed until they are exhausted, and the tears are running down their faces.

The simplicity and innocence and sincerity and unconsciousness of the old farmer are perfectly simulated, and the result is a performance which is thoroughly charming and delicious. This is art—and fine and beautiful, and only a master can compass it; but a machine could tell the other story.

To string incongruities and absurdities together in a wandering and sometimes purposeless way, and seem innocently unaware that they are absurdities, is the basis of the American art, if my position is correct. Another feature is the slurring of the point.

A third is the dropping of a studied remark apparently without knowing it, as if one were thinking aloud. The fourth and last is the pause.

Artemus Ward dealt in numbers three and four a good deal. He would begin to tell with great animation something which he seemed to think was wonderful; then lose confidence, and after an apparently absent-minded pause add an incongruous remark in a soliloquizing way; and that was the remark intended to explode the mine—and it did.

For instance, he would say eagerly, excitedly, "I once knew a man in New Zealand who hadn't a tooth in his head"—here his animation would die out; a silent, reflective pause would follow, then he would say dreamily, and as if to himself, "and yet that man could beat a drum better than any man I ever saw."

The pause is an exceedingly important feature in any kind of story, and a frequently recurring feature, too. It is a dainty thing, and delicate, and also uncertain and treacherous; for it must be exactly the right length—no more and no less—or it fails of its purpose and makes trouble. If the pause is too short the impressive point is passed, and the audience have had time to divine that a surprise is intended—and then you can't surprise them, of course.

On the platform I used to tell a negro ghost story that had a pause in front of the snapper on the end, and that pause was the most important thing in the whole story. If I got it the right length precisely, I could spring the finishing ejaculation with effect enough to make some impressible girl deliver a startled little yelp and jump out of her seat—and that was what I was after. This story was called "The Golden Arm," and was told in this fashion. You can practise with it yourself—and mind you look out for the pause and get it right.

THE GOLDEN ARM

Once 'pon a time dey wuz a monsus mean man, en he live 'way out in de prairie all 'lone by hisself, 'cep'n he had a wife. En bimeby she died, en he tuck en toted her way out dah in de prairie en buried her. Well, she had a golden arm—all solid gold, fum de shoulder down. He wuz pow'ful mean—pow'ful; en dat night he couldn't sleep, caze he want dat golden arm so bad.

When it come midnight he couldn't stan' it no mo'; so he git

up, he did, en tuck his lantern en shoved out thoo de storm en
dug her up en got de golden arm; en he bent his head down 'gin
de win', en plowed en plowed en plowed thoo de snow. Den all
on a sudden he stop (make a considerable pause here, and look
startled, and take a listening attitude) en say: "My *lan'*, what's
dat!"

En he listen—en listen—en de win' say (set your teeth together
and imitate the wailing and wheezing singsong of the wind),
"Bzzz-z-zzz"—en den, way back yonder whah de grave is, he
hear a *voice!*—he hear a voice all mix' up in de win'—can't
hardly tell 'em 'part—"Bzzz-zzz—W-h-o—g-o-t—m-y—g-o-l-d-e-n
arm?—zzz—zzz—W-h-o g-o-t m-y g-o-l-d-e-n *arm?* (You must
begin to shiver violently now.)

En he begin to shiver en shake, en say, "Oh, my! *Oh*, my
lan'!" en de win' blow de lantern out, en de snow en sleet blow
in his face en mos' choke him, en he start a-plowin' knee-deep
towards home mos' dead, he so sk'yerd—en pooty soon he hear
de voice agin, en (pause) it 'us comin' *after* him! "Bzzz—zzz—
zzz-W-h-o—g-o-t—m-y—g-o-l-d-e-n—*arm?*"

When he git to de pasture he hear it agin—closter now, en
a-*comin'!*—a-comin' back dah in de dark en de storm—(repeat
the wind and the voice). When he git to de house he rush
upstairs en jump in de bed en kiver up, head and years, en lay
dah shiverin' en shakin'—en den way out dah he hear it
agin!—en a-*comin'!* En bimeby he hear (pause—awed, listening
attitude)—pat—pat—pat—*hit's* a-*comin' up-stairs!* Den he hear de
latch, en he *know* it's in de room!

Den pooty soon he know it's a-*stannin' by de bed!* (Pause.)
Den—he know it's a-*bendin' down over him*—en he cain't
skasely git his breath! Den—den—he seem to feel someth'n
c-o-l-d, right down 'most agin his head! (Pause.)

Den de voice say, *right at his year*—"W-h-o—g-o-t—m-y—
g-o-l-d-e-n *arm?*" (You must wail it out very plaintively and
accusingly; then you stare steadily and impressively into the
face of the farthest-gone auditor—a girl, preferably—and let that
awe-inspiring pause begin to build itself in the deep hush. When
it has reached exactly the right length, jump suddenly at that
girl and yell, "*You've* got it!")

If you've got the *pause* right, she'll fetch a dear little yelp and
spring right out of her shoes. But you *must* get the pause right;
and you will find it the most troublesome and aggravating and
uncertain thing you ever undertook.

10. ON SOME PROBLEMS OF COMPOSITION*

There has never been a time in the past thirty-five years[1] when my literary shipyard hadn't two or more half-finished ships on the ways, neglected and baking in the sun; generally there have been three or four; at present there are five. This has an unbusiness-like look but it was not purposeless, it was intentional. As long as a book would write itself I was a faithful and interested amanuensis and my industry did not flag, but the minute that the book tried to shift to *my* head the labor of contriving its situations, inventing its adventures and conducting its conversations, I put it away and dropped it out of my mind. Then I examined my unfinished properties to see if among them there might not be one whose interest in itself had revived through a couple of years' restful idleness and was ready to take me on again as amanuensis.

It was by accident that I found out that a book is pretty sure to get tired along about the middle and refuse to go on with its work until its powers and its interest should have been refreshed by a rest and its depleted stock of raw materials reinforced by lapse of time. It was when I had reached the middle of *Tom Sawyer* that I made this invaluable find. At page 400 of my manuscript the story made a sudden and determined halt and refused to proceed another step. Day after day it still refused. I was disappointed, distressed and immeasurably astonished, for I knew quite well that the tale was not finished and I could not understand why I was not able to go on with it. The reason was very simple—my tank had run dry; it was empty; the stock of

* The selection constitutes Chapter 53 in *The Autobiography of Mark Twain*, edited by Charles Neider; copyright © 1959 by The Mark Twain Company, copyright © 1959 by Charles Neider. Reprinted by permission of Harper & Row Publishers, Inc., and Chatto and Windus Ltd.

[1] Written August 30, 1906.

materials in it was exhausted; the story could not go on without materials; it could not be wrought out of nothing.

When the manuscript had lain in a pigeonhole two years I took it out one day and read the last chapter that I had written. It was then that I made the great discovery that when the tank runs dry you've only to leave it alone and it will fill up again in time, while you are asleep—also while you are at work at other things and are quite unaware that this unconscious and profitable cerebration is going on. There was plenty of material now and the book went on and finished itself without any trouble.

Ever since then, when I have been writing a book I have pigeonholed it without misgivings when its tank ran dry, well knowing that it would fill up again without any of my help within the next two or three years, and that then the work of completing it would be simple and easy. *The Prince and the Pauper* struck work in the middle because the tank was dry, and I did not touch it again for two years. A dry interval of two years occurred in *A Connecticut Yankee in King Arthur's Court.* A like interval had occurred in the middle of other books of mine. Two similar intervals have occurred in a story of mine called "Which Was It?" In fact, the second interval has gone considerably over time, for it is now four years since that second one intruded itself. I am sure that the tank is full again now and that I could take up that book and write the other half of it without a break or any lapse of interest—but I shan't do it. The pen is irksome to me. I was born lazy, and dictating has spoiled me. I am quite sure I shall never touch a pen again; therefore that book will remain unfinished—a pity, too, for the idea of it is (actually) new and would spring a handsome surprise upon the reader at the end.

There is another unfinished book, which I should probably entitle "The Refuge of the Derelicts." It is half finished and will remain so. There is still another one, entitled "The Adventures of a Microbe During Three Thousand Years—by a Microbe." It is half finished and will remain so. There is yet another—*The Mysterious Stranger*. It is more than half finished. I would dearly like to finish it and it causes me a real pang to reflect that it is not be be.[2] These several tanks are full now and those books would go gaily along and complete themselves if I would hold the pen, but I am tired of the pen.

[2] Although he was unaware of the fact he had already finished this work.

There was another of these half-finished stories. I carried it as far as thirty-eight thousand words four years ago, then destroyed it for fear I might some day finish it. Huck Finn was the teller of the story and of course Tom Sawyer and Jim were the heroes of it. But I believed that that trio had done work enough in this world and were entitled to a permanent rest.

In Rouen in '93 I destroyed $15,000 worth of manuscript, and in Paris in the beginning of '94 I destroyed $10,000 worth—I mean, estimated as magazine stuff. I was afraid to keep those piles of manuscript on hand lest I be tempted to sell them, for I was fairly well persuaded that they were not up to standard. Ordinarily there would have been no temptation present and I would not think of publishing doubtful stuff—but I was heavily in debt then and the temptation to mend my condition was so strong that I burnt the manuscript to get rid of it. My wife not only made no objection but encouraged me to do it, for she cared more for my reputation than for any other concern of ours.

About that time she helped me put another temptation behind me. This was an offer of $16,000 a year, for five years, to let my name be used as editor of a humorous periodical. I praise her for furnishing her help in resisting that temptation, for it is her due. There was no temptation about it, in fact, but she would have offered her help just the same if there had been one. I can conceive of many wild and extravagant things when my imagination is in good repair but I can conceive of nothing quite so wild and extravagant as the idea of my accepting the editorship of a humorous periodical. I should regard that as the saddest (for me) of all occupations. If I should undertake it I should have to add to it the occupation of undertaker, to relieve it in some degree of its cheerlessness. I could edit a serious periodical with relish and a strong interest but I have never cared enough about humor to qualify me to edit it or sit in judgment upon it.

There are some books that refuse to be written. They stand their ground year after year and will not be persuaded. It isn't because the book is not there and worth being written—it is only because the right form for the story does not present itself. There is only one right form for a story and if you fail to find that form the story will not tell itself. You may try a dozen wrong forms but in each case you will not get very far before you discover that you have not found the right one—then that story will always stop and decline to go any further. In the story of *Joan of Arc* I made six wrong starts and each time that I offered the result to Mrs. Clemens she responded with the same deadly criticism—silence. She didn't say a word but her silence spoke with the voice of thunder. When at last I found the right form I recognized at once that it was the right one and I knew what she would say. She said it, without doubt or hesitation.

In the course of twelve years I made six attempts to tell a simple little story which I knew would tell itself in four hours if I could ever find the right starting point. I scored six failures; then one day in London I offered the text of the story to Robert McClure and proposed that he publish that text in the magazine and offer a prize to the person who should tell it best. I became greatly interested and went on talking upon the text for half an hour; then he said, "You have told the story yourself. You have nothing to do but put it on paper just as you have told it."

I recognized that this was true. At the end of four hours it was finished, and quite to my satisfaction. So it took twelve years and four hours to produce that little bit of a story, which I have called "The Death Wafer."

To start right is certainly an essential. I have proved this too many times to doubt it. Twenty-five or thirty years ago I began a story which was to turn upon the marvels of mental telegraphy. A man was to invent a scheme whereby he could synchronize two minds, thousands of miles apart, and enable them to freely converse together through the air without the aid of a wire. Four times I started it in the wrong way and it wouldn't go. Three times I discovered my mistake after writing about a hundred pages. I discovered it the fourth time when I had written four hundred pages—then I gave it up and put the whole thing in the fire.

11. ON PUBLIC AND PRIVATE OPINIONS*

Two or three weeks ago[1] Elinor Glyn called on me one afternoon and we had a long talk, of a distinctly unusual character, in the library. It may be that by the time this chapter reaches print she may be less well known to the world than she is now, therefore I will insert here a word or two of information about her. She is English. She is an author. The newspapers say she is visiting America with the idea of finding just the right kind of a hero for the principal character in a romance which she is purposing to write. She has come to us upon the stormwind of a vast and sudden notoriety.

The source of this notoriety is a novel of hers called *Three Weeks*. In this novel the hero is a fine and gifted and cultivated young English gentleman of good family, who imagines he has fallen in love with the ungifted, uninspired, commonplace daughter of the rector. He goes to the Continent on an outing and there he happens upon a brilliant and beautiful young lady of exceedingly foreign extraction, with a deep mystery hanging over her. It transpires later that she is the childless wife of a king or kinglet, a coarse and unsympathetic animal whom she does not love.

She and the young Englishman fall in love with each other at sight. The hero's feeling for the rector's daughter was pale, not to say colorless, and it is promptly consumed and extinguished in the furnace fires of his passion for the mysterious stranger— passion is the right word, passion is what the pair of strangers feel for each other, what they recognize as real love—the only real love, the only love worthy to be called by that great

* The selection constitutes Chapter 75 from *The Autobiography of Mark Twain,* eidted by Charles Neider; copyright ©1959 by The Mark Twain Company, copyright ©1959 by Charles Neider. Reprinted by permission of Harper & Row Publishers, Inc., and Chatto and Windus Ltd.

[1] Written January 13, 1908.

name—whereas the feeling which the young man had for the
rector's daughter is perceived to have been only a passing
partiality.

The queenlet and the Englishman flit away privately to the
mountains and take up sumptuous quarters in a remote and
lonely house there—and then business begins. They recognize
that they were highly and holily created for each other and that
their passion is a sacred thing, that it is their master by divine
right and that its commands must be obeyed. They get to
obeying them at once and they keep on obeying them and
obeying them, to the reader's intense delight and disapproval,
and the process of obeying them is described, several times,
almost exhaustively, but not quite—some little rag of it being
left to the reader's imagination, just at the end of each
infraction, the place where his imagination is to take up and do
the finish being indicated by stars.

The unstated argument of the book is that the laws of Nature
are paramount and properly take precedence of the interfering
and impertinent restrictions obtruded upon man's life by man's
statutes.

Mme. Glyn called, as I have said, and she was a picture!
Slender, young, faultlessly formed and incontestably beautiful—a blonde with blue eyes, the incomparable English complexion and crowned with a glory of red hair of a very peculiar,
most rare and quite ravishing tint. She was clad in the choicest
stuffs and in the most perfect taste. There she is, just a beautiful
girl; yet she has a daughter fourteen years old. She isn't
winning; she has no charm but the charm of beauty and youth
and grace and intelligence and vivacity; she *acts* charm and does
it well, exceedingly well in fact, but it does not convince, it
doesn't stir the pulse, it doesn't go to the heart, it leaves the
heart serene and unemotional. Her English hero would have
prodigiously admired her; he would have loved to sit and look
at her and hear her talk, but he would have been able to get
away from that lonely house with his purity in good repair, if
he wanted to.

I talked with her with daring frankness, frequently calling a
spade a spade instead of coldly symbolizing it as a snow shovel;
and on her side she was equally frank. It was one of the
damnedest conversations I have ever had with a beautiful
stranger of her sex, if I do say it myself that shouldn't. She
wanted my opinion of her book and I furnished it. I said its

literary workmanship was excellent and that I quite agreed with her view that in the matter of the sexual relation man's statutory regulations of it were a distinct interference with a higher law, the law of Nature. I went further and said I couldn't call to mind a written law of any kind that had been promulgated in any age of the world in any statute book or any Bible for the regulation of man's conduct in *any* particular, from assassination all the way up to Sabbath-breaking, that wasn't a violation of the law of Nature, which I regarded as the highest of laws, the most peremptory and absolute of all laws—Nature's laws being in my belief plainly and simply the laws of God, since He instituted them, He and no other, and the said laws, by authority of this divine origin, taking precedence of all the statutes of man. I said that her pair of indelicate lovers were obeying the clearly enunciated law of God, and in His eyes must manifestly be blameless.

Of course what she wanted of me was support and defense—I knew that but I said I couldn't furnish it. I said we were the servants of convention; that we could not subsist, either in a savage or a civilized state, without conventions; that we must accept them and stand by them, even when we disapproved of them; that while the laws of Nature, that is to say the laws of God, plainly made every human being a law unto himself, we must steadfastly refuse to obey those laws, and we must as steadfastly stand by the conventions which ignore them, since the statutes furnish us peace, fairly good government and stability, and therefore are better for us than the laws of God, which would soon plunge us into confusion and disorder and anarchy if we should adopt them. I said her book was an assault upon certain old and well-established and wise conventions and that it would not find many friends, and indeed would not deserve many.

She said I was very brave, the bravest person she had ever met (gross flattery which could have beguiled me when I was very very young), and she implored me to publish these views of mine, but I said, "No, such a thing is unthinkable." I said that if I, or any other wise, intelligent and experienced person, should suddenly throw down the walls that protect and conceal his *real* opinions on almost any subject under the sun, it would at once be perceived that he had lost his intelligence and his wisdom and ought to be sent to the asylum. I said I had been revealing to her my private sentiments, *not* my public ones; that I, like all the other human beings, expose to the world only my trimmed and perfumed and carefully barbered public opinions and conceal carefully, cautiously, wisely, my private ones.

I explained that what I meant by that phrase "public opinions" was *published* opinions, opinions spread broadcast in print. I said I was in the common habit, in private conversation with friends, of revealing every private opinion I possessed relating to religion, politics and men, but that I should never dream of *printing* one of them, because they are individually and collectively at war with almost everybody's public opinion while at the same time they are in happy agreement with almost everybody's private opinion. As an instance, I asked her if she had ever encountered an intelligent person who privately believed in the Immaculate Conception[2]—which of course she hadn't; and I also asked her if she had ever seen an intelligent person who was daring enough to publicly deny his belief in that fable and print the denial. Of course she hadn't encountered any such person.

I said I had a large cargo of most interesting and important private opinions about every great matter under the sun, but that they were not for print. I reminded her that we all break over the rule two or three times in our lives and fire a disagreeable and unpopular private opinion of ours into print, but we never do it when we can help it, we never do it except when the desire to do it is too strong for us and overrides and conquers our cold, calm wise judgment. She mentioned several instances in which I had come out publicly in defense of unpopular causes, and she intimated that what I had been saying about myself was not perhaps in strict accordance with the facts; but I said they were merely illustrations of what I had just been saying, that when I publicly attacked the American missionaries in China and some other iniquitous persons and causes, I did not do it for any reason but just the one: that the inclination to do it was stronger than my diplomatic instincts, and I had to obey and take the consequences. But I said I was not moved to defend her book in public; that it was not a case where inclination was overpowering and unconquerable, and that therefore I could keep diplomatically still and should do it.

The lady was young enough and inexperienced enough to

---

[2] "Throughout Mark Twain's writing, he confuses the doctrine of the Immaculate Conception with that of the Virgin Birth of Christ." (DeVoto.)

imagine that whenever a person has an unpleasant opinion in stock which could be of educational benefit to Tom, Dick and Harry it is his *duty* to come out in print with it and become its champion. I was not able to get that juvenile idea out of her head. I was not able to convince her that we never do *any* duty for duty's sake but only for the mere personal satisfaction we get out of doing that duty. The fact is, she was brought up just like the rest of the world, with the ingrained and stupid superstition that there is such a thing as *duty for duty's sake*, and so I was obliged to let her abide in her darkness. She believed that when a man held a private unpleasant opinion of an educational sort which would get him hanged if he published it he ought to publish it anyway and was a coward if he didn't. Take it all around, it was a very pleasant conversation and glaringly unprintable, particularly those considerable parts of it which I haven't had the courage to more than vaguely hint at in this account of our talk.

Some days afterward I met her again for a moment and she gave me the startling information that she had written down every word I had said, just as I had said it, without any softening and purifying modifications, and that it was "just splendid, just wonderful." She said she had sent it to her husband in England. Privately I didn't think that that was a very good idea, and yet I believed it would interest him. She begged me to let her publish it and said it would do infinite good in the world, but I said it would damn me before my time and I didn't wish to be useful to the world on such expensive conditions.

12. WILLIAM DEAN HOWELLS
"Mark Twain; An Inquiry"*

Two recent events have concurred to offer criticism a fresh excuse, if not a fresh occasion, for examining the literary work of Mr. Samuel L. Clemens, better known to the human family by his pseudonym of Mark Twain. One of these events is the publication of his writings in a uniform edition, which it is to be hoped will remain indefinitely incomplete; the other is his return to his own country after an absence so long as to form a psychological perspective in which his characteristics make a new appeal.

The uniform edition of Mr. Clemens's writings is of that dignified presence which most of us have thought their due in moments of high pleasure with their quality, and high dudgeon with their keeping in the matchlessly ugly subscription volumes of the earlier issues. Yet now that we have them in this fine shape, fit every one, in its elect binding, paper, and print, to be set on the shelf of a gentleman's library, and not taken from it without some fear of personal demerit, I will own a furtive regret for the hideous blocks and bricks of which the visible temple of the humorist's fame was first builded. It was an advantage to meet the author in a guise reflecting the accidental and provisional moods of a unique talent finding itself out; and the pictures which originally illustrated the process were helps to the imagination such as the new uniform edition does not afford. In great part it could not retain them, for reasons which the recollection of their uncouth vigor will suggest, but these reasons do not hold in all cases, and especially in the case of Mr. Dan Beard's extraordinarily sympathetic and interpretative pictures for *The Connecticut Yankee in King Arthur's Court*. The illustrations of the uniform edition, in fact, are its weak side, but it can be said that they do not detract from one's delight in the literature; no illustrations could do that; and, in compensation for their defeat, the reader has the singularly intelligent and

* The selection constitutes the entire essay, "Mark Twain: An Inquiry" by William Dean Howells, first published in *The North American Review,* February, 1901.

agreeable essay of Mr. Brander Matthews on Mr. Clemens's work by way of introduction to the collection. For the rest one may acquit one's self of one's whole duty to the uniform edition by reminding the reader that in the rich variety of its inclusion are those renowning books *The Innocents Abroad* and *Roughing It*; the first constructive fiction on the larger scale, *Tom Sawyer* and *Huckleberry Finn*; the later books of travel, *A Tramp Abroad* and *Following the Equator*; the multiplicity of tales, sketches, burlesques, satires, and speeches, together with the spoil of Mr. Clemens's courageous forays in the region of literary criticism; and his later romances, *The Connecticut Yankee*, *The American Claimant*, and *Joan of Arc.* These complete an array of volumes which the most unconventional reviewer can hardly keep from calling goodly, and which is responsive to the spirit of the literature in a certain desultory and insuccessive arrangement.

So far as I know, Mr. Clemens is the first writer to use in extended writing the fashion we all use in thinking, and to set down the thing that comes into his mind without fear or favor of the thing that went before or the thing that may be about to follow. I, for instance, in putting this paper together, am anxious to observe some sort of logical order, to discipline such impressions and notions as I have of the subject into a coherent body which shall march columnwise to a conclusion obvious if not inevitable from the start. But Mr. Clemens, if he were writing it, would not be anxious to do any such thing. He would take whatever offered itself to his hand out of that mystical chaos, that divine ragbag, which we call the mind, and leave the reader to look after relevancies and sequences for himself. These there might be, but not of that hard-and-fast sort which I am eager to lay hold of, and the result would at least be satisfactory to the author, who would have shifted the whole responsibility to the reader, with whom it belongs, at least as much as with the author. In other words, Mr. Clemens uses in work on the larger scale the method of the elder essayists, and you know no more where you are going to bring up in *The Innocents Abroad* or *Following the Equator* than in an essay of Montaigne. The end you arrive at is the end of the book, and you reach it amused but edified, and sorry for nothing but to be there. You have noted the author's thoughts, but not his order of thinking; he has not attempted to trace the threads of association between the things that have followed one another; his reason, not his logic, has convinced you, or, rather, it has persuaded you, for you have not been brought under conviction. It is not certain that this method is of design with Mr. Clemens; that might spoil it; and possibly he will be as much surprised as any one to know that it is his method. It is imaginable that he pursues it from no wish but to have pleasure of his work, and not to fatigue either himself or his reader; and his method may be the secret of his vast popularity, but it cannot be the whole secret of it. Any one may compose a scrapbook, and offer it to the public with nothing of Mark Twain's good-fortune. Everything seems to depend upon the nature of the scraps, after all; his scraps might have been consecutively arranged, in a studied order, and still have immensely pleased; but there is no doubt that people like things that have at least the appearance of not having been drilled into line. Life itself has that sort of appearance as it goes on; it is an essay with moments of drama in it rather than a drama; it is a lesson, with the precepts appearing haphazard, and not precept upon precept; it is a school, but not always a school-room; it is a temple, but the priests are not always in their sacerdotal robes; sometimes they are eating the sacrifice behind the altar and pouring the libations for the god through the channels of their dusty old throats. An instinct of something chaotic, ironic, empiric in the order of experience seems to have been the inspiration of our humorist's art, and what finally remains with the reader, after all the joking and laughing, is not merely the feeling of having had a mighty good time, but the conviction that he has got the worth of his money. He has not gone through the six hundred pages of *The Innocents Abroad*, or *Following the Equator*, without having learned more of the world as the writer saw it than any but the rarest traveller is able to show for his travel; and possibly, with his average practical American public, which was his first tribunal, and must always be his court of final appeal, Mark Twain justified himself for being so delightful by being so instructive. If this bold notion is admissible, it seems the moment to say that no writer ever imparted information more inoffensively.

But his great charm is his absolute freedom in a region where most of us are fettered and shackled by immemorial convention. He saunters out into the trim world of letters, and lounges across its neatly kept paths, and walks about on the grass at will, in spite of all the signs that have been put up from the beginning of literature, warning people of dangers and penalties for the slightest trespass.

One of the characteristics I observe in him is his single-minded use of words, which he employs as Grant did to express the plain, straight meaning their common acceptance has given them with no regard to their structural significance or their philological implications. He writes English as if it were a primitive and not a derivative language, without Gothic or Latin or Greek behind it, or German and French beside it. The result is the English in which the most vital works of English literature are cast, rather than the English of Milton and Thackeray and Mr. Henry James. I do not say that the English of the authors last named is less than vital, but only that it is not the most vital. It is scholarly and conscious; it knows who its grandfather was; it has the refinement and subtlety of an old patriciate. You will not have with it the widest suggestion, the largest human feeling, or perhaps the loftiest reach of imagination, but you will have the keen joy that exquisite artistry in words can alone impart, and that you will not have in Mark Twain. What you will have in him is a style which is as personal, as biographical as the style of any one who has written, and expresses a civilization whose courage of the chances, the preferences, the duties, is not the measure of its essential modesty. It has a thing to say, and it says it in the word that may be the first or second or third choice, but will not be the instrument of the most fastidious ear, the most delicate and exacting sense, though it will be the word that surely and strongly conveys intention from the author's mind to the reader's. It is the Abraham Lincolnian word, not the Charles Sumnerian; it is American, Western.

Now that Mark Twain has become a fame so worldwide, we should be in some danger of forgetting, but for his help, how entirely American he is, and we have already forgotten, perhaps, how truly Western he is, though his work, from first to last, is always reminding us of the fact. But here I should like to distinguish. It is not alone in its generous humor, with more honest laughter in it than humor ever had in the world till now, that his work is so Western. Any one who has really known the West (and really to know it one must have lived it) is aware of the profoundly serious, the almost tragical strain which is the fundamental tone in the movement of such music as it has. Up to a certain point, in the presence of the mystery which we call

life, it trusts and hopes and laughs; beyond that it doubts and
fears, but it does not cry. It is more likely to laugh again, and in
the work of Mark Twain there is little of the pathos which is
supposed to be the ally of humor, little suffusion of apt tears
from the smiling eyes. It is too sincere for that sort of play; and
if after the doubting and the fearing it laughs again, it is with a
suggestion of that resentment which youth feels when the
disillusion from its trust and hope comes, and which is the grim
second-mind of the West in the presence of the mystery. It is
not so much the race-effect as the region-effect; it is not the
Anglo-American finding expression, it is the Westerner, who is
not more thoroughly the creature of circumstances, of conditions, but far more dramatically their creature than any prior
man. He found himself placed in them and under them, so near
to a world in which the natural and primitive was obsolete, that
while he could not escape them, neither could he help challenging them. The inventions, the appliances, the improvements
of the modern world invaded the hoary eld of his rivers and
forests and prairies, and, while he was still a pioneer, a hunter, a
trapper, he found himself confronted with the financier, the
scholar, the gentleman. They seemed to him, with the world
they represented, at first very droll, and he laughed. Then they
set him thinking, and, as he never was afraid of anything, he
thought over the whole field and demanded explanations of all
his prepossessions—of equality, of humanity, of representative
government, and revealed religion. When they had not their
answers ready, without accepting the conventions of the modern world as solutions or in any manner final, he laughed again,
not mockingly, but patiently, compassionately. Such, or somewhat like this, was the genesis and evolution of Mark Twain.

Missouri was Western, but it was also Southern, not only in
the institution of slavery, to the custom and acceptance of
which Mark Twain was born and bred without any applied
doubt of its divinity, but in the peculiar social civilization of the
older South from which his native State was settled. It would be
reaching too far out to claim that American humor, of the now
prevailing Western type, is of Southern origin, but without
staying to attempt it I will say that I think the fact could be
established; and I think one of the most notably Southern traits
of Mark Twain's humor is its power of seeing the fun of
Southern seriousness, but this vision did not come to him till
after his liberation from neighborhood in the vaster Far West.

He was the first, if not the only, man of his section to betray a consciousness of the grotesque absurdities in the Southern inversion of the civilized ideals in behalf of slavery, which must have them upside down in order to walk over them safely. No American of Northern birth or breeding could have imagined the spiritual struggle of Huck Finn in deciding to help the negro Jim to his freedom, even though he should be forever despised as a negro thief in his native town, and perhaps eternally lost through the blackness of his sin. No Northerner could have come so close to the heart of a Kentucky feud, and revealed it so perfectly, with the whimsicality playing through its carnage, or could have so brought us into the presence of the sardonic comi-tragedy of the squalid little river town where the store-keeping magnate shoots down his drunken tormentor in the arms of the drunkard's daughter, and then cows with bitter mockery the mob that comes to lynch him. The strict religiosity compatible in the Southwest with savage precepts of conduct is something that could make itself known in its amusing contrast only to the native Southwesterner, and the revolt against it is as constant in Mark Twain as the enmity to New England orthodoxy is in Doctor Holmes. But he does not take it with such serious resentment as Doctor Holmes is apt to take his inherited Puritanism, and it may be therefore that he is able to do it more perfect justice, and impart it more absolutely. At any rate, there are no more vital passages in his fiction than those which embody character as it is affected for good as well as evil by the severity of the local Sunday-schooling and church-going.

I find myself, in spite of the discipline I intend for this paper, speaking first of the fiction, which by no means came first in Mark Twain's literary development. It is true that his beginnings were in short sketches, more or less inventive, and studies of life in which he let his imagination play freely; but it was not till he had written *Tom Sawyer* that he could be called a novelist. Even now I think he should rather be called a romancer, though such a book as *Huckleberry Finn* takes itself out of the order of romance and places itself with the great things in picaresque fiction. Still, it is more poetic than picaresque, and of a deeper psychology. The probable and credible soul that the author divines in the son of the town-drunkard is one which we might each own brother, and the art which portrays this nature at first hand in the person and language of the hero, without pose or affectation, is fine art. In the boy's history the author's fancy works realistically to an end as high as it has reached elsewhere, if not higher; and I who like *The Connecticut Yankee in King Arthur's Court* so much have half a mind to give my whole heart to *Huckleberry Finn*.

Both *Huckleberry Finn* and *Tom Sawyer* wander in episodes loosely related to the main story, but they are of a closer and more logical advance from the beginning to the end than the fiction which preceded them, and which I had almost forgotten to name before them. We owe to *The Gilded Age* a type in Colonel Mulberry Sellers which is as likely to endure as any fictitious character of our time. It embodies the sort of Americanism which survived through the Civil War, and characterized in its boundlessly credulous, fearlessly adventurous, unconsciously burlesque excess the period of political and economic expansion which followed the war. Colonel Sellers was, in some rough sort, the American of that day, which already seems so remote, and is best imaginable through him. Yet the story itself was of the fortuitous structure of what may be called the autobiographical books, such as *The Innocents Abroad* and *Roughing It*. Its desultory and accidental character was heightened by the co-operation of Mr. Clemens's fellow-humorist, Charles Dudley Warner, and such coherence as it had was weakened by the diverse qualities of their minds and their irreconcilable ideals in literature. These never combined to a sole effect or to any variety of effects that left the reader very clear what the story was all about; and yet from the cloudy solution was precipitated at least one character which, as I have said, seems of as lasting substance and lasting significance as any which the American imagination has evolved from the American environment.

If Colonel Sellers is Mr. Clemens's supreme invention, as it seems to me, I think that his *Connecticut Yankee* is his highest achievement in the way of a greatly imagined and symmetrically developed romance. Of all the fanciful schemes in fiction, it pleases me most, and I give myself with absolute delight to its notion of a keen East Hartford Yankee finding himself, by a retroactionary spell, at the court of King Arthur of Britain, and becoming part of the sixth century with all the customs and ideas of the nineteenth in him and about him. The field for humanizing satire which this scheme opens is illimitable; but the ultimate achievement, the last poignant touch, the most exquisite triumph of the book, is the return of the Yankee to his own century, with this look across the gulf of the ages at the period of which he had been a part and his vision of the sixth-century woman he had loved holding their child in her arms.

It is a great fancy, transcending in aesthetic beauty the invention in *The Prince and the Pauper*, with all the delightful and affecting implications of that charming fable, and excelling the heartrending story in which Joan of Arc lives and prophesies and triumphs and suffers. She is, indeed, realized to the modern sense as few figures of the past have been realized in fiction; and is none the less of her time and of all time because her supposititious historian is so recurrently of ours. After Sellers, and Huck Finn, and Tom Sawyer, and the Connecticut Yankee, she is the author's finest creation; and if he had succeeded in portraying no other woman-nature, he would have approved himself its fit interpreter in her. I do not think he succeeds so often with that nature as with the boy-nature or the man-nature, apparently because it does not interest him so much. He will not trouble himself to make women talk like women at all times; oftentimes they talk too much like him, though the simple, homely sort express themselves after their kind; and Mark Twain does not always write men's dialogue so well as he might. He is apt to burlesque the lighter colloquiality, and it is only in the more serious and most tragical junctures that his people utter themselves with veracious simplicity and dignity. That great, burly fancy of his is always tempting him to the exaggeration which is the condition of so much of his personal humor, but which when it invades the drama spoils the illusion. The illusion renews itself in the great moments, but I wish it could be kept intact in the small, and I blame him that he does not rule his fancy better. His imagination is always dramatic in its conceptions, but not always in its expressions; the talk of his people is often inadequate caricature in the ordinary exigencies, and his art contents itself with makeshift in the minor action. Even in *Huck Finn*, so admirably proportioned and honestly studied, you find a piece of lawless extravagance hurled in, like the episode of the two strolling actors in the flatboat; their broad burlesque is redeemed by their final tragedy—a prodigiously real and moving passage—but the friend of the book cannot help wishing the burlesque was not there. One laughs, and then despises one's self for laughing, and this is not what Mark Twain often makes you do. There are things in him that shock, and more things that we think shocking, but this may not be so much because of their nature as because of our want of naturalness; they wound our conventions rather than our convictions. As most women are more the subjects of convention than men, his humor is not for most women; but I have a theory that, when women like it, they like it far beyond men. Its very excess must satisfy that demand of their insatiate nerves for something that there is enough of; but I offer this conjecture with instant readiness to withdraw it under correction. What I feel rather surer of is that there is something finally feminine in the inconsequence of his ratiocination, and his beautiful confidence that we shall be able to follow him to his conclusion in all those turnings and twistings and leaps and bounds by which his mind carries itself to any point but that he seems aiming at. Men, in fact, are born of women, and possibly Mark Twain owes his literary method to the colloquial style of some far ancestress who was more concerned in getting there, and amusing herself on the way, than in ordering her steps.

Possibly, also, it is to this ancestress that he owes the instinct of right and wrong which keeps him clear as to the conditions that formed him, and their injustice. Slavery in a small Missouri River town could not have been the dignified and patriarchal institution which Southerners of the older South are fond of remembering or imagining. In the second generation from Virginia ancestry of this sort, Mark Twain was born to the common necessity of looking out for himself, and, while making himself practically of another order of things, he felt whatever was fine in the old and could regard whatever was ugly and absurd more tolerantly, more humorously than those who bequeathed him their enmity to it. Fortunately for him, and for us who were to enjoy his humor, he came to his intellectual consciousness in a world so large and free and safe that he could be fair to any wrong while seeing the right so unfailingly; and nothing is finer in him than his gentleness with the error which is simply passive and negative. He gets fun out of it, of course, but he deals almost tenderly with it, and hoards his violence for the superstitions and traditions which are arrogant and active. His pictures of that old river-town, Southwestern life, with its faded and tattered aristocratic ideals and its squalid democratic realities, are pathetic, while they are so unsparingly true and so inapologetically and unaffectedly faithful.

The West, when it began to put itself into literature, could do so without the sense, or the apparent sense, of any older or politer world outside of it; whereas the East was always looking fearfully over its shoulder at Europe, and anxious to account for itself as well as represent itself. No such anxiety as this entered Mark Twain's mind, and it is not claiming too much for the Western influence upon American literature to say that the final liberation of the East from this anxiety is due to the West, and to its ignorant courage or its indifference to its difference from the rest of the world. It would not claim to be superior, as the South did, but it could claim to be humanly equal, or, rather, it would make no claim at all, but would simply be, and what it was, show itself without holding itself responsible for not being something else.

The Western boy of forty or fifty years ago grew up so close to the primeval woods or fields that their inarticulate poetry became part of his being, and he was apt to deal simply and uncritically with literature when he turned to it, as he dealt with nature. He took what he wanted, and left what he did not like; he used it for the playground, not the workshop of his spirit. Something like this I find true of Mark Twain in peculiar and uncommon measure. I do not see any proof in his books that he wished at any time to produce literature, or that he wished to reproduce life. When filled up with an experience that deeply interested him, or when provoked by some injustice or absurdity that intensely moved him, he burst forth, and the outbreak might be altogether humorous, but it was more likely to be humorous with a groundswell of seriousness carrying it profoundly forward. In all there is something curiously, not very definably, elemental, which again seems to me Western. He behaves himself as if he were the first man who was ever up against the proposition in hand. He deals as newly, for instance, with the relations of Shelley to his wife, and with as personal and direct an indignation, as if they had never attracted critical attention before; and this is the mind or the mood which he brings to all literature. Life is another affair with him; it is not a discovery, not a surprise; every one else knows how it is; but here is a new world, and he explores it with a ramping joy, and shouts for the reader to come on and see how, in spite of all the lies about it, it is the same old world of men and women, with really nothing in it but their passions and prejudices and hypocrisies. At heart he was always deeply and essentially romantic, and once must have expected life itself to be a fairy dream. When it did not turn out so he found it tremendously amusing still, and his expectation not the least amusing thing in it, but without rancor, without grudge or bitterness in his disillusion, so that his latest word is as sweet as his first. He is deeply and essentially romantic in his literary conceptions, but when it comes to working them out he is helplessly literal and real; he is the impassioned lover, the helpless slave of the concrete. For this reason, for his wish, his necessity, first to ascertain his facts, his logic is as irresistible as his laugh.

All life seems, when he began to find it out, to have the look of a vast joke, whether the joke was on him or on his fellow-beings, or if it may be expressed without irreverence, on their common creator. But it was never wholly a joke, and it was not long before his literature began to own its pathos. The sense of this is not very apparent in *The Innocents Abroad*, but in *Roughing It* we began to be distinctly aware of it, and in the successive books it is constantly imminent, not as a clutch at the heartstrings, but as a demand of common justice, common sense, the feeling of proportion. It is not sympathy with the under dog merely as under dog that moves Mark Twain; for the under dog is sometimes rightfully under. But the probability is that it is wrongfully under, and has a claim to your inquiry into the case which you cannot ignore without atrocity. Mark Twain never ignores it; I know nothing finer in him than his perception that in this curiously contrived mechanism men suffer for their sorrows rather oftener than they suffer for their sins; and when they suffer for their sorrows they have a right not only to our pity but to our help. He always gives his help, even when he seems to leave the pity to others, and it may be safely said that no writer has dealt with so many phases of life with more unfailing justice. There is no real telling how any one comes to be what he is; all speculation concerning the fact is more or less impudent or futile conjecture; but it is conceivable that Mark Twain took from his early environment the custom of clairvoyance in things in which most humorists are purblind, and that being always in the presence of the under dog, he came to feel for him as under with him. If the knowledge and vision of slavery did not tinge all life with potential tragedy, perhaps it was this which lighted in the future humorist the indignation at injustice which glows in his page. His indignation relieves itself as often as not in a laugh; injustice is the most ridiculous thing in the world, after all, and indignation with it feels its own absurdity.

It is supposable, if not more than supposable, that the ludicrous incongruity of a slaveholding democracy nurtured upon the Declaration of Independence, and the comical spectacle of white labor owning black labor, had something to do in quickening the sense of contrast which is the fountain of humor, or is said to be so. But not to drive too hard a conjecture which must remain conjecture, we may reasonably hope to find in the untrammelled, the almost unconditional life of the later and farther West, with its individualism limited by nothing but individualism, the outside causes of the first overflow of the spring. We are so fond of classification, which we think is somehow interpretation, that one cannot resist the temptation it holds out in the case of the most unclassifiable things; and I must yield so far as to note that the earliest form of Mark Twain's work is characteristic of the greater part of it. The method used in *The Innocents Abroad* and in *Roughing It* is the method used in *Life on the Mississippi*, in *A Tramp Abroad*, and in *Following the Equator*, which constitute in bulk a good half of all his writings, as they express his dominant aesthetics. If he had written the fictions alone, we should have had to recognize a rare inventive talent, a great imagination and dramatic force; but I think it must be allowed that the personal books named overshadow the fictions. They have the qualities that give character to the fictions, and they have advantages that the fictions have not and that no fiction can have. In them, under cover of his pseudonym, we come directly into the presence of the author, which is what the reader is always longing and seeking to do; but unless the novelist is a conscienceless and tasteless recreant to the terms of his art, he cannot admit the reader to his intimacy. The personal books of Mark Twain have not only the charm of the essay's inconsequent and desultory method, in which invention, fact, reflection, and philosophy wander after one another in any following that happens, but they are of an immediate and most informal hospitality which admits you at once to the author's confidence, and makes you frankly welcome not only to his thought but to his way of thinking. He takes no trouble in the matter, and he asks you to take none. All that he requires is that you will have common sense, and be able to tell a joke when you see it. Otherwise the whole furnishing of his mental mansion is at your service, to make such use as you can of it, but he will not be always directing your course, or requiring you to enjoy yourself in this or that order. In the case of the fictions, he conceives that his first affair is to tell a story, and a story when you are once launched upon it does not admit of deviation without some hurt to itself. In Mark Twain's novels, whether they are for boys or for men, the episodes are only those that illustrate the main narrative or relate to it, though he might have allowed himself somewhat larger latitude in the old-fashioned tradition which he had oftenest observed in them. When it comes to the critical writings, which again are personal, and which, whether they are criticisms of literature or of life, are always so striking, he is quite relentlessly logical and coherent. Here there is no lounging or sauntering, with entertaining or edifying digressions. The object is in view from the first, and the reasoning is straightforwardly to it throughout. This is as notable in the admirable paper on the Jews, or on the Austrian situation, as in that on Harriet Shelley, or that on Cooper's novels. The facts are first ascertained with a conscience uncommon in critical writing of any kind, and then they are handled with vigor and precision till the polemic is over. It does not so much matter whether you agree with the critic or not; what you have to own is that here is a man of strong convictions, clear ideas, and ardent sentiments, based mainly upon common sense of extraordinary depth and breadth.

In fact, what finally appeals to you in Mark Twain, and what may hereafter be his peril with his readers, is his common sense. It is well to eat humble pie when one comes to it at the table d'hôte of life, and I wish here to offer my brother literary men a piece of it that I never refuse myself. It is true that other men do not really expect much common sense of us, whether we are poets or novelists or humorists. They may enjoy our company, and they may like us or pity us, but they do not take us very seriously, and they would as soon we were fools as not if we will only divert or comfort or inspire them. Especially if we are humorists do they doubt our practical wisdom; they are apt at first sight to take our sense for a part of the joke, and the humorist who convinces them that he is a man of as much sense as any of them, and possibly more, is in the parlous case of having given them hostages for seriousness which he may not finally be able to redeem.

I should say in the haste to which every inquiry of this sort seems subject, that this was precisely the case with Mark Twain.

The exceptional observer must have known from the beginning that he was a thinker of courageous originality and penetrating sagacity, even when he seemed to be joking; but in the process of time it has come to such a pass with him that the wayfaring man can hardly shirk knowledge of the fact. The fact is thrown into sudden and picturesque relief by his return to his country after the lapse of time long enough to have let a new generation grow up in knowledge of him. The projection of his reputation against a background of foreign appreciation, more or less luminous, such as no other American author has enjoyed, has little or nothing to do with his acceptance on the new terms. Those poor Germans, Austrians, Englishmen, and Frenchmen who have been, from time to time in the last ten years, trying to show their esteem for his peculiar gifts could never come as close to the heart of his humor as we could; we might well doubt if they could fathom all his wisdom, which begins and ends in his humor; and if ever they seemed to chance upon his full significance, we naturally felt a kind of grudge, when we could not call it their luck, and suspected him of being less significant in the given instances than they supposed. The danger which he now runs with us is neither heightened nor lessened by the spread of his fame, but is an effect from intrinsic causes. Possibly it might not have been so great if he had come back comparatively forgotten; it is certain only that in coming back more remembered than ever, he confronts a generation which began to know him not merely by his personal books and his fiction, but by those criticisms of life and literature which have more recently attested his interest in the graver and weightier things.

Graver and weightier, people call them, but whether they are really more important than the lighter things, I am by no means sure. What I am amused with, independently of the final truth, is the possibility that his newer audience will exact this serious mood of Mr. Clemens, whereas we of his older world only suffered it, and were of a high conceit with our liberality in allowing a humorist sometimes to be a philosopher. Some of us indeed, not to be invidiously specific as to whom, were always aware of potentialities in him, which he seemed to hold in check, or to trust doubtfully to his reader, as if he thought they might be thought part of the joke. Looking back over his work now, the later reader would probably be able to point out to earlier readers the evidence of a constant growth in the direction of something like recognized authority in matters of public import, especially those that were subject to the action of the public conscience as well as the public interest, until now hardly any man writing upon such matters is heard so willingly by all sorts of men. All of us, for instance, have read somewhat of the conditions in South Africa which have eventuated in the present effort of certain British politicians to destroy two free republics in the interest of certain British speculators; but I doubt if we have found the case anywhere so well stated as in the closing chapters of Mark Twain's *Following the Equator*. His estimate of the military character of the belligerents on either side is of the prophetic cast which can come only from the thorough assimilation of accomplished facts; and in those passages the student of the actual war can spell its anticipative history. It is by such handling of such questions, unpremeditated and almost casual as it seems, that Mark Twain has won his claim to be heard on any public matter, and achieved the odd sort of primacy which he now enjoys.

But it would be rather awful if the general recognition of his prophetic function should implicate the renunciation of the humor that has endeared him to mankind. It would be well for his younger following to beware of reversing the error of the elder, and taking everything in earnest, as these once took nothing in earnest from him. To reverse that error would not be always to find his true meaning, and perhaps we shall best arrive at this by shunning one another's mistakes. In the light of the more modern appreciation, we elders may be able to see some things seriously that we once thought pure drolling, and from our experience his younger admirers may learn to receive as drolling some things that they might otherwise accept as preaching. What we all should wish to do is to keep Mark Twain what he has always been: a comic force unique in the power of charming us out of our cares and troubles, united with as potent an ethic sense of the duties, public and private, which no man denies in himself without being false to other men. I think we may hope for the best he can do to help us deserve our self-respect, without forming Mark Twain societies to read philanthropic meanings into his jokes, or studying the Jumping Frog as the allegory of an imperializing republic. I trust the time may be far distant when the Meditation at the Tomb of Adam shall be memorized and declaimed by ingenuous youth as a mystical appeal for human solidarity.

IV. Henry James:
The Varieties of Experience

Like his contemporaries, William Dean Howells and Mark Twain, Henry James (1843-1916) identified the romance with pre-Civil War America, realism with the new postwar generation to which he belonged. A major theme in the critical biography of Nathaniel Hawthorne (1879) is the limiting provinciality of the world Hawthorne knew. James, in effect, reverses Howells' attack upon the romance. It is not that the false morality or inflated ideals of the romance misled Americans, but rather that the slender social opportunities of American society forced even the most creative of American authors into the vapid, idealized formulas the romance offered. James is less forgiving of his subject than Howells who, in *Criticism and Fiction*, suggests that Hawthorne's best works were "strictly speaking, novels rather than romances." To James it seemed that a novel could not be written by so inexperienced a man, one who lived out his creative life in Salem and Concord, with an occasional summer in the Berkshires. It requires, James asserts, "such an accumulation of history and custom, such a complexity of manners and types, to form a fund of suggestion for the novelist." Critics have found his rolling catalogue of the missing elements in American life unforgettable: "No sovereign, no court, no personal loyalty, no aristocracy, no church . . . no Oxford, nor Eton, nor Harrow; no literature, no novels, no museums, no pictures, no political society, no sporting class—no Epsom nor Ascot!" and so on. Without such materials, even the most perceptive writer cannot, James suggests, bring a novel into being. It is not enough to say that, for James, the novel is the "novel of manners." His own practice went far beyond such traditional limits. He is, in fact, sometimes called a "psychological realist"—an awkward term which nonetheless implies his concern with the private, inner life as opposed to institutional reality. But the *knowledgeability* of the writer was, to him, always important. Upon various occasions, as a critic, he wondered how Balzac and Zola, chained to the schedule of their enormous productions and researches, came to know "life." Hawthorne, however, had no opportunities. Like other Americans of his generation, he was "simple and uncritical" because he had seen so little of the world. The "new American" of James' own generation had, at least, experienced the national tragedy of Civil War. He would be a "realist," James felt, because his simple and patriotic optimism had been shattered. Having learned the lesson of uncalculated "eventualities," he would be "more critical" and "an observer" of a newly complex society.

Given such early sentiments it is not surprising that James soon became (like T. S. Eliot in a later generation) a "Transatlantic" American. Yet his fiction always had an American audience. Indeed, an early novelette, *Daisy Miller* (1879), inspired a momentarily popular expression, "Daisy Millerism," to describe the mannerless, apparently ambitious, American girl. Most of James' American characters, however, seem removed from the actualities of this business culture. They are well-to-do, free to travel abroad, separated by thousands of well-invested dollars from the economic burdens Howells described in his portraits of the contemporary middle class, and even further removed, by wealth and experience, from the small-town Middle Western life that Twain portrayed. It is significant that James' one venture into the "social novel," *The Princess Casamassima* (1886), is set in London and treats the life of English poor.

James' criticism, too, was largely concerned with European movements, especially the development of the novel in nineteenth-century France. Like Balzac, Flaubert, and Zola, he understood the novel as a serious effort to capture the essence of life and contemporary society. A pamphlet urging amusement in fiction by the Englishman, Walter Besant, inspired James' essay "The Art of Fiction" (1884).

In this defense of serious fiction, James is most concerned with defining the importance of the artist, his unique imagination and intelligence, in the creation of the novel. His vision of the "true" or "real" is far more liberal than that of most realists. He is not limited by any version of Howells' formula that "truth" resides in "human nature, known to us all." The "commonplace," as Howells or Twain employed it, is equally foreign to James' theory. He also avoids the semistatistical interest in the "facts" that characterized the work of Balzac and Zola. For James, the novelist's "truth" is simply "what he assumes, the premises that we must grant him, whatever they may be." Each observer has to offer his own record of his observations. It may be that there is a universal human nature. Certainly, James does not deny it, but he suggests that if such a universal nature exists, it is too broad and undefined to provide meaningful limits for the writer of fiction:

> Humanity is immense, and reality has myriad forms; the most one can affirm is that some of the flowers of fiction have the odour of it and others have not . . . It is equally excellent and inconclusive to say that one must write from experience . . . Experience is never limited, and it is never complete . . . It is the very atmosphere of the mind . . .

The word "experience" is crucial, for it emphasizes the function of the experiencing individual. Facts may be compiled by statisticians and confirmed, checked, and rechecked by elegant machines. But experience is the wholly human record of things we have known. Thus the center of the novel is not "reality" but "realization," first in the artist and then in his *dramatis personae*.

The critic should not accordingly judge the facts with which the writer begins, but only his execution. It is not, for example, the *data* of Balzac's novels that James admires (these records of francs and centimes he wryly attributes to "the spirit of edification" in their author), but rather the "infinite reach in him of the painter and the poet" which imaginatively gives such dull facts life. And the facts themselves are no sufficient basis for the artist. What is great in Balzac is "his unequalled power of putting people on their feet, planting them before us in their habit as they lived—a faculty nourished by observation as much as one will, but with the inner vision all the while wide-awake, the vision for which ideas are as living as facts and assume an equal intensity." As a novelist, this is James' achievement also: the presentation of ideas as "living," in fact more alive, than all the facts of finance, furnishing, or social conditions which most realists understood as necessary to their art.

So opposed is James to the realistic fondness for reportage and the commonplace situation that both his fiction and his criticism might seem to fall outside of the realistic tradition. His work, especially his interest in evoking "the spirit of the place," might be called impressionistic. But his comments on the art of fiction belong to the debate on realism because he is intelligently concerned with "the sense of life" and the record of an understanding observer of human nature. He wisely corrects both realistic and naturalistic theorists who seem to value accuracy more than the artistic imitation of life. The practice of the novelist's art which James proposes is more complex than that based on social purpose or the need for verisimilitude. It also forces the writer to recognize his function as the observer who interprets the life he describes. In his preface to *The Portrait of A Lady* (1881) written for the New York edition of his works (1907-09) James metaphorically described his view of the writer's relation to "reality":

> The house of fiction has . . . not one window, but a million—a number of possible windows not to be reckoned, rather; every one of which has been pierced, or is still pierceable, in its vast front, by the need of the individual vision and by the pressure of the individual will. These apertures, of dissimilar shape and size, hang so, all together, over the human scene that we might have expected of them a greater sameness of report than we find. They are but windows at the best, mere holes in a dead wall, disconnected, perched aloft; they are not hinged doors opening straight upon life. But they have this mark of their own that at each of them stands a figure with a pair of eyes, or at least with a field-glass, which forms, again and again, for observation, a unique instrument, insuring to the person making use of it an impression distinct from every other. He and his neighbours are watching the same show, but one seeing more where the other sees less, one seeing black where the other sees white, one seeing big where the other sees small, one seeing coarse where the other sees fine. And so on, and so on; there is fortunately no saying on what, for the particular pair of eyes, the window may *not* open; "fortunately" by reason, precisely, of this incalculability of range. The spreading field, the human scene, is the "choice of subject"; the pierced aperture, either broad or balanced or slit-like and low-browed, is the "literary form"; but they are, singly or together, as nothing without the posted presence of the

watcher—without, in other words, the consciousness of the artist. Tell me what the artist is, and I will tell you of what he has *been* conscious. Thereby I shall express to you at once his boundless freedom and his "moral" reference.

During the many years he lived abroad, James became, to many of his contemporaries, more English—or European—than American. In the literary journal of his American tour of 1904, *The American Scene* (1907), he himself claims that he returned as an "inquiring stranger" to his native land. The memoir by Edith Wharton (1862-1937)—who was, more than any other turn-of-the-century American author, James' disciple—places him in his American context. Though he lived well into the era when this country became an urban industrial power, he belonged to an earlier period in the nation's history, the "old America" of Mrs. Wharton's own youth in the 1860's and 1870's, the New England culture of Boston and Cambridge, and the close-knit family he celebrated in his anecdotes of the "Emmetry." Like William Dean Howells and Mark Twain, the America of which James wrote was, by the end of the nineteenth century, past or passing. His theory of fiction, more than theirs, made that past current and universal.

Selections

13. ON NATHANIEL HAWTHORNE*

. . . I know not at what age he began to keep a diary; the first entries in the American volumes are of the summer of 1835. There is a phrase in the preface to his novel of *Transformation*, which must have lingered in the minds of many Americans who have tried to write novels and to lay the scene of them in the western world. "No author, without a trial, can conceive of the difficulty of writing a romance about a country where there is no shadow, no antiquity, no mystery, no picturesque and gloomy wrong, nor anything but a commonplace prosperity, in broad and simple daylight, as is happily the case with my dear native land." The perusal of Hawthorne's American *Note-Books* operates as a practical commentary upon this somewhat ominous text. It does so at least to my own mind; it would be too much perhaps to say that the effect would be the same for the usual English reader. An American reads between the lines—he completes the suggestions—he constructs a picture. I think I am not guilty of any gross injustice in saying that the picture he constructs from Hawthorne's American diaries, though by no means without charms of its own, is not, on the whole, an interesting one. It is characterized by an extraordinary blankness—a curious paleness of color and paucity of detail. Hawthorne, as I have said, has a large and healthy appetite for detail, and one is therefore the more struck with the lightness of the diet to which his observation was condemned. For myself, as I turn the pages of his journals, I seem to see the image of the crude and simple society in which he lived. I use these epithets, of course, not invidiously, but descriptively; if one desire to enter as closely as possible into Hawthorne's situation, one must endeavor to reproduce his circumstances. We are struck with the large number of elements

* The selection is taken from *Hawthorne* by Henry James (1880, 1879).

that were absent from them, and the coldness, the thinness, the blankness, to repeat my epithet, present themselves so vividly that our foremost feeling is that of compassion for a romancer looking for subjects in such a field. It takes so many things, as Hawthorne must have felt later in life, when he made the acquaintance of the denser, richer, warmer European spectacle—it takes such an accumulation of history and custom, such a complexity of manners and types, to form a fund of suggestion for a novelist. If Hawthorne had been a young Englishman, or a young Frenchman of the same degree of genius, the same cast of mind, the same habits, his consciousness of the world around him would have been a very different affair; however obscure, however reserved, his own personal life, his sense of the life of his fellow-mortals would have been almost infinitely more various. The negative side of the spectacle on which Hawthorne looked out, in his contemplative saunterings and reveries, might, indeed, with a little ingenuity, be made almost ludicrous; one might enumerate the items of high civilization, as it exists in other countries, which are absent from the texture of American life, until it should become a wonder to know what was left. No State, in the European sense of the word, and indeed barely a specific national name. No sovereign, no court, no personal loyalty, no aristocracy, no church, no clergy, no army, no diplomatic service, no country gentlemen, no palaces, no castles, nor manors, nor old country houses, nor parsonages, nor thatched cottages, nor ivied ruins; no cathedrals, nor abbeys, nor little Norman churches; no great universities nor public schools—no Oxford, nor Eton, nor Harrow; no literature, no novels, no museums, no pictures, no political society, no sporting class—no Epsom nor Ascot! Some such list as that might be drawn up of the absent things in American life—especially in the American life of forty years ago, the effect of which, upon an English or a French imagination, would probably as a general thing be appalling. The natural remark, in the almost lurid light of such an indictment, would be that if these things are left out, everything is left out. The American knows that a good deal remains; what it is that remains—that is his secret, his joke, as one may say. It would be cruel, in this terrible denudation, to deny him the consolation of his national gift, that "American humor" of which of late years we have heard so much.

But in helping us to measure what remains, our author's

diaries, as I have already intimated, would give comfort rather
to persons who might have taken the alarm from the brief
sketch I have just attempted of what I have called the negative
side of the American social situation, than do those reminding
themselves of its fine compensations. Hawthorne's entries are to
a great degree accounts of walks in the country, drives in
stage-coaches, people he met in taverns. The minuteness of the
things that attract his attention and that he deems worthy of
being commemorated is frequently extreme, and from this fact
we get the impression of a general vacancy in the field of vision.
"Sunday evening, going by the jail, the setting sun kindled up
the windows most cheerfully; as if there were a bright, comfortable light within its darksome stone wall." "I went yesterday with Monsieur S—— to pick raspberries. He fell through an
old log bridge, thrown over a hollow; looking back, only his
head and shoulders appeared through the rotten logs and among
the bushes.—A shower coming on, the rapid running of a little
barefooted boy, coming up unheard, and dashing swiftly past
us, and showing us the soles of his naked feet as he ran down
the path and up the opposite side." In another place he devotes
a page to a description of a dog whom he saw running round
after its tail; in still another he remarks, in a paragraph by
itself—"The aromatic odor of peat-smoke in the sunny autum-
nal air is very pleasant." The reader says to himself that when a
man turned thirty gives a place in his mind—and his inkstand—
to such trifles as these, it is because nothing else of superior
importance demands admission. Everything in the notes indicates a simple, democratic, thinly-composed society; there is no
evidence of the writer finding himself in any variety or intimacy
of relations with anyone or with anything. We find a good deal
of warrant for believing that if we add that statement of Mr.
Lathrop's about his meals being left at the door of his room, to
rural rambles of which an impression of the temporary phases
of the local apple-crop were the usual, and an encounter with an
organ-grinder, or an eccentric dog, the rarer, outcome, we
construct a rough image of our author's daily life during the
several years that preceded his marriage. He appears to have
read a good deal, and that he must have been familiar with the
sources of good English we see from his charming, expressive,
slightly self-conscious, cultivated, but not too cultivated, style.
Yet neither in these early volumes of his *Note-Books* nor in the

later is there any mention of his reading. There are no literary judgments or impressions—there is almost no allusion to works or to authors. The allusions to individuals of any kind are indeed much less numerous than one might have expected; there is little psychology, little description of manners. . . .

The House of the Seven Gables was written at Lenox, among the mountains of Massachusetts, a village nestling, rather loosely, in one of the loveliest corners of New England, to which Hawthorne had betaken himself after the success of *The Scarlet Letter* became conspicuous, in the summer of 1850, and where he occupied for two years an uncomfortable little red house which is now pointed out to the inquiring stranger. The inquiring stranger is now a frequent figure at Lenox, for the place has suffered the process of lionization. It has become a prosperous watering-place, or at least (as there are no waters), as they say in America, a summer resort. It is a brilliant and generous landscape, and thirty years ago a man of fancy, desiring to apply himself, might have found both inspiration and tranquillity there. Hawthorne found so much of both that he wrote more during his two years of residence at Lenox than at any period of his career. He began with *The House of the Seven Gables*, which was finished in the early part of 1851. This is the longest of his three American novels, it is the most elaborate, and in the judgment of some persons it is the finest. It is a rich, delightful, imaginative work, larger and more various than its companions, and full of all sorts of deep intentions, of interwoven threads of suggestion. But it is not so rounded and complete as *The Scarlet Letter*; it has always seemed to me more like a prologue to a great novel than a great novel itself. I think this is partly owing to the fact that the subject, the *donnée*, as the French say, of the story, does not quite fill it out, and that we get at the same time an impression of certain complicated purposes on the author's part, which seem to reach beyond it. I call it larger and more various than its companions, and it has indeed a greater richness of tone and density of detail. The color, so to speak, of *The House of the Seven Gables* is admirable. But the story has a sort of expansive quality which never wholly fructifies, and as I lately laid it down, after reading it for the third time, I had a sense of having interested myself in a magnificent fragment. Yet the book has a great fascination, and of all of those of its author's productions which I have read over while writing this sketch, it is perhaps the one that has gained most by re-perusal. If it be true of the others that the pure, natural quality of the imaginative strain is their great merit, this is at least as true of *The House of the Seven Gables*, the charm of which is in a peculiar degree of the kind that we fail to reduce to its grounds—like that of the sweetness of a piece of music, or the softness of fine September weather. It is vague, indefinable, ineffable; but it is the sort of thing we must always point to in justification of the high claim that we make for Hawthorne. In this case, of course, its vagueness is a drawback, for it is difficult to point to ethereal beauties; and if the reader whom we have wished to inoculate with our admiration inform us after looking a while that he perceives nothing in particular, we can only reply that, in effect, the object is a delicate one.

The House of the Seven Gables comes nearer being a picture of contemporary American life than either of its companions; but on this ground it would be a mistake to make a large claim for it. It cannot be too often repeated that Hawthorne was not a realist. He had a high sense of reality—his *Note-Books* superabundantly testify to it; and fond as he was of jotting down the items that make it up, he never attempted to render exactly or closely the actual facts of the society that surrounded him. I have said—I began by saying—that his pages were full of its spirit, and of a certain reflected light that springs from it; but I was careful to add that the reader must look for his local and national quality between the lines of his writing and in the *indirect* testimony of his tone, his accent, his temper, of his very omissions and suppressions. *The House of the Seven Gables* has, however, more literal actuality than the others, and if it were not too fanciful an account of it, I should say that it renders, to an initiated reader, the impression of a summer afternoon in an elm-shadowed New England town. It leaves upon the mind a vague correspondence to some such reminiscence, and in stirring up the association it renders it delightful. The comparison is to the honor of the New England town, which gains in it more than it bestows. The shadows of the elms, in *The House of the Seven Gables*, are exceptionally dense and cool; the summer afternoon is peculiarly still and beautiful; the atmosphere has a delicious warmth, and the long daylight seems to pause and rest. But the mild provincial quality is there,

the mixture of shabbiness and freshness, the paucity of ingredients. The end of an old race—this is the situation that
Hawthorne has depicted, and he has been admirably inspired in
the choice of the figures in whom he seeks to interest us. They
are all figures rather than characters—they are all pictures rather
than persons. But if their reality is light and vague, it is
sufficient, and it is in harmony with the low relief and dimness
of outline of the objects that surround them. They are all types,
to the author's mind, of something general, of something that is
bound up with the history, at large, of families and individuals,
and each of them is the center of a cluster of those ingenious
and meditative musings, rather melancholy, as a general thing,
than joyous, which melt into the current and texture of the
story and give it a kind of moral richness. A grotesque old
spinster, simple, childish, penniless, very humble at heart, but
rigidly conscious of her pedigree; an amiable bachelor, of an
epicurean temperament and an enfeebled intellect, who has
passed twenty years of his life in penal confinement for a crime
of which he was unjustly pronounced guilty; a sweet-natured
and bright-faced young girl from the country, a poor relation of
these two ancient decrepitudes, with whose moral mustiness her
modern freshness and soundness are contrasted; a young man
still more modern, holding the latest opinions, who has sought
his fortune up and down the world, and, though he has not
found it, takes a genial and enthusiastic view of the future:
these, with two or three remarkable accessory figures, are the
persons concerned in the little drama. The drama is a small one,
but as Hawthorne does not put it before us for its own
superficial sake, for the dry facts of the case, but for something
in it which he holds to be symbolic and of large application,
something that points a moral and that it behooves us to
remember, the scenes in the rusty wooden house whose gables
give its name to the story, have something of the dignity both
of history and of tragedy. Miss Hepzibah Pyncheon, dragging
out a disappointed life in her paternal dwelling, finds herself
obliged in her old age to open a little shop for the sale of penny
toys and gingerbread. This is the central incident of the tale,
and, as Hawthorne relates it, it is an incident of the most
impressive magnitude and most touching interest. Her dishon-
ored and vague-minded brother is released from prison at the
same moment, and returns to the ancestral roof to deepen her
perplexities. But, on the other hand, to alleviate them, and to

introduce a breath of the air of the outer world into this
long-unventilated interior, the little country cousin also arrives,
and proves the good angel of the feebly distracted household.
All this episode is exquisite—admirably conceived, and executed
with a kind of humorous tenderness, an equal sense of everything in it that is picturesque, touching, ridiculous, worthy of
the highest praise. Hepzibah Pyncheon, with her near-sighted
scowl, her rusty joints, her antique turban, her map of a great
territory to the eastward which ought to have belonged to her
family, her vain terrors and scruples and resentments, the
inaptitude and repugnance of an ancient gentlewoman to the
vulgar little commerce which a cruel fate has compelled her to
engage in—Hepzibah Pyncheon is a masterly picture. I repeat
that she is a picture, as her companions are pictures; she is a
charming piece of descriptive writing, rather than a dramatic
exhibition. But she is described, like her companions, too, so
subtly and lovingly that we enter into her virginal old heart and
stand with her behind her abominable little counter. Clifford
Pyncheon is a still more remarkable conception, though he is
perhaps not so vividly depicted. It was a figure needing a much
more subtle touch, however, and it was of the essence of his
character to be vague and unemphasized. Nothing can be more
charming than the manner in which the soft, bright, active
presence of Phoebe Pyncheon is indicated, or than the account
of her relations with the poor dimly-sentient kinsman for whom
her light-handed sisterly offices, in the evening of a melancholy
life, are a revelation of lost possibilities of happiness. "In her
aspect," Hawthorne says of the young girl, "there was a familiar
gladness, and a holiness that you could play with, and yet
reverence it as much as ever. She was like a prayer offered up in
the homeliest beauty of one's mother tongue. Fresh was
Phoebe, moreover, and airy, and sweet in her apparel; as if
nothing that she wore—neither her gown, nor her small straw
bonnet, nor her little kerchief, any more than her snowy
stockings—had ever been put on before; or if worn, were all the
fresher for it, and with a fragrance as if they had lain among the
rosebuds." Of the influence of her maidenly salubrity upon
poor Clifford, Hawthorne gives the prettiest description, and
then, breaking off suddenly, renounces the attempt in language
which, while pleading its inadequacy, conveys an exquisite
satisfaction to the reader. I quote the passage for the sake of its

extreme felicity, and of the charming image with which it concludes.

But we strive in vain to put the idea into words. No adequate expression of the beauty and profound pathos with which it impresses us is attainable. This being, made only for happiness, and heretofore so miserably failing to be happy—his tendencies so hideously thwarted that some unknown time ago, the delicate springs of his character, never morally or intellectually strong, had given way, and he was now imbecile—this poor forlorn voyager from the Islands of the Blest, in a frail bark, on a tempestuous sea, had been flung by the last mountain-wave of his shipwreck into a quiet harbor. There, as he lay more than half lifeless on the strand, the fragrance of an earthly rose-bud had come to his nostrils, and, as odors will, had summoned up reminiscences or visions of all the living and breathing beauty amid which he should have had his home. With his native susceptibility of happy influences, he inhales the slight ethereal rapture into his soul, and expires!

I have not mentioned the personage in *The House of the Seven Gables* upon whom Hawthorne evidently bestowed most pains, and whose portrait is the most elaborate in the book; partly because he is, in spite of the space he occupies, an accessory figure, and partly because, even more than the others, he is what I have called a picture rather than a character. Judge Pyncheon is an ironical portrait, very richly and broadly executed, very sagaciously composed and rendered—the portrait of a superb, full-blown hypocrite, a large-based, full-nurtured Pharisee, bland, urbane, impressive, diffusing about him a "sultry" warmth of benevolence, as the author calls it again and again, and basking in the noontide of prosperity and the consideration of society; but in reality hard, gross, and ignoble. Judge Pyncheon is an elaborate piece of description, made up of a hundred admirable touches, in which satire is always winged with fancy, and fancy is linked with a deep sense of reality. It is difficult to say whether Hawthorne followed a model in describing Judge Pyncheon; but it is tolerably obvious that the picture is an impression—a copious impression—of an individual. It has evidently a definite starting-point in fact, and the author is able to draw, freely and confidently, after the image established in his mind. Holgrave, the modern young man, who has been a Jack-of-all-trades and is at the period of the story a daguerreotypist, is an attempt to render a kind of national type—that of the young citizen of the United States whose fortune is simply in his lively intelligence, and who stands naked, as it were, unbiased and unencumbered alike, in the center of the far-stretching level of American life. Holgrave is intended as a contrast; his lack of traditions, his democratic stamp, his condensed experience, are opposed to the desiccated prejudices and exhausted vitality of the race of which poor feebly-scowling, rusty-jointed Hepzibah is the most heroic representative. It is perhaps a pity that Hawthorne should not have proposed to himself to give the old Pyncheon qualities some embodiment which would help them to balance more fairly with the elastic properties of the young daguerreotypist—should not have painted a lusty conservative to match his strenuous radical. As it is, the mustiness and moldiness of the tenants of the House of the Seven Gables crumble away rather too easily. Evidently, however, what Hawthorne designed to represent was not the struggle between an old society and a new, for in this case he would have given the old one a better chance; but simply, as I have said, the shrinkage and extinction of a family. This appealed to his imagination; and the idea of long perpetuation and survival always appears to have filled him with a kind of horror and disapproval. Conservative, in a certain degree, as he was himself, and fond of retrospect and quietude and the mellowing influences of time, it is singular how often one encounters in his writings some expression of mistrust of old houses, old institutions, long lines of descent. He was disposed apparently to allow a very moderate measure in these respects, and he condemns the dwelling of the Pyncheons to disappear from the face of the earth because it has been standing a couple of hundred years. In this he was an American of Americans; or rather he was more American than many of his countrymen, who, though they are accustomed to work for the short run rather than the long, have often a lurking esteem for things that show the marks of having lasted. I will add that Holgrave is one of the few figures, among those which Hawthorne created, with regard to which the absence of the realistic mode of treatment is felt as a loss. Holgrave is not sharply enough characterized; he lacks features; he is not an individual, but a type. But my last word about this admirable novel must not be a restrictive one. It is a large and generous production, pervaded with that vague hum, that indefinable echo, of the whole multitudinous life of man, which is the real sign of a great work of fiction. . . .

Insofar, however, as Hawthorne suffered the penalties of celebrity at the hands of intrusive fellow-citizens, he was soon to escape from this honorable incommodity. On the fourth of March, 1853, his old college-mate and intimate friend, Franklin Pierce, was installed as President of the United States. He had been the candidate of the Democratic party, and all good Democrats, accordingly, in conformity to the beautiful and rational system under which the affairs of the great Republic were carried on, began to open their windows to the golden sunshine of Presidential patronage. When General Pierce was put forward by the Democrats, Hawthorne felt a perfectly loyal and natural desire that his good friend should be exalted to so brilliant a position, and he did what was in him to further the good cause, by writing a little book about its hero. His *Life of Franklin Pierce* belongs to that class of literature which is known as the "campaign biography," and which consists of an attempt, more or less successful, to persuade the many-headed monster of universal suffrage that the gentleman on whose behalf it is addressed is a paragon of wisdom and virtue. Of Hawthorne's little book there is nothing particular to say, save that it is in very good taste, that he is a very fairly ingenious advocate, and that if he claimed for the future President qualities which rather faded in the bright light of a high office, this defect of proportion was essential to his undertaking. He dwelt chiefly upon General Pierce's exploits in the war with Mexico (before that, his record, as they say in America, had been mainly that of a successful country lawyer), and exercised his descriptive powers so far as was possible in describing the advance of the United States troops from Vera Cruz to the city of the Montezumas. The mouthpieces of the Whig party spared him, I believe, no reprobation for "prostituting" his exquisite genius; but I fail to see anything reprehensible in Hawthorne's lending his old friend the assistance of his graceful quill. He wished him to be President—he held afterwards that he filled the office with admirable dignity and wisdom—and as the only thing he could do was to write, he fell to work and wrote for him. Hawthorne was a good lover and a very sufficient partisan, and I suspect that if Franklin Pierce had been made even less of the stuff of a statesman, he would still have found in the force of old associations an injunction to hail him as a ruler. Our hero was an American of the earlier and simpler type—the type of which it is doubtless premature to say that it has wholly passed away, but of which it may at least be said that the circumstances that produced it have been greatly modified. The generation to which he belonged, that generation which grew up with the century, witnessed during a period of fifty years the immense, uninterrupted material development of the young Republic; and when one thinks of the scale on which it took place, of the prosperity that walked in its train and waited on its course, of the hopes it fostered and the blessings it conferred, of the broad morning sunshine, in a word, in which it all went forward, there seems to be little room for surprise that it should have implanted a kind of superstitious faith in the grandeur of the country, its duration, its immunity from the usual troubles of earthly empires. This faith was a simple and uncritical one, enlivened with an element of genial optimism, in the light of which it appeared that the great American state was not as other human institutions are, that a special Providence watched over it, that it would go on joyously forever, and that a country whose vast and blooming bosom offered a refuge to the strugglers and seekers of all the rest of the world, must come off easily, in the battle of the ages. From this conception of the American future the sense of its having problems to solve was blissfully absent; there were no difficulties in the program, no looming complications, no rocks ahead. The indefinite multiplication of the population, and its enjoyment of the benefits of a common-school education and of unusual facilities for making an income—this was the form in which, on the whole, the future most vividly presented itself, and in which the greatness of the country was to be recognized of men. There was indeed a faint shadow in the picture—the shadow projected by the "peculiar institution" of the Southern states; but it was far from sufficient to darken the rosy vision of most good Americans, and, above all, of most good Democrats. Hawthorne alludes to it in a passage of his life of Pierce, which I will quote not only as a hint of the trouble that was in store for a cheerful race of men, but as an example of his own easy-going political attitude.

It was while in the lower house of Congress that Franklin Pierce took that stand on the Slavery question from which he has never since swerved by a hair's-breadth. He fully recognized by his votes and his voice the rights pledged to the South by the Constitution. This, at the period when he declared himself, was an easy thing to do. But when it became more difficult, when the first imperceptible murmur of agitation had grown almost to a convulsion, his course was still the same. Nor did he ever shun the obloquy that sometimes threatened to pursue the Northern man who dared to love that great and sacred reality—his whole united country—better than the mistiness of a philanthropic theory.

This last invidious allusion is to the disposition, not infrequent at the North, but by no means general, to set a decisive limit to further legislation in favor of the cherished idiosyncrasy of the other half of the country. Hawthorne uses the license of a sympathetic biographer in speaking of his hero's having incurred obloquy by his conservative attitude on the question of Slavery. The only class in the American world that suffered in the smallest degree, at this time, from social persecution, was the little band of Northern Abolitionists, who were as unfashionable as they were indiscreet—which is saying much. Like most of his fellow-countrymen, Hawthorne had no idea that the respectable institution which he contemplated in impressive contrast to humanitarian "mistiness" was presently to cost the nation four long years of bloodshed and misery, and a social revolution as complete as any the world has seen. When this event occurred, he was therefore proportionately horrified and depressed by it; it cut from beneath his feet the familiar ground which had long felt so firm, substituting a heaving and quaking medium in which his spirit found no rest. Such was the bewildered sensation of that earlier and simpler generation of which I have spoken; their illusions were rudely dispelled, and they saw the best of all possible republics given over to fratricidal carnage. This affair had no place in their scheme, and nothing was left for them but to hang their heads and close their eyes. The subsidence of that great convulsion has left a different tone from the tone it found, and one may say that the Civil War marks an era in the history of the American mind. It introduced into the national consciousness a certain sense of proportion and relation, of the world being a more complicated place than it had hitherto seemed, the future more treacherous, success more difficult. At the rate at which things are going, it is obvious that good Americans will be more numerous than ever; but the good American, in days to come, will be a more critical person than his complacent and confident grandfather. He has eaten of the tree of knowledge. He will not, I think, be a skeptic, and still less, of course, a cynic; but he will be, without discredit to his well-known capacity for action, an observer. He will remember that the ways of the Lord are inscrutable, and that this is a world in which everything happens; and eventualities, as the late Emperor of the French used to say, will not find him intellectually unprepared. The good American of which Hawthorne was so admirable a specimen was not critical, and it was perhaps for this reason that Franklin Pierce seemed to him a very proper President.

14. THE ART OF FICTION*

I should not have affixed so comprehensive a title to these few remarks, necessarily wanting in any completeness upon a subject the full consideration of which would carry us far, did I not seem to discover a pretext for my temerity in the interesting pamphlet lately published under this name by Mr. Walter Besant. Mr. Besant's lecture at the Royal Institution—the original form of his pamphlet—appears to indicate that many persons are interested in the art of fiction, and are not indifferent to such remarks, as those who practise it may attempt to make about it. I am therefore anxious not to lose the benefit of this favourable association, and to edge in a few words under cover of the attention which Mr. Besant is sure to have excited. There is something very encouraging in his having put into form certain of his ideas on the mystery of story-telling.

It is a proof of life and curiosity—curiosity on the part of the brotherhood of novelists as well as on the part of their readers. Only a short time ago it might have been supposed that the English novel was not what the French call *discutable*. It had no air of having a theory, a conviction, a consciousness of itself behind it—of being the expression of an artistic faith, the result of choice and comparison. I do not say it was necessarily the worse for that: it would take much more courage than I possess to intimate that the form of the novel as Dickens and Thackeray (for instance) saw it had any taint of incompleteness. It was, however, *naif* (if I may help myself out with another French word); and evidently if it be destined to suffer in any way for having lost its *naïveté* it has now an idea of making sure of the corresponding advantages. During the period I have alluded to

---

* The selection constitutes the entire essay "The Art of Fiction" by Henry James, in *Partial Portraits* (1894).

there was a comfortable, good-humoured feeling abroad that a novel is a novel, as a pudding is a pudding, and that our only business with it could be to swallow it. But within a year or two, for some reason or other, there have been signs of returning animation—the era of discussion would appear to have been to a certain extent opened. Art lives upon discussion, upon experiment, upon curiosity, upon variety of attempt, upon the exchange of views and the comparison of standpoints; and there is a presumption that those times when no one has anything particular to say about it, and has no reason to give for practice or preference, though they may be times of honour, are not times of development—are times, possibly even, a little of dulness. The successful application of any art is a delightful spectacle, but the theory too is interesting; and though there is a great deal of the latter without the former I suspect there has never been a genuine success that has not had a latent core of conviction. Discussion, suggestion, formulation, these things are fertilising when they are frank and sincere. Mr. Besant has set an excellent example in saying what he thinks, for his part, about the way in which fiction should be written, as well as about the way in which it should be published; for his view of the "art," carried on into an appendix, covers that too. Other labourers in the same field will doubtless take up the argument, they will give it the light of their experience, and the effect will surely be to make our interest in the novel a little more what it had for some time threatened to fail to be—a serious, active, inquiring interest, under protection of which this delightful study may, in moments of confidence, venture to say a little more what it thinks of itself.

It must take itself seriously for the public to take it so. The old superstition about fiction being "wicked" has doubtless died out in England; but the spirit of it lingers in a certain oblique regard directed toward any story which does not more or less admit that it is only a joke. Even the most jocular novel feels in some degree the weight of the proscription that was formerly directed against literary levity: the jocularity does not always succeed in passing for orthodoxy. It is still expected, though perhaps people are ashamed to say it, that a production which is after all only a "make-believe" (for what else is a "story"?) shall be in some degree apologetic—shall renounce the pretension of attempting really to represent life. This, of course, any sensible, wide-awake story declines to do, for it quickly perceives that the tolerance granted to it on such a condition is only an attempt to stifle it disguised in the form of generosity. The old evangelical hostility to the novel, which was as explicit as it was narrow, and which regarded it as little less favourable to our immortal part than a stage-play, was in reality far less insulting. The only reason for the existence of a novel is that it does attempt to represent life. When it relinquishes this attempt, the same attempt that we see on the canvas of the painter, it will have arrived at a very strange pass. It is not expected of the picture that it will make itself humble in order to be forgiven; and the analogy between the art of the painter and the art of the novelist is, so far as I am able to see, complete. Their inspiration is the same, their process (allowing for the different quality of the vehicle), is the same, their success is the same. They may learn from each other, they may explain and sustain each other. Their cause is the same, and the honour of one is the honour of another. The Mahometans think a picture an unholy thing, but it is a long time since any Christian did, and it is therefore the more odd that in the Christian mind the traces (dissimulated though they may be) of a suspicion of the sister art should linger to this day. The only effectual way to lay it to rest is to emphasise the analogy to which I just alluded—to insist on the fact that as the picture is reality, so the novel is history. That is the only general description (which does it justice) that we may give of the novel. But history also is allowed to represent life; it is not, any more than painting, expected to apologise. The subject-matter of fiction is stored up likewise in documents and records, and if it will not give itself away, as they say in California, it must speak with assurance, with the tone of the historian. Certain accomplished novelists have a habit of giving themselves away which must often bring tears to the eyes of people who take their fiction seriously. I was lately struck, in reading over many pages of Anthony Trollope, with his want of discretion in this particular. In a digression, a parenthesis or an aside, he concedes to the reader that he and this trusting friend are only "making believe." He admits that the events he narrates have not really happened, and that he can give his narrative any turn the reader may like best. Such a betrayal of a sacred office seems to me, I confess, a terrible crime; it is what I mean by the attitude of apology, and it shocks me every whit as much in Trollope as it would have shocked me in Gibbon or Macaulay. It implies that the novelist is less occupied in looking for the truth (the truth, of course I mean, that he assumes, the premises that we must grant him, whatever they may be), than the historian, and in doing so it deprives him at a stroke of all his standing-room. To represent and illustrate the past, the actions of men, is the task of either writer, and the only difference that I can see is, in proportion as he succeeds, to the honour of the novelist, consisting as it does in his having more difficulty in collecting his evidence, which is so far from being purely literary. It seems to me to give him a great character, the fact that he has at once so much in common with the philosopher and the painter; this double analogy is a magnificent heritage.

It is of all this evidently that Mr. Besant is full when he insists upon the fact that fiction is one of the *fine* arts, deserving in its turn of all the honours and emoluments that have hitherto been reserved for the successful profession of music, poetry, painting, architecture. It is impossible to insist too much on so important a truth, and the place that Mr. Besant demands for the work of the novelist may be represented, a trifle less abstractly, by saying that he demands not only that it shall be reputed artistic, but that it shall be reputed very artistic indeed. It is excellent that he should have struck this note, for his doing so indicates that there was need of it, that his proposition may be to many people a novelty. One rubs one's eyes at the thought; but the rest of Mr. Besant's essay confirms the revelation. I suspect in truth that it would be possible to confirm it still further, and that one would not be far wrong in saying that in addition to the people to whom it has never occurred that a novel ought to be artistic, there are a great many others who, if this principle were urged upon them, would be filled with an indefinable mistrust. They would find it difficult to explain their repugnance, but it would operate strongly to put them on their guard. "Art," in our Protestant communities, where so many things have got so strangely twisted about, is supposed in certain circles to have some vaguely injurious effect upon those who make it an important consideration, who let it weigh in the balance. It is assumed to be opposed in some mysterious manner to morality, to amusement, to instruction. When it is embodied in the work of the painter (the sculptor is another affair!) you know what it is: it stands there before you, in the honesty of pink and green and a gilt frame; you can see the worst of it at a glance, and you can be on your guard. But when it is introduced into literature it becomes more insidious—there is danger of its hurting you before you know it. Literature should be either instructive or amusing, and there is in many minds an impression that these artistic preoccupations, the search for form, contribute to neither end, interfere indeed with both. They are too frivolous to be edifying, and too serious to be diverting; and they are moreover priggish and paradoxical and superfluous. That, I think, represents the manner in which the latent thought of many people who read novels as an exercise in skipping would explain itself if it were to become articulate. They would argue, of course, that a novel ought to be "good," but they would interpret this term in a fashion of their own, which indeed would vary considerably from one critic to another. One would say that being good means representing virtuous and aspiring characters, placed in prominent positions; another would say that it depends on a "happy ending," on a distribution at the last of prizes, pensions, husbands, wives, babies, millions, appended paragraphs, and cheerful remarks. Another still would say that it means being full of incident and movement, so that we shall wish to jump ahead, to see who was the mysterious stranger, and if the stolen will was ever found, and shall not be distracted from this pleasure by any tiresome analysis or "description." But they would all agree that the "artistic" idea would spoil some of their fun. One would hold it accountable for all the description, another would see it revealed in the absence of sympathy. Its hostility to a happy ending would be evident, and it might even in some cases render any ending at all impossible. The "ending" of a novel is, for many persons, like that of a good dinner, a course of dessert and ices, and the artist in fiction is regarded as a sort of meddlesome doctor who forbids agreeable aftertastes. It is therefore true that this conception of Mr. Besant's of the novel as a superior form encounters not only a negative but a positive indifference. It matters little that as a work of art it should really be as little or as much of its essence to supply happy endings, sympathetic characters, and an objective tone, as if it were a work of mechanics: the association of ideas, however incongruous, might easily be too much for it if an eloquent voice were not sometimes raised to call attention to the fact that it is at once as free and as serious a branch of literature as any other.

Certainly this might sometimes be doubted in presence of the enormous number of works of fiction that appeal to the credulity of our generation, for it might easily seem that there could be no great character in a commodity so quickly and easily produced. It must be admitted that good novels are much compromised by bad ones, and that the field at large suffers discredit from overcrowding. I think, however, that this injury is only superficial, and that the superabundance of written fiction proves nothing against the principle itself. It has been vulgarised, like all other kinds of literature, like everything else to-day, and it has proved more than some kinds accessible to vulgarisation. But there is as much difference as there ever was between a good novel and a bad one: the bad is swept with all the daubed canvases and spoiled marble into some unvisited limbo, or infinite rubbish-yard beneath the back-windows of the world, and the good subsists and emits its light and stimulates our desire for perfection. As I shall take the liberty of making but a single criticism of Mr. Besant, whose tone is so full of the love of his art, I may as well have done with it at once. He seems to me to mistake in attempting to say so definitely beforehand what sort of an affair the good novel will be. To indicate the danger of such an error as that has been the purpose of these few pages; to suggest that certain traditions on the subject, applied *a priori*, have already had much to answer for, and that the good health of an art which undertakes so immediately to reproduce life must demand that it be perfectly free. It lives upon exercise, and the very meaning of exercise is freedom. The only obligation to which in advance we may hold a novel, without incurring the accusation of being arbitrary, is that it be interesting. That general responsibility rests upon it, but it is the only one I can think of. The ways in which it is at liberty to accomplish this result (of interesting us) strike me as innumerable, and such as can only suffer from being marked out or fenced in by prescription. They are as various as the temperament of man, and they are successful in proportion as they reveal a particular mind, different from others. A novel is in its broadest definition a personal, a direct impression of life: that, to begin with, constitutes its value, which is greater or less according to the intensity of the impression. But there will be no intensity at all, and therefore no value, unless there is freedom to feel and say. The tracing of a line to be followed, of a tone to be taken, of a form to be filled out, is a limitation of that freedom and a suppression of the very thing that we are most curious about. The form, it seems to me, is to be appreciated after the fact; then the author's choice has been made, his standard has been indicated; then we can follow lines and directions and compare tones and resemblances. Then in a word we can enjoy one of the most charming of pleasures, we can estimate quality, we can apply the test of execution. The execution belongs to the author alone; it is what is most personal to him, and we measure him by that. The advantage, the luxury, as well as the torment and responsibility of the novelist, is that there is no limit to what he may attempt as an executant—no limit to his possible experiments, efforts, discoveries, successes. Here it is especially that he works, step by step, like his brother of the brush, of whom we may always say that he has painted his picture in a manner best known to himself. His manner is his secret, not necessarily a jealous one. He cannot disclose it as a general thing if he would; he would be at a loss to teach it to others. I say this with a due recollection of having insisted on the community of method of the artist who paints a picture and the artist who writes a novel. The painter *is* able to teach the rudiments of his practice, and it is possible, from the study of good work (granted the aptitude), both to learn how to paint and to learn how to write. Yet it remains true, without injury to the *rapprochement*, that the literary artist would be obliged to say to his pupil much more than the other, "Ah, well, you must do it as you can!" It is a question of degree, a matter of delicacy. If there are exact sciences, there are also exact arts, and the grammar of painting is so much more definite that it makes the difference.

I ought to add, however, that if Mr. Besant says at the beginning of his essay that the "laws of fiction may be laid down and taught with as much precision and exactness as the laws of harmony, perspective, and proportion," he mitigates what might appear to be an extravagance by applying his remark to "general" laws, and by expressing most of these rules in a manner with which it would certainly be unaccommodating to disagree. That the novelist must write from his experience, that his "characters must be real and such as might be met with in actual life;" that "a young lady brought up in a quiet country village should avoid descriptions of garrison life," and "a writer whose friends and personal experiences belong to the lower middle-class should carefully avoid introducing his characters into society;" that one should enter one's notes in a commonplace book; that one's figures should be clear in outline; that making them clear by some trick of speech or of carriage is a bad method, and "describing them at length" is a worse one; that English Fiction should have a "conscious moral purpose;" that "it is almost impossible to estimate too highly the value of careful workmanship—that is, of style;" that "the most important point of all is the story," that "the story is everything": these are principles with most of which it is surely impossible not to sympathise. That remark about the lower middle-class writer and his knowing his place is perhaps rather chilling; but for the rest I should find it difficult to dissent from any one of these recommendations. At the same time, I should find it difficult positively to assent to them, with the exception, perhaps, of the injunction as to entering one's notes in a common-place book. They scarcely seem to me to have the quality that Mr. Besant attributes to the rules of the novelist—the "precision and exactness" of "the laws of harmony, perspective, and proportion." They are suggestive, they are even inspiring, but they are not exact, though they are doubtless as much so as the case admits of: which is a proof of that liberty of interpretation for which I just contended. For the value of these different injunctions—so beautiful and so vague—is wholly in the meaning one attaches to them. The characters, the situation, which strike one as real will be those that touch and interest one most, but the measure of reality is very difficult to fix. The reality of Don Quixote or of Mr. Micawber is a very delicate shade; it is a reality so coloured by the author's vision that, vivid as it may be, one would hesitate to propose it as a model: one would expose one's self to some very embarrassing questions on the part of a pupil. It goes without saying that you will not write a good novel unless you possess the sense of reality; but it will be difficult to give you a recipe for calling that sense into being. Humanity is immense, and reality has myriad forms; the most one can affirm is that some of the flowers of fiction have the odour of it, and others have not; as for telling you in advance how your nosegay should be composed, that is another affair. It is equally excellent and inconclusive to say that one must write from experience; to our supposititious aspirant such a declaration might savour of mockery. What kind of experience is intended, and where does it begin and end? Experience is never limited, and it is never complete; it is an immense sensibility, a kind of huge spiderweb of the finest silken threads suspended in the chamber of consciousness, and catching every airborne particle in its tissue. It is the very atmosphere of the mind; and when the mind is imaginative—much more when it happens to be that of a man of genius—it takes to itself the faintest hints of life, it converts the very pulses of the air into revelations. The young lady living in a village has only to be a damsel upon whom nothing is lost to make it quite unfair (as it seems to me) to declare to her that she shall have nothing to say about the military. Greater miracles have been seen than that, imagination assisting, she should speak the truth about some of these gentlemen. I remember an English novelist, a woman of genius, telling me that she was much commended for the impression she had managed to give in one of her tales of the nature and way of life of the French Protestant youth. She had been asked where she learned so much about this recondite being, she had been congratulated on her peculiar opportunities. These opportunities consisted in her having once, in Paris, as she ascended a staircase, passed an open door where, in the household of a *pasteur*, some of the young Protestants were seated at table round a finished meal. The glimpse made a picture; it lasted only a moment, but that moment was experience. She had got her direct personal impression, and she turned out her type. She knew what youth was, and what Protestantism; she also had the advantage of having seen what it was to be French, so that she converted these ideas into a concrete image and produced a reality. Above all, however, she was blessed with the faculty which when you give it an inch takes an ell, and which for the artist is a much greater source of strength than any accident of residence or of place in the social scale. The power to guess the unseen from the seen, to trace the implication of things, to judge the whole piece by the pattern, the condition of feeling life in general so completely that you are well on your way to knowing any particular corner of it—this cluster of gifts may almost be said to constitute experience, and they occur in country and in town, and in the most differing stages of education. If experience consists of impressions, it may be said that impressions *are* experience, just as (have we not seen it?) they are the very air we breathe. Therefore, if I should certainly say to a novice, "Write from experience and experience only," I should feel that this was rather a tantalising monition if I were not careful immediately to add, "Try to be one of the people on whom nothing is lost!"

I am far from intending by this to minimise the importance of exactness—of truth of detail. One can speak best from one's own taste, and I may therefore venture to say that the air of reality (solidity of specification) seems to me to be the supreme virtue of a novel—the merit on which all its other merits (including that conscious moral purpose of which Mr. Besant speaks) helplessly and submissively depend. If it be not there they are all as nothing, and if these be there, they owe their effect to the success with which the author has produced the illusion of life. The cultivation of this success, the study of this exquisite process, form, to my taste, the beginning and the end of the art of the novelist. They are his inspiration, his despair, his reward, his torment, his delight. It is here in very truth that he competes with life; it is here that he competes with his brother the painter in *his* attempt to render the look of things, the look that conveys their meaning, to catch the colour, the relief, the expression, the surface, the substance of the human spectacle. It is in regard to this that Mr. Besant is well inspired when he bids him take notes. He cannot possibly take too many, he cannot possibly take enough. All life solicits him, and to "render" the simplest surface, to produce the most momentary illusion, is a very complicated business. His case would be easier, and the rule would be more exact, if Mr. Besant had been able to tell him what notes to take. But this, I fear, he can never learn in any manual; it is the business of his life. He has to take a great many in order to select a few, he has to work them up as he can, and even the guides and philosophers who might have most to say to him must leave him alone when it comes to the application of precepts, as we leave the painter in communion with his palette. That his characters "must be clear in outline," as Mr. Besant says—he feels that down to his boots; but how he shall make them so is a secret between his good angel and himself. It would be absurdly simple if he could be taught that a great deal of "description" would make them so, or that on the contrary the absence of description and the cultivation of dialogue, or the absence of dialogue and the multiplication of "incident," would rescue him from his difficulties. Nothing, for instance, is more possible than that he be of a turn of mind for which this odd, literal opposition of description and dialogue, incident and description, has little meaning and light. People often talk of these things as if they had a kind of internecine distinctness, instead of melting into each other at every breath, and being intimately associated parts of one general effort of expression. I cannot imagine composition existing in a series of blocks, nor conceive, in any novel worth discussing at all, of a passage of description that is not in its intention narrative, a passage of dialogue that is not in its intention descriptive, a touch of truth of any sort that does not partake of the nature of incident, or an incident that derives its interest from any other source than the general and only source of the success of a work of art—that of being illustrative. A novel is a living thing, all one and continuous, like any other organism, and in proportion as it lives will it be found, I think, that in each of the parts there is something of each of the other parts. The critic who over the close texture of a finished work shall pretend to trace a geography of items will mark some frontiers as artificial, I fear, as any that have been known to history. There is an old-fashioned distinction between the novel of character and the novel of incident which must have cost many a smile to the intending fabulist who was keen about his work. It appears to me as little to the point as the equally celebrated distinction between the novel and the romance—to answer as little to any reality. There are bad novels and good novels, as there are bad pictures and good pictures; but that is the only distinction in which I see any meaning, and I can as little imagine speaking of a novel of character as I can imagine speaking of a picture of character. When one says picture one says of character, when one says novel one says of incident, and the terms may be transposed at will. What is character but the determination of incident? What is incident but the illustration of character? What is either a picture or a novel that is *not* of character? What else do we seek in it and find in it? It is an incident for a woman to stand up with her hand resting on a table and look out at you in a certain way; or if it be not an incident I think it will be hard to say what it is. At the same time it is an expression of character. If you say you don't see it (character in *that—allons donc!*), this is exactly what the artist who has reasons of his own for thinking he *does* see it undertakes to show you. When a young man makes up his mind that he has not faith enough after all to enter the church as he intended, that is an incident, though you may not hurry to the end of the chapter to see whether perhaps he doesn't change once more. I do not say that these are extraordinary or startling incidents. I do not pretend to estimate the degree of interest proceeding from them, for this will depend upon the skill of the painter. It sounds almost puerile to say that some incidents are intrinsically much more important than others, and I need not take this precaution after having professed my sympathy for the major ones in remarking that the only classification of the novel that I can understand is into that which has life and that which has it not.

The novel and the romance, the novel of incident and that of character—these clumsy separations appear to me to have been made by critics and readers for their own convenience, and to help them out of some of their occasional queer predicaments, but to have little reality or interest for the producer, from whose point of view it is of course that we are attempting to consider the art of fiction. The case is the same with another shadowy category which Mr. Besant apparently is disposed to set up—that of the "modern English novel"; unless indeed it be that in this matter he has fallen into an accidental confusion of standpoints. It is not quite clear whether he intends the remarks in which he alludes to it to be didactic or historical. It is as difficult to suppose a person intending to write a modern English as to suppose him writing an ancient English novel: that is a label which begs the question. One writes the novel, one paints the picture, of one's language and of one's time, and calling it modern English will not, alas! make the difficult task any easier. No more, unfortunately, will calling this or that work of one's fellow-artist a romance—unless it be, of course, simply for the pleasantness of the thing, as for instance when Hawthorne gave this heading to his story of *Blithedale*. The French, who have brought the theory of fiction to remarkable completeness, have but one name for the novel, and have not attempted smaller things in it, that I can see, for that. I can think of no obligation to which the "romancer" would not be held equally with the novelist; the standard of execution is equally high for each. Of course it is of execution that we are talking—that being the only point of a novel that is open to contention. This is perhaps too often lost sight of, only to produce interminable confusions and cross-purposes. We must grant the artist his subject, his idea, his *donnée*: our criticism is applied only to what he makes of it. Naturally I do not mean that we are bound to like it or find it interesting: in case we do not our course is perfectly simple—to let it alone. We may believe that of a certain idea even the most sincere novelist can make nothing at all, and the event may perfectly justify our belief; but the failure will have been a failure to execute, and it is in the execution that the fatal weakness is recorded. If we pretend to respect the artist at all, we must allow him his freedom of choice, in the face, in particular cases, of innumerable presumptions that the choice will not fructify. Art derives a considerable part of its beneficial exercise from flying in the face of presumptions, and some of the most interesting experiments of which it is capable are hidden in the bosom of common things. Gustave Flaubert has written a story about the devotion of a servant-girl to a parrot, and the production, highly finished as it is, cannot on the whole be called a success. We are perfectly free to find it flat, but I think it might have been interesting; and I, for my part, am extremely glad he should have written it; it is a contribution to our knowledge of what can be done—or what cannot. Ivan Turgénieff has written a tale about a deaf and dumb serf and a lap-dog, and the thing is touching, loving, a little masterpiece. He struck the note of life where Gustave Flaubert missed it—he flew in the face of a presumption and achieved a victory.

Nothing, of course, will ever take the place of the good old fashion of "liking" a work of art or not liking it: the most improved criticism will not abolish that primitive, that ultimate test. I mention this to guard myself from the accusation of intimating that the idea, the subject, of a novel or a picture, does not matter. It matters, to my sense, in the highest degree, and if I might put up a prayer it would be that artists should select none but the richest. Some, as I have already hastened to admit, are much more remunerative than others, and it would be a world happily arranged in which persons intending to treat them should be exempt from confusions and mistakes. This fortunate condition will arrive only, I fear, on the same day that critics become purged from error. Meanwhile, I repeat, we do not judge the artist with fairness unless we say to him, "Oh, I grant you your starting-point, because if I did not I should seem to prescribe to you, and heaven forbid I should take that responsibility. If I pretend to tell you what you must not take, you will call upon me to tell you then what you must take; in which case I shall be prettily caught. Moreover, it isn't till I have accepted your data that I can begin to measure you. I have the standard, the pitch; I have no right to tamper with your flute and then criticise your music. Of course I may not care for your idea at all; I may think it silly, or stale, or unclean; in which case I wash my hands of you altogether. I may content myself with believing that you will not have succeeded in being interesting, but I shall, of course, not attempt to demonstrate it, and you will be as indifferent to me as I am to you. I needn't remind you that there are all sorts of tastes: who can know it better? Some people, for excellent reasons, don't like to read about carpenters; others, for reasons even better, don't like to read about courtesans. Many object to Americans. Others (I believe they are mainly editors and publishers) won't look at Italians. Some readers don't like quiet subjects; others don't like bustling ones. Some enjoy a complete illusion, others the consciousness of large concessions. They choose their novels accordingly, and if they don't care about your idea they won't, *a fortiori*, care about your treatment."

So that it comes back very quickly, as I have said, to the liking: in spite of M. Zola, who reasons less powerfully than he represents, and who will not reconcile himself to this absoluteness of taste, thinking that there are certain things that people ought to like, and that they can be made to like. I am quite at a loss to imagine anything (at any rate in this matter of fiction) that people *ought* to like or to dislike. Selection will be sure to take care of itself, for it has a constant motive behind it. That motive is simply experience. As people feel life, so they will feel the art that is most closely related to it. This closeness of relation is what we should never forget in talking of the effort of the novel. Many people speak of it as a factitious, artificial form, a product of ingenuity, the business of which is to alter and arrange the things that surround us, to translate them into conventional, traditional moulds. This, however, is a view of the matter which carries us but a very short way, condemns the art to an eternal repetition of a few familiar *clichés*, cuts short its development, and leads us straight up to a dead wall. Catching the very note and trick, the strange irregular rhythm of life, that is the attempt whose strenuous force keeps Fiction upon her feet. In proportion as in what she offers us we see life *without* rearrangement do we feel that we are touching the truth; in proportion as we see it *with* rearrangement do we feel that we are being put off with a substitute, a compromise and convention. It is not uncommon to hear an extraordinary assurance of remark in regard to this matter of rearranging, which is often spoken of as if it were the last word of art. Mr. Besant seems to me in danger of falling into the great error with his rather unguarded talk about "selection." Art is essentially selection, but it is a selection whose main care is to be typical, to be inclusive. For many people art means rose-coloured window-panes, and selection means picking a bouquet for Mrs. Grundy. They will tell you glibly that artistic considerations have nothing to do with the disagreeable, with the ugly; they will rattle off shallow commonplaces about the province of art and the limits of art till you are moved to some wonder in return as to the province and the limits of ignorance. It appears to me that no one can ever have made a seriously artistic attempt without becoming conscious of an immense increase—a kind of revelation—of freedom. One perceives in that case—by the light of a heavenly ray—that the province of art is all life, all feeling, all observation, all vision. As Mr. Besant so justly intimates, it is all experience. That is a sufficient answer to those who maintain that it must not touch the sad things of life, who stick into its divine unconscious bosom little prohibitory inscriptions on the end of sticks, such as we see in public gardens—"It is forbidden to walk on the grass; it is forbidden to touch the flowers; it is not allowed to introduce dogs or to remain after dark; it is requested to keep to the right." The young aspirant in the line of fiction whom we continue to imagine will do nothing without taste, for in that case his freedom would be of little use to him; but the first advantage of his taste will be to reveal to him the absurdity of the little sticks and tickets. If he have taste, I must add, of course he will have ingenuity, and my disrespectful reference to that quality just now was not meant to imply that it is useless in fiction. But it is only a secondary aid; the first is a capacity for receiving straight impressions.

Mr. Besant has some remarks on the question of "the story" which I shall not attempt to criticise, though they seem to me to contain a singular ambiguity, because I do not think I understand them. I cannot see what is meant by talking as if there were a part of a novel which is the story and part of it which for mystical reasons is not—unless indeed the distinction be made in a sense in which it is difficult to suppose that any one should attempt to convey anything. "The story," if it represents anything, represents the subject, the idea, the *donnée*

of the novel; and there is surely no "school"—Mr. Besant speaks
of a school—which urges that a novel should be all treatment
and no subject. There must assuredly be something to treat;
every school is intimately conscious of that. This sense of the
story being the idea, the starting-point, of the novel, is the only
one that I see in which it can be spoken of as something
different from its organic whole; and since in proportion as the
work is successful the idea permeates and penetrates it, informs
and animates it, so that every word and every punctuation-point
contribute directly to the expression, in that proportion do we
lose our sense of the story being a blade which may be drawn
more or less out of its sheath. The story and the novel, the idea
and the form, are the needle and thread, and I never heard of a
guild of tailors who recommended the use of the thread without
the needle, or the needle without the thread. Mr. Besant is not
the only critic who may be observed to have spoken as if there
were certain things in life which constitute stories, and certain
others which do not. I find the same odd implication in an
entertaining article in the *Pall Mall Gazette*, devoted, as it
happens, to Mr. Besant's lecture. "The story is the thing!" says
this graceful writer, as if with a tone of opposition to some
other idea. I should think it was, as every painter who, as the
time for "sending in" his picture looms in the distance, finds
himself still in quest of a subject—as every belated artist not
fixed about his theme will heartily agree. There are some
subjects which speak to us and others which do not, but he
would be a clever man who should undertake to give a rule—an
index expurgatorius—by which the story and the no-story
should be known apart. It is impossible (to me at least) to
imagine any such rule which shall not be altogether arbitrary.
The writer in the *Pall Mall* opposes the delightful (as I suppose)
novel of *Margot la Balafrée* to certain tales in which "Bostonian
nymphs" appear to have "rejected English dukes for psychological reasons." I am not acquainted with the romance just
designated, and can scarcely forgive the *Pall Mall* critic for not
mentioning the name of the author, but the title appears to
refer to a lady who may have received a scar in some heroic
adventure. I am inconsolable at not being acquainted with this
episode, but am utterly at a loss to see why it is a story when
the rejection (or acceptance) of a duke is not, and why a reason,
psychological or other, is not a subject when a cicatrix is. They
are all particles of the multitudinous life with which the novel

deals, and surely no dogma which pretends to make it lawful to touch the one and unlawful to touch the other will stand for a moment on its feet. It is the special picture that must stand or fall, according as it seem to possess truth or to lack it. Mr. Besant does not, to my sense, light up the subject by intimating that a story must, under penalty of not being a story, consist of "adventures." Why of adventures more than of green spectacles? He mentions a category of impossible things, and among them he places "fiction without adventure." Why without adventure, more than without matrimony, or celibacy, or parturition, or cholera, or hydropathy, or Jansenism? This seems to me to bring the novel back to the hapless little *rôle* of being an artificial, ingenious thing—bring it down from its large, free character of an immense and exquisite correspondence with life. And what *is* adventure, when it comes to that, and by what sign is the listening pupil to recognise it? It is an adventure—an immense one—for me to write this little article; and for a Bostonian nymph to reject an English duke is an adventure only less stirring, I should say, than for an English duke to be rejected by a Bostonian nymph. I see dramas within dramas in that, and innumerable points of view. A psychological reason is, to my imagination, an object adorably pictorial; to catch the tint of its complexion—I feel as if that idea might inspire one to Titianesque efforts. There are few things more exciting to me, in short, than a psychological reason, and yet, I protest, the novel seems to me the most magnificent form of art. I have just been reading, at the same time, the delightful story of *Treasure Island*, by Mr. Robert Louis Stevenson and, in a manner less consecutive, the last tale from M. Edmond de Goncourt, which is entitled *Chérie*. One of these works treats of murders, mysteries, islands of dreadful renown, hairbreadth escapes, miraculous coincidences and buried doubloons. The other treats of a little French girl who lived in a fine house in Paris, and died of wounded sensibility because no one would marry her. I call *Treasure Island* delightful, because it appears to me to have succeeded wonderfully in what it attempts; and I venture to bestow no epithet upon *Chérie*, which strikes me as having failed deplorably in what it attempts—that is in tracing the development of the moral consciousness of a child. But one of these productions strikes me as exactly as much of a novel as the other, and as having a "story" quite as much. The moral consciousness of a child is as much a part of life as the islands of the Spanish Main, and the one sort of geography seems to me to have those "surprises" of which Mr. Besant speaks quite as much as the other. For myself (since it comes back in the last resort, as I say, to the preference of the individual), the picture of the child's experience has the advantage that I can at successive steps (an immense luxury, near to the "sensual pleasure" of which Mr. Besant's critic in the *Pall Mall* speaks) say Yes or No, as it may be, to what the artist puts before me. I have been a child in fact, but I have been on a quest for a buried treasure only in supposition, and it is a simple accident that with M. de Goncourt I should have for the most part to say No. With George Eliot, when she painted that country with a far other intelligence, I always said Yes.

The most interesting part of Mr. Besant's lecture is unfortu- nately the briefest passage—his very cursory allusion to the "conscious moral purpose" of the novel. Here again it is not very clear whether he be recording a fact or laying down a principle; it is a great pity that in the latter case he should not have developed his idea. This branch of the subject is of immense importance, and Mr. Besant's few words point to considerations of the widest reach, not to be lightly disposed of. He will have treated the art of fiction but superficially who is not prepared to go every inch of the way that these considera- tions will carry him. It is for this reason that at the beginning of these remarks I was careful to notify the reader that my reflections on so large a theme have no pretension to be exhaustive. Like Mr. Besant, I have left the question of the morality of the novel till the last, and at the last I find I have used up my space. It is a question surrounded with difficulties, as witness the very first that meets us, in the form of a definite question, on the threshold. Vagueness, in such a discussion, is fatal, and what is the meaning of your morality and your conscious moral purpose? Will you not define your terms and explain how (a novel being a picture) a picture can be either moral or immoral? You wish to paint a moral picture or carve a moral statue: will you not tell us how you would set about it? We are discussing the Art of Fiction; questions of art are questions (in the widest sense) of execution; questions of morality are quite another affair, and will you not let us see how it is that you find it so easy to mix them up? These things are so clear to Mr. Besant that he has deduced from them a law which he sees embodied in English Fiction, and which is "a truly admirable thing and a great cause for congratulation." It is a great cause for congratulation indeed when such thorny problems become as smooth as silk. I may add that in so far as Mr. Besant perceives that in point of fact English Fiction has addressed itself preponderantly to these delicate questions he will appear to many people to have made a vain discovery. They will have been positively struck, on the contrary, with the moral timidity of the usual English novelist; with his (or with her) aversion to face the difficulties with which on every side the treatment of reality bristles. He is apt to be extremely shy (whereas the picture that Mr. Besant draws is a picture of boldness), and the sign of his work, for the most part, is a cautious silence on certain subjects. In the English novel (by which of course I mean the American as well), more than in any other, there is a traditional difference between that which people know and that which they agree to admit that they know, that which they see and that which they speak of, that which they feel to be a part of life and that which they allow to enter into literature. There is the great difference, in short, between what they talk of in conversation and what they talk of in print. The essence of moral energy is to survey the whole field, and I should directly reverse Mr. Besant's remark and say not that the English novel has a purpose, but that it has a diffidence. To what degree a purpose in a work of art is a source of corruption I shall not attempt to inquire; the one that seems to me least dangerous is the purpose of making a perfect work. As of our novel, I may say lastly on this score that as we find it in England to-day it strikes me as addressed in a large degree to "young people," and that this in itself constitutes a presumption that it will be rather shy. There are certain things which it is generally agreed not to discuss, not even to mention, before young people. That is very well, but the absence of discussion is not a symptom of the moral passion. The purpose of the English novel—"a truly admirable thing, and a great cause for congratulation"—strikes me therefore as rather negative.

There is one point at which the moral sense and the artistic sense lie very near together; that is in the light of the very obvious truth that the deepest quality of a work of art will always be the quality of the mind of the producer. In proportion as that intelligence is fine will the novel, the picture, the statue partake of the substance of beauty and truth. To be constituted of such elements is, to my vision, to have purpose enough. No good novel will ever proceed from a superficial mind; that seems to me an axiom which, for the artist in fiction, will cover all needful moral ground: if the youthful aspirant take it to heart it will illuminate for him many of the mysteries of "purpose." There are many other useful things that might be said to him, but I have come to the end of my article, and can only touch them as I pass. The critic in the *Pall Mall Gazette*, whom I have already quoted, draws attention to the danger, in speaking of the art of fiction, of generalising. The danger that he has in mind is rather, I imagine, that of particularising, for there are some comprehensive remarks which, in addition to those embodied in Mr. Besant's suggestive lecture, might without fear of misleading him be addressed to the ingenuous student. I should remind him first of the magnificence of the form that is open to him, which offers to sight so few restrictions and such innumerable opportunities. The other arts, in comparison, appear confined and hampered; the various conditions under which they are exercised are so rigid and definite. But the only condition that I can think of attaching to the composition of the novel is, as I have already said, that it be sincere. This freedom is a splendid privilege, and the first lesson of the young novelist is to learn to be worthy of it. "Enjoy it as it deserves," I should say to him; "take possession of it, explore it to its utmost extent, publish it, rejoice in it. All life belongs to you, and do not listen either to those who would shut you up into corners of it and tell you that it is only here and there that art inhabits, or to those who would persuade you that this heavenly messenger wings her way outside of life altogether, breathing a superfine air, and turning away her head from the truth of things. There is no impression of life, no manner of seeing it and feeling it, to which the plan of the novelist may not offer a place; you have only to remember that talents so dissimilar as those of Alexandre Dumas and Jane Austen, Charles Dickens and Gustave Flaubert have worked in this field with equal glory. Do not think too much about optimism and pessimism; try and catch the colour of life itself. In France to-day we see a prodigious effort (that of Emile Zola, to whose solid and serious work no explorer of the capacity of the novel can allude without respect), we see an extraordinary effort vitiated by a spirit of pessimism on a narrow basis. M. Zola is magnificent, but he strikes an English reader as ignorant; he has an air of working in the dark; if he had as much light as energy, his results would be of the highest value. As for the aberrations of a shallow optimism, the ground (of English fiction especially) is strewn with their brittle particles as with broken glass. If you must indulge in conclusions, let them have the taste of a wide knowledge. Remember that your first duty is to be as complete as possible—to make as perfect a work. Be generous and delicate and pursue the prize."

15. HONORÉ DE BALZAC*

1

Stronger than ever, even than under the spell of first acquaintance and of the early time, is the sense—thanks to a renewal of intimacy and, I am tempted to say, of loyalty—that Balzac stands signally apart, that he is the first and foremost member of his craft, and that above all the Balzac-lover is in no position till he has cleared the ground by saying so. The Balzac-lover alone, for that matter, is worthy to have his word on so happy an occasion as this[1] about the author of *La Comédie humaine*, and it is indeed not easy to see how the amount of attention so inevitably induced could at the worst have failed to find itself turning to an act of homage. I have been deeply affected, to be frank, by the mere refreshment of memory, which has brought in its train moreover consequences critical and sentimental too numerous to figure here in their completeness. The authors and the books that have, as we say, done something for us, become part of the answer to our curiosity when our curiosity had the freshness of youth, these particular agents exist for us, with the lapse of time, as the substance itself of knowledge: they have been intellectually so swallowed, digested and assimilated that we take their general use and suggestion for granted, cease to be aware of them because they have passed out of sight. But they have passed out of sight simply by having passed into our lives. They have become a part of our personal history, a part of ourselves, very often, so far as we may have succeeded in best expressing ourselves. Endless, however, are the uses of great persons and great things, and it may easily happen in these cases

* From *Notes on Novelists with Some Other Notes* by Henry James; copyright, 1914, by Charles Scribner's Sons, 1942, by Henry James; used by permission of Charles Scribner's Sons.
[1] The appearance of a translation of the *Deux Jeunes Mariées* in A Century of French Romance.

that the connection, even as an 'excitement'—the form mainly of the connections of youth—is never really broken. We have largely been living on our benefactor—which is the highest acknowledgment one can make; only, thanks to a blest law that operates in the long run to rekindle excitement, we are accessible to the sense of having neglected him. Even when we may not constantly have read him over the neglect is quite an illusion, but the illusion perhaps prepares us for the finest emotion we are to have owed to the acquaintance. Without having abandoned or denied our author we yet come expressly back to him, and if not quite in tatters and in penitence like the Prodigal Son, with something at all events of the tenderness with which we revert to the parental threshold and hearthstone, if not, more fortunately, to the parental presence. The beauty of this adventure, that of seeing the dust blown off a relation that had been put away as on a shelf, almost out of reach, at the back of one's mind, consists in finding the precious object not only fresh and intact, but with its firm lacquer still further figured, gilded and enriched. It is all overscored with traces and impressions—vivid, definite, almost as valuable as itself—of the recognitions and agitations it originally produced in us. Our old—that is our young—feelings are very nearly what page after page most gives us. The case has become a case of authority *plus* association. If Balzac in himself is indubitably wanting in the sufficiently common felicity we know as charm, it is this association that may on occasion contribute the grace.

The impression then, confirmed and brightened, is of the mass and weight of the figure and of the extent of ground it occupies; a tract on which we might all of us together quite pitch our little tents, open our little booths, deal in our little wares, and not materially either diminish the area or impede the circulation of the occupant. I seem to see him in such an image moving about as Gulliver among the pigmies, and not less good-natured than Gulliver for the exercise of any function, without exception, that can illustrate his larger life. The first and the last word about the author of *Les Contes drolatiques* is that of all novelists he is the most serious—by which I am far from meaning that in the human comedy as he shows it the comic is an absent quantity. His sense of the comic was on the scale of his extraordinary senses in general, though his expression of it suffers perhaps exceptionally from that odd want of elbow-room—the penalty somehow of his close-packed, pressed-down contents—which reminds us of some designedly beautiful thing but half-disengaged from the clay or the marble. It is the scheme and the scope that are supreme in him, applying this moreover not to mere great intention, but to the concrete form, the proved case, in which we possess them. We most of us aspire to achieve at the best but a patch here and there, to pluck a sprig or a single branch, to break ground in a corner of the great garden of life. Balzac's plan was simply to do everything that could be done. He proposed to himself to 'turn over' the great garden from north to south and from east to west; a task—immense, heroic, to this day immeasurable—that he bequeathed us the partial performance of, a prodigious ragged clod, in the twenty monstrous years representing his productive career, years of concentration and sacrifice the vision of which still makes us ache. He had indeed a striking good fortune, the only one he was to enjoy as an harassed and exasperated worker: the great garden of life presented itself to him absolutely and exactly in the guise of the great garden of France, a subject vast and comprehensive enough, yet with definite edges and corners. This identity of his universal with his local and national vision is the particular thing we should doubtless call his greatest strength were we preparing agreeably to speak of it also as his visible weakness. Of Balzac's weaknesses, however, it takes some assurance to talk; there is always plenty of time for them; they are the last signs we know him by—such things truly as in other painters of manners often come under the head of mere exuberance of energy. So little in short do they earn the invidious name even when we feel them as defects.

What he did above all was to read the universe, as hard and as loud as he could, *into* the France of his time; his own eyes regarding his work as at once the drama of man and a mirror of the mass of social phenomena the most rounded and registered, most organized and administered, and thereby most exposed to systematic observation and portrayal, that the world had seen. There are happily other interesting societies, but these are for schemes of such an order comparatively loose and incoherent, with more extent and perhaps more variety, but with less of the great enclosed and exhibited quality, less neatness and sharpness of arrangement, fewer categories, subdivisions, juxtapositions. Balzac's France was both inspiring enough for an immense prose epic and reducible enough for a report or a chart. To allow his achievement all its dignity we should doubtless say also treat-

able enough for a history, since it was as a patient historian, a
Benedictine of the actual, the living painter of his living time,
that he regarded himself and handled his material. All painters
of manners and fashions, if we will, are historians, even when
they least don the uniform: Fielding, Dickens, Thackeray,
George Eliot, Hawthorne among ourselves. But the great difference between the great Frenchman and the eminent others is
that, with an imagination of the highest power, an unequalled
intensity of vision, he saw his subject in the light of science as
well, in the light of the bearing of all its parts on each other,
and under pressure of a passion for exactitude, an appetite, the
appetite of an ogre, for *all* the kinds of facts. We find I think in
the union here suggested something like the truth about his
genius, the nearest approach to a final account of him. Of
imagination on one side all compact, he was on the other an
insatiable reporter of the immediate, the material, the current
combination, and perpetually moved by the historian's impulse
to fix, preserve and explain them. One asks one's self as one
reads him what concern the poet has with so much arithmetic
and so much criticism, so many statistics and documents, what
concern the critic and the economist have with so many
passions, characters and adventures. The contradiction is always
before us; it springs from the inordinate scale of the author's
two faces; it explains more than anything else his eccentricities
and difficulties. It accounts for his want of grace, his want of
the lightness associated with an amusing literary form, his
bristling surface, his closeness of texture, so rough with richness, yet so productive of the effect we have in mind when we
speak of not being able to see the wood for the trees.

A thorough-paced votary, for that matter, can easily afford to
declare at once that this confounding duality of character does
more things still, or does at least the most important of
all—introduces us without mercy (mercy for ourselves I mean)
to the oddest truth we could have dreamed of meeting in such a
connection. It was certainly *a priori* not to be expected we
should feel it of him, but our hero is after all not in his
magnificence totally an artist: which would be the strangest
thing possible, one must hasten to add, were not the smallness
of the practical difference so made even stranger. His endowment and his effect are each so great that the anomaly makes at
the most a difference only by adding to his interest for the
critic. The critic worth his salt is indiscreetly curious and wants

ever to know how and why—whereby Balzac is thus a still rarer
case for him, suggesting that exceptional curiosity may have
exceptional rewards. The question of what makes the artist on a
great scale is interesting enough; but we feel it in Balzac's
company to be nothing to the question of what on an equal
scale frustrates him. The scattered pieces, the *disjecta membra*
of the character are here so numerous and so splendid that they
prove misleading; we pile them together, and the heap assuredly
is monumental; it forms an overtopping figure. The genius this
figure stands for, none the less, is really such a lesson to the
artist as perfection itself would be powerless to give; it carries
him so much further into the special mystery. Where it carries
him, at the same time, I must not in this scant space attempt to
say—which would be a loss of the fine thread of my argument. I
stick to our point in putting it, more concisely, that the artist of
the *Comédie humaine* is half smothered by the historian. Yet it
belongs as well to the matter also to meet the question of
whether the historian himself may not be an artist—in which
case Balzac's catastrophe would seem to lose its excuse. The
answer of course is that the reporter, however philosophic, has
one law, and the originator, however substantially fed, has
another; so that the two laws can with no sort of harmony or
congruity make, for the finer sense, a common household.
Balzac's catastrophe—so to name it once again—was in this
perpetual conflict and final impossibility, an impossibility that
explains his defeat on the classic side and extends so far at times
as to make us think of his work as, from the point of view of
beauty, a tragic waste of effort.

What it would come to, we judge, is that the irreconcilability
of the two kinds of law is, more simply expressed, but the
irreconcilability of two different ways of composing one's
effect. The principle of composition that his free imagination
would have, or certainly might have, handsomely imposed on
him is perpetually dislocated by the quite opposite principle of
the earnest seeker, the inquirer to a useful end, in whom
nothing is free but a born antipathy to his yokefellow. Such a
production as *Le Curé de village*, the wonderful story of
Madame Graslin, so nearly a masterpiece yet so ultimately not
one, would be, in this connection, could I take due space for it,
a perfect illustration. If, as I say, Madame Graslin's creator was
confined by his doom to patches and pieces, no piece is finer
than the first half of the book in question, the half in which the

picture is determined by his unequalled power of putting people on their feet, planting them before us in their habit as they lived—a faculty nourished by observation as much as one will, but with the inner vision all the while wide-awake, the vision for which ideas are as living as facts and assume an equal intensity. This intensity, greatest indeed in the facts, has in Balzac a force all its own, to which none other in any novelist I know can be likened. His touch communicates on the spot to the object, the creature evoked, the hardness and permanence that certain substances, some sorts of stone, acquire by exposure to the air. The hardening medium, for the image soaked in it, is the air of his mind. It would take but little more to make the peopled world of fiction as we know it elsewhere affect us by contrast as a world of rather gray pulp. This mixture of the solid and the vivid is Balzac at his best, and it prevails without a break, without a note not admirably true, in *Le Curé de village*—since I have named that instance—up to the point at which Madame Graslin moves out from Limoges to Montégnac in her ardent passion of penitence, her determination to expiate her strange and undiscovered association with a dark misdeed by living and working for others. Her drama is a particularly inward one, interesting, and in the highest degree, so long as she herself, her nature, her behaviour, her personal history and the relations in which they place her, control the picture and feed our illusion. The firmness with which the author makes them play this part, the whole constitution of the scene and of its developments from the moment we cross the threshold of her dusky stuffy old-time birth-house, is a rare delight, producing in the reader that sense of local and material immersion which is one of Balzac's supreme secrets. What characteristically befalls, however, is that the spell accompanies us but part of the way—only until, at a given moment, his attention ruthlessly transfers itself from inside to outside, from the centre of his subject to its circumference.

This is Balzac caught in the very fact of his monstrous duality, caught in his most complete self-expression. He is clearly quite unwitting that in handing over his *data* to his twin-brother the impassioned economist and surveyor, the insatiate general inquirer and reporter, he is in any sort betraying our confidence, for his good conscience at such times, the spirit of edification in him, is a lesson even to the best of us, his rich robust temperament nowhere more striking, no more marked anywhere the great push of the shoulder with which he makes his theme move, overcharged though it may be like a carrier's van. It is not therefore assuredly that he loses either sincerity or power in putting before us to the last detail such a matter as, in this case, his heroine's management of her property, her tenantry, her economic opportunities and visions, for these are cases in which he never shrinks nor relents, in which positively he stiffens and terribly towers—to remind us again of M. Taine's simplifying word about his being an artist doubled with a man of business. Balzac was indeed doubled if ever a writer was, and to that extent that we almost as often, while we read, feel ourselves thinking of him as a man of business doubled with an artist. Whichever way we turn it the oddity never fails, nor the wonder of the ease with which either character bears the burden of the other. I use the word burden because, as the fusion is never complete—witness in the book before us the fatal break of 'tone,' the one unpardonable sin for the novelist—we are beset by the conviction that but for this strangest of dooms one or other of the two partners might, to our relief and to his own, have been disembarrassed. The disembarrassment, for each, by a more insidious fusion, would probably have conduced to the mastership of interest proceeding from form, or at all events to the search for it, that Balzac fails to embody. Perhaps the possibility of an artist constructed on such strong lines is one of those fine things that are not of this world, a mere dream of the fond critical spirit. Let these speculations and condonations at least pass as the amusement, as a result of the high spirits—if high spirits be the word—of the reader feeling himself again in touch. It was not of our author's difficulties—that is of his difficulty, the great one—that I proposed to speak, but of his immense clear action. Even that is not truly an impression of ease, and it is strange and striking that we are in fact so attached by his want of the unity that keeps surfaces smooth and dangers down as scarce to feel sure at any moment that we shall not come back to it with most curiosity. We are never so curious about successes as about interesting failures. The more reason therefore to speak promptly, and once for all, of the scale on which, in its own quarter of his genius, success worked itself out for him.

It is to that I *should* come back—to the infinite reach in him of the painter and the poet. We can never know what might have become of him with less importunity in his consciousness of the machinery of life, of its furniture and fittings, of all that, right and left, he causes to assail us, sometimes almost to suffocation, under the general rubric of *things*. Things, in this sense with him, are at once our delight and our despair; we pass from being inordinately beguiled and convinced by them to feeling that his universe fairly smells too much of them, that the larger ether, the diviner air, is in peril of finding among them scarce room to circulate. His landscapes, his 'local colour'—thick in his pages at a time when it was to be found in his pages almost alone—his towns, his streets, his houses, his Saumurs, Angoulêmes, Guérandes, his great prose Turner-views of the land of the Loire, his rooms, shops, interiors, details of domesticity and traffic, are a short list of the terms into which he saw the real as clamouring to be rendered and into which he rendered it with unequalled authority. It would be doubtless more to the point to make our profit to this consummation than to try to reconstruct a Balzac planted more in the open. We hardly, as the case stands, know most whether to admire in such an example as the short tale of 'La Grenadière' the exquisite feeling for 'natural objects' with which it overflows like a brimming wine-cup, the energy of perception and description which so multiplies them for beauty's sake and for the love of their beauty, or the general wealth of genius that can calculate, or at least count, so little and spend so joyously. The tale practically exists for the sake of the enchanting aspects involved—those of the embowered white house that nestles on its terraced hill above the great French river, and we can think, frankly, of no one else with an equal amount of business on his hands who would either have so put himself out for aspects or made them almost by themselves a living subject. A born son of Touraine, it must be said, he pictures his province, on every pretext and occasion, with filial passion and extraordinary breadth. The prime aspect in his scene all the while, it must be added, is the money aspect. The general money question so loads him up and weighs him down that he moves through the human comedy, from beginning to end, very much in the fashion of a camel, the ship of the desert, surmounted with a cargo. 'Things' for him are francs and centimes more than any others, and I give up as inscrutable, unfathomable, the nature, the peculiar avidity of his interest in them. It makes us wonder again and again what then is the use on Balzac's scale of the divine faculty. The imagination, as we all know, may be employed up to a certain point in inventing uses for money; but its office beyond that point is surely to make us forget that anything so odious exists. This is what Balzac never forgot; his universe goes on expressing itself for him, to its furthest reaches, on its finest sides, in the terms of the market. To say these things, however, is after all to come out where we want, to suggest his extraordinary scale and his terrible completeness. I am not sure that he does not see character too, see passion, motive, personality, as quite in the order of the 'things' we have spoken of. He makes them no less concrete and palpable, handles them no less directly and freely. It is the whole business in fine—that grand total to which he proposed to himself to do high justice—that gives him his place apart, makes him, among the novelists, the largest weightiest presence. There are some of his obsessions—that of the material, that of the financial, that of the 'social,' that of the technical, political, civil—for which I feel myself unable to judge him, judgment losing itself unexpectedly in a particular shade of pity. The way to judge him is to try to walk all round him—on which we see how remarkably far we have to go. He is the only member of his order really monumental, the sturdiest-seated mass that rises in our path. . . .

16. EDITH WHARTON:
"Henry James"*

1

. . . as for the date of the meeting which finally drew us together, without hesitations or preliminaries, we could neither of us ever recall when or where that happened. All we knew was that suddenly it was as if we had always been friends, and were to go on being (as he wrote to me in February 1910) "more and more never apart".

The explanation, of course, was that in the interval I had found myself, and was no longer afraid to talk to Henry James of the things we both cared about; while he, always so helpful and hospitable to younger writers, at once used his magic faculty of drawing out his interlocutor's inmost self. Perhaps it was our common sense of fun that first brought about our understanding. The real marriage of true minds is for any two people to possess a sense of humour or irony pitched in exactly the same key, so that their joint glances at any subject cross like interarching search-lights. I have had good friends between whom and myself that bond was lacking, but they were never really intimate friends; and in that sense Henry James was perhaps the most intimate friend I ever had, though in many ways we were so different.

The Henry James of the early meetings was the bearded Penseroso of Sargent's delicate drawing, soberly fastidious in dress and manner, cut on the approved pattern of the *homme du monde* of the 'eighties; whereas by the time we got to know each other well the compact upright figure had expanded to a rolling and voluminous outline, and the elegance of dress given way to the dictates of comfort, while a clean shave had revealed in all its sculptural beauty the noble Roman mask and the big dramatic mouth. The change typified something deep beneath the surface. In the interval two things had happened: Henry James had taken the measure of the fashionable society which

* The selection is taken from *A Backward Glance* by Edith Wharton, copyright 1933 by William Tyler. Reprinted by permission of A. Watkins, Inc., New York.

225

in youth had subjugated his imagination, as it had Balzac's, and was later to subjugate Proust's, and had fled from it to live in the country, carrying with him all the loot his adventure could yield; and in his new solitude he had come to grips with his genius. Exquisite as the early novels are—and in point of perfection probably none can touch "The Portrait of a Lady"— yet measured by what was to come Henry James, when he wrote them, had but skimmed the surface of life and of his art. Even the man who wrote, in "The Portrait of a Lady", the chapter in which Isabel broods over her fate at night by the fire, was far from the man in whom was already ripening that greater night-piece, the picture of Maggie looking in from the terrace at Fawns at the four bridge-players, and renouncing her vengeance as "nothing nearer to experience than a wild eastern caravan, looming into view with crude colours in the sun, fierce pipes in the air, high spears against the sky . . . but turning off short before it reached her and plunging into other defiles".

But though he had found his genius and broken away from the social routine, he never emancipated himself in small matters from the conformities. Though he now affected to humour the lumbering frame whose physical ease must be considered first, he remained spasmodically fastidious about his dress, and about other trifling social observances, and once when he was motoring with us in France in 1907, and suddenly made up his mind (at Poitiers, of all places!) that he must then and there buy a new hat, almost insuperable difficulties attended its selection. It was not until he had announced his despair of ever making the hatter understand "that what he wanted was a hat like everybody else's", and I had rather impatiently suggested his asking for a head-covering *"pour l'homme moyen sensuel"*, that the joke broke through his indecisions, and to a rich accompaniment of chuckles the hat was bought.

Still more particular about his figure than his dress, he resented any suggestion that his silhouette had lost firmness and acquired volume; and once, when my friend Jacques-Emile Blanche was doing the fine seated profile portrait which is the only one that renders him *as he really was*, he privately implored me to suggest to Blanche "not to lay such stress on the resemblance to Daniel Lambert".

The truth is that he belonged irrevocably to the old America out of which I also came, and of which—almost—it might paradoxically be said that to follow up its last traces one had to come to Europe; as I discovered when my French and English friends told me, on reading "The Age of Innocence", that they had no idea New York life in the 'seventies had been so like that of the English cathedral town, or the French *ville de province*", of the same date. As for the nonsense talked by critics of a later generation, who never knew James, much less the world he grew up in, about his having thwarted his genius by living in Europe, and having understood his mistake too late, as a witness of his long sojourns in America in 1904, 1905 and 1910, and of the reactions they produced (expressed in all the letters written at the time), I can affirm that he was never really happy or at home there. He came several times for long visits to the Mount, and during his first visit to America, in 1904-5, he also stayed with us for some time in New York; and responsive as he always was, interested, curious, and heroically hospitable to new ideas, new aspects, new people, the nostalgia of which he speaks so poignantly in one of his letters to Sir Edmund Gosse (written from the Mount) was never for a moment stilled. Henry James was essentially a novelist of manners, and the manners he was qualified by nature and situation to observe were those of the little vanishing group of people among whom he had grown up, or their more picturesque prototypes in older societies. For better or worse he had to seek that food where he could find it, for it was the only food his imagination could fully assimilate. He was acutely conscious of this limitation, and often bewailed to me his total inability to use the "material", financial and industrial, of modern American life. Wall Street, and everything connected with the big business world, remained an impenetrable mystery to him, and knowing this he felt he could never have dealt fully in fiction with the "American scene", and always frankly acknowledged it. The attempt to portray the retired financier in Mr. Verver, and to relate either him or his native "American City" to any sort of concrete reality, is perhaps proof enough of the difficulties James would have found in trying to depict the American money-maker in action.

On his first visit, however, he was still in fairly good health, and in excellent spirits, exhilarated (at first) by the novelty of the adventure, the success of his revolt against his own sedentary habit (he called me "the pendulum-woman" because I crossed the Atlantic every year!), and, above all, captivated by the new experience of motoring. It was the summer when we were experimenting with "Alfred de Musset" and "George"; in spite of many frustrations there were beautiful tours successfully carried out "in the Whartons' commodious new motor, which has fairly converted me to the sense of all the thing may do for one and one may get from it"; and this mode of locomotion seemed to him, as it had to me, an immense enlargement of life.

2

It is particularly regrettable in the case of Henry James that no one among his intimates had a recording mind, or rather that those who had did not apply it to noting down his conversation, for I have never known a case in which an author's talk and his books so enlarged and supplemented each other. Talent is often like an ornamental excrescence; but the quality loosely called genius usually irradiates the whole character. "If he but so much as cuts his nails," was Goethe's homely phrase of Schiller, "one saw at once that he was a greater man than any of them." This irradiation, so abundantly basked in by the friends of Henry James, was hidden from those who knew him slightly by a peculiarity due to merely physical causes. His slow way of speech, sometimes mistaken for affectation—or, more quaintly, for an artless form of Anglomania!—was really the partial victory over a stammer which in his boyhood had been thought incurable. The elaborate politeness and the involved phraseology that made off-hand intercourse with him so difficult to casual acquaintances probably sprang from the same defect. To have too much time in which to weigh each word before uttering it could not but lead, in the case of the alertest and most sensitive of minds, to self-consciousness and self-criticism; and this fact explains the hesitating manner that often passed for a mannerism. Once, in New York, when I had arranged a meeting between him and the great Mr. Dooley, whose comments on the world's ways he greatly enjoyed, I perceived, as I watched them after dinner, that Peter Dunne was floundering helplessly in the heavy seas of James's parentheses; and the next time we met, after speaking of his delight in having at last seen James, he added mournfully: "What a pity it takes him so long to say anything! Everything he said was so splendid—but I felt like telling him all the time: 'Just 'pit it right up into Popper's hand'."

To James's intimates, however, these elaborate hesitancies, far from being an obstacle, were like a cobweb bridge flung from his mind to theirs, an invisible passage over which one knew that silver-footed ironies, veiled jokes, tiptoe malices, were stealing to explode a huge laugh at one's feet. This moment of suspense, in which there was time to watch the forces of malice and merriment assembling over the mobile landscape of his face, was perhaps the rarest of all in the unique experience of a talk with Henry James.

His letters, delightful as they are, give but hints and fragments of his talk; the talk that, to his closest friends, when his health and the surrounding conditions were favourable, poured out in a series of images so vivid and appreciations so penetrating, the whole so sunned over by irony, sympathy and wide-flashing fun, that those who heard him at his best will probably agree in saying of him what he once said to me of M. Paul Bourget: "He was the first, easily, of all the talkers I ever encountered."

Of the qualities most impossible to preserve in his letters, because so impossible to explain with whatever fulness of foot-notes, was the quality of fun—often of sheer abstract "fooling"—that was the delicious surprise of his talk. His letter to Walter Berry "on the gift of a dressing-bag" is almost the only instance of this genial play that is intelligible to the general reader. From many of the letters to his most intimate group it was necessary to excise long passages of chaff, and recurring references to old heaped-up pyramidal jokes, huge cairns of hoarded nonsense. Henry James's memory for a joke was prodigious; when he got hold of a good one, he not only preserved it piously, but raised upon it an intricate superstructure of kindred nonsense into which every addition offered by a friend was skilfully incorporated. Into his nonsense-world, as four-dimensional as that of the Looking Glass, or the Land where the Jumblies live, the reader could hardly have groped his way without a preparatory course in each correspondent's private history and casual experience. The merest hint was usually enough to fire the train; and, as in the writing of his tales a tiny mustard-seed of allusion spread into a many-branched "subject", so his best nonsense flowered out of unremembered trifles.

I recall a bubbling over of this nonsense on one of our happy motor-trips among the hills of Western Massachusetts. We had motored so much together in Europe that allusions to Roman

ruins and Gothic cathedrals furnished a great part of the jests
with which his mind played over what he has called "the thin
empty lonely American beauty"; and one day, when his eye
caught the fine peak rising alone in the vale between Deerfield
and Springfield, with a wooden barrack of a "summer hotel" on
its highest ledge, I told him that the hill was Mount Tom, and
the building "the famous Carthusian monastery". "Yes, where
the monks make Moxie," he flashed back, referring to a
temperance drink that was blighting the landscape that summer
from a thousand hoardings.

Sometimes his chaff was not untinged with malice. I remember a painful moment, during one of his visits, when my
husband imprudently blurted out an allusion to "Edith's new
story—you've seen it in the last 'Scribner'?" My heart sank; I
knew it always embarrassed James to be called on, in the
author's presence, for an "appreciation". He was himself so
engrossed in questions of technique and construction—and so
increasingly detached from the short-story form as a medium—
that very few "fictions" (as he called them) but his own were of
interest to him, except indeed Mr. Wells's, for which he once
avowed to me an incurable liking, "because everything he writes
is so alive and kicking". At any rate I always tried to keep my
own work out of his way, and once accused him of ferreting out
and reading it just to annoy me—to which charge his sole
response was a guilty chuckle. In the present instance, as usual,
he instantly replied: "Oh, yes, my dear Edward, I've read the
little work—of course I've read it." A gentle pause, which I
knew boded no good; then he softly continued: "Admirable,
admirable; a masterly little achievement." He turned to me, full
of a terrifying benevolence. "Of course so accomplished a
mistress of the art would not, without deliberate intention, have
given the tale so curiously conventional a treatment. Though
indeed, in the given case, no treatment *but* the conventional was
possible; which might conceivably, my dear lady, on further
consideration, have led you to reject your subject as—er—in
itself a totally unsuitable one."

I will not deny that he may have added a silent twinkle to the
shout of laughter with which—on that dear wide sunny terrace
of the Mount—his fellow-guests greeted my "dressing-down".
Yet it would be a mistake to imagine that he had deliberately
started out to destroy my wretched tale. He had begun, I am
sure, with the sincere intention of praising it; but no sooner had

he opened his lips than he was overmastered by the need to speak the truth, and the whole truth, about anything connected with the art which was sacred to him. Simplicity of heart was combined in him with a brain that Mr. Percy Lubbock has justly called robust, and his tender regard for his friends' feelings was equalled only by the faithfulness with which, on literary questions, he gave them his view of their case when they asked for it—and sometimes when they did not. On all subjects but that of letters his sincerity was tempered by an almost exaggerated tenderness; but when *le métier* was in question no gentler emotion prevailed.

Another day—somewhat later in our friendship, since this time the work under his scalpel was "The Custom of the Country"—after prolonged and really generous praise of my book, he suddenly and irrepressibly burst forth: "But of course you know—as how should you, with your infernal keenness of perception, *not* know?—that in doing your tale you had under your hand a magnificent subject, which ought to have been your main theme, and that you used it as a mere incident and then passed it by?"

He meant by this that for him the chief interest of the book, and its most original theme, was that of a crude young woman such as Undine Spragg entering, all unprepared and unperceiving, into the mysterious labyrinth of family life in the old French aristocracy. I saw his point, and recognized that the contact between the Undine Spraggs and the French families they marry into was, as the French themselves would say, an "actuality" of immense interest to the novelist of manners, and one which as yet had been little dealt with; but I argued that in "The Custom of the Country" I was chronicling the career of a particular young woman, and that to whatever hemisphere her fortunes carried her, my task was to record her ravages and pass on to her next phase. This, however, was no argument to James; he had long since lost all interest in the chronicle-novel, and cared only for the elaborate working out on all sides of a central situation, so that he could merely answer, by implication if not openly: "Then, my dear child, you chose the wrong kind of subject."

Once when he was staying with us in Paris I had a still more amusing experience of this irresistible tendency to speak the truth. He had chanced to nose out the fact that, responding to an S.O.S. from the *Revue des Deux Mondes*, for a given number of which a promised translation of one of my tales had not been ready, I had offered to replace it by writing a story myself—in French! I knew what James would feel about such an experiment, and there was nothing I did not do to conceal the horrid secret from him; but he had found it out before arriving, and when in my presence some idiot challenged him with: "Well, Mr. James, don't you think it's remarkable that Mrs. Wharton should have written a story in French for the *Revue*?" the twinkle which began in the corner of his eyes and trickled slowly down to his twitching lips showed that his answer was ready. "Remarkable—most remarkable! An altogether astonishing feat." He swung around on me slowly. "I do congratulate you, my dear, on the way in which you've picked up every old worn-out literary phrase that's been lying about the streets of Paris for the last twenty years, and managed to pack them all into those few pages." To this withering comment, in talking over the story afterward with one of my friends, he added more seriously, and with singular good sense: "A very creditable episode in her career. *But she must never do it again.*"

He knew I enjoyed our literary rough-and-tumbles; and no doubt for that reason scrupled the less to hit straight from the shoulder; but with others, though he tried to be more merciful, what he really thought was no less manifest. My own experience has taught me that nothing is more difficult than to talk indifferently or insincerely on the subject of one's craft. The writer, without much effort, can reel off polite humbug about pictures, the painter about books; but to fib about the art one practises is incredibly painful, and James's overscrupulous conscience, and passionate reverence for letters, while always inclining him to mercy, made deception doubly impossible.

I think it was James who first made me understand that genius is not an indivisible element, but one variously apportioned, so that the popular system of dividing humanity into geniuses and non-geniuses is a singularly inadequate way of estimating human complexity. In connection with this, I once brought him a phrase culled in a literary review. "Mr.—— has *almost a streak* of genius". James, always an eager collector of verbal oddities, fell on the phrase with rapture, and earnest requests to every one to define the exact extent of "almost a streak" caused him amusement for months afterward. I mention this because so few people seem to have known in Henry James the ever-bubbling fountain of fun which was the delight of his intimates.

One of our joys, when the talk touched on any great example of prose or verse, was to get the book from the shelf, and ask one of the company to read the passage aloud. There were some admirable readers in the group, in whose gift I had long delighted; but I had never heard Henry James read aloud—or known that he enjoyed doing so—till one night some one alluded to Emily Brontë's poems, and I said I had never read "Remembrance". Immediately he took the volume from my hand, and, his eyes filling, and some far-away emotion deepening his rich and flexible voice, he began:

Cold in the earth, and the deep snow piled above thee,
Far, far removed, cold in the dreary grave,
Have I forgot, my only Love, to love thee,
Severed at last by Time's all-severing wave?

I had never before heard poetry read as he read it; and I never have since. He chanted it, and he was not afraid to chant it, as many good readers are, who, though they instinctively feel that the genius of the English poetical idiom requires it to be spoken *as poetry*, are yet afraid of yielding to their instinct because the present-day fashion is to chatter high verse as though it were colloquial prose. James, on the contrary, far from shirking the rhythmic emphasis, gave it full expression. His stammer ceased as by magic as soon as he began to read, and his ear, so sensitive to the convolutions of an intricate prose style, never allowed him to falter over the most complex prosody, but swept him forward on great rollers of sound till the full weight of his voice fell on the last cadence.

James's reading was a thing apart, an emanation of his inmost self, unaffected by fashion or elocutionary artifice. He read from his soul, and no one who never heard him read poetry knows what that soul was. Another day some one spoke of Whitman, and it was a joy to me to discover that James thought him, as I did, the greatest of American poets. "Leaves of Grass" was put into his hands, and all that evening we sat rapt while he wandered from "The Song of Myself" to "When lilacs last in the door-yard bloomed" (when he read "Lovely and soothing Death" his voice filled the hushed room like an organ adagio), and thence let himself be lured on to the mysterious music of "Out of the Cradle", reading, or rather crooning it in a mood of subdued ecstasy till the fivefold invocation to Death

tolled out like the knocks in the opening bars of the Fifth
Symphony.

James's admiration of Whitman, his immediate response to
that mighty appeal, was a new proof of the way in which, above
a certain level, the most divergent intelligences walk together
like gods. We talked long that night of "Leaves of Grass",
tossing back and forth to each other treasure after treasure; but
finally James, in one of his sudden humorous drops from the
heights, flung up his hands and cried out with the old stammer
and twinkle: "Oh, yes, a great genius; undoubtedly a very great
genius! Only one cannot help deploring his too-extensive acquaintance with the foreign languages."

3

I believe James enjoyed those days at the Mount as much as
he did (or could) anything connected with the American scene;
and the proof of it is the length of his visits and their frequency.
But on one occasion his stay with us coincided with a protracted heat-wave; a wave of such unusual intensity that even the
nights, usually cool and airy at the Mount, were as stifling as the
days. My own dislike of heat filled me with sympathy for
James, whose sufferings were acute and uncontrollable. Like
many men of genius he had a singular inability for dealing with
the most ordinary daily incidents, such as giving an order to a
servant, deciding what to wear, taking a railway ticket, or
getting from one place to another; and I have often smiled to
think how far nearer the truth than he could possibly have
known was the author of that cataclysmic sketch in the famous
"If—" series: "If Henry James had written Bradshaw."

During a heat-wave this curious inadaptability to conditions or
situations became positively tragic. His bodily surface, already
broad, seemed to expand to meet it, and his imagination to
become a part of his body, so that the one dripped words of
distress as the other did moisture. Always uneasy about his
health, he became visibly anxious in hot weather, and this
anxiety added so much to his sufferings that his state was
pitiful. Electric fans, iced drinks and cold baths seemed to give
no relief; and finally we discovered that the only panacea was
incessant motoring. Luckily by that time we had a car which
would really go, and go we did, daily, incessantly, over miles

and miles of lustrous landscape lying motionless under the still glaze of heat. While we were moving he was refreshed and happy, his spirits rose, the twinkle returned to lips and eyes; and we never halted except for tea on a high hillside, or for a "cooling drink" at a village apothecary's—on one of which occasions he instructed one of us to bring him "something less innocent than Apollinaris", and was enchanted when this was interpreted as meaning an "orange phosphate", a most sophisticated beverage for that day.

On another afternoon we had encamped for tea on a mossy ledge in the shade of great trees, and as he seemed less uneasy than usual somebody pulled out an anthology, and I asked one of the party to read aloud Swinburne's "Triumph of Time", which I knew to be a favourite of James's; but after a stanza or two I saw the twinkle of beatitude fade, and an agonized hand was lifted up. "Perhaps, in view of the abnormal state of the weather, our young friend would have done better to choose a poem of less inordinate length—" and immediately we were all bundled back into the car and started off again on the incessant quest for air.

James was to leave for England in about a fortnight; but his sufferings distressed me so much that, the day after this expedition, feeling sure that there was nothing to detain him in America if he chose to go, I asked a friend who was staying in the house to propose my telephoning for a passage on a Boston steamer which was sailing within two days. My ambassador executed the commission, and hurried back with the report that the mere hint of such a plan had thrown James into a state of helpless perturbation. To change his sailing date at two days' notice—to get from the Mount to Boston (four hours by train) in *two days*—how could I lightly suggest anything so impracticable? And what about his heavy luggage, which was at his brother William's in New Hampshire? And his wash, which had been sent to the laundry only the afternoon before? Between the electric fan clutched in his hand, and the pile of sucked oranges at his elbow, he cowered there, a mountain of misery, repeating in a sort of low despairing chant: "Good God, what a woman—what a woman! Her imagination boggles at nothing! She does not even scruple to project me in a naked flight across the Atlantic . . ." The heat collapse had been as nothing to the depths into which my rash proposal plunged him, and it took several hours to quiet him down and persuade him that, if he preferred enduring the weather to flying from it, we were only too glad to keep him at the Mount.

A similar perturbation could be produced (I later learned, to my cost) by asking him to explain any phrase in his books that did not seem quite clear, or any situation of which the motive was not adequately developed; and still more disastrous was the effect of letting him know that any of his writings had been parodied. I had always regarded the fact of being parodied as one of the surest evidences of fame, and once, when he was staying with us in New York, I brought him with glee a deliciously droll article on his novels by poor Frank Colby, the author of "Imaginary Obligations". The effect was disastrous. I shall never forget the misery, the mortification even, which tried to conceal itself behind an air of offended dignity. His ever-bubbling sense of fun failed him completely on such occasions; as it did also (I was afterward to find) when one questioned him, in a way that even remotely implied criticism, on any point in the novels. It was in England, I think—when he and I, and a party of intimate friends, were staying together at Howard Sturgis's—that I brought him, in all innocence, a passage from one of his books which, after repeated readings, I still found unintelligible. He took the book from me, read over the passage to himself, and handed it back with a lame attempt at a joke; but I saw—we all saw—that even this slight, and quite involuntary, criticism, had wounded his morbidly delicate sensibility.

Once again—and again unintentionally—I was guilty of a similar blunder. I was naturally much interested in James's technical theories and experiments, though I thought, and still think, that he tended to sacrifice to them that spontaneity which is the life of fiction. Everything, in the latest novels, had to be fitted into a predestined design, and design, in his strict geometrical sense, is to me one of the least important things in fiction. Therefore, though I greatly admired some of the principles he had formulated, such as that of always letting the tale, as it unfolded, be seen through the mind most capable of reaching to its periphery, I thought it was paying too dear even for such a principle to subordinate to it the irregular and irrelevant movements of life. And one result of the application of his theories puzzled and troubled me. His latest novels, for all their profound moral beauty, seemed to me more and more lacking in atmosphere, more and more severed from that thick nourishing human air in which we all live and move. The characters in "The Wings of the Dove" and "The Golden Bowl" seem isolated in a Crookes tube for our inspection: his stage was cleared like that of the Théâtre Français in the good old days when no chair or table was introduced that was not *relevant to the action* (a good rule for the stage, but an unnecessary embarrassment to fiction). Preoccupied by this, I one day said to him: "What was your idea in suspending the four principal characters in 'The Golden Bowl' in the void? What sort of life did they lead when they were not watching each other, and fencing with each other? Why have you stripped them of all the *human fringes* we necessarily trail after us through life?"

He looked at me in surprise, and I saw at once that the surprise was painful, and wished I had not spoken. I had assumed that his system was a deliberate one, carefully thought out, and had been genuinely anxious to hear his reasons. But after a pause of reflection he answered in a disturbed voice: "My dear—I didn't know I had!" and I saw that my question, instead of starting one of our absorbing literary discussions, had only turned his startled attention on a peculiarity of which he had been completely unconscious.

This sensitiveness to criticism or comment of any sort had nothing to do with vanity; it was caused by the great artist's deep consciousness of his powers, combined with a bitter, a life-long disappointment at his lack of popular recognition. I am not sure that Henry James had not secretly dreamed of being a "best seller" in the days when that odd form of literary fame was at its height; at any rate he certainly suffered all his life—and more and more as time went on—from the lack of recognition among the very readers who had most warmly welcomed his early novels. He could not understand why the success achieved by "Daisy Miller" and "The Portrait of a Lady" should be denied to the great novels of his maturity: and the sense of protracted failure made him miserably alive to the least hint of criticism, even from those who most completely understood, and sympathized with, his later experiments in technique and style.

4

Those long days at the Mount, in the deep summer glow or

the crisp glitter of autumn, the walks in the woods, motor-flights over hill and dale, evening talks on the moonlit terrace and readings around the library fire, come back with a mocking radiance as I write—and with them the figures of our other most beloved guests, Walter Berry, Bay Lodge, and three dear friends from England, Gaillard Lapsley, Robert Norton and John Hugh Smith.

Still others, friendly and delightful also, came and went; but these, with Henry James, if not by the actual frequency of their visits, yet from some secret quality of participation, had formed from the first the nucleus of what I have called the inner group. In this group an almost immediate sympathy had established itself between the various members, so that our common stock of allusions, cross-references, pleasantries was always increasing, and new waves of interest in the same book or picture, or any sort of dramatic event in life or letters, would simultaneously flood through our minds.

I think I may safely say that Henry James was never so good as with this little party at the Mount, or when some of its members were reunited, as often happened in after years, under Howard Sturgis's welcoming roof at Windsor. The mere fact that we had in common so many topics, and such innumerable allusions, made James's talk on such occasions easier and wider-ranging than I ever heard it elsewhere; and the free and rapid give-and-take of ideas animated his mind, which so easily drooped in dull company.

In one respect Henry James stood alone among the great talkers I have known, for while he was inexhaustible in repartee, and never had the least tendency to monopolize the talk, yet it was really in monologue that he was most himself. I remember in particular one summer evening, when we sat late on the terrace at the Mount, with the lake shining palely through dark trees, and one of us suddenly said to him (in response to some chance allusion to his Albany relations): "And now tell us about the Emmets—tell us all about them."

The Emmet and Temple families composed, as we knew, the main element of his vast and labyrinthine cousinship—"the Emmetry" as he called it—and for a moment he stood there brooding in the darkness, murmuring over to himself: "Ah, my dear, the Emmets—ah, the Emmets!" Then he began, forgetting us, forgetting the place, forgetting everything but the vision of his lost youth that the question had evoked, the long train of ghosts flung with his enchanter's wand across the wide stage of the summer night. Ghostlike indeed at first, wavering and indistinct, they glimmered at us through a series of disconnected ejaculations, epithets, allusions, parenthetical rectifications and restatements, till not only our brains but the clear night itself seemed filled with a palpable fog; and then, suddenly, by some miracle of shifted lights and accumulated strokes, there they stood before us as they lived, drawn with a million filament-like lines, yet sharp as an Ingres, dense as a Rembrandt; or, to call upon his own art for an analogy, minute and massive as the people of Balzac.

I often saw the trick repeated; saw figures obscure or famous summoned to the white square of his magic-lantern, flickering and wavering there, and slowly solidifying under the turn of his lens; but never perhaps anything so ample, so sustained, as that summoning to life of dead-and-gone Emmets and Temples, old lovelinesses, old follies, old failures, all long laid away and forgotten under old crumbling grave-stones. I wonder if it may not have been that very night, the place and his reawakened associations aiding, that they first came to him and constrained him to make them live for us again in the pages of "A Small Boy" and "A Son and Brother"?

5

In New York James was a different being. He hated the place, as his letters abundantly testify; its aimless ugliness, its noisy irrelevance, wore on his nerves, but he was amused by the social scene, and eager to leave nothing of it unobserved. During his visits, therefore, we invited many people to the house, and he dined out frequently, and went to the play—for he was still intensely interested in the theatre. But this mundane James, his attention scattered, his long and complex periods breaking against a dull wall of incomprehension, and dispersing themselves in nervous politenesses, was a totally different being from our leisurely companion at the Mount. I always enjoyed having him under my roof, wherever that good fortune befell me; but my hurried preoccupied New York guest seemed a mere fragment of the great "Henry" of our country hours.

New York in those days, though more cosmopolitan than in my youth, was still a small place, with so limited a range of intellectual interests and allusions that dinner-table talk was a good deal like the "local items" column in a country newspaper; and I remember depressing evenings when the hosts, contributing orchids and gold plate, remained totally unconscious of the royal gifts their guest had brought them in exchange.

James knew that his treasures were largely unmarketable in Fifth Avenue, but it perplexed and saddened him that they should, as a rule, be equally so in the world of letters, which he was naturally even more eager to explore. I remember one occasion when a dinner was especially arranged to make known to him a brilliant essayist whose books he greatly enjoyed. Unhappily the essayist's opaque countenance revealed nothing of the keenness within, and he on his part, though appreciative of James's genius, was obviously put off by his laborious hesitations. Their comments on the meeting were, on the essayist's side, a joke about James's stammer, and on James's the melancholy exclamation: "What a mug!"

I suspect that he was much happier, and more at his ease, in Boston than in New York. At Cambridge, in the houses of his brother, William James, and of Charles Eliot Norton, and their kindred circles, he had the best of Boston; and in Boston itself, where the sense of the past has always been so much stronger than in New York, he found all sorts of old affinities and relations and early Beacon Hill traditions, to act as life-belts in the vast ocean of strangeness. He had always clung to his cousinage, and to any one who represented old friendly associations, whether in Albany, New York or Boston, and I remember his once saying: "You see, my dear, they're so much easier to talk to, because I can always ask them questions about uncles and aunts, and other cousins." He had brought this question-asking system to a high state of perfection, and practised it not only on relations and old friends, but on transatlantic pilgrims to Lamb House, whom he would literally silence by a friendly volley of interrogations as to what train they had taken to come down, and whether they had seen all the cathedral towns yet, and what plays they had done; so that they went away aglow with the great man's cordiality, "and, you see, my dear, they hadn't time to talk to me about my books"—the calamity at all costs to be averted.

V. Hamlin Garland: Theorist of Localism

The slim volume of essays, entitled *Crumbling Idols*, by Hamlin Garland (1860-1940) has a unique and curious place in the history of American literary theory. Brief and journalistic as it is, it touches upon nearly all the literary issues of the 1890's: impressionism, the new European writers and artists, the scientific thought of Darwin and Spencer, local color literature, the decline of Boston as the cultural "hub" of America, the fading influence of New England's genteel "library poets," the rise of New York as a publishing center, the increased interest in stories from the Middle and Far West—especially Chicago and California. The title, *Crumbling Idols*, is deliberately revolutionary. Garland presents himself as a young man addressing young men, urging them to be original and personal. The idols he challenges are the values of the past. "Literary prostration," he announces in the introduction, "is as hopeless and sterile as prostration before Baal or Isis or Vishnu . . . I do not advocate an exchange of masters, but freedom from masters. Life, Nature,—these should be our teachers." Garland's urgent advocacy of the "new" has also a political aspect, as the closing paragraph of the chapter on "Literary Centres" indicates, and this strain has led some intellectual historians to see *Crumbling Idols* as nothing more nor less than Populism in a literary guise.

But Garland was neither firebrand nor politician, far less a consistent radical. A native son of the Middle Border, born in Wisconsin and raised in Iowa and South Dakota, he early abandoned the dreary life of a Western agricultural laborer and made his way to Boston, where he met William Dean Howells and established himself as a writer and lecturer on literary subjects. His memory of Western farm life—its pathetically narrow opportunities and economic hardship—provided material for several volumes of short stories, the best of which is *Main-Travelled Roads* (1891). In the late 1880's and early

1890's when he was writing the various pieces later collected in *Crumbling Idols*, Garland was established, as his reminiscence of Whitman self-consciously indicates, as a "Boston professor." From such heights, neither revolution nor provincialism was appropriate. Ambitious, a Westerner turned Easterner and something of the *parvenu*, Garland treats older American writers respectfully. Whitman (whose "Collect," Garland said, provided the motto for *Crumbling Idols*) is first among his literary masters. It is Whitman's "flaming thought" that, in the chapter called "Literary Prophecy," provides a "search-light of the profound deeps: All that the past was not, the future will be." Howells probably influenced Garland even more. Many of the new European writers Garland mentions in *Crumbling Idols* had been more fully discussed in essays and reviews by Howells. Garland's melioristic view of evolution and his conviction that literature "progresses" as society does is a more strident version of Howells' theory of the gradual improvement of literary taste in the nineteenth century. It is, of course, revealing that Garland praises the fiction of his older, well-established contemporary and awards it the accolade of his unique coinage: Howells' work is "veritistic."

The term "veritism" is Garland's special contribution to the vocabulary of American criticism. Adapted from the writings of Eugène Véron, it also recalls the Italian term *verismo*, which describes a literary movement marked by interest in provincial life, dialect, and local color. For Garland "veritism" is a battle cry, not an effort to define sharply a literary attitude. Years later, in *Roadside Meetings*, Garland testified that "realism," "veritism," and "Americanism" meant "practically the same thing."

Garland is often vague and allusive, but loose definitions serve him well. Throughout *Crumbling Idols* he proves himself an adroit synthesizer. The old morality is, for example, wedded to the new science. Garland accepts Howells' view of the moral and social effect of literature but offers a "scientific defense of this position. Spencer and Darwin, he argues, have shown that literature and art change as society does and that change is characterized by "progression" and "improvement." Assured that change is as inevitable as it is benevolent, the individual writer is happily freed from "the power of tradition," his "idols" crumble because they must, and he records his unique moment in the evolutionary process, contentedly aware that future writers will memorialize another time as different from his as is his present from all that preceded him. This vision of benign and ceaseless change underlies the individualism which Garland associates with "impressionism"—that "modern" style in painting and writing of which he learned from the group of young Boston painters who visited Paris in the 1880's. (Characteristically Garland notes that he was prepared for the theory of "blue shadows" both by his own experience and by reading a chapter on architecture by Herbert Spencer!) *Crumbling Idols* simplifies and Americanizes the theory of literary impressionism. In Garland's hands, Henry James' many-windowed "house of fiction" becomes an argument for local color in literature. The veritist is moved by his personal "powerful, sincere, emotional concept of life," but the truth he sees is necessarily embedded in his native regional life and landscape.

Like Howells' *Criticism and Fiction*, *Crumbling Idols* was assembled with scissors and paste. Parts of several chapters appeared earlier in the *Arena*, a liberal Boston journal edited by B. O. Flower; others were probably first delivered as lectures. But careless composition cannot account for all its inconsistencies. Garland theorizes piecemeal; he does not attempt close reasoning. On the one hand, he assures his readers that "literary power is not personal" but "at bottom sociologic. The power of the writer is derived from the society in which he lives . . ." On the other hand, the veritist is "a dreamer" who sees "life in terms of what it might be, as well as in terms of what it is." The artist is, somehow, both the product and the producer of his world: the creature of conditions and the prophet of a better world to come. Confusions of this sort are not uniquely Garland's. Later naturalists, like Dreiser, equally influenced by Spencer's social theory, are also inconsistent in their assertion that man is limited by his incomplete evolutionary development while some men—scientists or literary artists—transcend their evolutionary level and foresee the age to come. Without pressing too hard upon the theoretical problems Garland does not try to solve, we may recognize his amiable gestures toward the several philosophic, literary, and political positions he tried to link or merge. However awkwardly, *Crumbling Idols* joined the new science of evolution to the established values of American ("Bostonian" or "Howellsian") culture and made the still foreign art of impressionism serve not only refined, Europeanized authors, like Henry James, but also the simple recorders of life in the American West. Garland's plea for the "modern" was strident, but his views were melioristic and deeply patriotic. Howells seems to have measured his young compatriot exactly when he called him "unconsciously romantic at heart, and only kept to reality because [he] did not know unreality."

17. ON IMPRESSIONISM AND VERITISM*

My association with these artists [in Boston] resulted in a complete change in my personal appearance. I secured a Van Dyke cut to my brown beard and wore a loosely knotted Windsor tie. I became a regular caller at studios and joined in their discussions. I entered into the technical problems which engaged painters and sympathized with their resentments.

They were all strugglers. Some taught drawing, some painted portraits, others lived on borrowed money. It was a discouraging period in American art. Like fiction and poetry, painting was in process of change.

A new technique in the use of color was being developed and I heard much violent criticism of the "Old Hat" schools of Munich, of "landscapes done in brown gravy," of "mud"—"Oh, the Munich kind of thing!" was a frequent scornful remark. All the younger men fresh from Paris were open-air painters at war with "the bitumen school" who had studied in Germany and Holland, a war which I enjoyed without fully understanding its significance. Enneking's position was midway. He was an open-air painter but not an imitation Monet.

In calling on Dennis Bunker, a powerful young artist of a type not unlike Collins, I heard him say to Enneking, "I'm in a hole. I don't know how I shall come out but I show no more canvases till I have solved my problem."

His seriousness convinced me that his struggle was as real as mine, although I could not understand it. A little later Lilla Cabot Perry, one of Bunker's friends, brought back from Paris a group of vivid canvases by a man named Breck and so widened the influence of the new school.

If I am not mistaken I was taken to her house by Pellew, but however it came about, I recall seeing the paintings set on the floor and propped against the wall, each with its flare of primitive colors—reds, blues, and yellows, presenting "Impres-

* The selection is taken from *Roadside Meetings* by Hamlin Garland. It is reprinted here by permission of the author's daughters.

sionism," the latest word from Paris. They were un-American in subject as in treatment, and while they interested me, I held to my opinion that Enneking was the sounder artist, and I am certain that I would think so still although Enneking has been surpassed and subordinated by many of our later men.

My preparation for the acceptance of the blue and purple shadows of impressionism was singular in that it was scientific, for in a chapter on Architecture by Herbert Spencer I had happened upon a description of blue shadows on a marble building, and a discussion as to their probable cause. Furthermore I was a man of the outdoors. I had seen the blue shadows on snow when lit by the morning sun and it was easy for me to see lavender shadows on the sidewalk or on the beach.

This exhibition opened the campaign for Monet, Sisley, Pizarro, and other of the European painters who had sternly banished black and brown from their palettes, claiming that all the effects of nature could be obtained by the use of red, blue, and yellow pigment, a claim which rested on the scientific constitution of light.

Bunker died soon after, and when his paintings were exhibited, I understood something of the struggle which he had undergone in changing from "the school of mud" to the school of the open air, and the use of primary colors. In fact I began to write and to lecture on impressionism, a service which carried me ever deeper into the camp of the young revolutionaries. I retained, however, my admiration for the naturalistic art of those who granted the blue shadows and went calmly on completing a noble transcript of New England's hills, orchards, and streams.

II

Meanwhile, in carrying on a fight for truth in American fiction, I had adapted Veritism as the word which best described my theory, a word which I gained from reading Eugène Véron's "Esthetics" and Max Nordau's savage "Conventional Lies." Howells was the leader in the school of writers whose work was verifiable, and all the romantic novelists and their admirers had risen in bitter and vociferous opposition. It was a lively contest, and being strong for native art, I naturally took a fist in it.

This brings me back to Charles Hurd, for in his gentle way he influenced me more than any other of my acquaintances at this time. Through him I met Edgar Chamberlin, who conducted a column in the *Transcript* called "The Listener."

Though a hard-working journalist, Chamberlin was a loyal lover of nature, and spent every holiday in the country. He was a short man with brown hair and close-clipped mustache, low-spoken, thoughtful, and gentle. Despite his modest manner he was a determined individualist and had little patience with any socialistic scheme.

He came to hear me make my first speech on the Single Tax and filled his column in the *Transcript* next day with kindly criticism of my arraignment of our land system, a blaze of publicity which rather terrified me. In a letter to him I complained a bit of his stressing the poetry of my address rather than its logic, ending by saying, "We shall meet—at Philippi."

To this he responded: "I had a serious misgiving yesterday lest my account of the meeting might have wounded you; but I feel now that even if it did wound you, you have forgiven me. I was impressed with the meeting and wanted to tell the story of it and couldn't really describe it except as it appeared to me. As to the meeting at Philippi, I shall be glad to have it take place as soon as practicable. I am no good at an argument. I expect to be beaten."

This meeting took place in his home at West Medford, where I met Mary E. Wilkins, Bradford Torrey, Gertrude and Minna Smith, and a number of other young writers, a jolly and informal company. Chamberlin and his wife were ideal hosts and had the one open fire known to me and I recall that as we all sat about the hearth on this night, Mary Wilkins told ghost stories in the light of it, and my admiration of her grew with acquaintance. She was a fair, small, blue-eyed girl at this time, just beginning her work as a short-story writer. She was quiet, almost shy in the presence of strangers, but in Chamberlin's home she was ready, in her low-voiced way, to do her share of the entertainment.

In spite of my plaid Windsor tie and frock coat I think Chamberlin's friends liked me, and when I learned that he had spent his boyhood in Wisconsin and was filled with poetic recollections of it, I sought him out whenever possible, and often went walking with him. I read his column with care and valued his comment for its quiet depth of feeling. To the readers of the *Transcript* he was only an essayist, but to me he was a thinker of unusual powers, tenacious yet reasonable. With him I discussed American fiction and drama with greater freedom than with any other man. He was less remote, less of the desk than Hurd, with whom I never quite reached the same sense of comradeship.

Miss Wilkins was a charming talker, humorous in her laconic way, but her succinct, low-voiced comment was often lost in the joyous clamor of less important voices. Boston was just becoming aware of her rare quality and *Harper's Magazine* was printing her stories almost month by month. Her success, although marvelous in my eyes, aroused no envy. We had only admiration for her artless art.

Her home was in the suburban village of Randolph and I recall visiting her in a small white Colonial cottage, exactly appropriate to her. Her home might have been used as a typical illustration for her stories, and the supper which her companion served me was equally in character. Its cakes and pies, its hot biscuits and jam were exactly right. I felt large and rude like that man in one of her tales who came into the well-ordered sitting room of his sweetheart with such clumsy haste that he overturned her workbasket and sat down on the cat. That she was taking my measure at the same time that I was taking hers was certain. Her keen glance was almost as intimidating as that of Howells. As a student of minute forms of conduct, she had no superior. The amazing part of her genius lay in her ability to see the near-by life of her neighborhood in artistic perspective. In her ability to characterize elderly folk she had no superior.

In a letter to her I put certain questions concerning her work which drew forth this highly significant confession:

"Yes, I *do* consider that I am writing about the New England of the present day and the dialect is that which is daily in my ears. I have, however, a fancy that my characters belong to a present that is rapidly becoming *past* and that a few generations will cause them to disappear. Still this may be only a fancy."

Her only competitor in the New England short-story field was Sarah Orne Jewett, a graceful figure in Boston society. I read her stories, but I never met her. In fact I only saw her once at a public meeting. Her work was related to the school in which Mary Wilkins was an exemplar but she was more adroitly literary. There was a little more of the summer visitor in her stories of the New England villages which she celebrated.

I greatly admired her work and once wrote to her to say so. I received the following reply:

"I thank you for your letter and am much interested in what you say. I have often wondered why we read realistic sketches with such delight, when the scene is laid in foreign countries, and are apt to find equally truthful and truly artistic sketches of our own neighborhood a trifle dull. But perhaps I do wrong in insisting that we are always as artistic in our work as our foreign neighbors. It is not the accuracy of the likeness but the artistic quality of the work that does count and should count most.

"Octave Thanet's and Mrs. Cooke's and Mr. Chase-Wymans' and Miss Wilkins' stories are so much better than all but the very best of Russian and French stories.

"I listen to all that you say of the dark and troubled side of New England life. Mrs. Cooke has felt that and written it, but her Connecticut people are different from those I have known and thought most about. It is a harder fight with nature for the most part, and there were not such theologians in the old days here as in that part of New England. Yet the types of humanity are the same varied by the surroundings. I am often struck by the fact that the old-fashioned people here have small vocabularies and are sure to say least when they feel most."

There were others in this Boston group of writers who wrote occasional sketches with the color of New England in them, and so related themselves to the local-color movement in the South where Thomas Nelson Page was doing for Virginia something like the same work that Harris was doing for Georgia and Cable for Louisiana, a work in which Bret Harte and Joaquin Miller were leaders for the Coast. The importance of this local-color fiction increased with every month, for Gilder in the *Century* and Alden in *Harper's* welcomed it and encouraged it.

The reader will begin to understand how helpful Hurd, Chamberlin, and Enneking were in extending my knowledge of artists and writers, but it is only fair to say that I was spending from ten to twelve hours of each day in the library reading in preparation for my classes in literature. Furthermore, I had begun to write a book to be called "The Evolution of American Ideals," a sufficiently inclusive subject, you will say, which had been suggested by the writings of Herbert Spencer, De Tocqueville, and Walt Whitman. It was based on my reading but its philosophy was derivative.

III

My first attempt at story writing was highly sensational—at least in title. I called it "Ten Years Dead." It was a short story, a very short story—so short that it hardly got under motion before it stopped. I suspect it stopped because my invention gave out, but it is all so long ago that I had but a dim recollection of it as I was writing "A Son of the Middle Border."

Though so sensational of title it was studiedly veritistic. I met the man who had been ten years dead in the Boston Public Library—I mean that is the way the tale opened; and the calm current of the narrative was in careful contrast with the theme, which was the return to familiar scenes of a man who had in some singular fashion been as one dead for a space of ten years.

It was published by a Boston weekly periodical, and I don't remember being paid for it though perhaps I did receive a five-dollar check. It was a column or two in length, perhaps about fifteen or eighteen hundred words, and was written about 1885. I hope nobody will look it up, for it was a very boyish performance. I was only fumbling around with material. Some of my verse of this time I am still able to read in public, but that story would seem comical if not disconcerting to me now.

It comes to me dimly that it was a dream story; that is to say, the theme came to me in a dream. It was after Hawthorne—a long way after—and I only mention it now because it really was my first attempt and I can not tell a lie; that is to say, I consider it more interesting to tell the truth about it.

Meanwhile, more important still (as it afterwards proved), I had begun to do a little in the way of Western local color. One evening in November while at work in my attic in the home of Dr. Cross just at dusk, I heard the ring of a scoop shovel in the alley under my window (it was a truckman unloading a ton of coal) and this sound, combined with the moan of the wind in the elm trees over the roof, put me back into the gloom of an autumn sunset on an Iowa farm. Instantly I was shoveling corn from a wagon box into the crib at the close of a day's husking in a broad, bleak field.

18. *Crumbling Idols:*
NEW FIELDS*

The secret of every lasting success in art or literature lies, I believe, in a powerful, sincere, emotional concept of life first, and, second, in the acquired power to convey that concept to others. This leads necessarily to individuality in authorship, and to freedom from past models.

This *theory* of the veritist is, after all, a statement of his passion for truth and for individual expression. The passion does not spring from theory; the theory rises from the love of the verities, which seems to increase day by day all over the Western world.

The veritist, therefore, must not be taken to be dogmatic, only so far as he is personally concerned. He is occupied in stating his sincere convictions, believing that only in that way is the cause of truth advanced. He addresses himself to the mind prepared to listen. He destroys by displacement, not by attacking directly.

It is a settled conviction with me that each locality must produce its own literary record, each special phase of life utter its own voice. There is no other way for a true local expression to embody itself. The sun of truth strikes each part of the earth at a little different angle; it is this angle which gives life and infinite variety to literature. It is the subtle differences which life presents in California and Oregon, for example, which will produce, and justify, a Pacific-Coast literature.

In all that I have written upon local literature, I have told the truth as I saw it. That others did not see it in the same light, was to be expected. And in writing upon Pacific-Coast literature, undoubtedly I shall once more be stating the cause of veritism; for the question of Pacific-Coast literature is really the question of genuine American literature. The same principles apply to all sections of the land.

The mere fact that a writer happens to live in California or Oregon will not make him a part of that literature, any more

* The selection constitutes the entire essay "New Fields" in *Crumbling Idols* by Hamlin Garland (1894).

than Stevenson's life in Samoa will make him a Samoan author.
A nation, in the early part of its literary history, is likely to
sweep together all that can, by any construction, be called its
literature; but as it grows rich in real utterances, it eliminates
one after the other all those writings which its clearer judgment
perceives to be exotics.

The Pacific Coast is almost like another world. Its distance
from New York and Boston, its semi-tropic plants, its strange
occupations, place it in a section by itself, just as the rest of the
nation falls naturally into New England, the South, the Middle
States, and the Northwest; and, in the same way, from the
Pacific States will continue to come a distinct local literature.
Its vitality depends, in my judgment, upon this difference in
quality.

I say "continue to come," because we can never overlook the
great work done by Joaquin Miller and Bret Harte. They came
to this strange new land, young and impressionable. They
became filled with the life and landscape almost with the same
power and sincerity as if they had been born here. Miller,
especially, at his best, got far below superficial wonder. He
attained the love for his subjects which is essential to sincere
art. The best of his work could not have been produced
anywhere else. It is native as Shasta.

But neither of these men must be taken for model. Veritism,
as I understand it, puts aside all models, even living writers.
Whatever he may do unconsciously, the artist must consciously
stand alone before nature and before life. Nature and life have
changed since Miller and Harte wrote. The California of to-day
is quite different. The creative writer to-day, if true to himself,
finds himself interested in other subjects, and finds himself
believing in a different treatment of even the same material.

There is no necessity of treating the same material, however.
Vast changes, already in progress, invite the writer. The coming
in of horticulture, the immigration of farmers from all the
Eastern States; the mingling of races; the feudalistic ownership
of lands; the nomadic life of the farmhands, the growth of
cities, the passing Spanish civilization,—these are a few of the
subjects which occur to me as worthy [of] the best work of
novelist and dramatist.

Being "a farmer by birth and a novelist by occupation," I saw
most clearly the literary possibilities of the farmer's life in the
valleys of California and in the stupendous forests of Oregon.

I saw children moving along to school in the shadow of the most splendid mountains; I saw a youth plowing,—behind him rose a row of palms, against which he stood like a figure of bronze in relief; I saw young men and maidens walking down aisles of green and crimson pepper-trees, and the aisles led to blue silhouetted mountains; I saw men herding cattle where the sun beat with hot radiance, and strange cacti held out wild arms; I saw children playing about cabins, setting at defiance the illimitable width and sunless depths of the Oregon forests, —and I thought, "Perhaps one of these is the novelist or painter of the future."

Perhaps the future poet of these spaces is plowing somewhere like that, because it must be that from the splendor and dramatic contrast of such scenes the poet will rise. He always has, and he always will. His feet will be on the soil like Whittier's, and like Miller's; his song will differ from theirs because he will be an individual soul, and because his time and his environment will not be the same.

Why should the Western artists and poets look away to Greece and Rome and Persia for themes? I have met Western people who were writing blank-verse tragedies of the Middle Ages and painting pictures of sirens and cherubs, and still considered themselves Western writers and Western artists! The reason is not hard to find. They had not risen to the perception of the significant and beautiful in their own environment, or they were looking for effects, without regard to their sincere conviction. They were poets of books, not of life.

This insincerity is fatal to any great work of art. A man must be moved by something higher than money, by something higher than hope of praise; he must have a sleepless love in his heart urging him to re-create in the image the life he has loved. He must be burdened and without rest until he has given birth to his conception. He will not be questioned when he comes; he will be known as a product of some one time and place, a voice speaking the love of his heart.

There was much of dross and effectism in Miller's earlier work, but it was filled with an abounding love of Sierra mountains and forests and moving things, which made him the great figure of the Coast. But the literature which is to come from the Pacific slope, in my judgment, will be intimate and human beyond any California precedent. It will not dodge or equivocate. It will state the truth. It will not be spectacular, it will not deal with the outside (as a tourist must do). It will deal with the people and their home dramas, their loves and their ambitions. It will not seek themes. Themes will crowd upon them and move them.

The lovers who wander down the aisles of orange or lemon or pepper trees will not marvel at blooms and shrubs. Their presence and perfume will be familiar and lovely, not strange. The stark lines of the fir and the broadsword-thrust of the banana-leaf will not attract their surprised look. All will be as friendly and grateful as the maple or the Lombardy poplar to the Iowa school-boy.

A new literature will come with the generation just coming to manhood and womanhood on the Coast. If rightly educated, their eyes will turn naturally to the wheat-fields, the forests, the lanes of orange-trees, the ranges of unsurpassed mountains. They will try to express in the novel, the drama, in painting and in song, the love and interest they take in the things close at hand.

This literature will not deal with crime and abnormalities, nor with deceased persons. It will deal, I believe, with the wholesome love of honest men for honest women, with the heroism of labor, the comradeship of men,—a drama of average types of character, infinitely varied, but always characteristic.

In this literature will be the shadow of mountain-islands, the sweep of dun plains, and dark-blue mountain-ranges silhouetted against a burning yellow sky. It will deal with mighty forests and with man's brave war against the gloom and silence. It will have in it types of vanishing races, and prophecies of coming citizens. It will have the perfume of the orange and lemon trees, the purple dapple of spicy pepper-tree fruit, the grace of drooping, fern-like acacia leaves.

And in the midst of these sights and sounds, moving to and fro in the shadow of these mountains, and feeling the presence of this sea, will be men and women working out the drama of life in a new way, thinking new thoughts, building a happier, sunnier order of things, perhaps, where the laborer will face the winter always without fear and without despondency.

When the real Pacific literature comes, it will not be subject to misunderstanding. It will be such a literature as no other locality could produce, a literature that could not have been written in any other time, or among other surroundings. That is the test of a national literature.

19. *Crumbling Idols:*
THE QUESTION OF SUCCESS*

But the question forced on the young writer, even when he is well disposed toward dealing with indigenous material, is, Will it pay? Is there a market for me?

Let me answer by pointing out that almost every novelist who has risen distinctively out of the mass of story-writers in America, represents some special local life or some special social phase.

Mr. Cable stands for the Creole South; Miss Murfree speaks for the mountaineer-life in Tennessee; Joel Harris represents the new study of the negro; Miss Wilkins voices the thought of certain old New England towns; Mr. Howells represents truthful treatment of the cities of Boston and New York; Joseph Kirkland has dealt with early Illinois life; Harold Frederic has written two powerful stories of interior New York life; and so on through a list of equally brave and equally fine writers.

I think it may be said, therefore, that success in indigenous lines is every year becoming more certain. You will not find your market in the West yet, but the great magazines of the country are every year gaining in Americanism.

If we look away to England, we see the same principle illustrated. The most vital blood of the English novel to-day comes from the Provinces. Barrie with his "A Window in Thrums," Kipling with his "Tales of the Hills," Olive Schreiner with "An African Farm," Jane Barlow with "Irish Idyls," are putting to rout the two-volume British novel, which never leaves anything out or puts anything in. It is precisely the same movement which is going on in Norway, Holland, Hungary,—all over Europe, in fact. Wherever the common man rises to the

* The selection constitutes the entire essay "The Question of Success" by Hamlin Garland in *Crumbling Idols* (1894).

power of stating his interest in life, it takes the form of local fiction.

The consideration of success, however, is not the power which makes the true artist. Deeper yet must be the keen creative delight,—the sweetest, deepest pleasure the artist knows; the passion which sends him supperless to bed in order that his story shall reflect his own ideal, his own concept of life.

But it may be concluded that the encouragement of this local fiction will rob our literature of its dignity. There is no dignity in imitation, it is mere pretence; to seek dignity in form is like putting on stilts. The assumption of the epic by an American poet is like putting a chimney-pot hat on a child. If we insist on sincerity, the question of dignity will take care of itself. Truth is a fine preparation for dignity, and for beauty as well.

Art, I must insist, is an individual thing,—the question of one man facing certain facts and telling his individual relations to them. His first care must be to present his own concept. This is, I believe, the essence of veritism: "Write of those things of which you know most, and for which you care most. By so doing you will be true to yourself, true to your locality, and true to your time."

I am a Western man; my hopes and ambitions for the West arise from absolute knowledge of its possibilities. I want to see its prairies, its river banks and coules, its matchless skies, put upon canvas. I want to see its young writers writing better books, its young artists painting pictures that are true to the life they live and the life they know. I want to see the West supporting its own painters and musicians and novelists; and to that end I want to state my earnest belief, which I have carefully matched with the facts of literary history, that, to take a place in the long line of poets and artists in the English language, the Western writer must, above all other things, be true to himself and to his time. To imitate is fatal. *Provincialism (that is to say, localism) is no ban to a national literature.*

20. *Crumbling Idols:*
LITERARY PROPHECY*

It is interesting to observe that all literary movements in the past had little or no prevision. The question of their future, their permanence, did not disturb them. My reading does not disclose to me that Euphues or Spenser ever thought of the dark future. Each school lived for its day and time, apparently, without disturbing prophecy.

Pope, the monarch of the circumscribed, the emperor of literary lace and ruffles, so far as I have read, had no gloomy forebodings. His dictatorship was the most absolutely despotic and long-continued dictatorship the literary history of England has ever seen. He could be pardoned for never imagining that real flowers could come to be enjoyed better than gilt and scarlet paper roses, all alike. It is not to be wondered at that he had no prevision of Whitman or Ibsen, in the joyous jog-trot of his couplets.

It is probable that where any thought of the future troubled the artist, it unnerved him. Thomas Browne saw oblivion like a dark sea beneath him, but his view of life was mainly statical; he had no basis for optimistic outlook. His skies were hung with black.

Take larger movements,—the Reformation, for example. This movement, in its day, filled the whole religious history of Europe. It transformed empires, and planted colonies in the wilderness of the west. It dominated art, literature, architecture, laws, and yet it was but a phase of intellectual development. Its order was transitory; and had an evolutionist been born into that austere time, he would have predicted the reaction to enjoyment of worldly things which followed, and would have foretold the sure passing away of the whole world as it was then colored and dominated by puritanic thought.

In art, this narrowness and sincerity of faith in itself has been the principal source of power of every movement in the past.

* The selection constitutes the entire essay "Literary Prophecy" in *Crumbling Idols* by Hamlin Garland (1894).

To question was to weaken. Had Spenser suspected the prosiness and hollow absurdity of his combats (wherein the hero always wins), had he perceived something else in life better worth while than allegory and the endless recounting of tales of chivalry, he would have failed to embody as he did the glittering and caparisoned barbarism of his forbears. And the crown which Pope wore would have rested like a plat of thorns on his brow had he been visited by disturbing visions of a time when men would prefer their poetry in some other form than couplets or quatrains, and would even question whether the "Essay on Man" was poetry or not.

With no conception of what the world had been, they had no guiding line to point to that which the world was to be. The statical idea of life and literature held in all thought,—except where men believed the world was fallen from a golden age into darkness and decay, or that it was again declining to a fall.

Because Shakespeare and the group around him were feudalistic, and did not believe in the common personality; because the critics of Dryden's day believed Shakespeare was a savage; because each age believed in its art and in the world of thought around it,—therefore has each real age of literature embodied more or less faithfully its own outlook upon life, and gone peacefully, if not arrogantly, to its grave at last, in blessed ignorance of the green dust which the library of the future held in store for it.

In the thought of philosophers, so-called, the same traditional feeling held. The observer, the independent investigator of facts, could hardly be said to have existed. Tradition, the organized conceptions of the race, reigned over the individual, and men did not think. The scriptures had said it all. There was no room for science.

But while each age can be held in general terms to have had no prevision, it is probable that some few of its greatest minds caught a glimpse of coming change, and that this power of prophecy grew slowly, and the power of tradition grew less binding, until there came upon the world the splendid light of the development theory, uttered by Spencer and Darwin. I think it is not too much to say that, previous to the writing of these men, definite prevision, even on the broadest lines, was impossible, either in sociology or literature.

Until men came to see system and progression, and endless but definite succession in art and literature as in geologic change; until the law of progress was enunciated, no conception of the future and no reasonable history of the past could be formulated. Once prove literature and art subject to social conditions, to environment and social conformation, and the dominance of the epic in one age, and of the drama in another, became as easy to understand and to infer as any other fact of a people's history.

The study of evolution has made the present the most critical and self-analytical of all ages known to us. It has liberated the thought of the individual as never before, and the power of tradition grows fainter year by year.

It is not my purpose to write the history of the development of literature. I have drifted farther into the general subject than I intended. I am merely preparing the way for some more or less valuable ideas upon the future of American fiction.

Evolutionists explain the past by means of laws operative in the present, by survivals of change. In an analogous way, we may infer (broadly, of course) the future of society, and therefore its art, from changes just beginning to manifest themselves. The developed future is always prophesied in the struggling embryos of the present. In the mold of the present are the swelling acorns of future forests.

Fiction already commands the present in the form of the novel of life. It already outranks verse and the drama as a medium of expression. It is so flexible, admits of so many points of view, and comprehends so much (uniting painting and rhythm to the drama and the pure narrative), that it has come to be the highest form of expression in Russia, Germany, Norway, and France. It occupies with easy tolerance the high seats in the synagogue, and felicitates the other arts on having got in,—or rather stayed in at all. At its best it certainly is the most modern and unconventional of arts.

Taking it as it stands to-day in America, the novel not only shows its relation to the past and the present, but it holds within itself prophecies of impending change. No other medium of art expression is so sensitive to demand. Change is sure. What will it be?

We are about to enter the dark. We need a light. This flaming thought from Whitman will do for the search-light of the profound deeps: All that the past was not, the future will be.

If the past was bond, the future will be free. If the past was feudalistic, the future will be democratic. If the past ignored and trampled upon women, the future will place them side by side with men. If the child of the past was ignored, the future will cherish him. And fiction will embody these facts.

If the past was dark and battleful and bloody and barbarous, the future will be peaceful and sunny. If the past celebrated lust and greed and love of power, the future will celebrate continence and humility and altruism. If the past was the history of a few titled personalities riding high on obscure waves of nameless, suffering humanity, the future will be the day of high average personality, the abolition of all privilege, the peaceful walking together of brethren, equals before nature and before the law. And fiction will celebrate this life.

If the past was gross and materialistic in its religion, worshipping idols of wood and stone, demanding sacrifices to appease God, using creed as a club to make men conform to a single interpretation of man's relation to nature and his fellows, then the future will be high and pure and subtle in its religious interpretations; and there will be granted to individuals perfect freedom in the interpretation of nature's laws, a freedom in fact, as well as in name. And to fiction is given the task of subtilely embodying this splendid creed.

All that the past was not, the future will be. The question is not one of similarity, but of difference.

As we run swiftly over the development of literary history, we see certain elements being left behind while others are carried forward. Those which are carried forward are, however, extremely general and fundamental. They are the bones of art, not its curve of flesh or flush of blood.

One of these central elements of unchanging power, always manifest in every really great literature, is sincerity in method. This produces contemporaneousness. The great writers of the past did not write "for all time,"—not even for the future. They mainly were occupied in interesting some portion of their fellow-men. Shakespeare had no care and little thought of the eighteenth century in his writing.

He studied his time, and tried sincerely to state it in terms that would please those whom he considered his judicious friends. Thus he reflected (indirectly) the feudal age, for that was the dominant thought of his day. So Dryden and Pope, each at his best, portrayed his day, putting his sincere and original comment upon the life around him, flavoring every translation he made with the vice and lawlessness which he felt to be the prevailing elements of his immediate surroundings. In the main, they believed in themselves.

Measured by our standard, the writers of the Restoration period were artificial in manner and vile in thought. They smell always of the bawdy-house, and their dramas sicken us with the odor of the filth through which their writers reeled the night before. To themselves they were elegant, truthful, and worthy of being taken seriously at their best and forgiven for their worst.

The romantic school of fiction, while it reigned, was self-justifiable, at least in great figures like Scott and Hugo, because it was a sincere expression of their likings and dislikings. It reflected directly and indirectly their rebellion against the old, and put in evidence their conception of the office of literature. It was also wholesome, and, in Hugo, consciously humanitarian. The romancers did their work. It will never be done so well again, because all that follows their model will be imitative; theirs was the genuine romanticism.

The fiction of the future will not be romantic in any such sense as Scott or Hugo was romantic, because to do that would be to re-live the past, which is impossible; to imitate models, which is fatal. Reader and writer will both be wanting. The element of originality follows from the power of the element of sincerity. "All original art," says Taine, "is self-regulative." It does not imitate. It does not follow models. It stands before life, and is accountant to life and self only. Therefore, the fiction of the future must be original, and therefore self-regulative.

The fiction of the past dealt largely with types, often with abstractions or caricatures. It studied men in heroic attitudes. It concerned itself mainly with love and war. It did not study men intimately, except in vicious or criminal moods.

As fiction has come to deal more and more with men and less with abstractions, it will be safe to infer that this will continue. Eugène Véron covered the ground fully when he said, "We care no longer for gods or heroes; we care for men." This is true of veritism, whose power and influence augment daily; even the romance writers feel its influence, and are abandoning their swiftly running love-stories for studies of character. Like the romantic school of painting, they are affected by the influence they fear.

The novels of Bulwer, Scott, and Hugo, are, after all, mixed with aristocratic influence, though Hugo had much more of what might be called the modern spirit, even in his so-called historical studies.

It is safe to say that the fiction of the future will grow more democratic in outlook and more individualistic in method. Impressionism, in its deeper sense, means the statement of one's own individual perception of life and nature, guided by devotion to truth. Second to this great principle is the law that each impression must be worked out faithfully on separate canvases, each work of art complete in itself. Literalism, the book that can be quoted in bits, is like a picture that can be cut into pieces. It lacks unity. The higher art would seem to be the art that perceives and states the relations of things, giving atmosphere and relative values as they appeal to the sight.

Because the novels of the past were long, involved, given to discussion and comment upon the action, so the novel of the future will be shorter and simpler and less obvious in its method. It will put its lessons into general effect rather than into epigrams. Discussion will be in the relations of its characters, not on quotable lines or paragraphs. Like impressionism in painting, it will subordinate parts to the whole.

It will teach, as all earnest literature has done, by effect; but it will not be by direct expression, but by placing before the reader the facts of life as they stand related to the artist. This relation will not be put into explanatory notes, but will address itself to the perception of the reader.

Turning our attention for a moment to the actualities of modern fiction, we find destructive criticism to be the most characteristic literary expression of the present and of the immediate future, because of this slow rising of the literary mind to prevision of change in life.

Because the fictionist of to-day sees a more beautiful and peaceful future social life, and, in consequence, a more beautiful and peaceful literary life, therefore he is encouraged to deal truthfully and at close grapple with the facts of his immediate present. His comment virtually amounts to satire or prophecy, or both. Because he is sustained by love and faith in the future, he can be mercilessly true. He strikes at thistles, because he knows the unrotted seed of loveliness and peace needs but sun and the air of freedom to rise to flower and fragrance.

The realist or veritist is really an optimist, a dreamer. He sees life in terms of what it might be, as well as in terms of what it is; but he writes of what is, and, at his best, suggests what is to be, by contrast. He aims to be perfectly truthful in his delineation of his relation to life, but there is a tone, a color, which comes unconsciously into his utterance, like the sobbing stir of the muted violins beneath the frank, clear song of the clarionet; and this tone is one of sorrow that the good time moves so slowly in its approach.

He aims to hasten the age of beauty and peace by delineating the ugliness and warfare of the present; but ever the converse of his picture rises in the mind of the reader. He sighs for a lovelier life. He is tired of warfare and diseased sexualism, and Poverty, the mother of Envy. He is haggard with sympathetic hunger, and weary with the struggle to maintain his standing place on this planet, which he conceives was given to all as the abode of peace. With this hate in his heart and this ideal in his brain the modern man writes his stories of life. They are not always pleasant, but they are generally true, and always they provoke thought.

This element of sad severity will change as conditions change for the common man, but the larger element of sincerity, with resulting contemporaneousness, will remain. Fiction, to be important and successful, must be original and suited to its time. As the times change, fiction will change. This must always be remembered.

The surest way to write for all time is to embody the present in the finest form with the highest sincerity and with the frankest truthfulness. The surest way to write for other lands is to be true to our own land and true to the scenes and people we love, and love in a human and direct way without being educated up to it or down to it.

The people can never be educated to love the past, to love Shakespeare and Homer. Students may be taught to believe they believe, but the great masses of American readers want the modern comment. They want the past colored to suit their ideas of life,—that is, the readers of romance; on higher planes of reading they want sincere delineation of modern life and thought, and Shakespeare, Wordsworth, Dante, Milton, are fading away into mere names,—books we should read but seldom do.

Thus it will be seen that the fiction of the immediate future will be the working out of plans already in hand. There is small prophecy in it, after all. We have but to examine the ground closely, and we see the green shoots of the coming harvest beneath our very feet. We have but to examine closely the most naïve and local of our novels, and the coming literature will be foreshadowed there. The local novelist seems to be the coming woman! Local color is the royal robe.

21. *Crumbling Idols:*
LOCAL COLOR IN ART*

Local color in fiction is demonstrably the life of fiction. It is the native element, the differentiating element. It corresponds to the endless and vital charm of individual peculiarity. It is the differences which interest us; the similarities do not please, do not forever stimulate and feed as do the differences. Literature would die of dry rot if it chronicled the similarities only, or even largely.

Historically, the local color of a poet or dramatist is of the greatest value. The charm of Horace is the side light he throws on the manners and customs of his time. The vital in Homer lies, after all, in his local color, not in his abstractions. Because the sagas of the North delineate more exactly how men and women lived and wrought in those days, therefore they have always appealed to me with infinitely greater power than Homer.

Similarly, it is the local color of Chaucer that interests us to-day. We yawn over his tales of chivalry which were in the manner of his contemporaries, but the Miller and the Priest interest us. Wherever the man of the past in literature showed us what he really lived and loved, he moves us. We understand him, and we really feel an interest in him.

Historically, local color has gained in beauty and suggestiveness and humanity from Chaucer down to the present day. Each age has embodied more and more of its actual life and social conformation until the differentiating qualities of modern art make the best paintings of Norway as distinct in local color as its fiction is vital and indigenous.

Every great moving literature to-day is full of local color. It is this element which puts the Norwegian and Russian almost at

* The selection constitutes the entire essay "Local Color in Art" in *Crumbling Idols* by Hamlin Garland (1894).

the very summit of modern novel writing, and it is the comparative lack of this distinctive flavor which makes the English and French take a lower place in truth and sincerity.

Everywhere all over the modern European world, men are writing novels and dramas as naturally as the grass or corn or flax grows. The Provençal, the Hun, the Catalonian, the Norwegian, is getting a hearing. This literature is not the literature of scholars; it is the literature of lovers and doers; of men who love the modern and who have not been educated to despise common things.

These men are speaking a new word. They are not hunting themes, they are struggling to express.

Conventional criticism does not hamper or confine them. They are rooted in the soil. They stand among the cornfields and they dig in the peat-bogs. They concern themselves with modern and very present words and themes, and they have brought a new word which is to divide in half the domain of beauty.

They have made art the re-creation of the beautiful *and the significant*. Mere beauty no longer suffices. Beauty is the world-old aristocrat who has taken for mate this mighty young plebeian Significance. Their child is to be the most human and humane literature ever seen.

It has taken the United States longer to achieve independence of English critics than it took to free itself from old-world political and economic rule. Its political freedom was won, not by its gentlemen and scholars, but by its yeomanry; and in the same way our national literature will come in its fulness when the common American rises spontaneously to the expression of his concept of life.

The fatal blight upon most American art has been, and is to-day, its imitative quality, which has kept it characterless and factitious,—a forced rose-culture rather than the free flowering of native plants.

Our writers despised or feared the home market. They rested their immortality upon the "universal theme," which was a theme of no interest to the public and of small interest to themselves.

During the first century and a half, our literature had very little national color. It was quite like the utterance of corresponding classes in England. But at length Bryant and Cooper felt the influence of our mighty forests and prairies. Whittier uttered something of New England boy-life, and Thoreau prodded about among newly discovered wonders, and the American literature got its first start.

Under the influence of Cooper came the stories of wild life from Texas, from Ohio, and from Illinois. The wild, rough settlements could not produce smooth and cultured poems or stories; they only furnished forth rough-and-ready anecdotes, but in these stories there were hints of something fine and strong and native.

As the settlements increased in size, as the pressure of the forest and the wild beast grew less, expression rose to a higher plane; men softened in speech and manner. All preparations were being made for a local literature raised to the level of art.

The Pacific slope was first in the line. By the exceptional interest which the world took in the life of the gold fields, and by the forward urge which seems always to surprise the pessimist and the scholiast, two young men were plunged into that wild life, led across the plains set in the shadow of Mount Shasta, and local literature received its first great marked, decided impetus.

To-day we have in America, at last, a group of writers who have no suspicion of imitation laid upon them. Whatever faults they may be supposed to have, they are at any rate, themselves. American critics can depend upon a characteristic American literature of fiction and the drama from these people.

The corn has flowered, and the cotton-boll has broken into speech.

Local color—what is it? It means that the writer spontaneously reflects the life which goes on around him. It is natural and unstrained art.

It is, in a sense, unnatural and artificial to find an American writing novels of Russia or Spain or the Holy Land. He cannot hope to do it so well as the native. The best he can look for is that poor word of praise, "He does it very well, considering he is an alien."

If a young writer complain that there are no themes at home, that he is forced to go abroad for prospective and romance, I answer there is something wrong in his education or his perceptive faculty. Often he is more anxious to win a money success than to be patiently one of art's unhurried devotees.

I can sympathize with him, however, for criticism has not helped him to be true. Criticism of the formal kind and spontaneous expression are always at war, like the old man and the youth. They may politely conceal it, but they are mutually destructive.

Old men naturally love the past; the books they read are the master-pieces; the great men are all dying off, they say; the young man should treat lofty and universal themes, as they used to do. These localisms are petty. These truths are disturbing. Youth annoys them. Spontaneousness is formlessness, and the criticism that does not call for the abstract and the ideal and the beautiful is leading to destruction, these critics say.

And yet there is a criticism which helps, which tends to keep a writer at his best; but such criticism recognizes the dynamic force of a literature, and tries to spy out tendencies. This criticism to-day sees that local color means national character, and is aiding the young writer to treat his themes in the best art.

I assert it is the most natural thing in the world for a man to love his native land and his native, intimate surroundings. Born into a web of circumstances, enmeshed in common life, the youthful artist begins to think. All the associations of that childhood and the love-life of youth combine to make that web of common affairs, threads of silver and beads of gold; the near-at-hand things are the dearest and sweetest after all.

As the reader will see, I am using local color to mean something more than a forced study of the picturesque scenery of a State.

Local color in a novel means that it has such quality of texture and back-ground that it could not have been written in any other place or by any one else than a native.

It means a statement of life as indigenous as the plant-growth. It means that the picturesque shall not be seen by the author,— that every tree and bird and mountain shall be dear and companionable and necessary, not picturesque; the tourist cannot write the local novel.

From this it follows that local color must not be put in for the sake of local color. It must go in, it *will* go in, because the writer naturally carries it with him half unconsciously, or conscious only of its significance, its interest to him.

He must not stop to think whether it will interest the reader or not. He must be loyal to himself, and put it in because he loves it. If he is an artist, he will make his reader feel it through his own emotion.

What we should stand for is not universality of theme, but

beauty and strength of treatment, leaving the writer to choose his theme because he loves it.

Here is the work of the critic. Recognizing that the theme is beyond his control, let him aid the young writer to delineate simply and with unwavering strokes. Even here the critic can do little, if he is possessed of the idea that the young writer of to-day should model upon Addison or Macaulay or Swift.

There are new criterions to-day in writing as in painting, and individual expression is the aim. The critic can do much to aid a young writer to *not* copy an old master or any other master. Good criticism can aid him to be vivid and simple and unhackneyed in his technique, the subject is his own affair.

I agree with him who says, Local art must be raised to the highest levels in its expression; but in aiding this perfection of technique we must be careful not to cut into the artist's spontaneity. To apply ancient dogmas of criticism to our life and literature would be benumbing to [the] artist and fatal to his art.

22. *Crumbling Idols:*
LITERARY CENTRES*

A favorite proposition with the business-man of the West is this: "If the West had been settled first, the East would be a wilderness to-day, for the reason (as he goes on to explain) that the fertile soil, the vast cities, the ease of communication of the midland, would have made it the home of all ease, refinement, culture, and art. The East would have been only a fringe of seaport towns, with fine shooting and fishing lands as a background."

If he happens to be a business-man with an imagination (there are such), he will then say: "The East has therefore had its day as a commercial centre. The West has finally been discovered. The East has poured its millions of men and money into the Mississippi valley, and these millions of men have taken root in the soil; and to-day, in the year of 1894, the commercial dominance of the East is distinctly on the wane. Henceforth, the centre of commercial activity in the United States is to be the West. Henceforth, when men of the Old World speak of America, they will not think of Boston and New York and Philadelphia, they will mean Chicago and the Mississippi valley."

There is, of course, an element of exaggeration in this, but there is also in it a larger truth and a magnificent enthusiasm,—an enthusiasm which rises above commercial considerations. The man who really dares to face the future,—and, of course, the man who dares to face the future, is he who finds his interests served by it,—the man who can sit down and think of the on-coming millions of the great Mississippi valley, must admit that over-statement of its importance is quite impossible, given time enough for fulfilment.

---

* The selection constitutes the entire essay "Literary Centres" in *Crumbling Idols* by Hamlin Garland (1894).

Commercially, the West rushes toward the future. Cities rise with velocity hitherto inconceivable. True, they are mushrooms to some extent, and are founded upon greed and speculation to a sorrowful extent; but the people are coming on after all, people of higher wisdom and purer life, who will make these mushroom cities temples to art and song. This great basin, like Egypt, like Germany, is to be a "well of nations." It will continually revivify and reinvigorate the East, the extreme North, and the extreme South. It will be the base of food supply; the heart of the nation; the place of interchange.

This leads me to a proposition, which I make on my own account. Literary horizons also are changing with almost equal swiftness. Centres of art production are moving westward; that is to say, the literary supremacy of the East is passing away. There are other and subtler causes than commercial elements at work. Racial influences are at work, and changes in literary and social ideals are hastening a far-reaching subdivision, if not decentralization, of power.

In the West there is coming into expression and literary influence the great Scandinavian and Germanic element to which the traditions of English literature are very weak and unimportant, and to whom Boston and New York are of small account. They have their own race-traditions which neutralize those of the English language which they speak, and thus their minds are left free to choose the most modern things. It is impossible for them to take on the literary traditions of their adopted tongue with equal power, and they find their own less binding by change.

Again, literary traditions are weakening all along the line. The old is passing away, the new is coming on. As the old fades away, the strongholds of tradition and classic interest are forgotten and left behind. This mighty change is a silent one, but it is irresistible. This can be illustrated in the change which has swept over Boston, Concord, and Cambridge during the last ten or twenty years.

Boston has claimed and held supremacy in American literature for more than half a century. Made illustrious by Emerson, Hawthorne, Whittier, Longfellow, Holmes, Lowell, the New England group, it easily kept its place as the most important literary centre in America. New York was second, and Philadelphia third. This Cambridge group has been called "the polite group" and "the Library group." Its members took things for

the most part at second hand. They read many books, and
mainly wrote gentle and polite poems on books and events.
Whittier and Hawthorne, notwithstanding their larger originality, were, after all, related. They took things in a bookish way.
It would be absurd to say they were weak or poor, they were
very high and noble; but they belonged to another period. They
were more closely allied with the past, with English traditions,
than we, and were actuated by different ideals of life.

So long as this group lived, Boston was the literary autocrat of
the nation. But the school of book-poets is losing power. And,
with the change in literary creed, Boston has lost its high place,
and it is but natural that she should now take a rather mournful
view of American literature.

New York to-day claims to be, and is, the literary centre of
America. Boston artists one by one go to New York. Literary
men find their market growing there, and dying out in Boston.
They find quicker and warmer appreciation in New York, and
the critical atmosphere more hospitable. The present receives a
larger share of attention than in Boston. Henceforward New
York, and not Boston, is to be the great dictator of American
literature. New York already assumes to be able to make or
break a novelist or playwright. Certainly it is the centre of
magazine production; and the magazine is, on the whole, the
greatest outlet for distinctive American art.

We are more American in our illustrating and in our fiction
than in any other lines of artistic work. New York is the centre
of oil-painting as well as of illustration, and its markets exceed
those of almost all other American cities taken together. In
short, its supremacy in art must be conceded to be as complete
to-day as its commercial domination in railways and stocks.

And yet New York is in danger of assuming too much. She
must not forget that the writers and painters who make her
illustrious are very largely products of the South and West. One
needs but to run over the list of the leading magazine-writers of
the last ten years, to see how true this is. Ohio sends William D.
Howells; Virginia sends Thomas Nelson Page and Amélie Rives;
Indiana sends Edward Eggleston, James Whitcomb Riley, Mrs.
Catherwood. Tennessee is represented by the Murfree sisters.
Georgia, by Joel Harris and Richard Malcolm Johnston. Louisiana finds voice through George W. Cable and Ruth McEnnery
[sic] Stuart. Arkansas and Kentucky are represented by Alice
French and James Lane Allen; and so through a notable list.

These are but a few of the best known of the names. Thus, every part of the West or South is represented in the literary domination of New York.

It is not so much a victory of New York over Boston, it is the rising to literary power of the whole nation. New York is but the trumpet through which the whole nation is at last speaking. Let New York remember this and be humble, for the same causes that have cut away the pride of Boston will certainly bring about a corresponding change in the relation of New York to the South and West.

It was easy for Boston to maintain her literary supremacy while the whole population of the nation was less than forty millions, when the whole West was a frontier, and the South was a slave-country. It will be hard for New York to retain her present supremacy with a nation of seventy millions of people, with cities containing half a million people springing up in the interior and on the Western sea,—not to mention Chicago, whose shadow already menaces New York.

Already Chicago claims to have pushed New York from her seat as ruler of our commerce. The whole West and South are in open rebellion against her financial rule. Chicago equals, possibly outnumbers her, in population, and certainly outspeeds her in enterprise. The rise of Chicago as a literary and art centre is a question only of time, and of a very short time; for the Columbian Exposition has taught her her own capabilities in something higher than business. The founding of vast libraries and universities and art museums is the first formal step, the preparation-stage; expression will follow swiftly. Magazines and publishing-houses are to come.

The writers have already risen. Every literary man must have a beginning somewhere, and there are scores of original young writers and artists just rising to power in the West. They need only a channel for utterance; it will come, and they will speak.

It is not contended that the names quoted above are the best,—that they represent the perfect art of the new school. Most of them are young writers, all of them are significant of things to come, but many of them are already of national, even international, fame. The absolutist in his sneer at the rising young artists forgets that the literary masters he worships were once as helpless to reply to the question: What have you done?

It is not intended to say that New York has not her native share in this new movement; I aim merely to show that never again can a city or a group of States overshadow the whole of literary America. It is not merely a question of New York and Chicago now, it is the rise of literary centres all over the nation. Henceforth, St. Louis, New Orleans, Atlanta, Denver, San Francisco, Cincinnati, St. Paul, and Minneapolis, and a dozen more interior cities are to be reckoned with.

Like Avignon and Marseilles, they will have literary men and literary judgments of their own. The process is one of decentralization, together with one of unification.

Never again will any city dominate American literature; and, in my judgment, there will be no over-topping personalities in art. The average is rising; the peaks will seem to sink.

There are other reasons for the revolt against the domination of the East over the whole nation. New York, like Boston, is too near London. It is no longer American. It is losing touch with the people. Chicago is much more American, notwithstanding its foreign population. Its dominant population is splendidly American, drawn from the immediate States,—Indiana, Illinois, Iowa, Wisconsin, Kentucky, and Ohio. It does not profess to be exclusive; it professes to be a meeting-place. Of course, it has its tremulous and timid imitators of New York and Boston imitations of London and Paris; but these people are in a sad minority. The great body of men and women who give strength and originality to Chicago are people who care very little what New York thinks of their work, and the doings of London and Paris are not more vital.

No critic whose eyes are not fastened upon the past can imagine a hopeless literary future for this great nation. To the conservative, who thinks change necessarily destructive and hopeless, the future is a blank. To the radical, who feels change to be necessary and natural, the present and the future are filled with magnificent promise. The horizon widens each year, including more cities, more writers, more lovers of light and song, more makers of literature. Literary invention is as inevitable as the manipulation of the material universe. The material always subtends the intellectual. Activity in material comes ultimately to be expressed, and expression is commensurate with the deed.

"Bigness does not count," the East says in answer to the West. Yes, but it does! The prairies lead to general conceptions. The winds give strength and penetration and alertness. The mighty stretches of woods lead to breadth and generosity of intellectual conception. The West and South are coming to be something more than big, coming to the expression of a new world, coming to take their places in the world of literature, as in the world of action, and no sneer from gloomy prophets of the dying past can check or chill them.

The literature which is already springing up in those great interior spaces of the South and West is to be a literature, not of books, but of life. It will draw its inspiration from original contact with men and with nature. It will have at first the rough-hewn quality of first-hand work. It is to out-run the old-world limitations.

Its vitalizing element will be its difference of treatment, which will not be that of any other literature of any other place or time, and it is extremely improbable that it will ever submit to any central academy, whether in New York or Chicago.

This school will be one where most notably the individuality of each writer will be respected, and this forbids strict conformity to accepted models. When life is the model and truth the criterion and individualism the coloring element of a literature, the central academy has small power. There will be association as of equals, not slavish acceptance of dictation.

Then again, hero-worship in literature is weakening. In the days when there were few literary men, and these few men professedly held strange powers entirely distinct from their fellows, something of awe went with the reader's admiration. To-day, when the ranks of the poets are thick with adepts, and when the novelists write of comprehensible subjects and lay no claim to mystic power, both poet and novelist are approached without ceremony. This also weakens the hold of the central academy.

The blight upon the literature of the West, like that of all provinces, has been its timidity, its tendency to work in accepted modes, its childish desire to write for the applause of its masters in the East. This has been, in fact, the weakness of the entire output of American literature. The West only emphasizes the fact. In material things, America has boundless self-assertion, but in the arts it has imitated because of its failure to perceive its proper relation to the literature of the world. The West, reckoning itself an annex of the East, has imitated imitations.

Because the East considered itself English in general character, the West, so far as most of its writers are concerned, has acquiesced. As a matter of fact, the West is not English. The Northwest is more largely Teutonic and Scandinavian, and the people of Indiana, Ohio, and Illinois are far removed from England and from English conceptions of life; and this distance is sure to find its statement in literature. Wisconsin, Iowa, Minnesota, Dakota, and other Western States are half composed of men and women of Germanic or Scandinavian extraction. The literature rising from these people will not be English. It will be something new; it will be, and ought to be, American,— that is to say, a new composite.

The centre of this literature of national scope, therefore, cannot be in the East. It will not be dominated by English idea. It will have no reference to Tennyson or Longfellow or Arnold. Its reference to the north of Europe, to Norway or Germany, will have less of benumbing effect, for these northern peoples are not so deeply enslaved to the past as England is.

The West should work in accordance with the fundamental principles of good writing; that is, it should seek to attain the most perfect lucidity, expressiveness, flexibility, and grace. Its technique should be comprehensible, clear in outline, and infinitely suggestive, ready to be submitted to the world, but free to use new forms.

The choice of subject and the quality which enters into it, like a subtle flavor into wine, should be individual, not subject to any school or master.

The judgment of the East should take rank merely among other judgments; it should not be held all-important.

The purpose of this writing is not merely to combat literary centralization, but also to build up local centres. Wherever a human soul is moved by genuine love of nature and of men to the conscientious and faithful study of the expression of his emotions, there is a literary centre. Around him are grouped minds whose candid criticism can aid and direct him; but this criticism must not evade, nor demand conformity to tradition; it must demand of the young writer truth, sincerity, and individuality.

Let the critics of the local centres remember Mistral and Whitcomb Riley, who won their way among the people before the critical journals would take count of them. It is the man who has no knowledge of accepted forms, and who therefore refers every work of art back to nature, who is quickest to respond to the literature of life. The average American is quick to thrill to real emotion, only he wants it direct and unaffected.

I believe in the local magazine. With the growth of inland cities in wealth and refinement, the magazine will come to displace the mere newspaper, possibly the newspaper will grow into the magazine. The work of the local magazines like "The Southern," "The Californian," "The Midland," "The Overland," can be made of vast importance in the nation's life.

Let them keep close to the local life, developing the best—that is, the simplest and most natural—talent of their region, making their appeal constantly to the unspoiled yet discerning taste of the middle-conditioned people, and they will succeed. "They have always failed in the past," says the doubter; possibly, but the past is not the present or the future. Taste is rising. Culture is broadening swiftly. A new generation is coming on,—a generation of veritists. Conditions grow more hospitable to this local literature with great rapidity. What was true of local conditions five years ago will scarcely be true to-day.

O Sayers and Doers of this broad, free inland America of ours! to you is given the privilege of being broad and free in your life and letters. You should not be bound to a false and dying culture, you should not endeavor to re-enact the harsh and fierce and false social dramas of the Old World. You should not turn your face to the east, to the past. Your comment should be that of free men and women, loving equality, justice, truth.

Yours not to worship crumbling idols; your privilege and pleasure should be to face life and the material earth in a new way,—moulding old forms of government into new shapes, catching from earth and sea and air, new songs to sing, new thoughts to frame, new deeds to dare.

23. WILLIAM DEAN HOWELLS
Mr. Garland's Books*

The life of any man of letters who has lived long with strong convictions becomes part of the literary history of his time, though the history may never acknowledge it. Or, if the reader will not allow so much as this, then we may agree that inevitably such an author's life becomes bound up with that of his literary contemporaries, especially his younger contemporaries. He must have been friends or foes with nearly all of them; in the wireless of print, whether he ever met them otherwise or not, he must have exchanged with them flashes of reciprocity or repulsion, electrical thrills, which remain memories after they have ceased to be actual experiences. Shall I own at once that in this abstract case some such relation was concrete in me and the author of these admirable books; that he is the younger contemporary and I the man of letters who has lived long with strong conviction?

I suppose we were friends in the beginning, and never foes, because he had strong convictions too, and they were flatteringly like mine. When first we met, twenty years ago or more, in a pleasant suburb of Boston, there was nothing but common ground between us, and our convictions played over it together as freely and affectionately as if they had been fancies. He was a realist to the point of idealism, and he was perhaps none the less, but much the more, realist because he had not yet had time to show his faith by his works. I mean his inventive works, for he was already writing radiant criticism in behalf of what he called veritism, a word he had borrowed, with due thanks, from a French critic whom he was reading with generous devotion and talking into any body who would hear him. There were as

---

* The selection constitutes the essay "Mr. Garland's Books." Reprinted from *The North American Review,* October 1912, by permission of the University of Northern Iowa.

yet only a few years between him and the Wisconsin farm which
grew him as genuinely as if he had been a product of its soil. He
was as poor as he was young, but he was so rich in purpose of
high economic and social import that he did not know he was
poor. Some day, perhaps, he will himself tell the tale of that
struggle to make both ends meet, the artistic and the economic
ends, in those Boston days, and by teaching and lecturing to
earn the time that he wished to spend in literature. He gladly
wrote in the Boston newspapers for nothing, and in the best of
them he was given the free hand which was far better for his
future than a conditioned salary could have been. As to his
present, he was such an ardent believer in Henry George's plan
for abolishing poverty that with his heart and hopes fixed on a
glorious tomorrow for all men he took no thought of his own
narrow day.

He seems at that time to have gone about preaching Georgism
equally with veritism in the same generous self-forgetfulness. A
large public, much more intelligent than the public which reads
novels instead of listening to lectures, already knew him, but I
was never of this worthier public so far as hearing him speak
was concerned, while we continued of the same thinking about
fiction. When we both left Boston and came to New York,
neither of us experienced that mental expansion, not to call it
distension, which is supposed to await the provincial arriving in
the metropolis; we still remained narrow-mindedly veritistic.
This possibly was because we were both doubly provincial,
being firstly Middle Westerners, and secondarily Bostonians, but
for whatever reason it was he had already begun to show his
faith by his works, in those severely conscientious studies of
Wisconsin life, which I should not blame the reader for finding
the best of his doing in fiction. But it is not necessary to make
any such restriction in one's liking in order to vouch one's high
sense of the art and the fact in *Main-Travelled Roads* and *Other
Main-Travelled Roads*. The volumes are happily named: these
highways are truly the paths that the sore feet of common men
and women have trodden to and fro in the rude new country;
they are thick with the dust and the snow of fierce summers
and savage winters. I do not say but they lead now and then
through beautiful springtimes and mellow autumns; they mostly
seek the lonely farmers, but sometimes they tarry in sociable
villages where youth and love have their dances. I do not think
that I am wrong in taking "The Return of the Private" and "Up

the Coolly" for types of the bare reality prevailing with the hot pity which comes from the painter's heart for the conditions he depicts.

At the time he was telling these grim stories of farm life in the West—that is, in the later years of his Boston sojourn—our author was much in contact with that great and sincere talent James A. Hearne, whom it was a dramatic education to know. So far as one influenced the other I do not think Mr. Garland owed more to Hearne than Hearne to him in practising in their art the veritism which they both preached. If I may confess a dreadful secret, I suspected them both at that time of being unconsciously romantic at heart, and only kept to reality because they did not know unreality. Hearne, in spite of such cunningest pieces of excelling nature as "Margaret Fleming" and "Drifting Apart," was often tempted to do the thing that was not—beautifully not, as Mr. James might say—in his other plays, and was willing to please his public with it, for of course the thing that is not will mainly please any public. I have no doubt the author of these books did very greatly help to stay the dramatist in his allegiance to the thing that was, while on his part Hearne doubtless helped his younger friend to clarify his native dramatic perception. At any rate, some plays relating to the nearer and farther West which Mr. Garland wrote in the heyday of his Hearne friendship (it lasted to the end of the great player's life) may have been inspired by his association with a man who was to the heart of his true humanity essentially representative. As both were secretly romantic a little, so both were openly idyllic a good deal. Of course Mr. Garland's treatment of country life is more direct, more authentic, more instructive, and there is pretty sure always to be a thrill or a throe of indignant compassion in it which the milder poet did not impart to his hearers. Some plays which the novelist wrote at this time (notably "Under the Lion's Paw," a tragedy of Far Western farming) expressed this compassion, still more directly and explicitly than the stories of *Main-Travelled Roads*, and I believe it the loss of our theatre that they have never got upon the stage.

But no doubt fortune that kept him to the story written to be read was not so unintelligent as her enemies might like to imagine. In the invention of such a group of novels as *Rose of Dutcher's Coolly*, *The Eagle's Heart*, *Hesper*, *The Captain of the*

Gray-Horse Troop, *Money Magic*, and *Cavanagh* he has justified the constancy of purpose which the fickle goddess has shown in his case. She seems to have known what she was about in guiding his talent from West to Farther West, from the farms to the wilds, and liberating it to the freer and bolder adventure which he must always have loved.

If the work seems to lose at times in closeness of texture on its westering way, it gains in breadth. The workman does not change in it; he is always what he was: mindful of his own past, and tenderly loyal to the simplest life, as embracing not only the potentialities but the actualities of beauty, of sublimity.

Mr. Garland's books seem to me as indigenous, in the true sense, as any our country has produced. They are western American, it is true, but America is mostly western now. But that is a question apart from the question of the author's literature. I for my part find this wholesome and edifying: I like being in the company of a man who believes so cordially in man's perfectibility; who believes that wrongs can really be righted, and that even in our depraved conditions, which imply selfishness as the greatest personal good, teaches that generosity and honesty and duty are wiser and better things. I like stirring adventure without bloodshed, as I find it so often in these pages; I like love which is sweet and pure, chivalry which is in its senses, honor for women which recognizes that while all women ultimately are good and beautiful some women are better and beautifuler than others, and some are more foolish and potentially vile enough to keep the balance of the virtues even between the sexes.

This brings me to the question of something in the author's work which I suppose has given question of its advantage to other readers as well as myself. It is something which deals with character rather than incident, and has nothing of that bad allure of so much modern fiction in its dances of the seven veils. It puts the gross passions, the propensities to shame, rather than flatters or entices them; but it doesn't recognize the beast in the man's desire of the woman, the satyr leer which is the complement of the lover's worship. In *Rose of Dutcher's Coolly*, in *Hesper*, in *Money Magic*, measurably in them all, you find the refusal, when it comes to the fact, to ignore what cannot be denied. I am old-fashioned, and I have moments when I could wish that the author had not been of such unsparing conscience. That is all, and with this wish noted I can give myself to the entire pleasure which the purity and wholesomeness of his fiction offers me.

There is an apparent want of continuity in his work. He has ventured from the open day at times into the mystical regions of old night, but the books here are an unbroken series in which the average West and Far West may behold itself as in a mirror. There is throughout, and in spite of everything, a manly and hopeful belief in the perfectibility of man and things. Indians, soldiers, woods, water, he teaches me that they may all be considered to the national advantage. He does not allow me to despair of the hero, even of the heroine; he finds me new sorts of these in every sort of people and persuades me that they may still be naturally and charmingly in love with one another. He paints me a West in which the physiognomy of the East has put on new expression, kindlier, gentler, truer, he makes me imagine a life out there which has been somehow pacified and humbled and exalted as an escape from death and restored in gratitude to new usefulness in that new air on that new earth. He holds me with his story and he will not let me go till he has taught me something more than he has told me. Greater than this I do not think we ought to ask of any, and if we do I am sure we shall not get it.

At the end of my praise I feel that I should leave it largely unspoken if I did not specify the power with which certain characters and characteristics are enforced in this book and in that. With some hesitancy I choose *Money Magic* as possibly the most masterly of the author's books. More than any other since the stories of *The Main-Travelled Roads*, it expresses constancy to his old young ideal of veritism. He has not hesitated to take clay from the "rude breast of the unexhausted West," and he has molded it in shapes which breathe as with a life of their own like Bertha and Mart Haney (Marshall Haney); she the young, beautiful wife and he an old broken gambler, are heroine and hero on their own plane, where they may stand with the creations of great modern fiction. The make as well as the manner of the uneducated girl, derived from New England and bred on the frontier, but not with all her slang and Far Western freedom underbred, is not more credibly portrayed than the rough Irishman who has outlived the saloon-keeper and desperado and has re-entered as it were into the primitive goodness of his generous nature. In both the power and the

meaning of vast wealth is studied, what it can and what it
cannot do, as I do not remember to have found it studied
before. They seem the witnesses of its magic, rather than
sorcerers who work it. The situation is most interesting, and the
situation in Mr. Garland's book is what interests me more than
the action; if I can know what people are, rather than what they
do, I am the more content; and I have noted with the
satisfaction which I should like to have others feel the clear
conditioning of his people. In fact, his people mainly derive
their importance from that. A given book of his does not
present a problem for this or that character to solve it; it
describes a condition which shall test him. Sometimes it is an
unfriendly condition, sometimes not; but the business is to
show how he copes with it. In *Money Magic*, in *The Captain of
the Gray-Horse Troop*, in *Cavanagh*, in *Hesper*, in *The Eagle's
Heart*, it is always a sense of the conditions which remains with
me. I remember the persons from them as I learned to recognize
the persons from them in their full meaning. Perhaps this is so
in the novels of others, but I do not think it is, and I consider
Mr. Garland's novels for this reason particularly valuable as
materials of social history, no less than as very entertaining
personal history. One cannot read them (and if you begin on
them you *must* read them) without becoming more and more
convinced that it is our conditioning which determines our
characters, even though it does not always determine our
actions. The strong man, the good woman, grows stronger and
better for the struggle with them, though I am not sure that this
is what Mr. Garland is conscious of seeking to show. I dare say
that he paints them and cannot help painting them, because in
his own career he has been passionately sensible of their stress
even when he has not mastered all their meaning. As a singularly
American artist, too, he instinctively devotes himself to the
portrayal of conditions because America itself is all a novel
condition.

VI. Frank Norris: Adapting Naturalism

The most enthusiastic American advocate of the naturalistic novel was undoubtedly Frank Norris (1870-1902). Like his near contemporaries, Hamlin Garland and Stephen Crane (1871-1900), he was consciously "modern," and, perhaps by reason of his youth as well as his convictions, anxious to demonstrate and define his differences with the older literary establishment represented for him by William Dean Howells, above all. Fortunate circumstance afforded Norris wider intellectual opportunities than most writers of his generation enjoyed. The son of a wealthy jewelry merchant, he went to Europe, studied art in Paris at the Julian *atelier*, and made a grand tour of Africa, where he saw the Boer uprising. He spent four years at the University of California and a year at Harvard, where he studied writing with Professor Lewis E. Gates, to whom his novel *McTeague* (1899) is dedicated. Like all naturalists, Norris was well-versed in evolutionary theory, but it seems likely that he was most influenced not by Darwin or (as Theodore Dreiser was) by Spencer, but by another of his teachers, Professor Joseph Le Comte, with whom he studied at Berkeley. Le Comte was one of a number of American philosophers (or professors of philosophy) who labored mightily to square evolutionary theory with Christian theology and so to preserve the assurance of a guiding moral force at work in universal nature. Something of his position may be gathered from the title of his major work—*Evolution: Its Nature, Its Evidences, and Its Relation to Religious Thought* (1888). For such adaptations of Christian theology, Americans had, in some measure, been prepared by the work of liberal Protestant thinkers of the 1840's and 1850's. Of these the best known is Ralph Waldo Emerson. Any reader of Emerson's "Nature" will find a familiar note in Le Comte's statement that "God is immanent, resident in Nature. Nature is the house of many mansions in which he ever dwells . . . The objects of Nature are objectified, externalized—materialized states of Divine consciousness, or Divine

284

thoughts objectified by the Divine will."* Such assertions
relieve or negate the picture of amoral struggle which many
thinkers found and feared in purely scientific presentations of
evolutionary theory. Norris' acceptance of Le Comte's ideas
significantly modified the deterministic attitudes he found in
the naturalistic novels of Zola. The role of the "immanent"
Ideal may be traced in Norris' fiction. In his critical comments,
it may help to explain a strain of optimism, even propriety,
unparalleled in European naturalism. In the review entitled "A
Case in Point," William Dean Howells objected that the "picture
of life" Norris drew in *McTeague* "is not true, because it leaves
beauty out. Life is squalid and cruel and vile and hateful, but it
is noble and tender and pure and lovely, too." Norris, thanking
Howells for his review, agreed: "You were quite right," he
wrote, "in saying that the novel that is true to life cannot afford
to ignore the finer things."

As a critic, Norris is known for *The Responsibilities of the
Novelist* (1903). The essays in this volume first appeared in
various journals between 1901 and 1903. They were gathered
and published, unedited, in book form after Norris' death.
Hastily written, journalistic, and, of course, never intended as a
single volume, the various essays cannot be said to present a
fully developed theory of the novel. Nonetheless, *The Responsibilities of the Novelist* became, in the words of V. L.
Parrington, "the textbook of the young naturalists."

Throughout these essays, Norris carries on a friendly argument
with Howells and the genteel literary establishment he represents. Two central terms in this one-sided debate are "romanticism" and "the romance." For Howells in his criticism of the
1880's, "romanticism" meant exaggerated sentiment and inflated idealism, as well as misleading, morally dangerous, indifference to "actualities," the simple truths of commonplace experience. The "romance" for Howells was a tale, like those of Sir
Walter Scott or James Fenimore Cooper, which utilized improbable situations and heroic characters and was probably set in the
long ago or far away. In his attempt to rescue these terms from
critical "abuse," Norris tries to present new definitions. "Romanticism" is not, he insists, "sentimentalism." It is not, that is

* Joseph Le Comte, *Evolution: Its Nature, Its Evidences, and Its Relation to
Religious Thought* (1888) quoted in Donald Pizer, *The Novels of Frank Norris,*
(Bloomington, Indiana University Press, 1966). Pizer's discussion of Le Comte's
influence is thorough and convincing. I am indebted to it throughout.

to say, adequately represented by the popular romance. The "romance" itself should be known not by such properties as adventure, but by its attitude toward life. It is, Norris says, "the kind of fiction that takes cognizance of variations from the type of moral life." What "variations" means is suggested by his personification of Romance "prying, peeping, peering into the closets" of the house next door, searching out "a complete revelation of my neighbor's secretest life." It is not, apparently, the *abnormal* that she seeks but the private, personal, passionate life, or what Nathaniel Hawthorne called "the truths of the human heart."

Norris urges the revival of "romance" because "realism" (by which he means Howellsian realism) seems to him to provide inadequate accounts of life. His need to argue the case indicates how completely this style dominated American writing, and publishing, in the early 1900's. But realism seems to Norris limited because, in the first place, it is concerned only with the "surface of things." There is truth in this observation, but Norris seems impatient with the decorum of the realistic novel which at its best (as in the work of Jane Austen) conveys depths of feeling in small gestures and silences more effective than revelations. Norris also, more emphatically, complains that realism draws its materials from the commonplace, the dull average of everyday middle-class life. In an essay entitled "Zola as a Romantic Writer" (first published in 1896), he comments that

> We ourselves are Mr. Howells' characters, so long as we are well-behaved and ordinary and bourgeois, so long as we are not adventurous or not rich or not unconventional. If we are otherwise, if things commence to happen to us, if we kill a man or two, or get mixed up in a traffic affair, or do something on a large scale, such as the amassing of enormous wealth or power or fame, Mr. Howells cuts our acquaintance at once. He will none of us if we are out of the usual.

Realism, that is to say, tells only a part of the truth. It avoids the tragic and adventurous, which is also part of "life." But, more significantly, it depicts only a narrow segment of American society. It shows the affluent, urban world: "things that are likely to happen between lunch and supper, small passions, restricted emotions, dramas of the reception-room, tragedies of an afternoon call, crises involving cups of tea."

If one fault of realism is familiarity, the interest of romance is, in part, sensationalism. Thus Zola, whose materials are, Norris says, "extraordinary, imaginative, grotesque, even, with a vague note of terror quivering throughout like the vibration of an ominous and low-pitched diapason," is, for all his attention to the "facts," romantic. He writes of prostitutes and drunkards, strange adventures, disease, inhuman brutality, murder and lurid crimes, and so he awakens us (though Norris does not emphasize the point) to realms of suffering and injustice the bourgeois novel rarely even suggests. On the basis of the essays in *The Responsibilities of the Novelist*, it would be hard to affirm that Norris deliberately tried to present naturalism as an inevitable synthesis of the romance and the realistic novel, combining the drama of the one with the social conscience of the other. But this strong suggestion in his essays may explain their influence upon other young writers at the turn of the century. Norris' naturalism points the way to new materials—the grandeur of the epic West as well as the seamy depths of urban slums—but it also maintains the discipline of "fact" and relevance. It goes, of course, far beyond the localism or personalism Hamlin Garland advocated to suggest dramas of poverty and social injustice which, except in the abolition novels of the pre-Civil War decades, were still little known in American literature.

Even so Norris did not attack the fundamentally conservative basis of American literature. He accepted, as fully as Howells, the need for authorial self-restraint in fiction and the educational mission of the American writer. Reviewing *McTeague*, Howells worried that the day would come when "the old-fashioned American ideal of a novel as something which may be read by all ages and sexes," should be abandoned in favor of "the European notion" of the novel, "as something fit only for age and experience, and for men rather than women." Had he then read *The Responsibilities of the Novelist*, especially the chapter entitled "Salt and Sincerity," he would have known that Norris shared his tender concern for the innocent conscience of the American girl. Norris is deeply aware of the popular author's duty to his enormous and, it seems, most impressionable audience, those "one hundred and fifty thousand people who—unenlightened—*believe what he says*," and, less of an entertainer than a teacher, he shoulders the burden of bringing his readers "Truth."

24. *The Responsibilities of the Novelist:*
THE RESPONSIBILITIES OF THE NOVELIST*

It is not here a question of the "unarrived," the "unpublished"; these are the care-free irresponsibles whose hours are halcyon and whose endeavours have all the lure, all the recklessness of adventure. They are not recognized; they have made no standards for themselves, and if they play the *saltimbanque* and the charlatan nobody cares and nobody (except themselves) is affected.

But the writers in question are the successful ones who have made a public and to whom some ten, twenty or a hundred thousand people are pleased to listen. You may believe if you choose that the novelist, of all workers, is independent—that he can write what he pleases, and that certainly, certainly he should never "write down to his readers"—that he should never consult them at all.

On the contrary, I believe it can be proved that the successful novelist should be more than all others limited in the nature and character of his work more than all others he should be careful of what he says; more than all others he should defer to his audience; more than all others—more even than the minister and the editor—he should feel "his public" and watch his every word, testing carefully his every utterance, weighing with the most relentless precision his every statement; in a word, possess a sense of his responsibilities.

For the novel is the great expression of modern life. Each form of art has had its turn at reflecting and expressing its contemporaneous thought. Time was when the world looked to the architects of the castles and great cathedrals to truly reflect and embody its ideals. And the architects—serious, earnest men—produced such "expressions of contemporaneous

---

* The selection constitutes the entire essay "The Responsibilities of the Novelist" by Frank Norris in *The Responsibilities of the Novelist and Other Literary Essays* (1903).

thought" as the Castle of Coucy and the Church of Notre
Dame. Then with other times came other customs, and the
painters had their day. The men of the Renaissance trusted
Angelo and Da Vinci and Velasquez to speak for them, and
trusted not in vain. Next came the age of drama. Shakespeare
and Marlowe found the value of x for the life and the times in
which they lived. Later on contemporary life had been so
modified that neither painting, architecture nor drama was the
best vehicle of expression, the day of the longer poems arrived,
and Pope and Dryden spoke for their fellows.

Thus the sequence. Each age speaks with its own peculiar
organ, and has left the Word for us moderns to read and
understand. The Castle of Coucy and the Church of Notre
Dame are the spoken words of the Middle Ages. The Renaissance speaks—and intelligibly—to us through the sibyls of the
Sistine chapel and the Mona Lisa. "Macbeth" and "Tamerlane"
résumé the whole spirit of the Elizabethan age, while the "Rape
of the Lock" is a wireless message to us straight from the period
of the Restoration.

To-day is the day of the novel. In no other day and by no
other vehicle is contemporaneous life so adequately expressed;
and the critics of the twenty-second century, reviewing our
times, striving to reconstruct our civilization, will look not to
the painters, not to the architects nor dramatists, but to the
novelists to find our idiosyncrasy.

I think this is true. I think if the matter could in any way be
statisticized, the figures would bear out the assumption. There
is no doubt the novel will in time "go out" of popular favour as
irrevocably as the long poem has gone, and for the reason that it
is no longer the right mode of expression.

It is interesting to speculate upon what will take its place.
Certainly the coming civilization will revert to no former means
of expressing its thought or its ideals. Possibly music will be the
interpreter of the life of the twenty-first and twenty-second
centuries. Possibly one may see a hint of this in the characterization of Wagner's operas as the "Music of the Future."

This, however, is parenthetical and beside the mark. Remains
the fact that to-day is the day of the novel. By this one does not
mean that the novel is merely popular. If the novel was not
something more than a simple diversion, a means of whiling
away a dull evening, a long railway journey, it would not,
believe me, remain in favour another day.

If the novel, then, is popular, it is popular with a reason, a vital, inherent reason; that is to say, it is essential. Essential—to resume once more the proposition—because it expresses modern life better than architecture, better than painting, better than poetry, better than music. It is as necessary to the civilization of the twentieth century as the violin is necessary to Kubelik, as the piano is necessary to Paderewski, as the plane is necessary to the carpenter, the sledge to the blacksmith, the chisel to the mason. It is an instrument, a tool, a weapon, a vehicle. It is that thing which, in the hand of man, makes him civilized and no longer savage, because it gives him a power of durable, permanent expression. So much for the novel—the instrument.

Because it is so all-powerful to-day, the people turn to him who wields this instrument with every degree of confidence. They expect—and rightly—that results shall be commensurate with means. The unknown archer who grasps the bow of Ulysses may be expected by the multitude to send his shaft far and true. If he is not true nor strong he has no business with the bow. The people give heed to him only because he bears a great weapon. He himself knows before he shoots whether or no he is worthy.

It is all very well to jeer at the People and at the People's misunderstanding of the arts, but the fact is indisputable that no art that is not in the end understood by the People can live or ever did live a single generation. In the larger view, in the last analysis, the People pronounce the final judgment. The People, despised of the artist, hooted, caricatured and vilified, are after all, and in the main, the real seekers after Truth. Who is it, after all, whose interest is liveliest in any given work of art? It is not now a question of *esthetic* interest—that is, the artist's, the amateur's, the *cognoscente's*. It is a question of *vital* interest. Say what you will, Maggie Tulliver—for instance—is far more a living being for Mrs. Jones across the street than she is for your sensitive, fastidious, keenly critical artist, litterateur, or critic. The People—Mrs. Jones and her neighbours—take the life history of these fictitious characters, these novels, to heart with a seriousness that the esthetic cult have no conception of. The cult consider them almost solely from their artistic sides. The People take them into their innermost lives. Nor do the People discriminate. Omnivorous readers as they are to-day, they make little distinction between Maggie Tulliver and the heroine of the last "popular novel." They do not stop to separate true from false; they do not care.

How necessary it becomes, then, for those who, by the simple art of writing, can invade the heart's heart of thousands, whose novels are received with such measureless earnestness—how necessary it becomes for those who wield such power to use it rightfully. Is it not expedient to act fairly? Is it not in Heaven's name essential that the People hear, not a lie, but the Truth?

If the novel were not one of the most important factors of modern life; if it were not the completest expression of our civilization; if its influence were not greater than all the pulpits, than all the newspapers between the oceans, it would not be so important that its message should be true.

But the novelist to-day is the one who reaches the greatest audience. Right or wrong, the People turn to him the moment he speaks, and what he says they believe.

For the Million, Life is a contracted affair, is bounded by the walls of the narrow channel of affairs in which their feet are set. They have no horizon. They look to-day as they never have looked before, as they never will look again, to the writer of fiction to give them an idea of life beyond their limits, and they believe him as they never have believed before and never will again.

This being so, is it not difficult to understand how certain of these successful writers of fiction—these favoured ones into whose hands the gods have placed the great bow of Ulysses—can look so frivolously upon their craft? It is not necessary to specify. One speaks of those whose public is measured by "one hundred and fifty thousand copies sold." We know them, and because the gods have blessed us with wits beyond our deserving we know their work is false. But what of the "hundred and fifty thousand" who are not discerning and who receive this falseness as Truth, who believe this topsy-turvy picture of Life beyond their horizons is real and vital and sane?

There is no gauge to measure the extent of this malignant influence. Public opinion is made no one can say how, by infinitesimal accretions, by a multitude of minutest elements. Lying novels, surely, surely in this day and age of indiscriminate reading, contribute to this more than all other influences of present-day activity.

The Pulpit, the Press and the Novel—these indisputably are the

great moulders of public opinion and public morals to-day. But
the Pulpit speaks but once a week; the Press is read with
lightning haste and the morning news is waste-paper by noon.
But the novel goes into the home to stay. It is read word for
word; is talked about, discussed; its influence penetrates every
chink and corner of the family.

Yet novelists are not found wanting who write for money. I
do not think this is an unfounded accusation. I do not think it
asking too much of credulity. This would not matter if they
wrote the Truth. But these gentlemen who are "in literature for
their own pocket every time" have discovered that for the
moment the People have confounded the Wrong with the Right,
and prefer that which is a lie to that which is true. "Very well,
then," say these gentlemen. "If they want a lie they shall have
it;" and they give the People a lie in return for royalties.

The surprising thing about this is that you and I and all the
rest of us do not consider this as disreputable—do not yet
realize that the novelist has responsibilities. We condemn an
editor who sells his editorial columns, and we revile the pulpit
attainted of venality. But the venal novelist—he whose influence
is greater than either the Press or Pulpit—*him* we greet with a
wink and the tongue in the cheek.

This should not be so. Somewhere the protest should be
raised, and those of us who see the practice of this fraud should
bring home to ourselves the realization that the selling of one
hundred and fifty thousand books is a serious business. The
People have a right to the Truth as they have a right to life,
liberty and the pursuit of happiness. It is *not* right that they be
exploited and deceived with false views of life, false characters,
false sentiment, false morality, false history, false philosophy,
false emotions, false heroism, false notions of self-sacrifice, false
views of religion, of duty, of conduct and of manners.

The man who can address an audience of one hundred and
fifty thousand people who—unenlightened—*believe what he
says*, has a heavy duty to perform, and tremendous responsibilities to shoulder; and he should address himself to his task
not with the flippancy of a catch-penny juggler at the county
fair, but with earnestness, with soberness, with a sense of his
limitations, and with all the abiding sincerity that by the favour
and mercy of the gods may be his.

25. *The Responsibilities of the Novelist:*
THE NEED OF A LITERARY CONSCIENCE*

Pilate saith unto them: "what is truth?" and it is of record that he received no answer—and for very obvious reasons. For is it not a fact, that he who asks that question must himself find the answer, and that not even one sent from Heaven can be of hope or help to him if he is not willing to go down into his own heart and into his own life to find it?

To sermonize, to elaborate a disquisition on nice distinctions of metaphysics is not appropriate here. But it is—so one believes—appropriate to consider a certain very large class of present day novelists of the United States who seldom are stirred by that spirit of inquiry that for a moment disturbed the Roman, who do *not* ask what is truth, who do not in fact care to be truthful at all, and who—and this is the serious side of the business—are bringing the name of American literature perilously near to disrepute.

One does not quarrel for one instant with the fact that certain books of the writers in question have attained phenomenally large circulations. This is as it should be. There are very many people in the United States, and compared with such a figure as seventy million, a mere hundred thousand of books sold is no great matter.

But here—so it seems—is the point. He who can address a hundred thousand people is, no matter what his message may be, in an important position. It is a large audience, one hundred thousand, larger than any roofed building now standing could contain. Less than one one-hundredth part of that number nominated Lincoln. Less than half of it won Waterloo.

And it must be remembered that for every one person who

* The selection constitutes the entire essay "The Need of a Literary Conscience" by Frank Norris in *The Responsibilities of the Novelist and Other Literary Essays* (1903).

buys a book there are three who will read it and half a dozen
who will read what some one else has written about it, so that
the sphere of influence widens indefinitely, and the audience
that the writer addresses approaches the half-million mark.

Well and good; but if the audience is so vast, if the influence is
so far-reaching, if the example set is so contagious, it becomes
incumbent to ask, it becomes imperative to demand that the
half-million shall be told the truth and not a lie.

And this thing called truth—"what is it?" says Pilate, and the
average man conceives at once of an abstraction, a vague idea, a
term borrowed from the metaphysicians, certainly nothing that
has to do with practical, tangible, concrete work-a-day life.

Error! If truth is not an actual workaday thing, as practical as
a cable-car, as real and homely and workaday and commonplace
as a bootjack, then indeed are we of all men most miserable and
our preaching vain.

And truth in fiction is just as real and just as important as
truth anywhere else—as in Wall Street, for instance. A man who
does not tell the truth there, and who puts the untruth upon
paper over his signature, will be very promptly jailed. In the
case of the Wall Street man the sum of money in question may
be trivial—$100, $50. But the untruthful novelist who starts in
motion something like half a million dollars invokes not fear
nor yet reproach. If truth in the matter of the producing of
novels is not an elusive, intangible abstraction, what, then, is it?
Let us get at the hard nub of the business, something we can
hold in the hand. It is the thing that is one's own, the discovery
of a subject suitable for fictitious narration that has never yet
been treated, and the conscientious study of that subject and
the fair presentation of results. Not a difficult matter, it would
appear, not an abstraction, not a philosophical kink. Newspaper
reporters, who are not metaphysicians, unnamed, unrewarded,
despised, even, and hooted and hounded, are doing this every
day. They do it on a meager salary, and they call the affair a
"scoop." Is the standard of the novelist—he who is entrusted
with the good name of his nation's literature—lower than that
of a reporter?

"Ah, but it is so hard to be original," "ah, but it is so hard to
discover anything new." Great Heavens! when a new life comes
into the world for every tick of the watch in your pocket—a
new life with all its complications, and with all the thousand
and one other complications it sets in motion!

Hard to be original! when of all of those billion lives your own is as distinct, as individual, as "original," as though you were born out of season in the Paleozoic age and yours the first human face the sun ever shone upon.

Go out into the street and stand where the ways cross and hear the machinery of life work clashing in its grooves. Can the utmost resort of your ingenuity evolve a better story than any one of the millions that jog your elbow? Shut yourself in your closet and turn your eyes inward upon yourself—deep *into* yourself, down, down into the heart of you; and the tread of the feet upon the pavement is the systole and diastole of your own being—different only in degree. It is life; and it is that which you must have to make your book, your novel—life, not other people's novels.

Or look from your window. A whole Literature goes marching by, clamouring for a leader and a master hand to guide it. You have but to step from your doorway. And instead of this, instead of entering into the leadership that is yours by right divine, instead of this, you must toilfully, painfully endeavour to crawl into the armour of the chief of some other cause, the harness of the leader of some other progress.

But you will not fit into the panoply. You may never brace that buckler upon your arm, for by your very act you stand revealed as a littler man than he who should be chief—a littler man and a weaker; and the casque will fall so far over your face that it will only blind you, and the sword will trip you, and the lance, too ponderous, will falter in your grip, and all that life which surges and thunders behind you will in time know you to be the false leader, and as you stumble will trample you in its onrush, and leave you dead and forgotten upon the road.

And just as a misconception of the truth makes of this the simplest and homeliest of things, a vagary, an abstraction and a bugbear, so it is possible that a misconception of the Leader creates the picture of a great and dreadful figure wrapped in majesty, solemn and profound. So that perhaps for very lack of self-confidence, for very diffidence, one shrinks from lifting the sword of him and from enduing one's forehead with the casque that seems so ponderous.

In other causes no doubt the leader must be chosen from the wise and great. In science and finance one looks to him to be a strong man, a swift and a sure man. But the literature that to-day shouts all in vain for its chief needs no such a one as this.

Here the battle is not to the strong nor yet the race to the swift. Here the leader is no vast, stern being, profound, solemn, knowing all things, but, on the contrary, is as humble as the lowliest that follow after him. So that it need not be hard to step into that place of eminence. Not by arrogance, nor by assumption, nor by the achievement of the world's wisdom, shall you be made worthy of the place of high command. But it will come to you, if it comes at all, because you shall have kept yourself young and humble and pure in heart, and so unspoiled and unwearied and unjaded that you shall find a joy in the mere rising of the sun, a wholesome, sane delight in the sound of the wind at night, a pleasure in the sight of the hills at evening, shall see God in a little child and a whole religion in a brooding bird.

26. *The Responsibilities of the Novelist:*
A NEGLECTED EPIC*

Suddenly we have found that there is no longer any Frontier. The westward-moving course of empire has at last crossed the Pacific Ocean. Civilization has circled the globe and has come back to its starting point, the vague and mysterious East.

The thing has not been accomplished peacefully. From the very first it has been an affair of wars—of invasions. Invasions of the East by the West, and of raids North and South—raids accomplished by flying columns that dashed out from both sides of the main army. Sometimes even the invaders have fought among themselves, as for instance the Trojan War, or the civil wars of Italy, England and America; sometimes they have turned back on their tracks and, upon one pretext or another, reconquered the races behind them, as for instance Alexander's wars to the eastward, the Crusades, and Napoleon's Egyptian campaigns.

Retarded by all these obstacles, the march has been painfully slow. To move from Egypt to Greece took centuries of time. More centuries were consumed in the campaign that brought empire from Greece to Rome, and still more centuries passed before it crossed the Alps and invaded northern and western Europe.

But observe. Once across the Mississippi, the West—our Far West—was conquered in about forty years. In all the vast campaign from east to west here is the most signal victory, the swiftest, the completest, the most brilliant achievement—the wilderness subdued at a single stroke.

Now all these various fightings to the westward, these mysterious race-movements, migrations, wars and wanderings have produced their literature, distinctive, peculiar, excellent. And

* The selection constitutes the entire essay "A Neglected Epic" by Frank Norris in *The Responsibilities of the Novelist and Other Literary Essays* (1903).

this literature we call epic. The Trojan War gave us the "Iliad," the "Odyssey" and the "Aeneid"; the campaign of the Greeks in Asia Minor produced the "Anabasis"; a whole cycle of literature grew from the conquest of Europe after the fall of Rome—"The Song of Roland," "The Nibelungenlied," "The Romance of the Rose," "Beowulf," "Magnusson," "The Scotch Border Ballads," "The Poem of the Cid," "The Hemskringla," "Orlando Furioso," "Jerusalem Delivered," and the like.

On this side of the Atlantic, in his clumsy, artificial way, but yet recognized as a producer of literature, Cooper has tried to chronicle the conquest of the eastern part of our country. Absurd he may be in his ideas of life and character, the art in him veneered over with charlatanism; yet the man was solemn enough and took his work seriously, and his work is literature.

Also a cycle of romance has grown up around the Civil War. The theme has had its poets to whom the public have been glad to listen. The subject is vast, noble; is, in a word, epic, just as the Trojan War and the Retreat of the Ten Thousand were epic.

But when at last one comes to look for the literature that sprang from and has grown up around the last great epic event in the history of civilization, the event which in spite of stupendous difficulties was consummated more swiftly, more completely, more satisfactorily than any like event since the westward migration began—I mean the conquering of the West, the subduing of the wilderness beyond the Mississippi—What has this produced in the way of literature? The dime novel! The dime novel and nothing else. The dime novel and nothing better.

The Trojan War left to posterity the character of Hector; the wars with the Saracens gave us Roland; the folklore of Iceland produced Grettir; the Scotch border poetry brought forth the Douglas; the Spanish epic the Cid. But the American epic, just as heroic, just as elemental, just as important and as picturesque, will fade into history leaving behind no finer type, no nobler hero than Buffalo Bill.

The young Greeks sat on marble terraces overlooking the Aegean Sea and listened to the thunderous roll of Homer's hexameter. In the feudal castles the minstrel sang to the young boys, of Roland. The farm folk of Iceland to this very day treasure up and read to their little ones hand-written copies of the Gretla Saga chronicling the deeds and death of Grettir the

Strong. But the youth of the United States learn of their epic by paying a dollar to see the "Wild West Show."

The plain truth of the matter is that we have neglected our epic—the black shame of it be on us—and no contemporaneous poet or chronicler thought it worth his while to sing the song or tell the tale of the West because literature in the day when the West was being won was a cult indulged in by certain well-bred gentlemen in New England who looked eastward to the Old World, to the legends of England and Norway and Germany and Italy for their inspiration, and left the great, strong, honest, fearless, resolute deeds of their own countrymen to be defamed and defaced by the nameless hacks of the "yellow back" libraries.

One man—who wrote "How Santa Claus Came to Simpson's Bar"—one poet, one chronicler did, in fact, arise for the moment, who understood that wild, brave life and who for a time gave promise of bearing record of things seen.

One of the requirements of an epic—a true epic—is that its action must devolve upon some great national event. There was no lack of such in those fierce years after '49. Just that long and terrible journey from the Mississippi to the ocean is an epic in itself. Yet no serious attempt has ever been made by an American author to render into prose or verse this event in our history as "national" in scope, in origin and in results as the Revolution itself. The prairie schooner is as large a figure in the legends as the black ship that bore Ulysses homeward from Troy. The sea meant as much to the Argonauts of the fifties as it did to the ten thousand.

And the Alamo! There is a trumpet-call in the word; and only the look of it on the printed page is a flash of fire. But the very histories slight the deed, and to many an American, born under the same flag that the Mexican rifles shot to ribbons on that splendid day, the word is meaningless. Yet Thermopylae was less glorious, and in comparison with that siege the investment of Troy was mere wanton riot. At the very least the Texans in that battered adobe church fought for the honour of their flag and the greater glory of their country, not for loot or the possession of the person of an adultress. Young men are taught to consider the "Iliad," with its butcheries, its glorification of inordinate selfishness and vanity, as a classic. Achilles, murderer, egoist, ruffian and liar, is a hero. But the name of Bowie, the

name of the man who gave his life to his flag at the Alamo, is
perpetuated only in the designation of a knife. Crockett is the
hero only of a "funny story" about a sagacious coon; while
Travis, the boy commander who did what Gordon with an
empire back of him failed to do, is quietly and definitely
ignored.

Because we have done nothing to get at the truth about the
West; because our best writers have turned to the old-country
folklore and legends for their inspiration; because "melancholy
harlequins" strut in fringed leggings upon the street-corners, one
hand held out for pennies, we have come to believe that our
West, our epic, was an affair of Indians, road-agents and
desperadoes, and have taken no account of the brave men who
stood for law and justice and liberty, and for those great ideas
died by the hundreds, unknown and unsung—died that the West
might be subdued, that the last stage of the march should be
accomplished, that the Anglo-Saxon should fulfil his destiny
and complete the cycle of the world.

The great figure of our neglected epic, the Hector of our
ignored Iliad, is not, as the dime novels would have us believe, a
lawbreaker, but a lawmaker; a fighter, it is true, as is always the
case with epic figures, but a fighter for peace, a calm, grave,
strong man who hated the lawbreaker as the hound hates the
wolf.

He did not lounge in barrooms; he did not cheat at cards; he
did not drink himself to maudlin fury; he did not "shoot at the
drop of the hat." But he loved his horse, he loved his friend, he
was kind to little children; he was always ready to side with the
weak against the strong, with the poor against the rich. For
hypocrisy and pretense, for shams and subterfuges he had no
mercy, no tolerance. He was too brave to lie and too strong to
steal. The odds in that lawless day were ever against him; his
enemies were many and his friends were few; but his face was
always set bravely against evil, and fear was not in him even at
the end. For such a man as this could die no quiet death in a
land where law went no further than the statute books and life
lay in the crook of my neighbour's forefinger.

He died in defense of an ideal, an epic hero, a legendary
figure, formidable, sad. He died facing down injustice, dishonesty and crime; died "in his boots"; and the same world that has
glorified Achilles and forgotten Travis finds none too poor to
do him reverence. No literature has sprung up around him—this

great character native to America. He is of all the world-types the one distinctive to us—peculiar, particular and unique. He is dead and even his work is misinterpreted and misunderstood. His very memory will soon be gone, and the American epic, which, on the shelves of posterity, should have stood shoulder to shoulder with the "Hemskringla" and the "Tales of the Nibelungen" and the "Song of Roland," will never be written.

27. *The Responsibilities of the Novelist:*
A PLEA FOR ROMANTIC FICTION*

Let us at the start make a distinction. Observe that one speaks of romanticism and not sentimentalism. One claims that the latter is as distinct from the former as is that other form of art which is called Realism. Romance has been often put upon and overburdened by being forced to bear the onus of abuse that by right should fall to sentiment; but the two should be kept very distinct, for a very high and illustrious place will be claimed for romance, while sentiment will be handed down the scullery stairs.

Many people to-day are composing mere sentimentalism, and calling it and causing it to be called romance; so with those who are too busy to think much upon these subjects, but who none the less love honest literature, Romance, too, has fallen into disrepute. Consider now the cut-and-thrust stories. They are all labeled Romances, and it is very easy to get the impression that Romance must be an affair of cloaks and daggers, or moonlight and golden hair. But this is not so at all. The true Romance is a more serious business than this. It is not merely a conjurer's trick-box, full of flimsy quackeries, tinsel and claptraps, meant only to amuse, and relying upon deception to do even that. Is it not something better than this? Can we not see in it an instrument, keen, finely tempered, flawless—an instrument with which we may go straight through the clothes and tissues and wrappings of flesh down deep into the red, living heart of things?

Is all this too subtle, too merely speculative and intrinsic, too *precieuse* and nice and "literary"? Devoutly one hopes the contrary. So much is made of so-called Romanticism in present-day fiction that the subject seems worthy of discussion, and a protest against the misuse of a really noble and honest formula of literature appears to be timely—misuse, that is, in the sense of limited use. Let us suppose for the moment that a

* The selection constitutes the entire essay "A Plea for Romantic Fiction" by Frank Norris in *The Responsibilities of the Novelist and Other Literary Essays* (1903).

romance can be made out of a cut-and-thrust business. Good Heavens, are there no other things that are romantic, even in this—falsely, falsely called—humdrum world of to-day? Why should it be that so soon as the novelist addresses himself—seriously—to the consideration of contemporary life he must abandon Romance and take up that harsh, loveless, colourless, blunt tool called Realism?

Now, let us understand at once what is meant by Romance and what by Realism. Romance, I take it, is the kind of fiction that takes cognizance of variations from the type of normal life. Realism is the kind of fiction that confines itself to the type of normal life. According to this definition, then, Romance may even treat of the sordid, the unlovely—as for instance, the novels of M. Zola. (Zola has been dubbed a Realist, but he is, on the contrary, the very head of the Romanticists.) Also, Realism, used as it sometimes is as a term of reproach, need not be in the remotest sense or degree offensive, but on the other hand respectable as a church and proper as a deacon—as, for instance, the novels of Mr. Howells.

The reason why one claims so much for Romance, and quarrels so pointedly with Realism, is that Realism stultifies itself. It notes only the surface of things. For it, Beauty is not even skin deep, but only a geometrical plane, without dimensions and depth, a mere outside. Realism is very excellent so far as it goes, but it goes no further than the Realist himself can actually see, or actually hear. Realism is minute; it is the drama of a broken teacup, the tragedy of a walk down the block, the excitement of an afternoon call, the adventure of an invitation to dinner. It is the visit to my neighbour's house, a formal visit, from which I may draw no conclusions. I see my neighbour and his friends—very, oh, such very! probable people—and that is all. Realism bows upon the doormat and goes away and says to me, as we link arms on the sidewalk: "That is life." And I say it is not. It is not, as you would very well see if you took Romance with you to call upon your neighbour.

Lately you have been taking Romance a weary journey across the water—ages and the flood of years—and haling her into the fusty, musty, worm-eaten, moth-riddled, rust-corroded "Grandes Salles" of the Middle Ages and the Renaissance, and she has found the drama of a bygone age for you there. But would you take her across the street to your neighbour's front parlour (with the bisque fisher-boy on the mantel and the photograph of Niagara Falls on glass hanging in the front window); would you introduce her there? Not you. Would you take a walk with her on Fifth Avenue, or Beacon Street, or Michigan Avenue? No, indeed. Would you choose her for a companion of a morning spent in Wall Street, or an afternoon in the Waldorf-Astoria? You just guess you would not.

She would be out of place, you say—inappropriate. She might be awkward in my neighbour's front parlour, and knock over the little bisque fisher-boy. Well, she might. If she did, you might find underneath the base of the statuette, hidden away, tucked away—what? God knows. But something that would be a complete revelation of my neighbour's secretest life.

So you think Romance would stop in the front parlour and discuss medicated flannels and mineral waters with the ladies? Not for more than five minutes. She would be off upstairs with you, prying, peeping, peering into the closets of the bedroom, into the nursery, into the sitting-room; yes, and into that little iron box screwed to the lower shelf of the closet in the library; and into those compartments and pigeon-holes of the *secretaire* in the study. She would find a heartache (maybe) between the pillows of the mistress's bed, and a memory carefully secreted in the master's deed-box. She would come upon a great hope amid the books and papers of the study-table of the young man's room, and—perhaps—who knows—an affair, or, great Heavens, an intrigue, in the scented ribbons and gloves and hairpins of the young lady's bureau. And she would pick here a little and there a little, making up a bag of hopes and fears and a package of joys and sorrows—great ones, mind you—and then come down to the front door, and, stepping out into the street, hand you the bags and package and say to you—"That is Life!"

Romance does very well in the castles of the Middle Ages and the Renaissance chateaux, and she has the *entree* there and is very well received. That is all well and good. But let us protest against limiting her to such places and such times. You will find her, I grant you, in the chatelaine's chamber and the dungeon of the man-at-arms; but, if you choose to look for her, you will find her equally at home in the brownstone house on the corner and in the office-building downtown. And this very day, in this very hour, she is sitting among the rags and wretchedness, the dirt and despair of the tenements of the East Side of New York.

"What?" I hear you say, "look for Romance—the lady of the silken robes and golden crown, our beautiful, chaste maiden of

soft voice and gentle eyes—look for her among the vicious
ruffians, male and female, of Allen Street and Mulberry Bend?"
I tell you she is there, and to your shame be it said you will not
know her in those surroundings. You, the aristocrats, who
demand the fine linen and the purple in your fiction; you, the
sensitive, the delicate, who will associate with your Romance
only so long as she wears a silken gown. You will not follow her
to the slums, for you believe that Romance should only amuse
and entertain you, singing you sweet songs and touching the
harp of silver strings with rosy-tipped fingers. If haply she
should call to you from the squalour of a dive, or the awful
degradation of a disorderly house, crying: "Look! listen! This,
too, is life. These, too, are my children! Look at them, know
them and, knowing, help!" Should she call thus you would stop
your ears; you would avert your eyes and you would answer,
"Come from there, Romance. Your place is not there!" And
you would make of her a harlequin, a tumbler, a sword-dancer,
when, as a matter of fact, she should be by right divine a
teacher sent from God.

She will not often wear the robe of silk, the gold crown, the
jeweled shoon; will not always sweep the silver harp. An iron
note is hers if so she choose, and coarse garments, and stained
hands; and, meeting her thus, it is for you to know her as she
passes—know her for the same young queen of the blue mantle
and lilies. She can teach you if you will be humble to
learn—teach you by showing. God help you if at last you take
from Romance her mission of teaching; if you do not believe
that she has a purpose—a nobler purpose and a mightier than
mere amusement, mere entertainment. Let Realism do the entertaining with its meticulous presentation of teacups, rag carpets,
wall-paper and haircloth sofas, stopping with these, going no
deeper than it sees, choosing the ordinary, the untroubled, the
commonplace.

But to Romance belongs the wide world for range, and the
unplumbed depths of the human heart, and the mystery of sex,
and the problems of life, and the black, unsearched penetralia
of the soul of man. You, the indolent, must not always be
amused. What matter the silken clothes, what matter the
prince's houses? Romance, too, is a teacher, and if—throwing
aside the purple—she wears the camel's-hair and feeds upon the
locusts, it is to cry aloud unto the people, "Prepare ye the way
of the Lord; make straight his path."

28. *The Responsibilities of the Novelist:*
A PROBLEM IN FICTION*

So many people—writers more especially—claim stridently and with a deal of gesturing that because a thing has happened it is therefore true. They have written a story, let us say, and they bring it to you to criticize. You lay your finger upon a certain passage and say "Not true to life." The author turns on you and then annihilates you—in his own mind—with the words, "But it actually happened." Of course, then, it must be true. On the contrary, it is accurate only.

For the assumption is, that truth is a higher power of accuracy—that the true thing includes the accurate; and assuming this, the authors of novels—that are not successful—suppose that if they are accurate, if they tell the thing just as they saw it, that they are truthful. It is not difficult to show that a man may be as accurate as the spectroscope and yet lie like a Chinese diplomat. As for instance: Let us suppose you have never seen a sheep, never heard of sheep, don't know sheep from shavings. It devolves upon me to enlighten your ignorance. I go out into the field and select from the flock a black sheep, bring it before you, and, with the animal there under our eyes, describe it in detail, faithfully, omitting nothing, falsifying nothing, exaggerating nothing. I am painfully accurate. But you go away with the untrue conviction that all sheep are black! I have been accurate, but I have not been true.

So it is with very, very many novels, written with all earnestness and seriousness. Every incident has happened in real life, and because it is picturesque, because it is romantic, because, in a word, it is like some other novel, it is seized upon at once, and serves as the nucleus of a tale. Then, because this tale fails of success, because it fails to impress, the author blames the public, not himself. He thinks he has gone to life for his material, and so must be original, new and true. It is not so. Life itself is not always true; strange as it may seem, you may be able to say that life is not always true to life—from the point

* The selection constitutes the entire essay "A Problem in Fiction" by Frank Norris in *The Responsibilities of the Novelist and Other Literary Essays* (1903).

of view of the artist. It happened once that it was my
unfortunate duty to tell a certain man of the violent death of
his only brother, whom he had left well and happy but an hour
before. This is how he took it: He threw up both hands and
staggered back, precisely as they do in melodrama, exclaiming
all in a breath: "Oh, my God! This is terrible! What will mother
say?" You may say what you please, this man was not true to
life. From the point of view of the teller of tales he was
theatrical, false, untrue, and though the incident was an actual
fact and though the emotion was real, it had no value as
"material," and no fiction writer in his senses would have
thought of using it in his story.

Naturally enough it will be asked what, then, is the standard.
How shall the writer guide himself in the treatment of a pivotal,
critical scene, or how shall the reader judge whether or not he is
true. Perhaps, after all, the word "seem," and not the word
"true," is the most important. Of course no good novelist, no
good artist, can represent life as it actually is. Nobody can, for
nobody knows. Who is to say what life actually is? It seems
easy—easy for us who have it and live in it and see it and hear it
and feel it every millionth part of every second of the time. I
say that life is actually this or that, and you say it is something
else, and number three says "Lo! here," and number four says
"Lo! there." Not even science is going to help you; no two
photographs, even, will convey just the same impression of the
same actuality; and here we are dealing not with science, but
with art, that instantly involves the personality of the artist and
all that that means. Even the same artist will not see the same
thing twice exactly alike. His personality is one thing to-day and
another thing to-morrow—is one thing before dinner and another thing after it. How, then, to determine what life actually is?

The point is just this. In the fine arts we do not care one little
bit about what life actually is, but what it looks like to an
interesting, impressionable man, and if he tells his story or
paints his picture so that the majority of intelligent people will
say, "Yes, that must have been just about what would have
happened under those circumstances," he is true. His accuracy
cuts no figure at all. He need not be accurate if he does not
choose to be. If he sees fit to be inaccurate in order to make his
point—so only his point be the conveying of a truthful impression—that is his affair. We have nothing to do with that.
Consider the study of a French cuirassier by Detaille; where the

sunlight strikes the brown coat of the horse, you will see, if you look close, a mere smear of blue—light blue. This is inaccurate. The horse is not blue, nor has he any blue spots. Stand at the proper distance and the blue smear resolves itself into the glossy reflection of the sun, and the effect is true.

And in fiction: Take the fine scene in "Ivanhoe," where Rebecca, looking from the window, describes the assault upon the outer walls of the castle to the wounded knight lying on the floor in the room behind her. If you stop and think, you will see that Rebecca never could have found such elaborate language under the stress of so great excitement—those cleverly managed little climaxes in each phrase, building up to the great climax of the paragraph, all the play of rhetoric, all the nice chain and adjustment of adjectives; she could not possibly have done it. Neither you nor I, nor any of us, with all the thought and time and labour at our command, could have written the passage. But is it not admirably true—true as the truth itself? It is not accurate: it is grossly, ludicrously inaccurate; but the fire and leap and vigour of it; there is where the truth is. Scott wanted you to get an impression of that assault on the barbican, and you do get it. You can hear those axes on the outer gate as plainly as Rebecca could; you can see the ladders go up, can hear them splinter, can see and feel and know all the rush and trample and smashing of that fine fight, with the Fetterlock Knight always to the fore, as no merely accurate description—accurate to five points of decimals—could ever present it.

So that one must remember the distinction, and claim no more for accuracy than it deserves—and that's but little. Anybody can be accurate—the man with the foot-rule is that. Accuracy is the attainment of small minds, the achievement of the commonplace, a mere machine-made thing that comes with niggardly research and ciphering and mensuration and the multiplication table, good in its place, so only the place is very small. In fiction it can under certain circumstances be dispensed with altogether. It is not a thing to be striven for. To be true is the all-important business, and, once attaining that, "all other things shall be added unto you." Paint the horse pea-green if it suits your purpose; fill the mouth of Rebecca with gasconades and rhodomontades interminable: these things do not matter. It is truth that matters, and the point is whether the daubs of pea-green will look like horseflesh and the mouth-filling words create the impression of actual battle.

29. WILLIAM DEAN HOWELLS
A Case in Point*

The question of expansion in American fiction lately agitated
by a lady novelist of Chicago with more vehemence than power,
and more courage than coherence, seems to me again palpitant
in the case of a new book by a young writer, which I feel
obliged at once to recognise as altogether a remarkable book.
Whether we shall abandon the old-fashioned American ideal of a
novel as something which may be read by all ages and sexes, for
the European notion of it as something fit only for age and
experience, and for men rather than women; whether we shall
keep to the bounds of the provincial proprieties, or shall include
within the imperial territory of our fiction the passions and the
motives of the savage world which underlies as well as environs
civilisation, are points which this book sums up and puts
concretely; and it is for the reader, not for the author, to make
answer. There is no denying the force with which he makes the
demand, and there is no denying the hypocrisies which the
old-fashioned ideal of the novel involved. But society, as we
have it, is a tissue of hypocrisies, beginning with the clothes in
which we hide our nakedness, and we have to ask ourselves how
far we shall part with them at his demand. The hypocrisies are
the proprieties, the decencies, the morals; they are by no means
altogether bad; they are, perhaps, the beginning of civilisation;
but whether they should be the end of it is another affair. That
is what we are to consider in entering upon a career of imperial
expansion in a region where the Monroe Doctrine was never
valid. From the very first Europe invaded and controlled in our
literary world. The time may have come at last when we are to
invade and control Europe in literature. I do not say that it has
come, but if it has we may have to employ European means and
methods.

* The essay appeared in *Literature,* March 24, 1899.

It ought not to be strange that the impulse in this direction should have come from California, where, as I am always affirming rather than proving, a continental American fiction began. I felt, or fancied I felt, the impulse in Mr. Frank Norris' "Moran of the Lady Letty," and now in his "McTeague" I am so sure of it that I am tempted to claim the prophetic instinct of it. In the earlier book there were, at least, indications that forecast to any weather-wise eye a change from the romantic to the realistic temperature, and in the later we have it suddenly, and with the overwhelming effect of a blizzard. It is saying both too much and too little to say that Mr. Norris has built his book on Zolaesque lines, yet Zola is the master of whom he reminds you in a certain epical conception of life. He reminds you of Zola also in the lingering love of the romantic, which indulges itself at the end in an anticlimax worthy of Dickens. He ignores as simply and sublimely as Zola any sort of nature of character beyond or above those of Polk Street in San Francisco, but within the ascertained limits he convinces you, two-thirds of the time, of his absolute truth to them. He does not, of course, go to Zola's lengths, breadths, and depths; but he goes far enough to difference his work from the old-fashioned American novel.

Polite readers of the sort who do not like to meet in fiction people of the sort they never meet in society will not have a good time in "McTeague," for there is really not a society person in the book. They might, indeed, console themselves a little with an elderly pair of lovers on whom Mr. Norris wreaks all the sentimentality he denies himself in the rest of the story; and as readers of that sort do not mind murders as much as vulgarity, they may like to find three of them, not much varying in atrocity. Another sort of readers will not mind the hero's being a massive blond animal, not necessarily bad, though brutal, who has just wit enough to pick up a practical knowledge of dentistry and follow it as a trade; or the heroine's being a little, pretty, delicate daughter of German-Swiss emigrants, perfectly common in her experiences and ideals, but devotedly industrious, patient, and loyal. In the chemistry of their marriage McTeague becomes a prepotent ruffian, with always a base of bestial innocence; and Trina becomes a pitiless miser without altogether losing her housewifely virtues or ceasing to feel a woman's rapture in giving up everything but her money to the man who maltreats her more and more, and, finally, murders her.

This is rendering in coarse outline the shape of a story realized with a fulness which the outline imparts no sense of. It abounds in touches of character at once fine and free, in little miracles of observation, in vivid insight, in simple and subtle expression. Its strong movement carries with it a multiplicity of detail which never clogs it; the subordinate persons are never shabbed or faked; in the equality of their treatment their dramatic inferiority is lost; their number is great enough to give the feeling of a world revolving round the central figures without distracting the interest from these. Among the minor persons, Maria Macapa, the Mexican chorewoman, whose fable of a treasure of gold turns the head of the Polish Jew Zerkow, is done with rare imaginative force. But all these lesser people are well done; and there are passages throughout the book that live strongly in the memory, as only masterly work can live. The one folly is the insistence on the love-making of those silly elders, which is apparently introduced as an offset to the misery of the other love-making; the anti-climax is McTeague's abandonment in the alkali desert, hand-cuffed to the dead body of his enemy.

Mr. Norris has, in fact, learned his lesson well, but he has not learned it all. His true picture of life is not true, because it leaves beauty out. Life is squalid and cruel and vile and hateful, but it is noble and tender and pure and lovely, too. By and by he will put these traits in, and then his powerful scene will be a reflection of reality; by and by he will achieve something of the impartial fidelity of the photograph. In the mean time he has done a picture of life which has form, which has texture, which has color, which has what great original power and ardent study of Zola can give, but which lacks the spiritual light and air, the consecration which the larger art of Tolstoy gives. It is a little inhuman, and it is distinctly not for the walls of living-rooms, where the ladies of the family sit and the children go in and out. This may not be a penalty, but it is the inevitable consequence of expansion in fiction.

30. HAMLIN GARLAND
On Meeting Frank Norris*

. . . At Mrs. Herne's we met Frank Norris again. My record describes him as "a stunning fellow—an author who does not personally disappoint his admirers. He is perilously handsome, tall and straight, with keen brown eyes and beautifully modeled features. His face is as smooth as that of a boy of twenty, but his hair is almost white. I have never known a more engaging writer. He is a poet in appearance, but a close observer and a realist in his fiction. We had a lively evening together, really got at each other's prejudices as well as enthusiasms. He seems confident of his future, as well he may be, for his work is in demand and his mind in a glow of creative energy. I know of no one for whom I can more unhesitatingly predict a noble career.

"He told me of his grand scheme for 'a trilogy on wheat.' 'My first novel,' he said, 'deals with a California grain farm; the second will take up Chicago and the Wheat Pit.' He spoke of his first volume, 'The Octopus,' as 'The Squid,' and when I criticized it for its reminiscences of 'Germinal' and 'La Terre,' he admitted smilingly that Zola's work had been his highest admiration. I then reminded him of a wise admonition which Howells once gave me when I had laid before him a program for future work. 'Can you be sure of your continuing interest?' he had asked. 'In my experience I have repeatedly found that my grand schemes for the future grew cold before I attained to the writing of them; something more vital intervened.'

" 'As a matter of fact,' I said to Norris, 'I never got to the writing of that particular novel. As Howells foretold, it grew cold in my desk.' Norris was not much concerned. 'I have a third volume outlined,' he said."

* The selection is taken from *Companions on the Trail* by Hamlin Garland. It is reprinted here by permission of the author's daughters.

VII. Theodore Dreiser:
Native American Naturalist

The early life of America's most eminent naturalistic novelist, Theodore Dreiser (1871-1945) might itself be the subject of a naturalistic novel. A native Midwesterner, born in Terre Haute, Indiana, Dreiser did not, like Hamlin Garland, enjoy the security of New England ancestry or, like Frank Norris, the advantage of wealth, foreign study, and a Harvard education. His father was a hard-working but unsuccessful German immigrant whose stern piety seems to have aroused in his son a lifelong quarrel with conventional religion. Throughout Dreiser's childhood, the family was haunted by poverty. Years later, he remembered his mother sitting on the floor, stroking her feet and saying "See poor mother's shoes? Aren't you sorry she has to wear such torn shoes? See the hole here?" The contrast between such pathetic poverty and the semiofficial American faith in material success seems to have awakened in Dreiser that sense of the magic and glamor of wealth which he, more than any other American writer except F. Scott Fitzgerald, glowingly depicts. The struggle for survival, in terms of either racial or economic contest, hardly needs philosophic justification when the immediate rewards of success seem so large and charming. Time after time, in his novels and reminiscences, Dreiser shows impoverished and unsophisticated youth dazzled by the wealth and excitement of a city, hypnotized by the visible power of commerce and industry. In *A Book About Myself* (1922) Dreiser, then in his fifties, paid tribute to the lure of Chicago as he saw it in his early twenties. It was romantic and potent, a study in physical contrasts: "the lake with its pure white sails and its blue water; the Chicago River, with its black, oily water, its tall grain elevators and black coal packers; the great railroad yards, covering miles and miles of space with their cars." Dreiser was, in fact, one of the first of a group of Middle Western writers, among them Edgar Lee Masters and Carl Sandburg, to hymn the incongruous beauty and rough vitality of the city, "the poetry of Chicago." Like this first heroine, Carrie Meeber, Dreiser seems early to have imagined a secret knowledge possessed by the prosperous and secure inhabitants of the "walled city," the domain of commercial wealth and ease. Journalism offered both a living and an opportunity to probe the mysteries of the city, and so, barely twenty, he became a newspaperman.

His experience as a journalist served Dreiser well. By the time he began work on his first novel, *Sister Carrie* (1900), he was deeply acquainted with the urban life he chose to portray—the "facts" of its styles and its slang, costs, clothes, the decoration of hotels, bars, and inexpensive flats, all came readily to hand. He possessed the accurate materials which both realist and naturalist employ, but his knowledge did not smell of the library or laborious research. More like William Dean Howells than Frank Norris, Dreiser wrote directly from the life he knew. In the opinion of the critic F. O. Matthiessen, it is "idle to speak of Dreiser as a naturalistic novelist in the sense of having a system of human behavior he wished to illustrate," and it is equally "beside the point to speak of the development of his fiction in relation to the deliberate mechanical devices of Zola, of which he was mainly ignorant. Yet there is a wider and looser, but still authentic, sense in which he was a naturalist. From first to last he was driven to try to understand man's place in nature, to a far more profound degree than any of his American contemporaries in fiction . . ."*

That Dreiser knew little of Zola we know from his own later testimony, but we also know that he was, at the outset of his career as a novelist, deeply read in the works of an earlier French master, Balzac. Sister Carrie's Chicago is not unlike Balzac's Paris, another capital that lures young provincials and educates them in the harsh contrasts of great poverty and enormous wealth. In Dreiser's first novel, the influence of Herbert Spencer is even more obvious. It is the mechanism of evolution that gives meaning and purpose to life, and, at the same time, satisfactorily nullifies strict standards of personal morality, based on traditional Christianity, which Dreiser wished to disown. Above all, "science" and objectivity provide a basis for compassion and humanity which religion, as Dreiser

---

* F. O. Matthiessen, *Theodore Dreiser,* (William Sloane Associates, 1951), p. 236.

knew it, did not afford. Thus, for example, Dreiser excuses Drouet's seduction of Carrie and her acquiescence by an appeal to "the forces which sweep and play throughout the universe." The human race we know, Dreiser comments, is "even as a wisp in the wind, moved by every breath of passion," but we have "the consolation of knowing that evolution is ever in action, that the ideal is a light that cannot fail . . . When this jangle of free-will and instinct shall have been adjusted, when perfect understanding has given the former the power to replace the latter entirely, man will no longer vary. The needle of understanding will yet point steadfast and unwavering to the distant pole of 'truth.' "

Many modern readers find this hortatory "science" nearly as moralistic as a Sunday-school text. In an age almost unacquainted with chastity in fiction (except as a psychological problem demanding cure), it may be hard to imagine the moral indignation aroused by Dreiser's account of Carrie's relatively cautious sexual career. That revolution in the moral standards of popular fiction which was accomplished in the 1920's has, for better or worse, carried all of us before it. Yet there was a time when the story of Dreiser's struggle against censorship and his difficulties publishing *Sister Carrie* was a legend in liberal intellectual circles. Briefly, the facts are these. The novel was submitted to Doubleday, Page where it was read by Frank Norris, who greeted it as a "master-piece" and urged its publication. A contract was signed and the novel was set in type before the senior partner in the publishing house, Frank Doubleday—acting, probably, somewhat under the influence of his wife—expressed his disapproval of the novel. In the face of Doubleday's objections, Dreiser insisted that the contract to publish be fulfilled. A small edition was printed, but no effort was made to sell the novel and so *Sister Carrie* was not really "published" in this country until the English edition of 1901 and several American editions, brought out after 1907, made it generally available.

Almost inevitably, Dreiser became a vociferous opponent of "prudery" and literary censorship, whether explicit or, like Doubleday's, tacit. More than a decade later, after two other novels—*The Titan* (1914) and *The Genius* (1915)—had encountered somewhat similar difficulties, Dreiser, by then an established literary figure, actively took up his own defense, meeting charge with countercharge. "Life, Art and America" represents his sentiments in this period. America is, as he sees it, in the grips of "Bottom the Weaver," the essentially ignorant small businessman who pretends to cultural knowledge, and of "Comstock," the moralistic censor, who is his "henchman." This alliance of religion and trade, sometimes represented as the "Protestant ethic," has strangled our national arts, and all other creative intellectual endeavor. In fact, Dreiser, bitter, scornful, and apparently wronged, was one of the first to announce the antagonism between America and her artists which became a truism for emigrant writers of the 1920's. It is significant that in "Life, Art and America" Dreiser does not consider, or even seem to see, any of the issues arising from the popular effect of literature which both Howells and Norris recognized. Not that Dreiser lacked compassion for his readers or the perennially innocent American girl. Morally speaking, however, the shoe is on the other foot. For Dreiser, it is immoral to hide, disguise, or ignore the facts of life. It is hypocritical, as well as immoral, to tell less than the whole truth of human passion and desire. Atheism, evolutionary objectivity, and the new psychology, represented by Freud, had brought about a revolution of the spirit which fiction had only to recognize.

"Life, Art and America" was included in Dreiser's first collection of philosophical essays, *Hey, Rub-A-Dub-Dub* (1920). There it falls into place as one piece in the growing pattern of Dreiser's disillusionment. The cosmic optimism he bore away from his first reading of Spencer has vanished, though the evolutionary system and the machinery of "forces" remains. "The Essential Tragedy of Life" describes his new position. Man's tragedy lies in his sense of forces that govern the universe and his pathetic awareness of his inability to control them. There is no room in this dark vision for the essentially sentimental assurance that "the ideal is a light that cannot fail" for this light may never dawn. The seemingly empty title of the collection captures Dreiser's cynicism. "Hey, rub-a-dub-dub!" is the meaningless call of the circus barker. According to Dreiser, "Life—like the title . . . is without meaning and has no objective."

Always serious and thoughtful, Dreiser never acquired artistic polish. (H. L. Mencken wittily wondered that he could take any pleasure in writing so badly.) It is, perhaps, surprising that such an "unwriterly" writer should have been widely admired by other writers of his time. Yet he captained the battle for free expression in the novel and courageously refused to bow to social pressure or to echo conventional idealistic formulas. Colleagues admired his honesty and determination as much as his art. Edgar Lee Masters' poem captures the appeal of Dreiser's intellectual austerity. Sherwood Anderson's *apologia* justified Dreiser's rough style and sometimes brutal subject matter on the good realistic grounds of American "truth." The most influential partisan in the battle against prudery and censorship was, however, H. L. Mencken, to whom the attack on Dreiser's novels seemed but another example of the confining influence of the "booboisie." Though he was Dreiser's close personal friend for many years, Mencken maintained his distance in criticizing Dreiser's work. Certainly he was right to note that, in contrast with Joseph Conrad, Dreiser is often inconsistent and intellectually provincial. Few would disagree with Mencken's view that Dreiser, "for all his achievement, [is] in the transition stage between Christian endeavor and civilization; between Warsaw, Indiana, and the Socratic grove." Yet Mencken and Dreiser fought together for the right of American authors to depict all aspects of life without fear of censorship. Their dedication to this cause inspired the admiration of younger contemporaries like F. Scott Fitzgerald who, early in his career, proclaimed "H. L. Mencken and Theodore Dreiser the greatest men living in the country today."

Selections

31. ON THE INSPIRATION OF CHICAGO*

During the year 1890 I had been formulating my first dim notion as to what it was I wanted to do in life. For two years and more I had been reading Eugene Field's "Sharps and Flats," a column he wrote daily for the Chicago *Daily News*, and through this, the various phases of life which he suggested in a humorous though at times romantic way, I was beginning to suspect, vaguely at first, that I wanted to write, possibly something like that. Nothing else that I had so far read—novels, plays, poems, histories—gave me quite the same feeling for constructive thought as did the matter of his daily notes, poems, and aphorisms, which were of Chicago principally, whereas nearly all others dealt with foreign scenes and people.

But this comment on local life here and now, these trenchant bits on local street scenes, institutions, characters, functions, all moved me as nothing hitherto had. To me Chicago at this time seethed with a peculiarly human or realistic atmosphere. It is given to some cities, as to some lands, to suggest romance, and to me Chicago did that hourly. It sang, I thought, and in spite of what I deemed my various troubles—small enough as I now see them—I was singing with it. These seemingly drear neighborhoods through which I walked each day, doing collecting for an easy-payment furniture company, these ponderous regions of large homes where new-wealthy packers and manufacturers dwelt, these curiously foreign neighborhoods of almost all nationalities; and, lastly, that great downtown area, surrounded on two sides by the river, on the east by the lake, and on the south by railroad yards and stations, the whole set with these new tall buildings, the wonder of the western world, fascinated me. Chicago was so young, so blithe, so new, I thought.

* The selection is taken from Chapter 1 in *A Book About Myself* by Theodore Dreiser. It is reprinted here by permission of The Dreiser Trust.

Florence in its best days must have been something like this to young Florentines, or Venice to the young Venetians.

Here was a city which had no traditions but was making them, and this was the very thing that every one seemed to understand and rejoice in. Chicago was like no other city in the world, so said they all. Chicago would outstrip every other American city, New York included, and become the first of all American, if not European or world, cities. . . . This dream many hundreds of thousands of its citizens held dear. Chicago would be first in wealth, first in beauty, first in art achievement. A great World's Fair was even then being planned that would bring people from all over the world. The Auditorium, the new Great Northern Hotel, the amazing (for its day) Masonic Temple twenty-two stories high, a score of public institutions, depots, theaters and the like, were being constructed. It is something wonderful to witness a world metropolis springing up under one's very eyes, and this is what was happening here before me.

Nosing about the city in an inquiring way and dreaming half-formed dreams of one and another thing I would like to do, it finally came to me, dimly, like a bean that strains at its enveloping shell, that I would like to write of these things. It would be interesting, so I thought, to describe a place like Goose Island in the Chicago River, a mucky and neglected realm then covered with shanties made of upturned boats sawed in two, and yet which seemed to me the height of the picturesque; also a building like the Auditorium or the Masonic Temple, that vast wall of masonry twenty-two stories high and at that time actually the largest building in the world; or a seething pit like that of the Board of Trade, which I had once visited and which astonished and fascinated me as much as anything ever had. That roaring, yelling, screaming whirlpool of life! And then the lake, with its pure white sails and its blue water; the Chicago River, with its black, oily water, its tall grain elevators and black coal pockets; the great railroad yards, covering miles and miles of space with their cars.

How wonderful it all was! As I walked from place to place collecting I began betimes to improvise rhythmic, vaguely formulated word-pictures or rhapsodies anent these same and many other things—free verse, I suppose we should call it now—which concerned everything and nothing but somehow expressed the seething poetry of my soul and this thing to me. Indeed I was crazy with life, a little demented or frenzied with

romance and hope. I wanted to sing, to dance, to eat, to love.
My word-dreams and maunderings concerned my day, my age,
poverty, hope, beauty, which I mouthed to myself, chanting
aloud at times. Sometimes, because on a number of occasions I
had heard the Reverend Frank W. Gunsaulus and his like spout
rocket-like sputterings on the subjects of life and religion, I
would orate, pleading great causes as I went. I imagined myself
a great orator with thousands of people before me, my gestures
and enunciation and thought perfect, poetic, and all my hearers
moved to tears or demonstrations of wild delight.

After a time I ventured to commit some of these things to
paper, scarcely knowing what they were, and in a fever for
self-advancement I bundled them up and sent them to Eugene
Field. In his column and elsewhere I had read about geniuses
being occasionally discovered by some chance composition or
work noted by one in authority. I waited for a time, with great
interest but no vast depression, to see what my fate would be.
But no word came and in time I realized that they must have
been very bad and had been dropped into the nearest waste
basket. But this did not give me pause nor grieve me. I seethed
to express myself. I bubbled. I dreamed. And I had a singing
feeling, now that I had done this much, that some day I should
really write and be very famous into the bargain.

But how? How? My feeling was that I ought to get into
newspaper work, and yet this feeling was so nebulous that I
thought it would never come to pass. I saw mention in the
papers of reporters calling to find out this, or being sent to do
that, and so the idea of becoming a reporter gradually formulated itself in my mind, though how I was to get such a place I had
not the slightest idea. Perhaps reporters had to have a special
training of some kind; maybe they had to begin as clerks behind
a counter, and this made me very somber, for those glowing
business offices always seemed so far removed from anything to
which I could aspire. Most of them were ornate, floreate, with
onyx or chalcedony wall trimmings, flambeaux of bronze or
copper on the walls, imitation mother-of-pearl lights in the
ceilings—in short, all the gorgeousness of a sultan's court
brought to the outer counter where people subscribed or paid
for ads. Because the newspapers were always dealing with signs
and wonders, great functions, great commercial schemes, great
tragedies and pleasures, I began to conceive of them as wonder-
lands in which all concerned were prosperous and happy. I

painted reporters and newspaper men generally as receiving fabulous salaries, being sent on the most urgent and interesting missions. I think I confused, inextricably, reporters with ambassadors and prominent men generally. Their lives were laid among great people, the rich, the famous, the powerful; and because of their position and facility of expression and mental force they were received everywhere as equals. Think of me, new, young, poor, being received in that way!

32. AT FORTY, ON AMERICAN LITERATURE*

BARFLEUR TAKES ME IN HAND

I have just turned forty. I have seen a little something of life. I have been a newspaper man, editor, magazine contributor, author and, before these things, several odd kinds of clerk before I found out what I could do.

Eleven years ago I wrote my first novel, which was issued by a New York publisher and suppressed by him, Heaven knows why. For, the same year they suppressed my book because of its alleged immoral tendencies, they published Zola's "Fecundity" and "An Englishwoman's Love Letters." I fancy now, after eleven years of wonder, that it was not so much the supposed immorality, as the book's straightforward, plain-spoken discussion of American life in general. We were not used then in America to calling a spade a spade, particularly in books. We had great admiration for Tolstoi and Flaubert and Balzac and de Maupassant at a distance—some of us—and it was quite an honor to have handsome sets of these men on our shelves, but mostly we had been schooled in the literature of Dickens, Thackeray, George Eliot, Charles Lamb and that refined company of English sentimental realists who told us something about life, but not everything. No doubt all of these great men knew how shabby a thing this world is—how full of lies, make-believe, seeming and false pretense it all is, but they had agreed among themselves, or with the public, or with sentiment generally, not to talk about that too much. Books were always to be built out of facts concerning "our better natures." We were always to be seen as we wish to be seen. There were villains to be sure—liars, dogs, thieves, scoundrels—

---

* The selection is taken from Chapter I of *A Traveler at Forty*. Reprinted by permission of The Dreiser Trust.

but they were strange creatures, hiding away in dark, unconventional places and scarcely seen save at night and peradventure; whereas we, all clean, bright, honest, well-meaning people, were living in nice homes, going our way honestly and truthfully, going to church, raising our children believing in a Father, a Son and a Holy Ghost, and never doing anything wrong at any time save as these miserable liars, dogs, thieves, et cetera, might suddenly appear and make us. Our books largely showed us as heroes. If anything happened to our daughters it was not their fault but the fault of these miserable villains. Most of us were without original sin. The business of our books, our church, our laws, our jails, was to keep us so.

I am quite sure that it never occurred to many of us that there was something really improving in a plain, straightforward understanding of life. For myself, I accept now no creeds. I do not know what truth is, what beauty is, what love is, what hope is. I do not believe any one absolutely and I do not doubt any one absolutely. I think people are both evil and well-intentioned.

33. THE ESSENTIAL TRAGEDY OF LIFE*

The Serpent to Eve, Genesis iii, 3-5: *"For God doth know that in the day ye eat thereof"* (the Tree of Knowledge) *"then your eyes shall be opened and ye shall be as gods, knowing good and evil."*

Jehovah to the Serpent, Genesis iii, 14; 15: *"Because thou hast done this"* (urged Eve to seek wisdom by eating of the Fruit of the Tree of Knowledge) *"thou art cursed above all cattle, and every beast of the field; upon thy belly shalt thou go, and dust shalt thou eat all the days of thy life; and I will put enmity between thee and the woman, and between thy seed and her seed; it shall bruise thy head and thou shalt bruise his heel."*

Jehovah to Eve, for attempting to obtain wisdom via eating the Fruit of the Tree, Genesis iv, 16: *"I will greatly multiply thy sorrow and thy conception; in sorrow shalt thou bring forth children; and thy desire shall be to thy husband and he shall rule over thee."*

Jehovah to Adam, because of his following the advice of Eve: *"Because thou hast hearkened unto the voice of thy wife and hast eaten of the Tree, cursed is the ground for thy sake; in sorrow shalt thou eat of it all the days of thy life; thorns and thistles shall it bring forth to thee, and thou shalt eat the herb of the field. In the sweat of thy face shalt thou eat bread till thou return unto the ground."*

"Prometheus (forethought), son of the Titan Iapeius and Clymene, and brother of Atlas, Menoetius and Epimetheus (after-thought), is represented as the creator of man, out of earth and water, and his great benefactor, having given him, in

---

* The selection constitutes the entire essay "The Essential Tragedy of Life" by Theodore Dreiser in *Hey, Rub-A-Dub-Dub*. Reprinted by permission of The Dreiser Trust.

*spite of Zeus who was apparently opposed to it all, a portion of
all the qualities possessed by the other animals. He also stole
fire from heaven in a hollow tube, and taught mortals all useful
arts. In order to punish Prometheus for this, Zeus gave Pandora
to Epimetheus, his brother, in consequence of which diseases
and sufferings of every kind befell mortals. He also chained
Prometheus to a rock on Mount Caucasus, where during the
daytime an eagle consumed his liver, which was restored each
succeeding night. Prometheus was thus exposed to perpetual
torture; but Hercules (strength) killed the eagle and with the
consent of Zeus, who in this way had an opportunity of
allowing his son to gain immortal fame, delivered the sufferer."*

Smaller Classical Dictionary

The significance of these several references to and quotations
from the supposed creative power of the elder pagan world is, if
anything, that man is a waif and an interloper in Nature (or
things celestial or intelligent), a machine or toy, created by
something which desires to use him or work through him in
some way, with no essential power to make his own way and no
"right" to seek either knowledge or wisdom, lest, in the words
attributed to Jehovah, his Creator, in Genesis, he becomes "as
one of us," a minor god, for instance, as the Creator via this
phrase writes himself down to be; not the Supreme Ruler of the
Universe, by any means. And in this phrase ("one of us") is
contained a hint of a possible condition or order in the universe
which, since the Christian era, has been put aside as untrue,
namely, that the Creator of man, our two billion two-legged
citizens stalking this earth, may be but (to use a very crude and
yet for that reason understandable description) a "side-line"
manufacturer, as it were, or a lower-level competitor for life and
pleasure, along with many others of his kind—Creators or
"Gods" or avatars of, let us say, mosquitoes, flies, bulls, cats,
dogs; in other words the specific and singular Creator of some
one thing as opposed to other Gods or powers who might well
be creators of other things of equal rank. And these "Gods," in
turn, should one choose to follow the thought, might well be
the special product of some greater "God" or manufacturer or
Creator who is finding a rather peculiar expression through
them and their creations in turn; also the various rivalries which
exist between man and the lower animals for the possession of

the earth might thereby be explained or have something to do with that.

The thought is not new. Alfred Russel Wallace, co-discoverer with Darwin, Lamarck and Spencer of the theory of evolution, has pointed out that "the organising mind which actually carries out the development of the life world need not be infinite, need not be what is usually meant by the term God or Deity. The main cause of the antagonism between religion and science seems to me to be the assumption by both that there are no existences capable of taking part in the work of creation other than blind forces on the one hand and the infinite, eternal, omnipotent God on the other. The apparently gratuitous creation by theologians of a hierarchy of angels and archangels, with no defined duties but those of attendants and messengers of the Deity, perhaps increases this antagonism." He then proceeds to develop a theory of his own in which (I quote) "the vast, the infinite chasm between ourselves and the Deity is to some extent occupied by an almost infinite series of grades of beings, each successive grade having higher and higher powers in regard to the origination, the development and the control of the universe." He goes on to show how this might be done by them—all to the one end: namely, the creation and preparation of man via experiences here, presumably for a higher place in the control of the universe at large, always under the Supreme Ruler of course and his lesser, yet in so far as man is concerned greater, agents. In other words, under these sub-Gods.

The idea is interesting only it does not, although it may be too much to say that it cannot, explain the endless bickering and chaffering in the universe at large, the utter failure of various movements and types here on earth and apparently elsewhere, the astonishing selection of so minute a mote in the material universe as this particular planet for the purpose of working out a higher type of assistant or worshipper of God Himself. It may be true, but the idea is a little fantastic and suggests the labours of an ignorant and yet hopeful being endeavouring to account for himself, his presence, in the best way he can.

To my humble way of thinking, the ancient Greeks and the various theogonies of the ancient pagan world (Egyptian, Chaldean, Hindu) were at least as plausible in their apprehension of a troublesome disorder. The Old Testament and all other forms of ancient pagan literature suggest the general and very natural conception, based on the evidence of life itself, that various gods were or are contending via various forms of life (animal, vegetable and mineral) for some form of expression here on earth, and that the various things which they make (or the one thing which each makes, its image and likeness perhaps) is opposed to all others here. Pagan thought reeked with the feeling of contests between gods or creators or controllers of this, that and the other, and in the Sinaitic interpretation of life just quoted we see something of the same thing; also in what small consideration man was held by his alleged special Creator. Evidently the conclusion reached by the thinking elders of the pagan world was that man, in so far as his own special Creator was concerned, was viewed with sinister opposition by the power which made him. It did not want him to amount to anything. Indeed he was very, very plainly conscious of the inimical attitude of Nature, or rather man's especial God or Creator, toward him. He was not as yet deluded by the Christian phantasm that man is made in the image and likeness of his Creator, who is highly considerate of him, and that the world was made for man, or that because of faith, good deeds, special forms of self-abnegation and self-effacement he is to be reserved to eternal bliss hereafter although there is no especial reward for him here and now. And this is excellent indeed as illustrating a force or forces of a creative turn which might wish to use man as man uses any other minor implement for the accomplishment of any purpose he may have, but not very complimentary to him as an illustration of his own free and creative powers.

And, curiously, modern chemistry with its various tropisms—helio, magnetic, stereo and chemo—together with its legal part, physics, does little better by him. Already they tend to show that he is merely—and, what is worse, accidentally so—an evoluted arrangement of attractions and repulsions, arranged by chemicals and forces which desire or cannot escape whorls or epitomes of complicated motions and emotions or attractions which take the odd forms presented by men and animals.

But aside from this the most effective illustration of the essential nothingness of man is his plain *individual* weakness here and now as contrasted with his mass ideals and the huge vanity or tendency toward romance which causes him to wish to seem to be more than he really is or can ever hope to be. For plainly every life, in the last analysis, however useful to an assumed and carefully directing Creator, or however successful from a momentary analysis it may appear, is a failure. We hear of that curious thing, "a successful life." It is in the main a myth, a self-delusion. How could there possibly be success for a watery, bulbous, highly limited and specially functioned creature, lacking (in the case of man, for instance) many of the superior attributes of other animals—wings, a sense of direction, foreknowledge and the like—and manufactured every forty years by hundreds of millions, century in and century out, made apparently not in the image and likeness of anything superior to himself but in that of an accidentally compelled pattern, due to an accidental arrangement of chemicals, his every move and aspiration anticipated and accounted for by a formula and an accidentally evolved system long before he arrives, and he himself born puling, compact of vain illusions in regard to himself, his "mission," his dominant relation to the enormous schemes of Nature, and ending, if "life" endures so long, in toothless senility and watery decay, dissolution. And in addition some have scientifically placed the creative as well as the generative period of man between his twentieth and fortieth years—twenty years! Others generously extend it to fifty and even sixty. Few venture to carry it beyond that. At seventy old Nestor drools and repeats his fables of his few years and many troubles. At fifty, even forty-five, most men are busy recounting the deeds, adventures and creations of their earlier years!

To me the most astonishing thing in connection with man is this same vanity or power of romanticising everything relating to himself, so that whereas in reality he is what he is, a structure of brief import and minute social or any other form of energy, left by his loving Creator to contest in the most drastic and often fatal way with thousands, one might almost say millions of inimical powers and only significant really in so far as he or it is interlocked with others in some larger unity, either (for illustration) as a soldier in an army or its delegated commander or as a delegated or acknowledged representative of some moving or mass or race impulse, still he has this astonishing power of viewing himself as a tremendous force in himself, a god, a hero, an enduring and undying figure of glory and beauty—as significant almost as the Creator Himself, in whose image and likeness he is supposed to be made!

The wonder! The beauty even!

Sometimes I think all this is the almost inevitable result of something inherently weak but with one clear power: that of visualising or perceiving strength in other things and so, by contrast, its own weakness; and, by reflex action merely, attempting to salve itself against its own ineffectiveness by imagining itself to be that which it may never be: a victor, a Colossus bestriding the world, an undying potentate, ruling for ever, and so gaining strength to go on. For individuals are never masters in any remarkable way. They merely and at best borrow or direct the energies of many, and in the main to no important result to themselves. A Napoleon slaves and starves to the end that he may die on St. Helena and bring considerable profit to many who never heard of him and care not at all. A Caesar toils endlessly at organisation and the development and preservation of Rome, only to be stabbed to death in his fifty-sixth year, practically unrewarded. A Hannibal slaves for Carthage, enduring endless hardships, only to die by his own hand. The category might be extended indefinitely. And yet the world is full of laudations of the powers of men, their satisfactions, their vast, vast rewards and glories; while so many decayed steles and temple doorways, and data unending, bear testimony to their utter material and subsequent spiritual futility.

And when I say this I wish to make it perfectly clear that I am by no means confusing the race with the individual, or vice versa. What a race may do, and what man may, are two very different things. The race, representing the totality of active creations and pushed on by dynamic forces from below, may be, and in so far as one can guess is, a huge success. The God or force or forces using man in various aspects here and now (two billion men at the present moment) may be and no doubt is finding self-expression through and in him and may well be tremendously satisfied with the result. But in what way does that, or can it, add to the comfort or bliss of the particular individual? Endlessly repeated, an oyster-like copy of every other man that has ever been, a mere minute portion of something the significance or import of which he cannot even surmise. And within the race itself one need only think of the various types—preacher, actor, lawyer, doctor, merchant, thief, writer, poet, artist, prize-fighter, all very much alike and all repeated and repeated *ad infinitum*—to see how impossible the idea of individuality is. The very idea of extreme individuality, even under the most special and favoured circumstances, is seen to be all but an impossibility. We are at best, even in our arts and highest forms of special adaptions, copies of things which are and have been as common as pig-tracks—generals, philosophers, statesmen, society *grande dames* and the like not excepted. Over and over and over we appear, one and all, even our exact gestures, smiles, glances. Who has not seen it in so short a space as three generations? And we speak of individuality, of special destinies!

Herein lies the pathos, and this is the outstanding fact, that man is essentially a creation or mechanism, accidental or not as you wish, or a force or forces which in so far as anyone can determine is or are, far more than he in his wildest flights of fancy suspects, the thing which he most craves to be, individual, enduring, but of which he is only a part and of which he is constantly seeking more—*life*. The thing is which makes and repeats over and over *ad infinitum* and *is* two billions of men, or anything else into which it chooses to form itself, may be thought of as having life, personality, success and the like, but as for individual man or any of its minute atoms! Indeed man might as well think of the minute atoms of his internal mechanism as having success, fame, a great life or future, as himself. His day, like theirs, is measured by a minute fraction of time and labour and energy, and so is nothing. Quite obviously there is something which is to man what man in his entirety as an individual is to the least ion or molecule of his inner cosmos: a thing of so vast a magnitude comparatively as to be as far outside his reckoning as must he be to the ion of his inner body. And as for size or force and import, that which creates him is as far above him as he is above the ion. Indeed, although man, in his capacity or proportion as an individual and as contrasted with the least of the electrons of his being, is beyond computation for size, yet viewed again in contrast with his external world he sinks into a mere fumbling, briefly-ended mote and tool. Like the ion of his inner cosmos, in this vast etheric or ionic something which is outside of him and which we see blazing as worlds or suns or existing as immeasurable space, he is too minute and too brief to be discussed. Even the great earth which he treads with so much pride is to this external thing quite as minute as man's electron is to him; and yet his relationship even to this is almost as nothing. For on this so minute thing which, sidereally speaking, is as nothing, he appears nevertheless, insect-wise, by the billion every forty (or whatever the average life of man may be) years, to say nothing of innumerable other forms which have the ion or the molecule as the base of their material presence or structure. Still he permits himself to believe that he is something, and in facing all has the stupendous or fortunate ignorance to write himself down as Lord, Master, Great Guider of Things Terrestrial!

One of the things which might modify this supreme romantic estimate of himself, if such a thing were either desirable or possible, would be an even slightly technical examination of the process by which he arrives, as well as the extreme simplicity of the mechanical and chemical formula by which, throughout endless ages, he and all his fellows have been created. There is no longer any vast mystery about it; we are even getting relatively close to the secret, or could if we were permitted to go on undisturbed for a period by wars, let us say, or religious and educational illusions and furies (put forward by what? How brought about?), a persistent inherent mass opposition to thought and change in man himself. What subtle force ever invented that as a race quieter?

As biologists and anthropologists present man and his allied species, the original type structure on which all are more or less modelled is not so wonderful: two eyes, two ears, two nostrils, two feet and two hands or four feet, two of them antecedents of the present hands; or two feet and two wings, the latter successors of former feet; a lung or air-breathing system, not unlike that of any tree or plant; a root or arterial system, modified to meet various conditions and situations as in birds, fishes, moles; a nervous or sensory system of an allied character—no marked diversity in anything indeed, and all brought about by the inescapable chemical and physical reactions and compulsions of seemingly blind forces, as Crile and Loeb have shown. Even now chemists and physicists are at work upon the balances and equations involved in the mechanical and chemical construction of man, the leverage by which he moves, the combinations which control his form or aspect, as well as the chemical combinations which can induce motion or self-propulsion. Even as to his so-called thought how close are the Behaviourists to the material mechanics which produce it? His thoughts also are apparently little more than compelled reactions of one chemical upon another which he can no more escape than can he his form or motions. The one unsolved mystery apparently is why a machine so easily made and controlled should be able to speculate as to the reason for his being or to worry over it.

And yet just here another interesting fact stands out, and that is that whether or not he is a machine, Nature, or his Creator, appears to be quite definitely opposed to his finding out about himself or even to his delving into the matter, and throughout recorded science there is no evidence of the least willingness on the part of Nature or the life constructing forces to yield a single fact of any kind without a struggle. Man has fumbled and stumbled, dying by billions in one erroneous way, or another, until at last, by mere chance apparently, he has stumbled upon one helpful fact or another. It is as if the fable of Prometheus or that other of Adam and Eve were true. The seekers after knowledge of any kind have almost invariably been fought or their work brought to nothing, and even where man has apparently proved victorious or where he has seemingly been aided only that has been yielded which has tended to further him as an ignorant and yet useful machine, never as a thinker. No one who has tended to throw a clear light on the internecine struggles of Nature herself, her cruelties and brutalities, has prospered. If one doubts this he has only to consider the fumbling, haphazard progress of man, his warring notions as to his source and import, his strange aberrant evolution and the persistent and discouraging hindrances cast in the way of his intellectual evolution; i.e. the rise of impossible and even ridiculous leaders and religious theories—Christianity, Shintoism, Mohammedanism—and the arrival of such dark figures as Attila (self-styled "the scourge of God"), Alaric, and Mohammed with his houris' dream, upon the scene of fairly acceptable intellectual conditions. The deaths of endless prying inventors, their pursuit by the religionists in darker ages, the periodic rise of -isms and world-sweeping folderol, political and other notions, all seem to point to but one thing: Nature's indifference if not opposition to man's tendency to develop intelligence and desire to know—if such a thing can be assumed, for it cannot be proved. For since when has the dullness of the mass, or man, his ignorance or indifference, apparently calculated and conditional, not stood its ground against the overtures of intelligence, science, the arts, philosophy? Nothing flourishes on earth so well as vain theory. Energetic thought is all but taboo. False dreams and false hopes are invariably encouraged by apparently some chemical or mechanical condition in the so-called brain of man himself. It is scarcely so much that he dare not as that he cannot.

And if he should but stop to consider this cloak-and-suit-model repetition of himself previously suggested, this system or pattern after which he and all the endless decillions which have preceded and will follow him are made, do you suppose he could exact anything which suggested individuality or personal persistence as a spirit or thought—self-generated thought—out of it? Is one button wiser or much more important than any other, or at all more likely to outlast another spiritually? Is it in any way essential that it should? The original model for the button might be important, but as for the endless copies! Indeed in the whole programme of repetition, in so far as man or any of the animals or insects or of matter itself is concerned, there is but one ray of light or hope, and that is that the ion or electron of which all and everything appears to be composed may after all be the only true base or unit of expression of the so-called controlling spirit or force or forces of life, not the various contesting combinations of them, and that this ionic sea or mass, while controlled by the necessity of division and recombination, if it wishes to express itself at all ("The Kinetic Theory," J. C. Vogt), is still so large and so involute in its creative processes as to be necessarily more or less indifferent to any form of ionic self-expression or combination that might occur under or with it. So that the mere fact that groups or volumes of itself (ions) should combine for any purpose or generate themselves into any special forms of life (via combination, of course)—suns, planets, animals, races, nations, and their special developments again—might be to it a matter of absolutely no consequence. What matter if the electrons of some minute part of itself should organise and set up some special sun or planet or race of individuals, so long as they did not prove troublesome to the rest of the ionic sea? Supposing there are vast galaxies of self-generated suns in space—endless space, composed of but a part of the total ionic mass—so long as they are a mere negligible nothing to the totality of enduring force; what of it? If such were the case it is entirely conceivable that anything might arise for a time, any system of suns or race-life on suns or planets, and also the domination of one organised group of ions over another, but all subject nevertheless in the course of time and according to some equational and inescapable law to the totality of primary ionic or universal force.

In that case such a statement as occurs in Genesis iii, 5, would be plain enough. Some self-generated combination of ions looking upon itself as a creator in its own right (for a period anyhow), and having sub-invented man for some purpose of its own, self-expression or comfort, or the use of other enslaved ions to do its bidding, might say just that ("For God doth know," etc.); and it would be true.

On the other hand man, via the force of the numbers of the ions collected within himself, his race, and by degrees so gaining in numbers, and so power or intelligence equal to that of the ions which had originally enslaved him, might rise and question of this other elemental ionic combination its right to lordship over him. And again, by reason of *laissez-faire* conditions which apparently hold throughout all Nature and force, he would then be able to overthrow this higher ionic combination and so set up a lordship of his own—as in some ways even now he appears to be doing. For one need only observe his growing command of machinery and the apparently indifferent streams of ionic energy everywhere moving, upon the backs of which or to the streams of which he attaches his wires and dynamos and engines and permits them to do a part of his work for him, in order to see how this might be. For if we are not an illustration of one ionic combination using another, what are we? And if that which is above us is not a combination of ions using us, what is it? Science has no other answer. At the same time, of course, man would be fought, as apparently he is being fought now, attacked and delayed by the powers which hitherto have made and are still using him. In that case the remarks of Jehovah in Genesis would be explicable enough.

And I here venture this prediction, based on this idea, that in case man is ever capable of awaking from his dream of spiritual enslavement and considers the higher creative reality which makes suns and his own immediate God as well, and sees also that he is the victim of a purely gratuitous overlordship of which he is no more than an hypnotic victim, he may well be able to invent crawling and winged things with some primary system of nervous response and intelligence, quite as he was invented in the first place, which will serve him in some dull, hopeless way, just as he himself now serves a higher power. Already he has invented most complicated machinery, and what else may he not invent? For ions are ions, wherever found, in whatever form of life, amoeba, or man or sun, and they are everywhere. Obviously they may not rule save in combination and by force, one combined group seizing on other uncombined and therefore helpless ions so to do, and is that not our method in all phases of life here on earth now? But once the ions of men finding themselves in combination, by whatsoever process contrived, it may not be so easy longer to control them. Rebellions may occur, and probably will. The great thing seems to be to get enough of them in combination. Time perhaps is the great factor in all these things. At the same time it might be true, and at present so appears, that the generative group of ions which evolved man and all of his so-called superior combinations and results here, might be so jealous of its own creative skill in this respect that, seeing man or his ionic content attempting to gain knowledge of how to proceed and do, it might at once set out to undo him. The fable of Prometheus and of Adam and Eve may not be so impossible, after all. Yet should his "God" not be able to completely destroy him he may yet well imitate his Creator and create.

But will he be allowed so to do?

34. LIFE, ART AND AMERICA*

I do not pretend to speak with any historic or sociologic knowledge of the sources of the American ethical, and therefore critical, point of view, though I suspect the origin, but I am at least convinced that, whatever its source or sense, it does not accord with the facts of life as I have noted or experienced them. To me the average or somewhat standardised American is an odd, irregularly developed soul, wise and even forward in matters of mechanics, organisations and anything that relates to technical skill in connection with material things, but absolutely devoid of true spiritual insight, correct knowledge of the history of literature or art, and confused by and mentally lost in or overcome by the multiplicity of the purely material and inarticulate details by which he finds himself surrounded.

As a boy in the small towns of the middle West I had no slightest opportunity to get a correct or even partially correct estimate of what might be called the mental A B abs of life. I knew nothing of history, and there was not a book in any of the schools which I attended, labelled either history or science or art, containing the least suggestion of the rationale which I subsequently came to feel to be relatively true, or at least acceptable to me. If I remember correctly, in the history of the world which was labelled Swinton's, the defeat of Napoleon, not his career, was pointed out as having had a great moral if not Christian value to the world. His end on St. Helena, not the Code Napoleon or the hieratic and ultra-economic arrangement of his material forces, was supposed to have achieved something for society! Similarly Socrates and his death were descanted upon as having almost a religious if not a Christian import. His

* The selection constitutes the entire essay "Life, Art and America" by Theodore Dreiser, in *Hey, Rub-A-Dub-Dub*. Reprinted by permission of The Dreiser Trust.

death was painted as having been brought about by his low private deeds, not his higher moral views. The true significance of the man as illustrated by the exact details of his life was utterly ignored.

Because my father was a Catholic and I was baptised in that faith, I was supposed to accept all the dogma, as well as the legends, of the Church as true. In the life about me I saw flourishing the Methodist, the Baptist, the United Brethren, the Christian, the Congregationalist, the what-not churches, each representing, according to its adherents, the exact historic and truthful development and interpretation of life or the world. As a fourteen- or fifteen-year-old boy I listened to sermons on hell, where it was, and what was the nature of its torments. As rewards for imaginary good behaviour I have been given colour-ed picture cards containing exact reproductions of heaven! Every newspaper that I have ever read, or still read, has had an exact code of morals by the light of which one may detect at once Mr. Bad Man and Mr. Good Man and so save oneself from the machinations of the former! The books which I was advised to read, and for the neglect of which I was frowned upon, were of that naïve character known as pure. One should read only good books—which meant of course books from which any reference to sex had been eliminated, and what followed as a natural consequence was that all intelligent interpretation of character and human nature was immediately discounted.

A picture of a nude or partially nude woman was sinful; a statue equally so. The dance in our home and our town was taboo. The theatre was an institution which led to crime, the saloon a centre of low, even bestial vices. The existence of such a thing as an erring or fallen woman, let alone a house of prostitution, was a crime, scarcely a fact to be considered. There were forms and social appearances which we were taught to wear, quite as one wears a suit of clothes. One had to go to church on Sunday whether one wished to or not. It was considered good business, if you please, to be connected with some religious organisation; and, by the same token, this commercialised religiosity was transmuted into glistening virtue. We were taught persistently to shun most human experiences as either dangerous or degrading or destructive. The less you knew about life the better; the more you knew about the fictional heaven and hell ditto. People walked about in a kind of sanctified maze or dream, hypnotised or self-hypnotised by an erratic and impossible theory of human conduct which had grown up heaven knows where or how, and had finally cast its amethystine spell over all America, if not over all the world.

Now I have no particular quarrel with this save that it is so impossible, so inane. In my day there were apparently no really bad men who were not known as such to all the world, or at least quickly detected, and few if any good men who were not sufficiently rewarded by the glorious fruits of their good deeds here and now! Success—mere commercial success—was in its way all but synonymous with greatness. Positively, and I stake my solemn word on this, until I was between seventeen and eighteen I had scarcely begun to suspect any other human being of harbouring the erratic and sinful thoughts which occasionally flashed through my own mind.

At that time I was just beginning to suspect that some of the things which had been laid down to me by one authority and another were not true. All so-called good men were not necessarily good, I was beginning to suspect, and all bad men not hopelessly bad. There were things in cities and town which, as I was coming to see, did not accord with the theories of the particular realm from which I had sprung and seemed to indicate another kind of human being, different from the type among which I had been raised. My mother, as I even then saw, admire her as I might, was a mere woman, not an angel; my father a mere, mere crotchety man. My sisters and brothers were individuals such as I soon began to find were breasting the stormy waters of life outside, and not very different from all other brothers and sisters, not perfect souls set apart from life and happy in the contemplation of each other's perfections. In short, I was beginning to find the world a seething, stormy, bitter, gay, rewarding and destroying realm, in which the strong and the subtle and the charming and the magnetic were apt to be victors, and the weak and the homely and the ignorant and the dull were apt to be deprived of any interesting share, not because of any innate depravity but rather because of the lacks by which they were handicapped and which they could not possibly overcome.

And there were other phases which previously I had scarcely suspected. The race was to the swift and the battle to the strong. All great successes, as I was beginning to discover for myself, were relatively gifts, the teachings of the self-helpers and virtue-mongers to the contrary notwithstanding. Artists, singers, actors, policemen, statesmen, generals, were born and not made. Sunday-school maxims, outside of the narrowest precincts, did not apply. People might preach one thing on Sunday or in the bosom of their families or in the meeting-places of conventional social groups, but they did not practise them except under compulsion, particularly in the marts of trade and exchange. Mark the phrase "under compulsion." I admit a vast compulsion which has nothing to do with the individual desires or tastes or impulses of individuals. That compulsion springs from the settling processes of forces which we do not in the least understand, over which we have no control and in whose grip we are as grains of dust or sand, blown hither and thither, for what purpose we cannot even suspect. Politics, as I found in working as a newspaper man, was a low mess; religion, both as to its principles and its practitioners, a ghastly fiction based on sound and fury, signifying nothing; trade was a seething war in which the less subtle and the less swift or strong went under, while the more cunning succeeded; the professions were largely gathering-places of weaklings, mediocrities or mercenaries, to be bought by, or sold to, the highest bidder.

The individual, as I found, was trying to do one thing: make himself happy principally; life was plainly trying to do another, or at least what it was doing involved no great concern for the welfare of any particular individual. He might live, he might die; he might be well fed, he might be hungry; he might, accidentally or by taking thought, ally himself with successful movements, or he might inherently, by some incapacity or fatality of disposition, involve himself in the drifts toward failure; he might be weak, he might be strong; he might be wise, he might be dull or narrow. Life in the large thrashing sense in which we see it to move about us cared no whit for him. Why so many failures? I was constantly asking myself; so many early deaths, so many accidents, crass and unexplained? Why so many fires? So many cyclones? So many destroying epidemics? So many breaks in health or in trade or by reason of vice or crime or mere increasing age and mood? So many, many individuals going down into the limbo of nothingness or failure, so few attaining to that vast and lonesome supremacy which all were seeking? Why? Why? I persistently asked myself; and I have yet to find the answer in any current code of morals or ethics or the dogma of any religion.

If you should chance to consult a Methodist, a Baptist, a Presbyterian, a Lutheran, or any other current American sectarian, on this subject you would find (which after all is a dull thing to point out at this day and date) that his conception of the things which he sees about him is bounded by what he was taught in his Sunday school or his church, or what he has stored up or gathered from the conventions of his native town. (His native town! Kind heaven!) And although the world has stored up endless treasures in chemistry, sociology, history, philosophy, still the millions and millions who tramp the streets and occupy the stores and fill the highways and by-ways and the fields and the tenements have no faintest knowledge of this, or of anything else that can be said to be intellectually "doing." They live in theories and isms, and under codes dictated by a church or a state or an order of society which has no least regard for or relationship to their natural mental development. The darkest side of democracy, like that of autocracy, is that it permits the magnetic and the cunning and the unscrupulous among the powerful individuals to sway vast masses of the mob, not so much to their own immediate destruction as to the curtailment of their natural privileges and the ideas which they should be allowed to entertain if they could think at all—and incidentally to the annoying and sometimes undoing of individuals who have the truest brain interests of the race at heart: *vide* Giordano Bruno! Jan Huss! Savonarola! Tom Paine! Walt Whitman! Edgar Allan Poe!

For after all the great business of life and mind is life. We are here, I take it, not merely to moon and vegetate, but to do a little thinking about this state in which we find ourselves, or at least to try. It is perfectly legitimate, all priests and theories and philosophies to the contrary, to go back, in so far as we may, to the primary sources of thought, i.e. the visible scene, the actions and thoughts of people, the movements of Nature and its chemical and physical subtleties, in order to draw original and radical conclusions for ourselves. The great business of the individual, if he has any time after struggling for life and a reasonable amount of entertainment or sensory satiation, should be this very thing. He should question the things he sees—not some things, but everything—stand, as it were, in the centre of this whirling storm of contradiction which we know as life, and ask of it its source and its import. Else why a brain at all? If only one could induce or enable a moderate number of the individuals who pass this way and come no more apparently to pause and think about life and take an individual point of view, the freedom and individuality and interest of the world might be greatly enhanced. We complain of the world as dull. If it is so, lack of thinking by individuals is the reason. But to ask the poor, half-equipped mentality of the mass to think, to be individual—what an anachronism! You might as well ask of a rock to move or a tree to fly.

Here in America, by reason of an idealistic Constitution which is largely a work of art and not a workable system, you see a nation dedicated to so-called intellectual and spiritual freedom, but actually devoted with an almost bee-like industry to the gathering and storing and articulation and organisation and use of purely material things. In spite of all our bass-drum announcement of our servitude to the intellectual ideals of the world (copied mostly, by the way, from England) no nation has ever contributed less, philosophically or artistically or spiritually, to the actual development of the intellect and the spirit. We have invented many things, it is true, which have relieved man from the crushing weight of a too-grinding toil, and this perhaps may be the sole mission of America in the world and the universe, its destiny, its end. Personally I think it is not a half bad thing to have done; the submarine and the flying machine and the armoured dreadnought, no less than the sewing-machine and the cotton-gin and the binder and the reaper and the cash register and the trolly-car if not the telephone, may prove in the end, or perhaps already have proved, as significant in breaking the chains of the physical and mental slavery of man as anything else. I do not know.

One thing I do know is that America seems profoundly interested in these things, to the exclusion of anything else. It has no time, you might almost say, no taste, to stop and contemplate life in the large, from an artistic or a philosophic point of view. Yet after all, when all the machinery for lessening man's burdens has been invented and all the safeguards for his preservation completed and possibly shattered by forces too deep or superior for his mechanical cunning, may not a phrase, a line of poetry, or a single act of some half-forgotten tragedy be all that is left of what we now see or dream of as materially perfect? For is it not thought alone, of many famous and powerful things that have already gone, that endures?—a thought most often conveyed by art as a medium?

But let me not become too remote or fine-spun in my conception of the ultimate significance of art itself. The point which I wish to make is just this: that in a land so devoted to the material, although dedicated by its Constitution to the ideal, the condition of intellectual freedom, let alone art, is certainly anomalous. Your trade and your trust builder, most obviously dominant in America at this time, is of all people most indifferent to, or most unconscious of, the ultimate and pressing claims of mind and spirit as expressed by art. If you doubt this you have only to look about you to see for what purposes, to what end, the increment of men of wealth and material power in America is most devoted. Stuffy, tasteless houses crowded with stuffy, tasteless antiques, safety deposit vaults stuffed with securities, the having and holding of purely material values always. In proof of which I may add that we have something like twenty-five hundred colleges and schools and institutions of various kinds, largely furthered by the money of American men of wealth, and all presumably devoted to the development of the mental equipment of man (or so we are told), yet nearly all set with flinty firmness against anything which is related to truly radical investigation, or thought, or action, or art. The inculcation of morality and patriotism is even now laid down as the true task and province of the so-called schools of higher learning by the educators themselves, or at least the presidents of most of the leading institutions—not the getting of knowledge at any cost, patriotic or other.

As a matter of fact, in spite of the American Constitution and the American oratorical address on all and sundry occasions, the average American school, college, university, institution, is as much against the development of the individual, in the true sense of that word, as any sect or religion. What it really wants is not an individual but an automatic copy of some altruistic and impossible ideal, which has been formulated here or elsewhere under the domination of Christianity or some other ism. I defy you to read any American college or university prospectus or address or plea which concerns the purposes or ideals of these institutions and not agree with me. They are not after individuals; they are after types of schools of individuals, all to be very much alike, all to be like themselves. And what type? Listen. I know of an American college professor in one of our successful State universities who had this to say of the male graduates of his institution, after having watched the output for a number of years: "They are all right, quite satisfactory as machines for the production of material wealth or for the maintenance of certain forms of professional skill, but as for ideas of their own or being creators or men with the normal impulses and passions of manhood they do not fulfil the requisite in any respect. They are little more than types, machines, made in the image and likeness of their college. They do not think; they cannot, because they are held hard and fast by the iron band of convention. They are afraid to think. They are moral young beings, Christian beings, model beings, but they are not men in the creative sense, and the large majority will never do a thing other than work for a corporation in a routine unindividual way, unless by chance or necessity the theories and the conventions imposed or generated by their training and surroundings are broken, and they become free, independent, self-thinking individuals."

In this connection I might say I know of one women's college, an American institution of the highest standing, which since its inception has sent forth into life some thousands of graduates and post-graduates to battle life as they may for individual supremacy or sensory comfort. They are (or were) supposed to be individuals capable of individual thought, procedure, invention, development; yet out of all of them not one has even entered upon any creative or artistic labour of any kind. Not one. (Write me for the name of the college, if you wish.) There is not a chemist, a physiologist, a botanist, a biologist, an historian, a philosopher, an artist, of any kind or repute among them; not one. They are secretaries to corporations, teachers, missionaries, college librarians, educators in any of the scores of pilfered meanings that may be attached to that much-abused word. They are curators, directors, keepers. They are not individuals in the true sense of that word; they have not been taught to think; they are not free. They do not invent, lead, create; they only copy or take care of, yet they are graduates of this college and its theory, mostly ultra-conventional, or, worse yet, anaemic, and glad to wear its collar, to clank the chains of its ideas or ideals—automata in a social scheme whose last and final detail was outlined to them in the class-rooms of their Alma Mater. That, to me, is one phase, amusing enough, of intellectual freedom in America.

But the above is a mere detail in any chronicle or picture of the social or intellectual state of the United States. Turn, for instance, if you will, to the legislative and judicial phases of our Government—those grand realms in which only statesmen and judicial students of our economic and social condition are supposed to move and rule, and what do we find?

As long ago as 1875 Ernst Häckel, the eminent German scientist, complained that the judges and legislatures of his day and country had "but a superficial acquaintance with that chief and peculiar object of their activity—the human organism and its most important function, the human mind," and that they had no time for anything save "an exhaustive study of beer and wine and the noble art of fencing." If that could be said of intellectual Germany in his day how much more and worse could be judicated of the American jurist and legislator in America to-day? The shabby mess which finance and trade rivalries make of our laws and our halls of legislation—the mental equipment of the average politician, his henchmen, the legislator and the judge—the hall boys of finance, and at the same time of religious and therefore arbitrary moral dogma which they have become, the petty ignoramuses we see on every hand legislating for the people or interpreting the laws once they are thus formulated! Häckel wrote sadly of the judges and law enactors in his day: "No one can maintain that their condition to-day is in harmony with our advanced knowledge of this world"—and, certainly, in America to-day, fifty years later, not a week passes in which we do not read of legislative deeds and legal decisions which make a thinking man sigh. Consider the slavish acceptance of religious and moral and financial dictation from self-interested and equally ignorant people, the running here and there to find what is temporarily expedient— what will satisfy or quiet the public for an hour; what will keep them from losing their petty jobs—by the politicians and legislators and so-called statesmen and judges; the complete ignorance of every congressman and senator and state legislator and judge and lawyer as to the commonest facts of biology, psychology, sociology, economics, and history! One President, Roosevelt, admitted that he could in no way understand economics. Yet once the average country or city law student has mastered a few hundred paragraphs of law he is ready to hire out to the nearest corporation, to legislate for the people, to prefix "Hon." to his name and set up in business as a judge or a statesman.

On the other hand, and in the very teeth of all this, no

country in the world, at least none that I know anything about, has such a peculiar, such a seemingly fierce determination, to make the Ten Commandments work. It would be amusing if it were not pitiful, their faith in these binding religious ideals. I have never been able to make up my mind whether this springs from the zealotry of the Puritans who landed at Plymouth Rock, or whether it is indigenous to the soil (which I doubt when I think of the Indians who preceded the white), or whether it is a product of the Federal Constitution, compounded by such idealists as Paine and Jefferson and Franklin and the more or less religious and political dreamers of the pre-Constitutional days. Certain it is that no such profound moral idealism animated the French in Canada, the Dutch in New York, the Swedes in New Jersey, or the mixed French and English in the extreme South and New Orleans.

The first shipload of white women ever brought to America was sold, almost at so much a pound. They were landed at Jamestown. The basis of all the first large fortunes was laid, to speak plainly, in graft—the most outrageous concessions obtained abroad. The history of our relations with the American Indians is sufficient to lay any claim to financial or moral virtue or worth in the white men who settled this country. We debauched, then robbed and murdered them; there is no other conclusion to be drawn from the facts covering that relationship as set down in any history worthy the name. As regards the development of our land, our canals, our railroads, and the vast organisations supplying our present-day necessities, their history is a complex of perjury, robbery, false witness, extortion, and indeed every crime to which avarice, greed and ambition are heir. If you do not believe this, examine the various congressional and State legislative investigations which have been held on an average of every six months since the Government was founded, and see for yourself. The cunning and unscrupulousness of American brains can be matched against any the world has ever known, not even excepting the English.

But an odd thing in connection with this financial and social criminality is that it has been consistently and regularly accompanied, outwardly at least, by a religious and a sex-puritanism which would be scarcely believable if it were not true. I do not say that the robbers and thieves who did so much to build up our great commercial and social structures were in themselves always religious or puritanically moral from the sex point of view, although in regard to the latter they most frequently made a show of so being; but I do say that the communities and the states and the nation in which they were committing their depredations have been individually and collectively, in so far as the written, printed and acted word are concerned, most loud in their pretensions. Why? I have a vague feeling that it is the American of Anglo-Saxon origin only who has been most vivid in his excitement over religion and morals where the written, printed, acted or painted word was concerned, yet who at the same time, and perhaps for this very reason, was failing or deliberately refusing to see the contrast which his ordinary and very human actions presented to all this. Was he a hypocrite? Is he one?

Your American of Anglo-Saxon or other origin is actually no better, spiritually or morally, than any other creature of this earth, be he Turk or Hindu or Chinese, except from a materially constructive or wealth-breeding point of view, but for some odd reason he thinks he is. The only real difference is that, cast out or spewed out by conditions over which he had no control elsewhere, he chanced to fall into a land overflowing with milk and honey. Nature in America was, and still is, kind to the lorn foreigner seeking a means of subsistence, and he seems to have immediately attributed this to three things: First, his inherent capacity to dominate and control wealth; second, the especial favour of God to him; third, of his superior and moral state (due, of course, to his possession of wealth). These three things, uncorrected as yet by any great financial pressure or any great natural or world catastrophe, have served to keep the American in his highly romantic state of self-deception. He still thinks that he is a superior spiritual and moral being, infinitely better than the creatures of any other land, and nothing short of a financial cataclysm, which will come with the pressure of population on resources, will convince him that he is not. But that he will yet be convinced is a certainty. You need not fear. Leave it to Nature.

One of the interesting phases of this puritanism or phariseeism is his attitude toward women and their morality and their purity. If ever a people has refined eroticism to a greater degree than the American I am not aware of it. Owing to a theory of the doctrinaire acceptance of the Mary legend possibly (Mariolatry, no less), the good American, capable of the same gross financial crimes previously indicated, has been able to look upon most women, but more particularly those above him in the social scale, as considerably more than human—angelic, no less, and possessed of qualities the like of which are not to be found in any breathing being, man, woman, child or animal. It matters not that his cities and towns, like those of any other nation, are rife with sex; that in each one are specific and often large areas devoted to Eros or Venus. While maintaining them he is still blind to their existence or import. He or his boys or his friends go—but——

Only a mentally one-sided nature or race such as the Anglo-Saxon could have built upon any such asinine theory as this. One would suppose that as they did, so they would have the courage to say, or at least cease this endless pother as to superior virtue. But no. The purity, the sanctity, the self-abnegation, the delicacy of women in America—how these qualities have been exaggerated and dinned into our ears, until at last the average scrubby non-reasoning male, quite capable of visiting the gardens of Venus or taking a girl off the street, is no more able clearly to visualise the creature before him than he is the central wilds of Africa which he has never seen. A princess, a goddess, a divine mother or creative principle, all the virtues, all the perfections, no vices, no weaknesses, no errors—some such hodge-podge as this has come to be the average Anglo-Saxon, or at least American, conception of the average American woman. I do not say that a portion of this illusion is not valuable, but as it stands now she is too good to be true, a paragon, a myth! Actually, she doesn't exist at all as he has been taught to imagine her. She is nothing more than a two-legged biped like the rest of us, but in consequence of this delusion sex itself, being a violation of this paragon, has become a crime. We enter upon the earth, it is true, in a none too artistic manner (conceived in iniquity and born in sin, is the Biblical phrasing of it), but all this has long since been glozed over, ignored, and to obviate its brutality as much as possible the male has been called upon to purify himself in thought and deed, to avoid all private speculation as to women and his relationship to them, and, much more than that, to avoid all public discussion, either by word of mouth or the printed page.

To think of women or to describe them, especially in our printed or publicly uttered word, as anything less than the paragon previously commented upon has become, by this process, not only a sin but a shameful infraction of the moral code. Women are now so good, the sex relationship so vile a thing that to think of the two at once is not to be thought of. They are supposed to have no connection. We must move in a mirage of illusion; we must trample fact underfoot and give fancy, in the guise of our so-called better natures, free rein. How this must affect or stultify the artistic and creative faculties of the race itself must be plain, yet that is exactly where we stand to-day, ethically and spiritually, in regard to sex and women, and that is what is the matter with American social life, letters and art. Imagine a Puritan or a moralist attempting anything in art, which is nothing if not a true reflection, emotional and intellectual, of insight into life! Imagine! And contrast this moral or art narrowness with the American's commercial or financial or agricultural freedom and sense, and note the difference. In regard to all the latter he is cool, sceptical, level-headed, understanding, natural, consequently well developed in those fields; in regard to this other he is disillusioned, theoretic, religious. In consequence he has no power, except for an occasional individual who may rise in spite of these untoward conditions (to be frowned upon), to understand, much less picture, life as it really is. Artistically, intellectually, philosophically we are weaklings; financially and in all ways commercial we are very powerful. So one-sided has been our development that in this latter respect we are almost giants. Strange, almost fabulous creatures have been developed here by this process, men so singularly devoid of a rounded human nature that they have become freaks in the matter of money-getting. I refer to Rockefeller, Gould, Sage, Vanderbilt the first, H. H. Rogers, Carnegie, Frick.

America I fear can be most aptly pictured as the land of Bottom the Weaver; and by Bottom I mean the tradesman or manufacturer who by reason of his enthusiasm for the sale of paints or powder or threshing-machines or coal has accumulated wealth, and in consequence and by reason of the haphazard privileges of democracy, has strayed into a position of counsellor, or even dictator, not in regard to the things about which he might readily be supposed to know, but about the many things about which he would be much more likely not to know: art, science, philosophy, morals, public policy in general. You recall Bottom, of course, in "A Midsummer Night's Dream," unconscious of his furry ears and also of the fact that he does not know how to play the lion's part; that it is more difficult than mere roaring. Here he is now, in America, enthroned as a lion, and in his way he is an epitome of the Anglo-Saxon temperament. Bottom is so wise in his own estimation. He never once suspects his furry ears or that he is not a perfect actor in the rôle of the lion—or, if you will take it for what it is meant, the arts. He is just a dull weaver really, made by this dream of our Constitution ("an exposition of sleep" come upon him) into a roaring lion—in his own estimation. No one must say that Bottom is not; he will be driven out of the country, deported or exiled. No one must presume to practise the arts save as Bottom understands them. If you do, presto, there is his henchman Comstock and all Comstockery to take you into custody. Men who have come here from foreign shores (England excepted) have been amazed at Bottom's ears and his presumption in passing upon what is a lion's part in life. Indeed he is the Anglo-Saxon temperament personified. He is convinced that liberty was not made for Oberon or Peas-blossom or Cobweb or Mustard-seed, but for bishops and executives and wholesale grocers and men who have become vastly rich canning tomatoes or selling oil. The great desire of Bottom is for all of us to have furry ears and long, and to believe that he is the greatest actor in the world. He is bewildered by a world that will not play Pyramus his way. Quince, Snug, Flute, Snout and Starveling (all those who came over with him in the *Mayflower*) agree that he is a great actor, but there are others, and Bottom is convinced that these others are in error, trying to wreck that dream, the American Constitution, which brought this "exposition of sleep" upon him and made him into a lion, "marvellous furry about the fact" and with great ears.

Alas, alas! for art in America. It has a hard, stubby row to hoe.

But my quarrel is not with America as a comfortable commercial and industrious atmosphere in which to move and have one's being, but largely because it is no more than that, because it tends to become a dull, conventionalised, routine, material world, duller even than its reputed mother, sacred England. We are drifting, unless most of the visible signs are deceiving, into the clutches of a commerical oligarchy whose mental standards outside of trade are so puerile as to be scarcely worth discussing. Contemplate, if you please, what has happened to one of the shibboleths or bulwarks of our sacred liberties and intellectual freedom, i.e. the newspaper, under the dominance of trade.

Look at it. I have not the time here to set forth *seriatim* all the charges that have been made, and in the main thoroughly substantiated, against the American newspaper; but consider for yourself the newspapers which you know and read. How much, I ask you, if you are in trade, do the newspapers you read know about trade? How far could you follow their trade judgment or understanding? And if you are a member of any profession, how much reported professional knowledge or news, as presented by a newspaper, can you rely on? If a newspaper reported a professional man's judgment or dictum in regard to any important professional fact, how fully would you accept it without other corroborative testimony?

You are a playgoer: do you believe the newspaper dramatic critics? You are a student of literature: do you accept the mouthings of their literary critics or even look to them for advice? You are an artist or a lover of art: do you follow the newspapers for anything more than the barest intelligence as to the whereabouts of anything artistic? I doubt it. And in regard to politics, finance, social movements and social affairs, are they not actually the darkest, the most misrepresentative, frequently the most biased and malicious guides in the world of the printed word? Newspaper criticism, like newspaper leadership, has long since come to be looked upon by the informed and intelligent as little more than the mouthings or bellowings of mercenaries or panderers to trade; or, worse still, rank incompetents. The newspaper man, *per se*, either does not know or cannot help himself. The newspaper publisher is very glad of this and uses his half intelligence or inability to further his own interests. Politicians, administrations, department stores, large interests and personalities of various kinds use or control or compel newspapers to do their bidding. This is a severe indictment to make against the Press in general, but is it not literally true?

Take again the large, almost dominant religious and commercial organisations of America. What relationship, if any, do they bear to a free mental development, a subtle understanding, art or life in its poetic or tragic moulds, its drift, its character? Would you personally look to the Methodist or the Presbyterian or the Catholic or the Baptist church to further individualism, or freedom of thought, or directness of mental action, or art in any form? Do not they really ask of all their adherents that they lay aside this freedom in favour of the reported word or dictum of a fabled, a non-historic, an imaginary ruler of the universe? Think of it! And they are among the powerful, constructive and controlling elements in government—in this government, to be accurate—dedicated and presumably devoted to individual liberty, not only of so-called conscience, but of constructive thought and art.

And our large corporations, with their dominant and controlling captains of industry so-called; what about their relationship to individuality, the freedom of the individual to think for himself, to grow mentally? Take, for instance, the tobacco trust, the oil trust, the milk trust, the coal trust—in what way do you suppose they help? Are they actively seeking a better code of ethics, a wider historic or philosophic perspective, a more delicate art perception for the individual, or are they definitely and permanently concerned with the customary bludgeoning tactics of trade, piling up fortunes out of which they are to be partially bled later by pseudo art collectors and swindling dealers in antiques and so-called historic art and literature? Of current life and its accomplishments, what do they actually know? Yet this is a democracy. Here, as in no other realm of the world, the individual is supposed to be permitted, even compelled, to seek his own material and mental salvation as best he may. Yet one trouble with a democracy, in so far as art and individal intelligence is concerned, as opposed to an autocracy with a line of titled idlers, is that the latter permits at least the gift of leisure and art indulgence to a few and there usually is a central force or group to foster art, to secure letters and art in their inalienable rights, to make of superior thought a noble and a sacred thing. I am not saying that democracy will not yet produce such a central force or group. I believe it may or can. It is entirely possible that when the time arrives it may prove to be better than any form of hereditary autocracy. But I am talking about the mental, the social, the artistic condition of America as it is to-day.

To me it is a thing for laughter, if not for tears; one hundred and twenty million Americans, rich (a fair percentage of them, anyhow) beyond the dreams of avarice, and scarcely a sculptor, a poet, a singer, a novelist, an actor, a musician, worthy the name. One hundred and forty years (almost two hundred, counting the Colonial days) of the most prosperous social conditions, a rich soil, incalculable deposits of gold, silver and precious and useful metals and fuels of all kinds, a land amazing in its mountains, its streams, its valley prospects, its wealth-yielding powers, and now its tremendous cities and far-flung facilities for travel and trade—and yet contemplate it. Artists, poets, thinkers, where are they? Has it produced a single philosopher of the first rank—a Spencer, a Nietzsche, a Schopenhauer, a Kant? Do I hear someone offering Emerson as an equivalent? Or James? Has it produced an historian of the force of either Macaulay or Grote or Gibbon? A novelist of the rank of Turgenev, de Maupassant or Flaubert? A scientist of the standing of Crookes or Röntgen or Pasteur? A critic of the insight and force of Taine, Sainte-Beuve or the de Goncourts? A dramatist the equivalent of Ibsen, Chekhov, Shaw, Hauptmann, Brieux? An actor, since Booth, of the force of Coquelin, Sonnenthal, Forbes-Robertson or Sarah Bernhardt? Since Whitman, one poet: Edgar Lee Masters. In painting a Whistler, an Inness, a Sargent. Who else? (And two of these shook the dust of our shores for ever.) Inventors, yes; by the hundreds, one might almost say thousands; some of them amazing enough, in all conscience, world figures, and enduring for all time. But of what relationship to art, the supreme freedom of the mind?

The most significant, and to me discouraging, manifestation in connection with the United States to-day is the tendency to even narrower and more puritanic standards than have obtained in the past. I am constantly astonished by the thousands of men, exceedingly capable in some mechanical or narrow technical sense, whose world or philosophic vision is that of a child. As a nation we accept and believe naïvely in such impossible things. I am not thinking alone of the primary tenets of all religions, which are manifestly based on nothing at all and which millions of Americans, along with the humbler classes of other countries, accept, but rather of those sterner truths which life itself teaches: the unreliability of human nature; the crass chance which strikes down and destroys our finest dreams; the fact that man in all his relations is neither good nor evil, but both. The American, by some hocus-pocus of atavism, has seemingly borrowed or retained from English lower middle-class Puritans all their folderol notions about making human nature perfect by fiat or edict—the written word, as it were, which goes with all religions. So, although by reason of the coarsest and most brutal methods we as a nation have built up one of the most interesting and domineering oligarchies in the world, we are still not aware of the fact.

All men, in the mind of the unthinking American, are still free and equal. They have in themselves certain inalienable rights; what they are when you come to test them no human being can discover. Life here, as elsewhere, comes down to the brutal methods of Nature itself. The rich strike the poor at every turn; the poor defend themselves and further their lives by all the tricks which stark necessity can conceive. No inalienable right keeps the average cost of living from rising steadily, while most of the salaries of our idealistic Americans are stationary. No inalienable right has ever yet prevented the strong from tricking or browbeating the weak. And although by degrees the average American feeling more and more keenly the sharpening struggle for existence, yet his faith in his impossible ideals is as fresh as ever. God will save the good American and seat him at His right hand on the Golden Throne.

With one hand the naïve American takes and executes with all the brutal insistence of Nature itself; with the other he writes glowing platitudes concerning brotherly love, virtue, purity, truth, etc. etc. A part of this right—or left-hand tendency, as the case may be, is seen in the constant desire of the American to reform something. No country in the world, not even England, the mother of folderol reforms, is so prolific in these frail ventures as this great country of ours. In turn we have had campaigns for the reform of the atheist, the drunkard, the lecher, the fallen woman, the buccaneer financier, the drug fiend, the dancer, the theatregoer, the reader of novels, the wearer of low-neck dresses and surplus jewellery—in fact every taste and frivolity, wherever sporadically it has chanced to manifest itself with any interesting human force. Your reformer's idea is that any human being, to be a successful one, must be a pale spindling sprout, incapable of any vice or crime. And all the while the threshing sea of life is sounding in his ears! The thief, the lecher, the drunkard, the fallen woman, the greedy, the inordinately vain, as in all ages past, pass by his door and are not the whit less numerous for the unending campaigns which have been launched to save them. In other words, human nature is human nature, but your American cannot be made to believe it.

Personally my quarrel is with America's quarrel with original thought. It is so painful to me to see one after another of our alleged reformers tilting Don Quixote-like at the giant windmills of fact. We are to have no pictures which the Puritan and the narrow, animated by an obsolete dogma, cannot approve of. We are to have no theatres, no motion pictures, no books, no public exhibitions of any kind, no speech even, which will in any way contravene his limited view of life. Finally we even contrived a President who was to have no more war! A few years ago it was the humble dealer in liquor whose life was anathematised and whose property was descended upon with torch, axe and bomb. A little later, our cities growing and the sections devoted to the worship of Venus becoming more manifest, the Vice Crusader was bred, and we now have the spectacle of whole areas of fallen women scattered to the four winds and allowed to practise separately what they cannot do collectively. Also came Mr. Comstock, vindictive, persistent, and with a nose and taste for the profane and erotic such as elsewhere has not been equalled since. Pictures, books, the theatre, the dance, the studio—all came under his watchful eye. During the twenty or thirty years in which he acted as a United States Post Office Inspector he was, because of his dull charging against things which he did not understand, never out of the white light of publicity which he so greatly craved. One month it would be a novel by d'Annunzio; another, a set of works by Balzac or de Maupassant, found in the shade of some grovelly bookseller's shop; the humble photographer attempting a nude; the painter who allowed his reverence for Raphael to carry him too far; the poet who attempted a recrudescence of Don Juan in modern iambics, was immediately seized upon and hauled before an equally dull magistrate, there to be charged with his offence and to be fined accordingly. All this is being continued with emphasis.

Then came the day of the armed White Slave Chasers, and now no American city and no backwoods Four Corners, however humble, is complete without a vice commission of some kind, or at least a local agent or representative charged with the duty of keeping the art, the literature, the press and the private lives of all those at hand up to that standard of perfection which only the dull can set for themselves. When the White Slave question was at its whitest heat the problem of giving expression to its fundamental aspects was divided between raiding plays which attempted to show the character of the crime in too graphic a manner, and licensing those which appealed to the intelligence of those who were foremost in the crusade. Thus we had the spectacle of an uncensored, but nevertheless approved, ten-reel film showing more details of the crime and better methods of securing white slaves than any other production of the day, running undisturbed to packed houses all over the country; while two somewhat more dramatic but far less effective distributors of information via plays were successfully harried from city to city and finally withdrawn.

Shakespeare has been ordered from the schools in some of the States. A production of "Antony and Cleopatra" has been raided in Chicago. Japanese prints of a high art value, intended for the seclusion of a private collection, have been seized and the most valuable of them destroyed. By turns, an artistic fountain to Heine in New York, loan exhibits of paintings in Denver, Kansas City and elsewhere, scores of books by Stevenson, James Lane Allen, Frances H. Burnett, have been attacked, not only, as in the case of the latter, with the airy weapons of the law, but in the case of the former with actual axes. A male dancer of repute and some artistic ability has been raided publicly by the Vice Crusaders for his shameless exposure of his person! No play, no picture, no book, no public or private jubilation of any kind is complete any more without its vice attack.

To me this sort of thing is dull and bespeaks the low state to which our mental activities have fallen. When it comes to the matter of serious letters it is the worst. In New York a literary region of terror has been and is now being attempted. The publisher of Freud's "Leonardo" is warned before he brings it out that he will be prosecuted—a work that probably has no more defect than that of being intelligent and true. Similarly, Mr. Przybyszewski's "Homo Sapiens," a by no means pornographic work, was at once seized on its appearance and the publishers frightened into withdrawing it. This was true of "Hagar Revelly," "Tess of the d'Urbervilles," "Sapho," "Jude the Obscure," "Rose of Dutchers Cooley," "A Lady of Quality," "A Summer in Arcady," and scores of others. Imagine banning a book like "A Summer in Arcady" from the public libraries! Even "The Sexual Question" by the eminent August Forel has been banned and of course all of Krafft-Ebing (Freud and Ellis are sold only on the written order of a doctor—a mental prescription as it were). Think of it—the work of a scientist of Freud's attainments!

This sort of interference with serious letters and science is to me the worst and most corrupting form of espionage which is conceivable to the human mind. It plumbs the depths of

ignorance and intolerance; if not checked it can and will dam
initiative and inspiration at the source. Life, if it is anything at
all, is a thing to be observed, studied, interpreted. We cannot
know too much about it because as yet we know nothing. It is
our one great realm of discovery. The artist, if left to himself,
may be safely trusted to observe, synchronise and articulate
human knowledge in the most comprehensive form. Human
nature will seek and have what it needs, the vice crusaders to
the contrary notwithstanding. There is no compulsion on
anyone to read; one must pay to do so. What is more, one must
have taste inherently to select, a brain and a heart to understand. With all these safeguards and a double score of capable
critics in every land to praise or blame, what need really is there
for a censor, or a dozen of them, each far less fitted than any of
the working critics to indulge his personal predilection and
opposition, and to appeal to the courts if he is disagreed with?

Personally I rise to protest. I look on this interference with
serious art and thought and serious minds as an outrage. I fear
for the ultimate intelligence of America, which in all conscience, judged by world standards, is low enough. Now comes a
band of wasp-like censors to put the finishing touches on a
literature and an art that has struggled all too feebly as it is.
Poe, Hawthorne, Whitman and Thoreau, each in turn was the
butt and jibe of unintelligent Americans, until by now we are
wellnigh the laughing-stock of the world. Where is it to end?
When will we lay aside our swaddling-clothes, enforced on us by
ignorant, impossible Puritans and their uneducated followers,
and stand up free-thinking men and women? Life is to be
learned as much from books and art as from life itself—almost
more so, in my judgment. Art is the stored honey of the human
soul, gathered on wings of misery and travail. Shall the dull and
the self-seeking and the self-advertising close this store on the
groping human mind?

Contemporary Comments

35. EDGAR LEE MASTERS
Theodore Dreiser*

Jack o'Lantern tall shouldered,
One eye set higher than the other,
Mouth cut like a scallop in a pie,
Aslant showing powerful teeth.
Swaying above the heads of others.
Jubilant with fixed eyes, scarcely sparkling.
Moving about rhythmically, exploding in laughter.
Touching fingers together back and forth,
Or toying with a handkerchief.
And the eyes burn like a flame at the end of a funnel.
And the ruddy face glows like a pumpkin
On Halloween!

Or else a gargoyle of bronze
Turning suddenly to life
And slipping suddenly down corners of stone
To eat you:
Full of questions, objections,
Distinctions, instances.
Contemptuous, ironical, remote,
Cloudy, irreverent, ferocious,
Fearless, grim, compassionate, yet hateful,
Old, yet young, wise but virginal.
To whom everything is new and strange:
Whence he stares and wonders,
Laughs, mocks, curses.
Disordered, yet with a passion for order
And classification—hence the habitual
Folding into squares of a handkerchief.

* The selection is taken from *The Great Valley* (The Macmillan Co., 1916).
Reprinted by permission of Mrs. Edgar Lee Masters.

Or else a well cultivated and fruitful valley,
But behind it unexplored fastnesses,
Gorges, precipices, and heights
Over which thunder clouds hang,
From which lightning falls,
Stirring up terrible shapes of prey
That slink about in the blackness.
The silence of him is terrifying
As if you sat before the sphinx.
The look of his eyes makes tubes of the air
Through which you are magnified and analyzed.
He needs nothing of you and wants nothing.
He is alone, but content,
Self-mastered and beyond friendship,
You could not hurt him.
If he would allow himself to have a friend
He would part from that friend forever
And in a moment be lost in wonder
Staring at a carved rooster on a doorstep,
Or at an Italian woman
Giving suck to a child
On a seat in Washington Square.

Soul enwrapped demi-urge
Walking the earth,
Stalking Life!

36. SHERWOOD ANDERSON
An Apology for Crudity*

For a long time I have believed that crudity is an inevitable quality in the production of a really significant present-day American literature. How indeed is one to escape the obvious fact that there is as yet no native subtlety of thought or living among us? And if we are a crude and childlike people how can our literature hope to escape the influence of that fact? Why indeed should we want it to escape?

If you are in doubt as to the crudity of thought in America, try an experiment. Come out of your offices, where you sit writing and thinking, and try living with us. Get on a train at Pittsburg and go west to the mountains of Colorado. Stop for a time in our towns and cities. Stay for a week in some Iowa corn-shipping town and for another week in one of the Chicago clubs. As you loiter about read our newspapers and listen to our conversations, remembering, if you will, that as you see us in the towns and cities, so we are. We are not subtle enough to conceal ourselves and he who runs with open eyes through the Mississippi Valley may read the story of the Mississippi Valley.

It is a marvelous story and we have not yet begun to tell the half of it. A little, I think I know why. It is because we who write have drawn ourselves away. We have not had faith in our people and in the story of our people. If we are crude and childlike, that is our story and our writing men must learn to dare to come among us until they know the story. The telling of the story depends, I believe, upon their learning that lesson and accepting that burden.

To my room, which is on a street near the loop in the city of Chicago, come men who write. They talk and I write. We are

* The selection constitutes the essay, first printed in *The Dial,* November 8, 1917. Copyright 1917 by Eleanor Anderson; renewed. Reprinted here by permission of Harold Ober Associates, Inc.

fools. We talk of writers of the old world and the beauty and
subtlety of the work they do. Below us the roaring city lies like
a great animal on the prairies, but we do not run out to the
prairies. We stay in our rooms and talk.

And so, having listened to talk and having myself talked
overmuch, I grow weary of talk and walk in the streets. As I
walk alone, an old truth comes home to me and I know that we
shall never have an American literature until we return to faith
in ourselves and to the facing of our own limitations. We must,
in some way, become in ourselves more like our fellows, more
simple and real.

For surely it does not follow that because we Americans are a
people without subtlety, we are a dull or uninteresting people.
Our literature is dull, but we are not. One remembers how
Dostoevsky had faith in the simplicity of the Russians and what
he achieved. He lived and he expressed the life of his time and
people. The thing that he did brings hope of achievement for
our men.

But let us first of all accept certain truths. Why should we
Americans aspire to a subtlety that belongs not to us but to old
lands and places? Why talk of intellectuality and of intellectual
life when we have not accepted the life that we have? There is
death on that road and following it has brought death into
much of American writing. Can you doubt what I say? Consider
the smooth slickness of the average magazine story. There is
often great subtlety of plot and phrase, but there is no reality.
Can such work live? The answer is that the most popular
magazine story or novel does not live in our minds for a month.

And what are we to do about it? To me it seems that as
writers we shall have to throw ourselves with greater daring into
the life here. We shall have to begin to write out of the people
and not for the people. We shall have to find within ourselves a
little of that courage. To continue along the road we are
travelling is unthinkable. To draw ourselves apart, to live in
little groups and console ourselves with the thought that we are
achieving intellectuality, is to get nowhere. By such a road we
can hope only to go on producing a literature that has nothing
to do with life as it is lived in these United States.

To be sure, the doing of the thing I am talking about will not
be easy. America is a land of objective writing and thinking.
New paths will have to be made. The subjective impulse is
almost unknown to us. Because it is close to life, it works out

into crude and broken forms. It leads along a road that such American masters of prose as James and Howells did not want to take, but if we are to get anywhere, we shall have to travel that road.

The road is rough and the times are pitiless. Who, knowing our America and understanding the life in our towns and cities, can close his eyes to the fact that life here is for the most part an ugly affair? As a people we have given ourselves to industrialism, and industrialism is not lovely. If anyone can find beauty in an American factory town, I wish he would show me the way. For myself, I cannot find it. To me, and I am living in industrial life, the whole thing is as ugly as modern war. I have to accept that fact and I believe a great step forward will have been taken when it is more generally accepted.

But why, I am asked, is crudity and ugliness necessary? Why cannot a man like Mr. Dreiser write in the spirit of the early Americans, why cannot he see fun in life? What we want is the note of health. In the work of Mark Twain there was something wholesome and sweet. Why cannot the modern man be also wholesome and sweet?

To this I make answer that to me a man, say like Mr. Dreiser, is wholesome. He is true to something in the life about him, and truth is always wholesome. Twain and Whitman wrote out of another age, out of an age and a land of forests and rivers. The dominant note of American life in their time was the noisy, swaggering raftsman and the hairy-breasted woodsman. To-day it is not so. The dominant note in American life to-day is the factory hand. When we have digested that fact, we can begin to approach the task of the present-day novelist with a new point of view.

It is, I believe, self-evident that the work of the novelist must always lie somewhat outside the field of philosophic thought. Your true novelist is a man gone a little mad with the life of his times. As he goes through life he lives, not in himself, but in many people. Through his brain march figures and groups of figures. Out of the many figures, one emerges. If he be at all sensitive to the life about him and that life be crude, the figure that emerges will be crude and will crudely express itself.

I do not know how far a man may go on the road of subjective writing. The matter, I admit, puzzles me. There is something approaching insanity in the very idea of sinking yourself too deeply into modern American industrial life.

But it is my contention that there is no other road. If one would avoid neat, slick writing, he must at least attempt to be brother to his brothers and live as the men of his time live. He must share with them the crude expression of their lives. To our grandchildren the privilege of attempting to produce a school of American writing that has delicacy and color may come as a matter of course. One hopes that will be true, but it is not true now. And that is why, with so many of the younger Americans, I put my faith in the modern literary adventurers. We shall, I am sure, have much crude, blundering American writing before the gift of beauty and subtlety in prose shall honestly belong to us.

37. H. L. MENCKEN
A Letter to Theodore Dreiser*

H.L. Mencken
1524 Hollins St.
Baltimore
April 23rd [1911]

DEAR DREISER:—

When "Jennie Gerhardt" is printed it is probable that more than one reviewer will object to its length, its microscopic detail, its enormous painstaking—but rest assured that Heinrich Ludwig von Mencken will not be in that gang. I have just finished reading the ms.—every word of it, from first to last—and I put it down with a clear notion that it should remain as it stands. The story comes upon me with great force; it touches my own experience of life in a hundred places; it preaches (or perhaps I had better say exhibits) a philosophy of life that seems to me to be sound; altogether I get a powerful effect of reality, stark and unashamed. It is drab and gloomy, but so is the struggle for existence. It is without humor, but so are the jests of that great comedian who shoots at our heels and makes us do our grotesque dancing.

I needn't say that it seems to me an advance above "Sister Carrie." Its obvious superiority lies in its better form. You strained (or perhaps even broke) the back of "Sister Carrie" when you let Hurstwood lead you away from Carrie. In "Jennie

---

* The selection, reproduced here in its entirety, is taken from *The American Scene: A Reader* by H. L. Mencken, edited by Huntington Cairns. Copyright © 1965 by Alfred A. Knopf, Inc. Reprinted by permission of the publisher.

Gerhardt" there is no such running amuck. The two currents of
interest, of spiritual unfolding, are very deftly managed. Even
when they do not actually coalesce, they are parallel and close
together. Jennie is never out of Kane's life, and after their first
meeting, she is never out of his. The reaction of will upon will,
of character upon character, is splendidly worked out and
indicated. In brief, the story hangs together; it is a complete
whole; consciously or unconsciously, you have avoided the
chief defect of "Sister Carrie."

It is difficult, just rising from the book, to describe the
impression I bring away. That impression is of a living whole,
not of a fabric that may be unraveled and examined in detail. In
brief, you have painted so smoothly and yet so vigorously that I
have no memory of brush strokes. But for one thing, the great
naturalness of the dialogue sticks in mind. In particular, you
have been extremely successful with Gerhardt. His speeches are
perfect: nothing could be nearer to truth. I am well aware that
certain persons are impatient of this photographic accuracy.
Well, let them choose their poison. As for me, I prefer the fact
to the fancy. You have tried to depict a German of a given
type—a type with which I, by chance, happen to be very
familiar. You have made him as thoroughly alive as Huck Finn.

These are random, disordered notes. When the time comes, I'll
reduce my thoughts to order and write a formal, intelligible
review. At the moment I am too near the book. I rather distrust
my own enthusiasm for it. Perhaps I read my own prejudices
and ideas into it. My interest is always in the subjective event,
seldom or never in the objective event. That is why I like "Lord
Jim." Here you have got very close to the very well-springs of
action. The march of episodes is nothing: the slow unfolding of
character is everything.

If anyone urges you to cut down the book bid that one be
damned. And if anyone argues that it is over-gloomy call the
police. Let it stand as it is. Its bald, forthright style; its
scientific, unemotional piling up of detail; the incisive truthfulness of its dialogue; the stark straightforwardness of it all—these
are merits that need no praise. It is at once an accurate picture
of life and a searching criticism of life. And that is my
definition of a good novel.

Here and there I noted minor weaknesses. For one thing, it is
doubtful that Jennie would have been able to conceal from so

sophisticated a man as Kane the fact that she had had a child. Child-bearing leaves physical marks, and those marks commonly persist for five or six years. But there are, of course, exceptions to this rule. Not many readers, I suppose, will raise the point. Again, if I remember correctly, you speak of L. S. & M. S. "shares" as being worth $1,000 par. Don't you mean bonds? If bonds, the income would be fixed and could not fluctuate. Again you give Kane $5,000 income from $75,000 at 6 per cent. A small thing—but everywhere else you are so utterly careful that small errors stick out.

A final word: the least satisfactory personage in the book is Jennie herself. Not that you do not account for her, from head to heels—but I would have preferred, had I the choice, a more typical kept woman. She is, in brief, uncompromisingly exceptional, almost unique, in several important details. Her connection with her mother and father and with the facts of her life grows, at times, very fragile. But I can well understand how her essential plausibility must have reacted upon you—how your own creation must have dragged you on. There is always Letty Pace to show Jennie's limitations. In her class she is a miracle, and yet she never quite steps out of that class.

But I go back to the effect of the book as a whole. That effect, believe me, is very powerful. I must go to Hardy and Conrad to find its like. David Phillips, I believe, might have done such a story had he lived, but the best that he actually wrote, to wit, "The Hungry Heart," goes to pieces beside "Jennie." I mean this in all seriousness. You have written a novel that no other American of the time could have written, and even in England there are not six men who, with your material, could have reached so high a level of reality. My earnest congratulations. By all means let me see that third book. "Jennie" shows immense progress in craftsmanship. As a work of art it is decidedly superior to "Sister Carrie."

I'll return the ms. by express tomorrow morning. Maybe chance will throw us together soon and we'll have a session over "Jennie." At the moment I am rather too full of the story as a human document to sit down in cold blood and discourse upon its merits and defects as a work of art. I know that it is immensely good, but I have still to get my reasons reduced to fluent words.

God keep you. As for me, I lately enjoyed the first of the

THEODORE DREISER:

season's rashers of crab à la creole. With genuine Muenchener to
flush the esophagus afterward.

Yours,
H. L. M.

Reading this over it seems damned cold. [What] I really want
to say is just—"Hurrah!" You have put over a truly *big* thing.

38. H. L. MENCKEN
Theodore Dreiser*

1

Out of the desert of American fictioneering, so populous and yet so dreary, Dreiser stands up—a phenomenon inescapably visible, but disconcertingly hard to explain. What forces combined to produce him in the first place, and how has he managed to hold out so long against the prevailing blasts—of disheartening misunderstanding and misrepresentation, of Puritan suspicion and opposition, of artistic isolation, of commercial seduction? There is something downright heroic in the way the man has held his narrow and perilous ground, disdaining all compromise, unmoved by the cheap success that lies so inviting around the corner. He has faced, in his day, almost every form of attack that a serious artist can conceivably encounter, and yet all of them together have scarcely budged him an inch. He still plods along in the laborious, cheerless way he first marked out for himself; he is quite as undaunted by baited praise as by bludgeoning, malignant abuse; his later novels are, if anything, more unyieldingly dreiserian than his earliest. As one who has long sought to entice him in this direction or that, fatuously presuming to instruct him in what would improve him and profit him, I may well bear a reluctant and resigned sort of testimony to his gigantic steadfastness. It is almost as if any change in his manner, any concession to what is usual and esteemed, any amelioration of his blind, relentless exercises of *force majeure*, were a physical impossibility. One feels him at last to be authentically no more than a helpless instrument (or victim) of that inchoate flow of forces which he himself is so fond of depicting as at once the answer to the riddle of life, and a riddle ten times more vexing and accursed. . . .

I have heard argument that he is a follower of Frank Norris,

* The selection is taken from *A Book of Prefaces.* Copyright 1917 by Alfred A. Knopf, Inc., and renewed copyright 1945 by H. L. Mencken. Reprinted by permission of the publisher.

and two or three facts lend it a specious probability. "McTeague" was printed in 1899; "Sister Carrie" a year later. Moreover, Norris was the first to see the merit of the latter book, and he fought a gallant fight, as literary advisor to Doubleday, Page & Co., against its suppression after it was in type. But this theory runs aground upon two circumstances, the first being that Dreiser did not actually read "McTeague," nor, indeed, grow aware of Norris, until after "Sister Carrie" was completed, and the other being that his development, once he began to write other books, was along paths far distant from those pursued by Norris himself. Dreiser, in truth, was a bigger man than Norris from the start; it is to the latter's unending honor that he recognized the fact instanter, and yet did all he could to help his rival. It is imaginable, of course, that Norris, living fifteen years longer, might have overtaken Dreiser, and even surpassed him; one finds an arrow pointing that way in "Vandover and the Brute" (not printed until 1914). But it swings sharply around in "The Epic of the Wheat." In the second volume of that incomplete trilogy, "The Pit," there is an obvious concession to the popular taste in romance; the thing is so frankly written down, indeed, that a play has been made of it, and Broadway has applauded it. And in "The Octopus," despite some excellent writing, there is a descent to a mysticism so fantastic and preposterous that it quickly passes beyond serious consideration. Norris, in his day, swung even lower—for example, in "A Man's Woman" and in some of his short stories. He was a pioneer, perhaps only half sure of the way he wanted to go, and the evil lures of popular success lay all about him. It is no wonder that he sometimes seemed to lose his direction.

Emile Zola is another literary father whose paternity grows dubious on examination. I once printed an article exposing what seemed to me to be a Zolaesque attitude of mind, and even some trace of the actual Zola manner, in "Jennie Gerhardt"; there came from Dreiser the news that he had never read a line of Zola, and knew nothing about his novels. Not a complete answer, of course; the influence might have been exerted at second hand. But through whom? I confess that I am unable to name a likely medium. The effects of Zola upon Anglo-Saxon fiction have been almost *nil*; his only avowed disciple, George Moore, has long since recanted and reformed; he has scarcely rippled the prevailing romanticism. . . . Thomas

Hardy? Here, I daresay, we strike a better scent. There are many obvious likenesses between "Tess of the D'Urbervilles" and "Jennie Gerhardt" and again between "Jude the Obscure" and "Sister Carrie." All four stories deal penetratingly and poignantly with the essential tragedy of women; all disdain the petty, specious explanations of popular fiction; in each one finds a poetical and melancholy beauty. Moreover, Dreiser himself confesses to an enchanted discovery of Hardy in 1896, three years before "Sister Carrie" was begun. But it is easy to push such a fact too hard, and to search for likenesses and parallels that are really not there. The truth is that Dreiser's points of contact with Hardy might be easily matched by many striking points of difference, and that the fundamental ideas in their novels, despite a common sympathy, are anything but identical. Nor does one apprehend any ponderable result of Dreiser's youthful enthusiasm for Balzac, which antedated his discovery of Hardy by two years. He got from both men a sense of the scope and dignity of the novel; they taught him that a story might be a good one, and yet considerably more than a story; they showed him the essential drama of the commonplace. But that they had more influence in forming his point of view, or even in shaping his technique, than any one of half a dozen other gods of those young days—this I scarcely find. In the structure of his novels, and in their manner of approach to life no less, they call up the work of Dostoevsky and Turgenev far more than the work of either of these men—but of all the Russians save Tolstoi (as of Flaubert) Dreiser himself tells us that he was ignorant until ten years after "Sister Carrie." In his days of preparation, indeed, his reading was so copious and so disorderly that antagonistic influences must have well-nigh neutralized one another, and so left the curious youngster to work out his own method and his own philosophy. . . .

. . . I see a far more potent influence in the chance discovery of Spencer and Huxley at twenty-three—the year of choosing! Who, indeed, will ever measure the effect of those two giants upon the young men of that era—Spencer with his inordinate meticulousness, his relentless pursuit of facts, his overpowering syllogisms, and Huxley with his devastating agnosticism, his insatiable questionings of the old axioms, above all, his brilliant style? Huxley, it would appear, has been condemned to the scientific hulks, along with bores innumerable and unspeakable;

one looks in vain for any appreciation of him in treatises on beautiful letters.[2] And yet the man was a superb artist in works, a master-writer even more than a master-biologist, one of the few truly great stylists that England has produced since the time of Anne. One can easily imagine the effect of two such vigorous and intriguing minds upon a youth groping about for self-understanding and self-expression. They swept him clean, he tells us, of the lingering faith of his boyhood—a medieval, Rhenish Catholicism;—more, they filled him with a new and eager curiosity, an intense interest in the life that lay about him, a desire to seek out its hidden workings and underlying causes. A young man set afire by Huxley might perhaps make a very bad novelist, but it is a certainty that he could never make a sentimental and superficial one. There is no need to go further than this single moving adventure to find the genesis of Dreiser's disdain of the current platitudes, his sense of life as a complex biological phenomenon, only dimly comprehended, and his tenacious way of thinking things out, and of holding to what he finds good. Ah, that he had learned from Huxley, not only how to inquire, but also how to report! That he had picked up a talent for that dazzling style, so sweet to the ear, so damnably persuasive, so crystal-clear!

But the more one examines Dreiser, either as writer or as theorist of man, the more his essential isolation becomes apparent. He got a habit of mind from Huxley, but he completely missed Huxley's habit of writing. He got a view of woman from Hardy, but he soon changed it out of all resemblance. He got a certain fine ambition and gusto out of Balzac, but all that was French and characteristic he left behind. So with Zola, Howells, Tolstoi and the rest. The tracing of likenesses quickly becomes rabbinism, almost cabalism. . . .

. 2 .

Once, seeking an analogy, I called him the Hindenburg of the novel. If it holds, then "The 'Genius' " is his Poland. The field

---

[2] For example, in "The Cambridge History of English Literature" which runs to fourteen large volumes and a total of nearly 10,000 pages, Huxley receives but a page and a quarter of notice, and his remarkable mastery of English is barely mentioned in passing. His two debates with Gladstone, in which he did some of the best writing of the century, are not noticed at all.

of action bears the aspect, at the end, of a hostile province meticulously brought under the yoke, with every road and lane explored to its beginning, and every crossroads village laboriously taken, inventoried and policed. Here is the very negation of Gallic lightness and intuition, and of all other forms of impressionism as well. Here is no series of illuminating flashes, but a gradual bathing of the whole scene with white light, so that every detail stands out.

And many of those details, of course, are trivial; even irritating. They do not help the picture; they muddle and obscure it; one wonders impatiently what their meaning is, and what the purpose may be of revealing them with such a precise, portentous air. . . . Turn to page 703 of "The 'Genius.' " By the time one gets there, one has hewn and hacked one's way through 702 large pages of fine print—97 long chapters, more than 250,000 words. And yet, at this hurried and impatient point, with the *coda* already begun, Dreiser halts the whole narrative to explain the origin, nature and inner meaning of Christian Science, and to make us privy to a lot of chatty stuff about Mrs. Althea Jones, a professional healer, and to supply us with detailed plans and specifications of the apartment house in which she lives, works her tawdry miracles, and has her being. Here, in sober summary, are the particulars:

1. That the house is "of conventional design."
2. That there is "a spacious areaway" between its two wings.
3. That these wings are "of cream-coloured pressed brick."
4. That the entrance between them is "protected by a handsome wrought-iron door."
5. That to either side of this door is "an electric lamp support of handsome design."
6. That in each of these lamp supports there are "lovely cream-coloured globes, shedding a soft luster."
7. That inside is "the usual lobby."
8. That in the lobby is "the usual elevator."
9. That in the elevator is the usual "uniformed Negro elevator man."
10. That this Negro elevator man (name not given) is "indifferent and impertinent."
11. That a telephone switchboard is also in the lobby.
12. That the building is seven stories in height.

In "The Financier" there is the same exasperating rolling up of irrelevant facts. The court proceedings in the trial of Cowperwood are given with all the exactness of a parliamentary report in the London *Times*. The speeches of the opposing counsel are set down nearly in full, and with them the remarks of the judge, and after that the opinion of the Appellate Court on appeal, with the dissenting opinions as a sort of appendix. In "Sister Carrie" the thing is less savagely carried out, but that is not Dreiser's fault, for the manuscript was revised by some anonymous hand, and the printed version is but little more than half the length of the original. In "The Titan" and "Jennie Gerhardt" no such brake upon exuberance is visible; both books are crammed with details that serve no purpose, and are as flat as ditch-water. Even in the two volumes of personal record, "A Traveler at Forty" and "A Hoosier Holiday," there is the same furious accumulation of trivialities. Consider the former. It is without structure, without selection, without reticence. One arises from it as from a great babbling, half drunken. On the one hand the author fills a long and gloomy chapter with the story of the Borgias, apparently under the impression that it is news, and on the other hand he enters into intimate and inconsequential confidences about all the persons he meets en route, sparing neither the innocent nor the obscure. The children of his English host at Bridgely Level strike him as fantastic little creatures, even as a bit uncanny—and he duly sets it down. He meets an Englishman on a French train who pleases him much, and the two become good friends and see Rome together, but the fellow's wife is "obstreperous" and "haughty in her manner" and so "loud-spoken in her opinions" that she is "really offensive"—and down it goes. He makes an impression on a Mlle Marcelle in Paris, and she accompanies him from Monte Carlo to Ventimiglia, and there gives him a parting kiss and whispers, *"Avril-Fontainebleau"*—and lo, this sweet one is duly spread upon the minutes. He permits himself to be arrested by a fair privateer in Piccadilly, and goes with her to one of the dens of sin that suffragettes see in their nightmares, and cross-examines her at length regarding her ancestry, her professional ethics and ideals, and her earnings at her dismal craft—and into the book goes a full report of the proceedings. He is entertained by an eminent Dutch jurist in Amsterdam—and upon the pages of the chronicle it appears that the gentleman is "waxy" and "a little pedantic," and that he is probably the sort of "thin, delicate, well barbered" professor that Ibsen had in mind when he cast about for a husband for the daughter of General Gabler.

Such is the art of writing as Dreiser understands it and practices it—an endless piling up of minutiae, an almost ferocious tracking down of ions, electrons and molecules, an unshakable determination to tell it all. One is amazed by the mole-like diligence of the man, and no less by his exasperating disregard for the ease of his readers. A Dreiser novel, at least of the later canon, cannot be read as other novels are read—on a winter evening or summer afternoon, between meal and meal, traveling from New York to Boston. It demands the attention for almost a week, and uses up the faculties for a month. If, reading "The 'Genius,' " one were to become engrossed in the fabulous manner described in the publishers' advertisements, and so find oneself unable to put it down and go to bed before the end, one would get no sleep for three days and three nights.

Worse, there are no charms of style to mitigate the rigors of these vast steppes and pampas of narration. Joseph Joubert's saying that "words should stand out well from the paper" is quite incomprehensible to Dreiser; he never imitates Flaubert by writing for *"la respiration et l'oreille."* There is no painful groping for the inevitable word, or for what Walter Pater called "the gipsy phrase"; the common, even the commonplace, coin of speech is good enough. On the first page of "Jennie Gerhardt" one encounters "frank, open countenance," "diffident manner," "helpless poor," "untutored mind," "honest necessity," and half a dozen other stand-bys of the second-rate newspaper reporter. In "Sister Carrie" one finds "high noon," "hurrying throng," "unassuming restaurant," "dainty slippers," "high-strung nature," and "cool, calculating world"—all on a few pages. Carrie's sister, Minnie Hanson, "gets" the supper. Hanson himself is "wrapped up" in his child. Carrie decides to enter Storm and King's office, "no matter what." In "The Titan" the word "trig" is worked to death; it takes on, toward the end, the character of a banal and preposterous refrain. In the other books one encounters mates for it—words made to do duty in as many senses as the American verb "to fix" or the journalistic "to secure." . . .

I often wonder if Dreiser gets anything properly describable as pleasure out of this dogged accumulation of threadbare, undistinguished, uninspiring nouns, adjectives, verbs, adverbs, pronouns, participles and conjunctions. To the man with an ear for verbal delicacies—the man who searches painfully for the perfect word, and puts the way of saying a thing above the thing said—there is in writing the constant joy of sudden discovery, of happy accident. A phrase springs up full blown, sweet and caressing. But what joy can there be in rolling up sentences that have no more life and beauty in them, intrinsically, than so many election bulletins? . . .

. 3 .

Of the general ideas which lie at the bottom of all of Dreiser's work it is impossible to be in ignorance, for he has exposed them at length in "A Hoosier Holiday" and summarized them in "Life, Art and America." In their main outlines they are not unlike the fundamental assumptions of Joseph Conrad. Both novelists see human existence as a seeking without a finding; both reject the prevailing interpretations of its meaning and mechanism; both take refuge in "I do not know." . . .

But to look into the blackness steadily, of course, is almost beyond the endurance of man. In the very moment that its impenetrability is grasped the imagination begins attacking it with pale beams of false light. All religions, I daresay, are thus projected from the questioning soul of man, and not only all religions, but also all great agnosticisms. Nietzsche, shrinking from the horror of that abyss of negation, revived the Pythagorean concept of *der ewigen Wiederkunft*—a vain and bloodcurdling sort of comfort. To it, after a while, he added explanations almost Christian—a whole repertoire of whys and wherefores, aims and goals, aspirations and significances. The late Mark Twain, in an unpublished work, toyed with an equally daring idea: that men are to some unimaginably vast and incomprehensible Being what the unicellular organisms of his body are to man, and so on *ad infinitum*. Dreiser occasionally inclines to much the same hypothesis; he likens the endless reactions going on in the world we know, the myriadal creation, collision and destruction of entities, to the slow accumulation and organization of cells *in utero*. He would make us specks in the insentient embryo of some gigantic Presence whose form is still unimaginable and whose birth must wait for Eons and Eons. Again, he turns to something not easily distinguishable from philosophical idealism, whether out of Berkeley or Fichte it is hard to make out—that is, he would interpret the whole phenomenon of life as no more than an appearance, a nightmare of some unseen sleeper or of men themselves, an "uncanny blur of nothingness"—in Euripides' phrase, "a song sung by an idiot, dancing down the wind." Yet again, he talks vaguely of the intricate polyphony of a cosmic orchestra, cacophonous to our dull ears. Finally, he puts the observed into the ordered, reading a purpose in the displayed event: "life was intended to sting and hurt" . . . But these are only gropings, and not to be read too critically. From speculations and explanations he always returns, Conrad-like, to the bald fact: to "the spectacle and stress of life." All he can make out clearly is "a vast compulsion which has nothing to do with the individual desires or tastes or impulses of individuals." That compulsion springs "from the settling processes of forces which we do not in the least understand, over which we have no control, and in whose grip we are as grains of dust or sand, blown hither and thither, for what purpose we cannot even suspect."[5] Man is not only doomed to defeat, but denied any glimpse or understanding of his antagonist. Here we come upon an agnosticism that has almost got beyond curiosity. What good would it do us, asks Dreiser, to know? In our ignorance and helplessness, we may at least get a slave's consolation out of cursing the unknown gods. Suppose we saw them striving blindly, too, and pitied them? . . .

But, as I say, this skepticism is often tempered by guesses at a possibly hidden truth, and the confession that this truth may exist reveals the practical unworkableness of the unconditioned system, at least for Dreiser. Conrad is far more resolute, and it is easy to see why. He is, by birth and training, an aristocrat. He has the gift of emotional detachment. The lures of facile doctrine do not move him. In his irony there is a disdain which plays about even the ironist himself. Dreiser is a product of far different forces and traditions, and is capable of no such escapement. Struggle as he may, and fume and protest as he may, he can no more shake off the chains of his intellectual and cultural heritage than he can change the shape of his nose. What that heritage is you may find out in detail by reading "A Hoosier Holiday," or in summary by glancing at the first few pages of "Life, Art and America." Briefly described, it is the burden of a believing mind, a moral attitude, a lingering

[5] "Life, Art and America," p. 5.

superstition. One-half of the man's brain, so to speak, wars with the other half. He is intelligent, he is thoughtful, he is a sound artist—but there come moments when a dead hand falls upon him, and he is once more the Indiana peasant, snuffing absurdly over imbecile sentimentalities, giving a grave ear to quackeries, snorting and eye-rolling with the best of them. One generation spans too short a time to free the soul of man. Nietzsche, to the end of his days, remained a Prussian pastor's son, and hence two-thirds a Puritan; he erected his war upon holiness, toward the end, into a sort of holy war. Kipling, the grandson of a Methodist preacher, reveals the tin-pot evangelist with increasing clarity as youth and its ribaldries pass away and he falls back upon his fundamentals. And that other English novelist who springs from the servants' hall—let us not be surprised or blame him if he sometimes writes like a bounder.

The truth about Dreiser is that he is still in the transition stage between Christian Endeavour and civilization, between Warsaw, Indiana and the Socratic grove, between being a good American and being a free man, and so he sometimes vacillates perilously between a moral sentimentalism and a somewhat extravagant revolt. "The 'Genius,' " on the one hand, is almost a tract for rectitude, a Warning to the Young; its motto might be *Scheut die Dirnen!* And on the other hand, it is full of a laborious truculence that can only be explained by imagining the author as heroically determined to prove that he is a plain-spoken fellow and his own man, let the chips fall where they may. So, in spots, in "The Financier" and "The Titan," both of them far better books. There is an almost moral frenzy to expose and riddle what passes for morality among the stupid. The isolation of irony is never reached; the man is still evangelical; his ideas are still novelties to him; he is as solemnly absurd in some of his floutings of the Code Américain as he is in his respect for Bouguereau, or in his flirtings with the New Thought, or in his naïve belief in the importance of novel-writing. Somewhere or other I have called all this the Greenwich Village complex. It is not genuine artists, serving beauty reverently and proudly, who herd in those cockroached cellars and bawl for art; it is a mob of half-educated yokels and cockneys to whom the very idea of art is still novel, and intoxicating—and more than a little bawdy.

Not that Dreiser actually belongs to this ragamuffin company. Far from it, indeed. There is in him, hidden deep down, a great instinctive artist, and hence the makings of an aristocrat. In his muddled way, held back by the manacles of his race and time, and his steps made uncertain by a guiding theory which too often eludes his own comprehension, he yet manages to produce works of art of unquestionable beauty and authority, and to interpret life in a manner that is poignant and illuminating. There is vastly more intuition in him than intellectualism; his talent is essentially feminine, as Conrad's is masculine; his ideas always seem to be deduced from his feelings. The view of life that got into "Sister Carrie," his first book, was not the product of a conscious thinking out of Carrie's problems. It simply got itself there by the force of the artistic passion behind it; its coherent statement had to wait for other and more reflective days. The thing began as a vision, not as a syllogism. . . .

. . . But whatever the process, the power of the image evoked is not to be gainsaid. It is not only brilliant on the surface, but mysterious and appealing in its depths. One swiftly forgets his intolerable writing, his mirthless, sedulous, repellent manner, in the face of the Athenian tragedy he instils into his seduced and soul-sick servant girls, his barbaric pirates of finances, his conquered and hamstrung supermen, his wives who sit and wait. He has, like Conrad, a sure talent for depicting the spirit in disintegration. Old Gerhardt, in "Jennie Gerhardt," is alone worth all the *dramatis personae* of popular American fiction since the days of "Rob o' the Bowl"; Howells could no more have created him, in his Rodinesque impudence of outline, than he could have created Tartuffe or Gargantua. Such a novel as "Sister Carrie" stands quite outside the brief traffic of the customary stage. It leaves behind it an unescapable impression of bigness, of epic sweep and dignity. It is not a mere story, not a novel in the customary American meaning of the word; it is at once a psalm of life and a criticism of life—and that criticism loses nothing by the fact that its burden is despair. Here, precisely, is the point of Dreiser's departure from his fellows. He puts into his novels a touch of the eternal *Weltschmerz*. They get below the drama that is of the moment and reveal the greater drama that is without end. They arouse those deep and lasting emotions which grow out of the recognition of elemental and universal tragedy. His aim is not merely to tell a tale; his aim is to show the vast ebb and flow of forces which sway and condition human destiny. One cannot imagine him consenting to Conan Doyle's statement of the purpose of fiction, quoted with characteristic approval by the New York *Times*: "to amuse

mankind, to help the sick and the dull and the weary." Nor is
his purpose to instruct; if he is a pedagogue it is only
incidentally and as a weakness. The thing he seeks to do is to
stir, to awaken, to move. One does not arise from such a book
as "Sister Carrie" with a smirk of satisfaction; one leaves it
infinitely touched.

. 6 .

. . . Dr. William Lyon Phelps, the Lampson professor of
English language and literature at Yale, opens his chapter on
Mark Twain in his "Essays on Modern Novelists" with a
humorous account of the critical imbecility which pursued
Mark in his own country down to his last years. The favorite
national critics of that era (and it extended to 1895, at the
least) were wholly blind to the fact that he was a great artist.
They admitted him, somewhat grudgingly, a certain low dexter-
ity as a clown, but that he was an imaginative writer of the first
rank, or even of the fifth rank, was something that, in their
insanest moments, never so much as occurred to them. Phelps
cites, in particular, an ass named Professor Richardson, whose
"American Literature," it appears, "is still a standard work"
and "a deservedly high authority"—apparently in colleges. In
the 1892 edition of this *magnum opus*, Mark is dismissed with
less than four lines, and ranked below Irving, Holmes and
Lowell—nay, actually below Artemus Ward, Josh Billings and
Petroleum V. Nasby! The thing is fabulous, fantastic, *un-
glaublich*—but nevertheless true. Lacking the "higher artistic
or moral purpose of the greater humorists" (*exempli gratia*,
Rabelais, Molière, Aristophanes!!), Mark is dismissed by this
Professor Balderdash as a hollow buffoon. . . . But stay! Do not
laugh yet! Phelps himself, indignant at the stupidity, now
proceeds to credit Mark with a moral purpose! . . . Turn to
"The Mysterious Stranger," or "What Is Man?" . . .
College professors, alas, never learn anything. The identical
gentleman who achieved this discovery about old Mark in 1910,
now seeks to dispose of Dreiser in the exact manner of
Richardson. That is to say, he essays to finish him by putting
him into Coventry, by loftily passing over him. "Do not speak
of him," said Kingsley of Heine; "he was a wicked man!"
Search the latest volume of the Phelps revelation, "The Advance

of the English Novel," and you will find that Dreiser is not once mentioned in it. The late O. Henry is hailed as a genius who will have "abiding fame"; Henry Sydnor Harrison is hymned as "more than a clever novelist," nay, "a valuable ally of the angels" (the right-thinker complex! art as a form of snuffling!), and an obscure Pagliaccio named Charles D. Stewart is brought forward as "the American novelist most worthy to fill the particular vacancy caused by the death of Mark Twain"—but Dreiser is not even listed in the index. And where Phelps leads with his baton of birch most of the other drovers of rah-rah boys follow. I turn, for example, to "An Introduction to American Literature," by Henry S. Pancoast, A.M., L.H.D., dated 1912. There are kind words for Richard Harding Davis, for Amélie Rives, and even for Will N. Harben, but not a syllable for Dreiser. Again, there is "A History of American Literature," by Reuben Post Halleck, A.M., LL.D., dated 1911. Lew Wallace, Marietta Holley, Owen Wister and Augusta Evans Wilson have their hearings, but not Dreiser. Yet again, there is "A History of American Literature Since 1870," by Prof. Fred Lewis Pattee,[8] instructor in "the English language and literature" somewhere in Pennsylvania. Pattee has praises for Marion Crawford, Margaret Deland and F. Hopkinson Smith, and polite bows for Richard Harding Davis and Robert W. Chambers, but from end to end of his fat tome I am unable to find the slightest mention of Dreiser.

So much for one group of heroes of the new Dunciad. That it includes most of the acknowledged heavyweights of the craft— the Babbitts, Mores, Brownells and so on—goes without saying; as Van Wyck Brooks has pointed out,[9] these magnificoes are austerely above any consideration of the literature that is in being. The other group, more courageous and more honest, proceeds by direct attack; Dreiser is to be disposed of by a moral *attentat*. Its leaders are two more professors, Stuart P. Sherman and H. W. Boynton, and in its ranks march the lady critics of the newspapers, with much shrill, falsetto clamor. Sherman is the only one of them who shows any intelligible reasoning. Boynton, as always, is a mere parroter of conventional phrases, and the objections of the ladies fade imperceptibly

8 New York: The Century Co.; 1916.

9 In *The Seven Arts*, May, 1917.

into a pious indignation which is indistinguishable from that of the professional suppressors of vice.

What, then, is Sherman's complaint? In brief, that Dreiser is a liar when he calls himself a realist; that he is actually a naturalist, and hence accursed. That "he has evaded the enterprise of representing human conduct, and confined himself to a representation of animal behavior." That he "imposes his own naturalistic philosophy" upon his characters, making them do what they ought not to do, and think what they ought not to think. That "he has just two things to tell us about Frank Cowperwood: that he has a rapacious appetite for money, and a rapacious appetite for women." That this alleged "theory of animal behavior" is not only incorrect but downright immoral, and that "when one-half the world attempts to assert it, the other half rises in battle."[10]

Only a glance is needed to show the vacuity of all this *brutum fulmen*. Dreiser, in point of fact, is scarcely more the realist or the naturalist, in any true sense, than H. G. Wells or the later George Moore, nor has he ever announced himself in either the one character or the other—if there be, in fact, any difference between them that any one save a pigeon-holing pedagogue can discern. He is really something quite different, and, in his moments, something far more stately. His aim is not merely to record, but to translate and understand; the thing he exposes is not the empty event and act, but the endless mystery out of which it springs; his pictures have a passionate compassion in them that it is hard to separate from poetry. If this sense of the universal and inexplicable tragedy, if this vision of life as a seeking without a finding, if this adept summoning up of moving images, is mistaken by college professors for the empty, meticulous nastiness of Zola in "Pot-Bouille"—in Nietzsche's phrase, for "the delight to stink"—then surely the folly of college professors, as vast as it seems, has been underestimated. What is the fact? The fact is that Dreiser's attitude of mind, his manner of reaction to the phenomena he represents, the whole of his alleged "naturalistic philosophy," stems directly, not from Zola, Flaubert, Augier and the younger Dumas, but from the Greeks. In the midst of democratic cocksureness and Christian sentimentalism, of doctrinaire shallowness and professorial smugness, he stands for a point of view which at least has something honest and courageous about it; here, at all events,

[10] The *Nation*. Dec. 2, 1915.

he is a realist. Let him put a motto to his books, and it might
be:

Ἰὼ γενεαὶ βροτῶν,
Ὡς ὑμᾶς ἴσα καὶ τὸ μηδὲν
Ζώσας ἐναριθμῶ.

If you protest against that as too harsh for Christians and
college professors, right-thinkers and forward-lookers, then you
protest against "Oedipus Rex." [11]

As for the animal behavior prattle of the learned headmaster,
it reveals, on the one hand, only the academic fondness for
seizing upon high-sounding but empty phrases and using them
to alarm the populace, and on the other hand, only the
academic incapacity for observing facts correctly and reporting
them honestly. The truth is, of course, that the behavior of such
men as Cowperwood and Witla and of such women as Carrie
and Jennie, as Dreiser describes it, is no more merely animal
than the behavior of such acknowledged and undoubted human
beings as Woodrow Wilson and Jane Addams. The whole point
of the story of Witla, to take the example which seems to
concern the horrified watchmen most, is this: that his life is a
bitter conflict between the animal in him and the aspiring soul,
between the flesh and the spirit, between what is weak in him
and what is strong, between what is base and what is noble.
Moreover, the good, in the end, gets its hooks into the bad: as
we part from Witla he is actually bathed in the tears of remorse,
and resolved to be a correct and godfearing man. And what have
we in "The Financier" and "The Titan"? A conflict, in the ego
of Cowperwood, between aspiration and ambition, between the
passion for beauty and the passion for power. Is either passion
animal? To ask the question is to answer it.

I single out Dr. Sherman, not because his pompous syllogisms
have any plausibility in fact or logic, but simply because he may
well stand as archetype of the booming, indignant corrupter of
criteria, the moralist turned critic. A glance at his paean to
Arnold Bennett[12] at once reveals the true gravamen of his

[11] 1186-1189. So translated by Floyd Dell: "O ye deathward-going tribes of man,
what do your lives mean except that they go to nothingness?"

[12] The New York *Evening Post,* Dec. 31, 1915.

objection to Dreiser. What offends him is not actually Dreiser's shortcoming as an artist, but Dreiser's shortcoming as a Christian and an American. In Bennett's volumes of pseudo-philosophy—*e.g.*, "The Plain Man and His Wife" and "The Feast of St. Friend"—he finds the intellectual victuals that are to his taste. Here we have a sweet commingling of virtuous conformity and complacent optimism, of sonorous platitude and easy certainty —here, in brief, we have the philosophy of the English middle classes—and here, by the same token, we have the sort of guff that the half-educated of our own country can understand. It is the calm, superior numskullery that was Victorian; it is by Samuel Smiles out of Hannah More. The offence of Dreiser is that he has disdained this revelation and gone back to the Greeks. Lo, he reads poetry into "the appetite for women"—he rejects the Pauline doctrine that all love is below the diaphragm! He thinks of Ulysses, not as a mere heretic and criminal, but as a great artist. He sees the life of man, not as a simple theorem in Calvinism, but as a vast adventure, an enchantment, a mystery. It is no wonder that respectable schoolteachers are against him. . . .

The comstockian attack upon "The 'Genius' " seems to have sprung out of the same muddled sense of Dreiser's essential hostility to all that is safe and regular—of the danger in him to that mellowed Methodism which has become the national ethic. The book, in a way, was a direct challenge, for though it came to an end upon a note which even a Methodist might hear as sweet, there were undoubted provocations in detail. Dreiser, in fact, allowed his scorn to make off with his taste—and *es ist nichts fürchterlicher als Einbildungskraft ohne Geschmack*. The Comstocks arose to the bait a bit slowly, but none the less surely. Going through the volume with the terrible industry of a Sundayschool boy dredging up pearls of smut from the Old Testament, they achieved a list of no less than 89 alleged floutings of the code—75 described as lewd and 14 as profane. An inspection of these specifications affords mirth of a rare and lofty variety; nothing could more cruelly expose the inner chambers of the moral mind. When young Witla, fastening his best girl's skate, is so overcome by the carnality of youth that he hugs her, it is set down as lewd. On page 51, having become an art student, he is fired by "a great, warm-tinted nude of Bouguereau"—lewd again. On page 70 he begins to draw from the figure, and his instructor cautions him that the female breast is round, not square—more lewdness. On page 151 he kisses a girl on mouth and neck and she cautions him: "Be careful! Mamma may come in"—still more. On page 161, having got rid of mamma, she yields "herself to him gladly, joyously" and he is greatly shocked when she argues that an artist (she is by way of being a singer) had better not marry—lewdness doubly damned. On page 245 he and his bride, being ignorant, neglect the principles laid down by Dr. Sylvanus Stall in his great works on sex hygiene—lewdness most horrible! But there is no need to proceed further. Every kiss, hug and tickle of the chin in the chronicle is laboriously snouted out, empanelled, exhibited. Every hint that Witla is no vestal, that he indulges his unchristian fleshliness, that he burns in the manner of I Corinthians, VII, 9, is uncovered to the moral inquisition.

On the side of profanity there is a less ardent pursuit of evidences, chiefly, I daresay, because their unearthing is less stimulating. (Beside, there is no law prohibiting profanity in books: the whole inquiry here is but so much *lagniappe*.) On page 408, in describing a character called Daniel C. Summerfield, Dreiser says that the fellow is "very much given to swearing, more as a matter of habit than of foul intention," and then goes on to explain somewhat lamely that "no picture of him would be complete without the interpolation of his various expressions." They turn out to be *God damn* and *Jesus Christ*—three of the latter and five or six of the former. All go down; the pure in heart must be shielded from the knowledge of them. (But what of the immoral French? They call the English *Goddams*.) Also, three plain *damns*, eight *hells*, one *my God*, five *by Gods*, one *go to the devil*, one *God Almighty* and one plain *God*. Altogether, 31 specimens are listed. "The 'Genius' " runs to 350,000 words. The profanity thus works out to somewhat less than one word in 10,000. . . . Alas, the comstockian proboscis, feeling for such offendings, is not as alert as when uncovering more savory delicacies. On page 191 I find an overlooked *by God*. On page 372 there are *Oh, God*, *God curse her*, and *God strike her dead*. On page 373 there are *Ah God, Oh God* and three other invocations of God. On page 617 there is *God help me*. On page 720 there is *as God is my judge*. On page 723 there is *I'm no damned good*. . . . But I begin to blush. . . .

VIII. John Steinbeck: Reevaluating Naturalism

In the course of a long career that began with the publication of *Cup of Gold* in 1929, John Steinbeck (b. 1902) had little to say about his method as a writer. His silence recalls the calculated ignorance of some earlier naturalists who presented themselves as spontaneous writers recording the life they knew with few theoretical or stylistic pretensions. In this vein Steinbeck recorded his suspicions of academic criticism Again, in the "Original Draft for the Dedication of *East of Eden*," he appeared as an innocent artist confronting the Big Businessmen of modern publishing, the "bookmakers" and "booksellers," the editors, proofreaders, and sales departments. His canny reticence was also of a piece with a desire he often stated in the early years of his career to avoid such personal publicity as Hemingway and Fitzgerald enjoyed that his works might stand by themselves.

Terse and infrequent as his critical statements were, Steinbeck said enough to indicate the theoretical and artistic concerns that influenced his writing. His critical ideas seemed to center on the problem of finding a literary form. Upon occasion, Steinbeck has adopted a natural or "organic" theory of organization which, in the American literary tradition, might be traced to Ralph Waldo Emerson. Thus, in the opening paragraph of *The Log from the Sea of Cortez* (which is the *locus classicus* for Steinbeck's scientific ideas), he stated, somewhat obliquely, that while the book is "a pattern of a reality . . . shaped by the mind of the writer," this particular work was allowed to "form itself." Presumably, the writer's mind, in some accord with nature, echoed and reformulated the patterns of the world it perceived. The book's design was not dictated by literary traditions or artificial laws of composition but by immediate experience: "a boat," "a sea," "a six weeks' charter time"— which is to say, a place and a time, or, as in Taine's famous formulation, *le milieu* and *le moment*. This attempt to draw the written word as close as possible to experience provides a literary parallel for Steinbeck's important distinction, in the "Easter Sunday" chapter of *The Log from the Sea of Cortez*, between "teleological thinking" which "considers changes and cures—what 'should be' in the terms of an end pattern" and "non-teleological ideas" which "derive through 'is' thinking, associated with natural selection as Darwin seems to have understood it." Clearly, this attempt to record external reality as it "is" without imposing upon it forms suggested by the imperative "should be" or the ultimate "why" is an effort to avoid traditional moral formulas. The attempt to see facts without "blaming"—especially when the "scientific" and statistical method reduces the individual's responsibility for what might otherwise be called his flaws and failures—provides a basis for Steinbeck's humanitarianism, at once impersonal and pitying. Indeed, the title of the "Easter Sunday" chapter is significant for it implies a contrast between a traditional faith based on universal love, pity, and redemption with the yet more forgiving stance of post-Darwinian science.

The examples cited in *The Log from the Sea of Cortez* suggest that Steinbeck identified "teleological thinking" with traditional religious and social attitudes, but these moral formulas are also deeply imbedded in folklore, myths, and traditional tales as well as in our formal literary heritage. It may therefore seem strange that Steinbeck so often built his works around traditional literary materials. Yet the "is" writing he attempts in *The Log from the Sea of Cortez* is not his customary style. As every reader of his novels knows, Steinbeck's prose constantly reflects his inheritance from the Bible, folklore, the Arthurian tales, and Walt Whitman—to name but a few obvious sources. In "My Short Novels," a brief piece of self-criticism (available in E. W. Tedlock, Jr., and C. V. Wicker, eds., *Steinbeck and His Critics*) Steinbeck discusses his conscious imitation of traditional literary forms. *Of Mice and Men*, he noted, was an attempt to crossbreed genres, "to write a novel in three acts to be played from the lines." *Tortilla Flat* was written in emulation of "the Arthurian cycle," which Steinbeck understood as "folklore," and *The Pearl* was another attempt to write "folklore." Strictly speaking, conscious art cannot, of course, be "folklore," but Steinbeck's use of the term is revealing. It suggests his desire to adopt a natural, unsophisticated literary form and to remain as close as possible to the simple perceptions of unlettered people. Such calculated "folklore" is, in fact, artificial "is" writing. And the "lore" of the folk is more than the simple record of experience. Tempered by retelling and common acceptance, it transcends the particular time and place it records. Preserved and enlarged by many narrators, it gains a timeless, universal quality. Steinbeck's conscious folklore seeks this transcendent quality most often through symbols and metaphors that suggest universal myths and the unceasing human quest for answers to the difficult question *"why."*

Such artifice certainly violates the scientific obligation of the naturalist to record what "is." But the scientific aspect of literary naturalism has never been hard or clear. From Darwin, as well as Zola, naturalists inherited two, often conflicting, obligations—to the "facts," on the one hand; to the grandeur of nature's supposed design, on the other. Many contemporary readers, wearied by "tough" determinists, like James T. Farrell or Erskine Caldwell, and by fiction that read like tracts on the hard facts of poverty, the class struggle, and economic injustice, found in Steinbeck's novels of the 1930's (an especially *The Grapes of Wrath* in 1939) welcome relief from dry reportage and doctrinaire hopelessness. His faith in universal man, implicit in analogies between simple, even impoverished moderns and men of the heroic past (between the Joads, for example, and the Israelites) reassured the reader, while his realistic treatments of social and economic problems satisfied those who demanded literature with a social conscience. It was this ability to join social realism to a personal brand of cosmic optimism reminiscent of the genial temper of the age of Howells and Twain ("the humanity, the gaiety, the wholeness, of realism in a more stable period"), which, as Alfred Kazin notes, won Steinbeck his unique place among writers of the Depression era. Many critics have tried to characterize the special flavor of Steinbeck's optimism, his altruism his transcendent and rhetorically affecting faith in man. Kazin calls this quality a "sense of fellowship," but he comments, ironically, that nothing in Steinbeck's books is "so dim significantly enough, as the human beings who live in them." Steinbeck's philosophy is his weakness as well as his strength. Certainly, his writing lacks the disciplined objectivity that gave realism the quality of hard, clear "truth." Kazin comments sharply that Steinbeck's "moral serenity" is "sterile" and can easily "slip into . . . calculated sentimentality." This judgment may seem to have been borne out in Steinbeck's later less successful novels.

The curious mixture of optimistic faith, scientific objectivity, and social conscience that characterize Steinbeck's best work need not, and probably cannot, be defended logically. It reflected the benign temper of American political liberalism in the years immediately before the Second World War. Steinbeck's success in that era seems to justify William Dean Howells' demand for a literature portraying life's more "smiling" aspects. It also suggests that, until very recently, many Americans did not feel that their lives demanded harsh deterministic treatment. Yet Steinbeck's achievement as an artist should not be confused with his personal faith or the public's approval of a hopeful doctrine. More fruitfully than most of his contemporaries, he explored the truly literary potential of the naturalistic novel. Enriched by his understanding of older literary forms, he devised not only a personal philosophy, but also a rhetoric based upon the tradition of Western literature and discovered analogies in the heroic past which provide dramatic parallels to the lives of his commonplace contemporaries. In other hands, the overarching theoretical structure of scientific speculation upon which naturalism is based had entered the novel awkwardly, as a sermon or authorial aside. By discovering imaginative mythic materials which convey a similar theoretical view, Steinbeck gave teleological optimism dramatic life.

Selections

39. THE DESIGN OF A BOOK*

The design of a book is the pattern of a reality controlled and shaped by the mind of the writer. This is completely understood about poetry or fiction, but it is too seldom realized about books of fact. And yet the impulse which drives a man to poetry will send another man into the tide pools and force him to try to report what he finds there. Why is an expedition to Tibet undertaken, or a sea bottom dredged? Why do men, sitting at the microscope, examine the calcareous plates of a sea-cucumber, and finding a new arrangement and number, feel an exaltation and give the new species a name, and write about it possessively? It would be good to know the impulse truly, not to be confused by the "services to science" platitudes or the other little mazes into which we entice our minds so that they will not know what we are doing.

We have a book to write about the Gulf of California. We could do one of several things about its design. But we have decided to let it form itself: its boundaries a boat and a sea; its duration a six weeks' charter time; its subject everything we could see and think and even imagine; its limits—our own without reservation. . . .

*The selection is taken from *The Log from the Sea of Cortez* by John Steinbeck. Reprinted by permission of the Viking Press, Inc., and McIntosh and Otis, Inc.

40. MARCH 24, EASTER SUNDAY*

. . . we discussed manners of thinking and methods of thinking, speculation which is not stylish any more. On a day like this the mind goes outward and touches in all directions. We discussed intellectual methods and approaches, and we thought that through inspection of thinking technique a kind of purity of approach might be consciously achieved—that non-teleological or "is" thinking might be substituted in part for the usual cause-effect methods.

The hazy Gulf, with its changes of light and shape, was rather like us, trying to apply our thoughts, but finding them always pushed and swayed by our bodies and our needs and our satieties. It might be well here to set down some of the discussions of non-teleological thinking.

During the depression there were, and still are, not only destitute but thriftless and uncareful families, and we have often heard it said that the county had to support them because they were shiftless and negligent. If they would only perk up and be somebody everything would be all right. Even Henry Ford in the depth of the depression gave as his solution to that problem, "Everybody ought to roll up his sleeves and get to work."

This view may be correct as far as it goes, but we wonder what would happen to those with whom the shiftless would exchange places in the large pattern—those whose jobs would be usurped, since at that time there was work for only about seventy percent of the total employable population, leaving the remainder as government wards.

This attitude has no bearing on what might be or could be if so-and-so happened. It merely considers conditions "as is." No matter what the ability or aggressiveness of the separate units of society, at that time there were, and still there are, great numbers necessarily out of work, and the fact that those numbers comprised the incompetent or maladjusted or unlucky units is in one sense beside the point. No causality is involved in

*The selection is taken from Chapter 14 of *The Log from the Sea of Cortez* by John Steinbeck and Edward F. Ricketts. Copyright 1941 by John Steinbeck & Edward F. Richetts, renewed 1951 by John Steinbeck, ©renewed 1969 by John Steinbeck & Edward F. Ricketts, Jr. Reprinted by permission of The Viking Press and McIntosh and Otis, Inc.

that; collectively it's just "so"; collectively it's related to the fact the animals produce more offspring than the world can support. The units may be blamed as individuals, but as members of society they cannot be blamed. Any given individual very possibly may transfer from the underprivileged into the more fortunate group by better luck or by improved aggressiveness or competence, but all cannot be so benefited whatever their strivings, and the large population will be unaffected. The seventy-thirty ratio will remain, with merely a reassortment of the units. And no blame, at least no social fault, imputes to these people; they are where they are "because" natural conditions are what they are. And so far as we selfishly are concerned we can rejoice that they, rather than we, represent the low extreme, since there must be one.

So if one is very aggressive he will be able to obtain work even under the most sub-normal economic conditions, but only because there are others, less aggressive than he, who serve in his stead as potential government wards. In the same way, the sight of a half-wit should never depress us, since his extreme, and the extreme of his kind, so affects the mean standard that we, hatless, coatless, often bewhiskered, thereby will be regarded only as a little odd. And similarly, we cannot justly approve the success manuals that tell our high school graduates how to get a job—there being jobs for only half of them!

This type of thinking unfortunately annoys many people. It may especially arouse the anger of women, who regard it as cold, even brutal, although actually it would seem to be more tender and understanding, certainly more real and less illusionary and even less blaming, than the more conventional methods of consideration. And the value of it as a tool in increased understanding cannot be denied.

As a more extreme example, consider the sea-hare *Tethys*, a shell-less, flabby sea-slug, actually a marine snail, which may be seen crawling about in tidal estuaries, somewhat resembling a rabbit crouched over. A California biologiest estimated the number of eggs produced by a single animal during a single breeding season to be more than 478 million. And the adults sometimes occur by the hundred! Obviously all these eggs cannot mature, all this potential cannot, *must not*, become reality, else the ocean would soon be occupied exclusively by sea-hares. There would be no kindness in that, even for the sea-hares themselves, for in a few generations they would overflow the earth; there would be nothing for the rest of us to eat, and nothing for them unless they turned cannibal. On the average, probably no more than the biblical one or two attain full maturity. Somewhere along the way all the rest will have been eaten by predators whose life cycle is postulated upon the presence of abundant larvae of sea-hares and other forms as food—as all life itself is based on such a postulate. Now picture the combination mother-father sea-hare (the animals are hermaphroditic, with the usual cross-fertilization) parentally blessing its offspring with these words: "Work hard and be aggressive, so you can grow into a nice husky *Tethys* like your ten-pound parent." Imagine it, the hypocrite, the illusionist, the Pollyanna, the genial liar, saying that to its millions of eggs *en masse*, with the dice loaded at such a ratio! Inevitably, 99.999 percent are destined to fall by the wayside. No prophet could foresee which specific individuals are to survive, but the most casual student could state confidently that no more than a few are likely to do so; any given individual has *almost* no chance at all—but still there is the "almost," since the race persists. And there is even a semblance of truth in the parent sea-hare's admonition, since even here, with this almost infinitesimal differential, the race is still to the swift and/or to the lucky.

What we personally conceive by the term "teleological thinking," as exemplified by the notion about the shiftless unemployed, is most frequently associated with the evaluating of causes and effects, the purposiveness of events. This kind of thinking considers changes and cures—what "should be" in the terms of an end pattern (which is often a subjective or an anthropomorphic projection); it presumes the bettering of conditions, often, unfortunately, without achieving more than a most superficial understanding of those conditions. In their sometimes intolerant refusal to face facts as they are, teleological notions may substitute a fierce but ineffectual attempt to change conditions which are assumed to be undesirable, in place of the understanding-acceptance which would pave the way for a more sensible attempt at any change which might still be indicated.

Non-teleological ideas derive through "is" thinking, associated with natural selection as Darwin seems to have understood it. They imply depth, fundamentalism, and clarity—seeing beyond traditional or personal projections. They consider events as outgrowths and expressions rather than as results; conscious acceptance as a desideratum, and certainly as an all-important prerequisite. Non-teleological thinking concerns itself primarily not with what should be, or could be, or might be, but rather with what actually "is"—attempting at most to answer the already sufficiently difficult questions *what* or *how*, instead of *why*.

An interesting parallel to these two types of thinking is afforded by the microcosm with its freedom or indeterminacy, as contrasted with the morphologically inviolable pattern of the macrocosm. Statistically, the electron is free to go where it will. But the destiny pattern of any aggregate, comprising uncountable billions of these same units, is fixed and certain, however much that inevitability may be slowed down. The eventual disintegration of a stick of wood or a piece of iron through the departure of the presumably immortal electrons is assured, even though it may be delayed by such protection against the operation of the second law of thermodynamics as is afforded by painting and rustproofing.

Examples sometimes clarify an issue better than explanations or definitions. Here are three situations considered by the two methods.

A. *Why are some men taller than others?*

Teleological "answer": because of the underfunctioning of the growth-regulating ductless glands. This seems simple enough. But the simplicity is merely a function of inadequacy and incompleteness. The finality is only apparent. A child, being wise and direct, would ask immediately if given this answer: "Well, why do the glands underfunction?" hinting instantly towards non-teleological methods, or indicating the rapidity with which teleological thinking gets over into the stalemate of first causes.

In the non-teleological sense there can be no "answer." There can be only pictures which become larger and more significant as one's horizon increases. In this given situation, the steps might be something like this:

(1) Variation is a universal and truly primitive trait. It occurs in any group of entities—razor blades, measuring-rods, rocks, trees, horses, matches, or men.

(2) In this case, the apropos variations will be towards shortness or tallness from a mean standard—the height of adult

men as determined by the statistics of measurements, or by common-sense observation.

(3) In men varying towards tallness there seems to be a constant relation with an underfunctioning of the growth-regulating ductless glands, of the sort that one can be regarded as an index of the other.

(4) There are other known relations consistent with tallness, such as compensatory adjustments along the whole chain of endocrine organs. There may even be other factors, separately not important or not yet discovered, which in the aggregate may be significant, or the integration of which may be found to wash over some critical threshold.

(5) The men in question are taller "because" they fall in a group within which there are the above-mentioned relations. In other words, "they're tall because they're tall."

This is the statistical, or "is," picture to date, more complex than the teleological "answer"—which is really no answer at all—but complex only in the sense that reality is complex; actually simple, inasmuch as the simplicity of the word "is" can be comprehended.

Understandings of this sort can be reduced to this deep and significant summary: "It's so because it's so." But exactly the same words can also express the hasty or superficial attitude. There seems to be no explicit method for differentiating the deep and participating understanding, the "all-truth" which admits infinite change or expansion as added relations become apparent, from the shallow dismissal and implied lack of further interest which may be couched in the very same words. . . .

. . . As a matter of fact there are three distinct types of thinking, two of them teleological. Physical teleology, the type we have been considering, is by far the commonest today. Spiritual teleology is rare. Formerly predominant, it now occurs metaphysically and in most religions, especially as they are popularly understood (but not, we suspect, as they were originally enunciated or as they may still be known to the truly adept). Occasionally the three types may be contrasted in a single problem Here are a couple of examples:

(1) Van Gogh's feverish hurrying in the Arles epoch, culminating in epilepsy and suicide.

Teleological "answer": Improper care of his health during times of tremendous activity and exposure to the sun and weather brought on his epilepsy out of which discouragement and suicide resulted.

Spiritual teleology: He hurried because he innately foresaw his imminent death, and wanted first to express as much of his essentiality as possible.

Non-teleological picture: Both the above, along with a good many other symptoms and expressions (some of which could probably be inferred from his letters), were parts of his essentiality, possibly glimpsable as his "lust for life."

(2) The thyroid-neurosis syndrome.

Teleological "answer": Over-activity of the thyroid gland irritates and over-stimulates the patient to the point of nervous breakdown.

Spiritual teleology: The neurosis is causative. Something psychically wrong drives the patient on to excess mental irritation which harries and upsets the glandular balance, especially the thyroid, through shock-resonance in the autonomic system in the sense that a purely psychic shock may spoil one's appetite, or may even result in violent illness. In this connection, note the army's acceptance of extreme homesickness as a reason for disability discharge.

Non-teleological picture: Both are discrete segments of a vicious circle, which may also include other factors as additional more or less discrete segments, symbols or maybe parts of an underlying but non-teleological pattern which comprises them and many others, the ramifications of which are n, and which has to do with causality only reflectedly.

Teleological thinking may even be highly fallacious, especially where it approaches the very superficial but quite common *post hoc, ergo propter hoc* pattern. Consider the situation with reference to dynamiting in a quarry. Before a charge is set off, the foreman toots warningly on a characteristic whistle. People living in the neighborhood come to associate the one with the other, since the whistle is almost invariably followed within a few seconds by the shock and sound of an explosion for which one automatically prepares oneself. Having experienced this many times without closer contact, a very naïve and unthinking person might justly conclude not only that there was a cause-effect relation, but that the whistle actually caused the explosion. A slightly wiser person would insist that the explosion caused the whistle, but would be hard put to explain the transposed time element. The normal adult would recognize that the whistle no more caused the explosion than the explosion caused the whistle, but that both were parts of a larger pattern out of which a "why" could be postulated for both, but more immediately and particularly for the whistle. Determined to chase the thing down in a cause-effect sense, an observer would have to be very wise indeed who could follow the intricacies of cause through more fundamental cause to primary cause, even in this largely man-made series about which we presumably know most of the motives, causes, and ramifications. He would eventually find himself in a welter of thoughts on production, and ownership of the means of production, and economic whys and wherefores about which there is little agreement.

The example quoted is obvious and simple. Most things are far more subtle than that, and have many of their relations and most of their origins far back in things more difficult of access than the tooting of a whistle calculated to warn bystanders away from an explosion. We know little enough even of a man-made series like this—how much less of purely natural phenomena about which also there is apt to be teleological pontificating!

Usually it seems to be true that when even the most definitely apparent cause-effect situations are examined in the light of wider knowledge, the cause-effect aspect comes to be seen as less rather than more significant, and the statistical or relational aspects acquire larger importance. It seems safe to assume that non-teleological is more "ultimate" than teleological reasoning. Hence the latter would be expected to prove to be limited and constricting except when used provisionally. But while it is true that the former is more open, for that very reason its employment necessitates greater discipline and care in order to allow for the dangers of looseness and inadequate control.

Frequently, however, a truly difinitive answer seems to arise through teleological methods. Part of this is due to wish-fulfillment delusion. When a person asks "Why?" in a given situation, he usually deeply expects, and in any case receives, only a relational answer in place of the definitive "because" which he thinks he wants. But he customarily accepts the actually relational answer (it couldn't be anything else unless it comprised the whole, which is unknowable except by "living into") as a definitive "because." Wishful thinking probably fosters that error, since everyone continually searches for absolutisms (hence the value placed on diamonds, the most permanent pysical things in the world) and imagines continually that he finds them. More justly, the relational picture should be regarded only as a glimpse—a challenge to consider also the rest of the relations as they are available—to envision the whole picture as well as can be done with given abilities and data. But one accepts it instead of a real "because," considers it settled, and, having named it, loses interest and goes on to something else.

Chiefly, however, we seem to arrive occasionally at difinitive answers through the workings of another primitive principle: the universality of quanta. No one thing ever merges gradually into anything else; the steps are discontinuous, but often so very minute as to seem truly continuous. If the investigation is carried deep enough, the factor in question, instead of being graphable as a continuous process, will be seen to function by discrete quanta with gaps or synapses between, as do quanta of energy, undulations of light. The apparently difinitive answer occurs when causes and effects both arise on the same large plateau which is bounded a great way off by the steep rise which announces the next plateau. If the investigation is extended sufficiently, that distant rise will, however, inevitably be encountered; the answer which formerly seemed definitive now will be seen to be at least slightly inadequate and the picture will have to be enlarged so as to include the plateau next further out. Everything impinges on everything else, often into radically different systems, although in such cases faintly. We doubt very much if there are any truly "closed systems." Those so called represent kingdoms of a great continuity bounded by the sudden discontinuity of great synapses which eventually must be bridged in any unified-field hypothesis. For instance, the ocean, with reference to waves of water, might be considered as a closed system. But anyone who has lived in Pacific Grove or Carmel during the winter storms will have felt the house tremble at the impact of waves half a mile or more away impinging on a totally different "closed" system.

But the greatest fallacy in, or rather the greatest objection to, teleological thinking is in connection with the emotional content, the belief. People get to believing and even to professing the apparent answers thus arrived at, suffering mental constrictions by emotionally closing their minds to any of the further and possibly opposite "answers" which might otherwise be

unearthed by honest effort—answers which, if faced realistically, would give rise to a struggle and to a possible rebirth which
might place the whole problem in a new and more significant
light. . . .

. . . The criterion of validity in the handling of data seems to
be this: that the summary shall say in substance, significantly
and understandingly, "It's so because it's so." Unfortunately
the very same words might equally derive through a most
superficial glance, as any child could learn to repeat from
memory the most abstruse of Dirac's equations. But to know a
thing emergently and significantly is something else again, even
though the understanding may be expressed in the self-same
words that were used superficially. In the following example[1]
note the deep significance of the emergent as contrasted with
the presumably satisfactory but actually incorrect original naïve
understanding. At one time an important game bird in Norway,
the willow grouse, was so clearly threatened with extinction
that it was thought wise to establish protective regulations and
to place a bounty on its chief enemy, a hawk which was known
to feed heavily on it. Quantities of the hawks were exter-
minated, but despite such drastic measures the grouse disap-
peared actually more rapidly than before. The naïvely applied
customary remedies had obviously failed. But instead of becoming discouraged and quietistically letting this bird go the
way of the great auk and the passenger pigeon, the authorities
enlarged the scope of their investigations until the anomaly was
explained. An ecological analysis into the relational aspects of
the situation disclosed that a parasitic disease, coccidiosis, was
endemic among the grouse. In its incipient stages, this disease so
reduced the flying speed of the grouse that the mildly ill
individuals became easy prey for the hawks. In living largely off
the slightly ill birds, the hawks prevented them from developing
the disease in its full intensity and so spreading it more widely
and quickly to otherwise healthy fowl. Thus the presumed
enemies of the grouse, by controlling the epidemic aspects of
the disease, proved to be friends in disguise.

In summarizing the above situation, the measure of validity
wouldn't be to assume that, even in the well-understood factor
of coccidiosis, we have the real "cause" of any beneficial or
untoward condition, but to say, rather, that in this phase we

[1] Abstracted from the article on ecology by Elton, *Encyclopaedia Britannica,* 14th
Edition, Vol. VII, p. 916.

have a highly significant and possibly preponderantly important relational aspect of the picture.

However, many people are unwilling to chance the sometimes ruthless-appearing notions which may arise through non-teleological treatments. They fear even to use them in that they may be left dangling out in space, deprived of such emotional support as had been afforded them by an unthinking belief in the proved value of pest control in the conservation of game birds; in the institutions of tradition; religion; science; in the security of the home or the family; or in a comfortable bank account. But for that matter emancipations in general are likely to be held in terror by those who may not yet have achieved them, but whose thresholds in those respects are becoming significantly low. . . .

As a matter of fact, whoever employs this type of thinking with other than a few close friends will be referred to as detached, hard-hearted, or even cruel. Quite the oppostie seems to be true. Non-teleological methods more than any other seem capable of great tenderness, of an all-embracingness which is rare otherwise. Consider, for instance, the fact that, once a given situation is deeply understood, no apologies are required. There are ample difficulties even to understanding conditions "as is." Once that has been accomplished, the "why" of it (known now to be simply a relation, though probably a near and important one) seems no longer to be preponderantly important. It needn't be condoned or extenuated, it just "is." . .

Strictly, the term non-teleological thinking ought not to be be applied to what we have in mind. Because it involves more than thinking, that term is inadequate. *Modus operandi* might be better—a method of handling data of any sort. The example cited just above concerns feeling more than thinking. The method extends beyond thinking even to living itself; in fact, by inferred definition it transcends the realm of thinking possibilities, it postulates "living into."

In the destitute-unemployed illustration, thinking, as being the evaluatory function chiefly concerned, was the point of departure, "the crust to break through." There the "blame approach" considered the situation in the limited and inadequate teleological manner. The non-teleological method included that viewpoint as correct but limited. . . .

Incidentally, there is in this connection a remarkable etiological similarity to be noted between cause in thinking and blame in feeling. One feels that one's neighbors are to be blamed for their hate or anger or fear. One thinks that poor pavements are "caused" by politics. The non-teleological picture in either case is the larger one that goes beyond blame or cause. And the non-causal or non-blaming viewpoint seems to us very often relatively to represent the "new thing," the Hegelian "Christ-child" which arises emergently from the union of two opposing viewpoints, such as those of physical and spiritual teleologies, especially if there is conflict as to causation between the two or within either. The new viewpoint very frequently sheds light over a larger picutre, providing a key which may unlock levels not accessible to either of the teleological viewpoints. There are interesting parallels here: to the triangle, to the Christian ideas of trinity, to Hegel's dialectic, and to Swedenborg's metaphysic of divine love (feeling) and divine wisdom (thinking).

The factors we have been considering as "answers" seem to be merely symbols or indices, relational aspects of things—of which they are integral parts—not to be considered in terms of causes and effects. The truest reason for anything's being so is that it *is*. This is actually and truly a reason, more valid and clearer than all the other separate reasons, or than any group of them short of the whole. Anything less than the whole forms part of the picture only, and the infinite whole is unknowable except by *being* it, by living into it.

A thing may be *so* "because" of a thousand and one reasons of greater or lesser importance, such as the man oversized because of glandular insufficiency. The integration of these many reasons which are in the nature of relations rather than reasons is that he *is*. The separate reasons, no matter how valid, are only fragmentary parts of the picture. And the whole necessarily includes all that it impinges on as object and subject, in ripples fading with distance or depending upon the original intensity of the vortex.

The frequent allusions to an underlying pattern have no implication of mysticism—except inasmuch as a pattern which comprises infinity in factors and symbols might be called mystic. But infinity as here used occurs also in the mathematical aspects of physiology and physics, both far away from mysticism as the term is ordinarily employed. Actually, the underlying pattern is probably nothing more than an integration of just such symbols and indices and mutual reference points as are already known, except that its power is n. Such an integration might include nothing more spectacular than we already know. But, equally, it *could* include anything, even events and entities as different from those already known as the vectors, tensors, scalars, and ideas of electrical charges in mathematical physics are different from the mechanical-model world of the Victorian scientists.

In such a pattern, causality would be merely a name for something that exists only in our partial and biased mental reconstructings. The pattern which it indexes, however, would be real, but not intellectually apperceivable because the pattern goes everywhere and is everything and cannot be encompassed by finite mind or by anything short of life—which it is. . . .

This deep underlying pattern inferred by non-teleological thinkung crops up everywhere—a relational thing, surely, relating opposing factors on different levels, as reality and potential are related. But it must not be considered as causative, it simply exists, it *is*, things are merely expressions of it as it is expressions of them. And they *are* it, also. As Swinburne, extolling Hertha, the earth goddess, makes her say: "Man, equal and one with me, man that is made of me, man that is I," so all things which are *that*—which is all—equally may be extolled. That pattern materializes everywhere in the sense that Eddington finds the mon-integar q "number" appearing everywhere, in the background of all fundamental equations,[2] in the sense that the speed of light, constant despite compoundings or subtractions, seemed at one time almost to be conspiring against investigation.

The whole is necessarily everything, the whole world of fact and fancy, body and psyche, physical fact and spiritual truth, individual and collective, life and death, macrocosm and microcosm (the greatest quanta here, the greatest synapse between these two), conscious and unconscious, subject and object. The whole picture is portrayed by *is*, the deepest word of deep ultimate reality, not shallow or partial as reasons are, but deeper and participating, possibly encompassing the Oriental concept of *being*.

And all this against the hot beach on an Easter Sunday, with the passing day and the passing time. . . .

[2] *The Nature of the Physical World*, pp. 208-10.

41. A LETTER ON CRITICISM*

Feb. 5, 1955

Dear Editors:

Thank you for your very kind letter and your offer to make space available for my comment on the two recent articles on the *Grapes of Wrath* which have appeared in the *Quarterly*. I wish I could so comment but I have no opinions nor ideas on the subject. Indeed, both pieces seem to me to be nearer to taxonomy than to criticism. Much of the new criticism with its specail terms and parochial approach is interesting to me, although I confess I don't understand it very well, but I cannot see that it has very much to do with the writing of novels good or bad. And since the new critics fight each other even more fiercely than they do the strapped down and laid open subjects of their study, it would seem to me that they do not have a

* JOHN STEINBECK wrote "A Letter on Criticism" in response to the invitation of the editor of *The Colorado Quarterly* to comment on two essays which had appeared in the pages of that periodical. The first of these essays, *"The Grapes of Wrath: a 'Wagons West' Romance,"* by Bernard Bowron, appeared in the Summer, 1954 issue. The quite inadequate, if not wholly mistaken view expressed in this article was partly corrected by the second piece, *"Another Look at The Grapes of Wrath,"* by Warren G. French, which appeared in the Winter, 1955 issue. Mr. Steinbeck's response to the editorial invitation was printed in the Autumn, 1955 issue.

table of constants. In less criticismal terms, I think it is a bunch of crap. As such I am not against it so long as it is understood that the process is a kind of ill tempered parlour game in which nobody gets kissed. What such an approach would do to a student beyond confusing him and perhaps making him shy away from reading, I have no idea. I do not read much criticism of my work any more. In the first place it is valueless as advice or castigation since the criticised piece is finished and I am not likely to repeat it. And in the second place, the intrafrontal disagreements only succeed in puzzling me. Recently a critic proved by parallel passages that I had taken my whole philosophy from a 17th century Frenchman of whom I had never heard. I usually know what I want to say and hope I have the technique to say it clearly and effectively. As Tennessee Williams once said, "I put it down that a way and that's the only way I know to put it down."

I don't think the *Grapes of Wrath* is obscure in what it tries to say. As to its classification and pickling, I have neither opinion nor interest. It's just a book, interesting I hope, instructive in the same way the writing instructed me. Its structure is very carefully worked out and it is no more intended to be inspected than is the skeletal structure of a pretty girl. Just read it, don't count it!

Please believe me when I say I have nothing against the scholarly or critical approach. It does seem to me to have very little to do with the writing or reading of books.

The writing of books is a lonely and difficult job, and it takes all the time I have. Remember the negro boy in Texas who when asked by a priest whether he was a catholic, replied, "Hell no, father, I'm having enough trouble just being a nigger." Well I'm having enough—just being a writer.

I am working now on a long novel, trying to get it straight and clear—trying to fit method to subject and tone to surround the whole—trying to fit the thousand details and people into the pattern. Imagine, if you will, the confusion if criticism should come now. No book would ever get written if the critic could get at the mind of a writer rather than his work. Afterwards, critics are hardly more destructive than silver fish.

Yours,
John Steinbeck

42. ORIGINAL DRAFT FOR THE DEDICATION OF EAST OF EDEN*

To Pascal Convici
Dear Pat.

I have decided for this, my book, *East of Eden*, to write dedication, prologue, argument, apology, epilogue and perhaps epitaph all in one.

The dedication is to you with all the admiration and affection that have been distilled from our singularly blessed association of many years. This book is inscribed to you because you have been part of its birth and growth.

As you know, a prologue is written last but placed first to explain the book's shortcomings and to ask the reader to be kind. But a prologue is also a note of farewell from the writer to his book. For years the writer and his book have been together—friends or bitter enemies but very close as only love and fighting can accomplish.

Then suddenly the book is done. It is a kind of death. This is the requiem.

Miguel Cervantes invented the modern novel and with his Don Quijote set a mark high and bright. In his prologue, he said best what writers feel—The gladness and The terror.

"Idling reader" Cervantes wrote, "you may believe me when I tell you that I should have liked this book, which is the child of my brain, to be The fairest. The sprightliest and The cleverest that could be imagined, but I have not been able to contravene the law of nature which would have it that like begets like—"

And so it is with me, Pat. Although some times I have felt that I held fire in my hands and spread a page with shining—I have

*The selection is taken from *Journal of a Novel: The East of Eden Letters* by John Steinbeck, copyright ©1969 by the Executors of John Steinbeck. All rights reserved. Reprinted by permission of The Viking Press, Inc. and McIntosh and Otis, Inc.

never lost the weight of clumsiness, of ignorance, of aching inability.

A book is like a man—clever and dull, brave and cowardly, beautiful and ugly. For every flowering thought there will be a page like a wet and mangy mongrel, and for every looping flight a tap on the wing and a reminder that wax cannot hold the feathers firm too near the sun.

Well—then the book is done. It has no virtue any more. The writer wants to cry out—"Bring it back! Let me rewrite it or better—Let me burn it. Don't let it out in the unfriendly cold in that condition."

As you know better than most, Pat, the book does not go from writer to reader. It goes first to the lions—editors, publishers, critics, copy readers, sales department. It is kicked and slashed and gouged. And its bloodied father stands attorney.

EDITOR
The book is out of balance. The reader expects one thing and you give him something else. You have written two books and stuck them together. The reader will not understand.

WRITER
No, sir. It goes together. I have written about one family and used stories about another family as well as counterpoint, as rest, as contrast in pace and color.

EDITOR
The reader won't understand. What you call counterpoint only slows the book.

WRITER
It has to be slowed—else how would you know when it goes fast.

EDITOR
You have stopped the book and gone into discussions of God knows what.

WRITER
Yes, I have. I don't know why. Just wanted to. Perhaps I was wrong.

EDITOR

Right in the middle you throw in a story about your mother and an airplane. The reader wants to know where it ties in and, by God, it doesn't tie in at all. That disappoints a reader.

WRITER

Yes, sir. I guess you're right. Shall I cut out the story of my mother and the airplane?

EDITOR

That's entirely up to you.

SALES DEPARTMENT

The book's too long. Costs are up. We'll have to charge five dollars for it. People won't pay five dollars. They won't buy it.

WRITER

My last book was short. You said then that people won't buy a short book.

PROOFREADER

The chronology is full of holes. The grammar has no relation to English. On page so-and-so you have a man look in the World Almanac for steamship rates. They aren't there. I checked. You've got Chinese New Year wrong. The characters aren't consistent. You describe Liza Hamilton one way and then have her act a different way.

EDITOR

You make Cathy too black. The reader won't believe her. You make Sam Hamilton too white. The reader won't believe him No Irishman ever talked like that.

WRITER

My grandfather did.

EDITOR

Who'll believe it.

SECOND EDITOR
No children ever talked like that.

WRITER
(losing temper as a refuge from despair)
God dam it. This is my book. I'll make the children talk any way I want. My book is about good and evil. Maybe the theme got into the execution. Do you want to publish it or not?

EDITORS
Let's see if we can't fix it up. It won't be much work. You want it to be good, don't you? For instance the ending. The reader won't understand it.

WRITER
Do you?

EDITOR
Yes, but the reader won't.

PROOFREADER
My god, how you do dangle a participle. Turn to page so-and-so.

There you are, Pat. You came in with a box of glory and there you stand with an armful of damp garbage.

And from this meeting a new character has emerged. He is called the Reader.

THE READER
He is so stupid you can't trust him with an idea.
He is so clever he will catch you in the least error.
He will not buy short books.
He will not buy long books.
He is part moron, part genius and part ogre.
There is some doubt as to whether he can read.

Well, by God, Pat, he's just like me, no stranger at all. He'll take from my book what he can bring to it. The dull witted will get dullness and the brilliant may find things in my book I didn't know were there.

And just as he is like me, I hope my book is enough like him so that he may find in it interest and recognition and some beauty as one find in a friend.

Cervantes ends his prologue with a lovely line. I want to use it, Pat, and then I will have done. He says to the reader:

"May God give you health—and may He be not unmindful of me, as well."

John Steinbeck

New York   1952

Contemporary Comment

43. ALFRED KAZIN
The Revival of Naturalism*

There were a few social realists in the period [the 1930's] who did promise something different from the automatism of contemporary naturalism and the cult of the hard-boiled, notably John Steinbeck; but his case has always been a curious one. Steinbeck's approach to the novel was interesting because he seemed to stand apart at a time when naturalism had divided writers into two mutually exclusive groups, since the negation of its starved and stunted spirit came more and more from writers who often had no sympathy with realism at all, and were being steadily pulled in the direction of surrealism and abstractionsim. Naturalism had made for so drearily uniform a conception of the novel, so mechanical an understanding of reality, that it is not strange to find many writers, and particularly so many young writers, revolting entirely against realism to work in *Innerlichkeit.* Just as the literary criticism of the crisis period was marked by the conflict of two groups of absolutists, one absorbed in "social significance," the other in technical problems, so it is significant to note the polarization in fiction between a grim surface realism and a literature of private sensibility. Inevitably, in a world where the public reality can seem so persistently oppressive and meaningless, while the necessity for new means of communication is so pressing, the more sensitive artist is steadily withdrawn into himself, into those reaches of the unconscious where "one can make a world within a world." But in this conflict between the outer and inner worlds of reality, between the fragmentary

*The selection is taken from *On Native Grounds,* by Alfred Kazin; copyright 1942, 1970 by Alfred Kazin. Reprinted by permission of Harcourt Brace Jovanovich, Inc.

realizations that each represents, the patterns of contemporary desperation can nullify one another.

Steinbeck, standing apart from both the contemporary naturalists and the new novel of sensibility that one finds in Faulkner and Wolfe, brought a fresh note into contemporary fiction because he promised a realism less terror-ridden than the depression novel, yet one consciously responsible to society, a realism mindful of the terror and disorganization of contemporary life, but not submissive to the spiritual stupor of the time; a realism equal in some measure, if only in its aspiration, to the humanity, the gaiety, the wholeness, of realism in a more stable period. It is the failure of so many contemporary American novelists to suggest even the urgency of such an achievement that marks their unconscious submission to the demoralization in contemporary life. Yet it cannot be said that Steinbeck's work, which has become more and more tenuous and even sentimental, has really answered to that need. With a writer like Farrell, oppressively narrow as his world is, one at least knows where he stands—his integrity, his materialism, the full range of his belief. Steinbeck is a greater humanist, and there is a poetry in some of his best work, particularly *The Long Valley* stories and *The Pastures of Heaven*, that naturalists of Farrell's stamp have never been able to conceive. But there is something imperfectly formed about Steinbeck's work; it has no creative character. For all his moral serenity, the sympathetic understanding of men under strain that makes a strike novel like *In Dubious Battle* so notable in the social fiction of the period, Steinbeck's people are always on the verge of becoming human, but never do. There is a persistent failure to realize human life fully in his books, where the characters in many American naturalistic novels have simply ceased to be human. After a dozen books Steinbeck still looks like a distinguished apprentice, and what is so striking in his work is its inconclusiveness, his moving approach to human life and yet his failure to be creative with it.

Steinbeck's moral advantage as a realist in the depression era was to be so different in his region—the Salinas Valley in California—his subject, as to seem different in kind. It was his famous "versatility" that first earned him his reputation—his ability to follow a *Tortilla Flat* with *In Dubious Battle*, *Of Mice and Men* with *The Grapes of Wrath*—but this was the least noteworthy thing about him and has come more and more to suggest not versatility but a need to feel his way. His great possession as a writer was not an interest in craft or an experimental spirit; it was an unusual and disinterested simplicity, a natural grace and tenderness and ease in his relation to his California world. Artistically, notably in early works like *To a God Unknown* and *The Pastures of Heaven*, these appeared as a shyly artful primitivism reminiscent of Sherwood Anderson, and in its boyish California mysticism, of Frank Norris. But at bottom Steinbeck's gift was not so much a literary resource as a distinctively harmonious and pacific view of life. In a period when so many better writers exhausted themselves, he had welded himself into the life of the Salinas Valley and enjoyed a spiritual stability by reporting the life cycles of the valley gardeners and mystics and adventurers, by studying and steeping himself in its growth processes out of a close and affectionate interest in the biology of human affairs. Steinbeck's absorption in the life of his native valley gave him a sympathetic perspective on the animal nature of human life, a means of reconciliation with people as people. The depression naturalists saw life as one vast Chicago slaughterhouse, a guerrilla war, a perpetual bombing raid. Steinbeck had picked up a refreshing belief in human fellowship and courage; he had learned to accept the rhythm of life. In one of the most beautiful stories in *The Long Valley*, "The Chrysanthemums," the heroine asks:

> Did you ever hear of planting hands? . . . It's when you're picking off the buds you don't want. Everything goes right down into your fingertips. You watch your fingers work. They do it themselves. You can see how it is. They pick and pick the buds. They never make a mistake. They're with the plant. Do you see? Your fingers and the plant. You can feel that, right up your arm. They know. They never make a mistake. You can feel it. When you're like that you can't do anything wrong.

It was this "unpanicky questioning of life," as Edmund Wilson put it, that gave Steinbeck's work its unusual tenderness, gave his valley-bred simplicity an advantageous perspective on contemporary social problems. With his deep amateur interest in biology, it gave him the necessary detachment and slow curiosity to approach the modern social struggle as a tragicomedy of animal instincts, which, as the best things in *The Grapes of*

Wrath and *In Dubious Battle* testify, meant an aroused compassion, an understanding of the pain that the human animal can suffer and the mistakes he can make. The Doctor in *In Dubious Battle*, speaking for Steinbeck, disputes the Communist organizer's instinctive terrorism, and says quietly:

> My senses aren't above reproach, but they're all I have. I want to see the whole picture—as nearly as I can. I don't want to put on the blinders of "good" and "bad," and limit my vision. If I used the term "good" on a thing I'd lose my license to inspect it, because there might be bad in it. Don't you see? I want to be able to look at the whole thing.

Later he adds reflectively: "Group-men are always getting some kind of infection."

This was the spirit of *The Long Valley*, the spirit of the old pioneer grandfather in "The Leader of the People," who, reminiscing of the westward migration, described it as "a whole bunch of people made into one big crawling beast. . . . Every man wanted something for himself, but the big beast that was all of them wanted only westering." People in Steinbeck's work, taken together, are often evil; a society moving on the principle of collective mass slowly poisons itself by corrupting its own members. But beyond his valley-bred conviction of the evil inherent in any society where men are at the mercy of each other's animalism, Steinbeck knew how to distinguish, in works like *The Long Valley*, *In Dubious Battle*, and *The Grapes of Wrath*, between the animal processes of life and social privation. Out of his slow curiosity, the strength of the agrarian tradition in him, Steinbeck was able to invest the migration of the Joads, if not his monochromatic characters, with a genuinely tragic quality precisely because he felt so deeply for them and had seen at first hand the gap between their simple belief in life and their degradation. He did not confuse the issue in *The Grapes of Wrath*; he was aroused by the man-made evil the Okies had to suffer, and he knew it as something remediable by men. And where another social realist might have confused the dark corners he described with the whole of life, Steinbeck had the advantage of his Western training, its plain confidence in men. The old pioneer grandfather in *The Long Valley*, remembering the brutality of men on the great trek, also remembered enough of its glory to say:

It wasn't Indians that were important, nor adventures, nor even getting out here. . . . When we saw the mountains at last, we cried—all of us. But it wasn't getting here that mattered, it was movement and westering. We carried life out here and set it down the way those ants carry eggs. And I was the leader. The westering was as big as God, and the slow steps that made the movement piled up and piled up until the continent was crossed.

It was these associations that contributed to the success of *The Grapes of Wrath* and made it the most influential social novel of the period. Though the book was as urgent and as obvious a social tract for its time as *Uncle Tom's Cabin* had been for another, it was also the first novel of its kind to dramatize the inflictions of the crisis without mechanical violence and hatred. The bitterness was there, as it should have been, the sense of unspeakable human waste and privation and pain. But in the light of Steinbeck's strong sense of fellowship, his simple indignation at so much suffering, the Joads, while essentially symbolic marionettes, did illuminate something more than the desperation of the time: they became a living and challenging part of the forgotten American procession. Though the characters were essentially stage creations, the book brought the crisis that had severed Americans from their history back into it by recalling what they had lost through it. It gave them a design, a sense of control, where out of other depression novels they could get only the aimless maniacal bombardment of rage. The lesson of the crisis, so often repeated in the proletarian novel and yet so lifeless in it, was suddenly luminous: it was an event in history, to be understood by history, to be transformed and remembered and taught in history. It was as if Steinbeck, out of the simplicity of his indignation, had been just primitive enough to call men back to their humanity, to remind drepression America that a culture is only the sum total of the human qualities that make it up, and that "life can give a periodical beating to death any time," as a contemporary poet put it, "if given a chance and some help."

It was this tonic sanity in a bad time, his understanding of the broad processes of human life, that gave Steinbeck his distinction among the depression realists. But no one can pretend, particularly after a book like *The Moon Is Down*, that it tells the whole story about him. For Steinbeck's primitivism is essentially uncreative, and for all his natural simplicity of spirit, there is a trickiness, a stage cunning, behind it that has become depressing. Though his interests have carried him squarely into certain central truths about the nature of life, he has not been able to establish them in human character. Nothing in his books is so dim, significantly enough, as the human beings who live in them, and a few of them are intensely imagined as human beings at all. It is obvious that his mind moves happily in realms where he does not have to work in very complex types—the *paisanos* in *Tortilla Flat*, the ranch hands in *Of Mice and Men*, the Okies in *The Grapes of Wrath*, the strikers in *In Dubious Battle*, the farmers in *The Long Valley*, the symbolic protagonists of democratic struggle and Nazi power in *The Moon Is Down*. But what one sees in his handling of these types is not merely a natural affection for this simplicity, but a failure to interest himself too deeply in them as individuals. It is not their simplicity that makes Lennie and George in *Of Mice and Men* into furry little animals, or the Joads into stage creations, or the characters in *The Moon Is Down* into manikins; it is Steinbeck's simplicity of characterization. It is not their paganism that makes the *paisanos* in *Tortilla Flat* so hard to take from one point of view; it is their undiluted cuteness. Steinbeck's perspective on human life always gives him a sense of process, an understanding of the circuits through which the human animal can move; but he cannot suggest the density of human life, for his characters are not fully human.

It is in this light that one can understand why Steinbeck's moral serenity is yet so sterile and why it is so easy for him to slip into the calculated sentimentality of *Of Mice and Men* and *The Moon Is Down*. In writers of a certain natural awkwardness, like Dreiser and Anderson, there is a sentimentality, an impurity, that follows from exaggeration and lack of control; but one is always conscious of the amplitude through which they move. Steinbeck is not awkward, no; but he is not ample. He is a simple writer who has acquired facility, but though he is restive in his simplicity, his imagination cannot rise above it. And it is that simplicity and facility, working together, a tameness of imagination operating slickly, that give his work its surface paradox of simplicity and trickiness, of integrity of emotion and endless contrivance of means. This does not mean a lack of sincerity; it does mean that Steinbeck is not so simple that he does not know how to please; or to take, as it were, advantage of himself. It is, after all, the cunning behind the poignant situation in *Of Mice and Men*, a certain Woollcott-like ambush of the heartstrings, that makes his little fable meretricious in its pathos, a moment's gulp; and it is the same air of calculation in *The Moon Is Down*, so much more glaring because of its subject, that makes this allegorical drama of the struggle of free men today merely depressing.

The Moon Is Down, published after Pearl Harbor, was heartily disliked by many people; but chiefly, as it would seem, because Steinbeck had not been tough and violent enough, had not portrayed his Nazis in Norway as the brutal gangsters that Nazis in Norway, as elsewhere, have been. But this demand for absolute realism was too shrill with war tension, and missed the root of the book's failure. What is really striking about the novel—so openly written, like *Of Mice and Men*, for the stage—is how fantastically simple the whole anti-Fascist struggle appeared to Steinbeck even as an allegory, and yet how easy it was for him to transcribe his naïveté into the shabbiest theater emotions. There is credulity here, even an essential innocence of spirit, and the kind of slow curiosity about all these war-haunted creatures that has always made Steinbeck's interest in the animal nature of life the central thing in his work. He does not appeal to the hatred of Hitlerism, no; he has never appealed to any hatred. The Doctor, with his patient wisdom, speaks for him here as another doctor, a student of human affairs, spoke in *In Dubious Battle*. But it is not the student's detachment that one remembers here; it is the facility that can turn this greatest of contemporary themes into a series of contrivances. We hear the affirmation of nobility Steinbeck wanted to make, as we hear it in all his work; but we cannot believe in it, for though it is intended to inspire us in the struggle against Hitlerism, there are no men and women here to fight it. . . . And Europe under Hitler, even a representative stage Europe, is not Monterey, where the *paisanos* had their fun; and it is not the Salinas Valley; and the people locked in its supreme struggle today are not Steinbeck's familiar primitives, only seeking to be human. No, they are not primitives at all. But Steinbeck's world is a kind of primitivism to the end—primitive, with a little cunning.

r—